Lighting by Design:
A Technical Guide

Other lighting books from Focal Press

Lighting by Design:
A Technical Guide

Brian Fitt
and
Joe Thornley

FOCAL PRESS

Focal Press
An imprint of Butterworth-Heinemann Ltd
Linacre House, Jordan Hill, Oxford OX2 8DP

A member of the Reed Elsevier plc group

OXFORD   LONDON   BOSTON
MUNICH   NEW DELHI   SINGAPORE   SYDNEY
TOKYO   TORONTO   WELLINGTON

First published 1992
Paperback edition 1995

British Library Cataloguing in Publication Data
Fitt, Brian
  Lighting by Design: Technical Guide
  I. Title   II. Thornley, Joe
  778.5

ISBN 0 240 51440 8

Library of Congress Cataloging in Publication Data
Fitt, Brian
  Lighting by design: a technical guide/Brian Fitt and Joe Thornley
  p.   cm.
  Includes bibliographical references and index.
  ISBN 0 240 51440 8
  1. Cinematography–Lighting.   2. Television–Lighting.
  I. Thornley, Joe.   II. Title.
  TR891.F58
  778.5′2343–dc20   92-17943
                                                             CIP

Composition by Genesis Typesetting, Laser Quay, Rochester, Kent
Printed and bound in Great Britain by
Hartnolls Ltd, Bodmin, Cornwall

Contents

Dedication

To two outstanding gentlemen of the lighting fraternity, Sam Barclay, who promoted television lighting to such a high standard of art, and Fred Bentham, who spent his whole working life interpreting theatre lighting designers' wishes into lighting products. Additionally, we would thank all our friends in the industry, particularly Mike Wood and Andy Collier, for their helpful suggestions. We also have to thank Brian's wife, Carole, who struggled valiantly against the authors' dictation techniques to type the manuscript in some form of English.

Preface

This book is aimed at those practitioners of lighting in the entertainment industry. In addition, it will interest those people who are involved with the stage, film, television and stills photography, particularly when the effects of lighting have a major influence on their contribution to the medium concerned.

Many times in our long careers in the entertainment industry, we have been asked by architects, structural engineers, mechanical and electrical engineers: 'Why the need for all this lighting ironmongery?' Hopefully, on looking through this book, they will find the answer!

Perhaps – and this must be our main wish – most readers will find the book interesting.

Brian Fitt
and Joe Thornley

Acknowledgements

The authors gratefully acknowledge the help of the following organizations: Arri (GB) Ltd.; A S Green & Co.; Department of Trade & Industry; Fuji Photo Film Co. Ltd.; G E Thorn Lighting; Great American Market; Health and Safety Executive; Institution of Electrical Engineers; J E M Smoke Machine Co. Ltd.; Lee Filters; Light & Sound Design; Minolta (UK) Ltd.; Osram; Philips Lighting; Roscolab Limited; Sony Broadcast & Communications Ltd.; Strand Lighting; Studio Five; TV World; BBC; Central TV and TVS.

1 Introduction

In the early 1960s when the authors began their romance with the lighting industry, television viewing had not taken the upper hand that it has today. It was still possible to walk through the West End of London and see productions of plays and musicals at many theatres filled to capacity, and in fact the theatre world was a vibrant, wonderful place in which to work. In those days, too, the British film industry was busy; the tendency to make films abroad in either Second or Third World countries on the grounds of cost had not yet commenced. The television world was still expanding after the creation of independent television in Great Britain in 1955. Commercial television companies were obviously having to build new studios and mini television centres, and the BBC had embarked on the creation of the Television Centre, at Shepherds Bush in London.

Although the techniques of the film industry – and for that matter the theatre – have changed very little over the past years, television has changed immeasurably. When the Television Centre opened in June 1960, black and white television was still the order of the day and BBC2 was some four years away. Many television productions were still broadcast live and most of the drama and music output came from the Television Centre, using multicamera techniques. Because of the need to utilize the studios as fully as possible, the BBC embarked on a system of saturated lighting which they still use to this day. Due to union agreements reached within the BBC, overnight working by some trades was possible, whereas in commercial television this was not the practice. Consequently, BBC studios had their scenery and lighting changed at night although the technical crews concerned with the production output only worked during the daytime period. Commercial television, on the other hand, by not utilizing studios at night, really required a longer period of time for each studio production and hence the numbers of studios used by commercial television to service the network were higher than those required by the BBC to service both BBC1 and BBC2.

With the advent of the colour television system, introduced in the late 1960s, production techniques were reviewed and the BBC decided that the same productivity had to be achieved out of the existing black and white studios. The effect of this was to bring about the introduction of the multipurpose luminaire as the main lighting tool in the studios. Commercial television, on the other hand, apart from using slightly larger light sources for the majority of the time, carried on in much the same way, and although it would probably be disputed by the BBC, their productivity was pretty good as well. At its peak, during the late 1960s and early 1970s, British television produced some wonderfully entertaining programmes, such as *Henry VIII* and *The Forsyte Saga* from the BBC, together with a string of musical productions such as *Barbra Streisand and Instruments* produced by ATV, all of these being shot in the studio with multicamera techniques. At the same time the British film industry was turning out superb James Bond movies, *Superman* was made at Pinewood and *Fiddler on the Roof* was produced using highly skilled British technicians for the stunning sound and pictures.

As the costs of television productions have risen so the programmes have changed. Both drama and musical programmes have become prohibitively high in cost and have unfortunately virtually disappeared from the television screens. The theatre is also suffering from increased production costs and today it is not abnormal to see big productions costing two million pounds or more being staged in the West End, although this is somewhat of a risk for the backers, who invariably look very closely at the next bright idea that comes along. Thus a large degree of hesitancy creeps into the whole scene. It has become cheaper to make films in Hungary or South America, much to the regret of our Spanish and Italian friends who thought they had captured the film industry for many years. At the present time, it would seem very difficult for the British film industry to arrest its decline and although the theatres still have excellent productions, more and more costly failures seem to be the order of the day.

The British television industry is going through a tremendous change; old companies are disappearing from the scene and new companies are emerging, but the basic fact remains that the costs of television production are rising all the time and this is causing problems with the quality of programmes. It is so much easier to put on the chat show, the panel game and audience participation shows rather than invest the money, where unfortunately large amounts are required, for drama and music. Production techniques have changed immeasurably over the years. Whereas a large-scale television production mounted in a studio would probably take five days of multicamera shooting, the same production now would probably be done on location using one or two hand-held cameras with many days of post-production techniques required to assemble the material. To reduce costs, 'in house' production is becoming less and less favoured and the rise of independent production houses has become a notable feature of the late 1980s and early 1990s. Why is this so? It is obviously cheaper to use facilities only when they are required, and not have them on a permanent basis. The average running cost of a large studio, whether it is being used or not, is probably of the order of a million pounds per annum – a high cost on the books if it is not used regularly. The television industry needs to be geared up rather like the aircraft industry, where it is important to keep the aircraft in the air – carrying fare paying passengers as much of the time as possible to recoup the enormous capital costs. For instance, to refurbish a major television studio with a highly sophisticated lighting system will probably cost anything from two million pounds upwards. The costs of lamps and filters rise all the time, therefore the operating costs are high.

The lighting industry looks for a panacea, such as highly efficient light sources, cheaper equipment and methods by which cost can be reduced generally. One problem that exists today is with too many manufacturers chasing too few customers, leading to a cut-throat industry that can only ultimately result in several business failures and a poorer service to the customer.

A visit to a bookshop which stocks technical books will reveal on the shelves a wealth of material for those people who work in the entertainment industry. One of the problems with the existing range of books is that they cover very specialist aspects of subjects such as film-making, television systems, video and photography. In the case of sound and lighting any literature is usually biased to the needs of the particular section of the industry. However, common to all disciplines is the requirement for illumination. Without light, which is possibly the most acute stimulation that we humans experience, communication in any form becomes exceedingly difficult.

Both authors, having worked in the entertainment industry for a considerable number of years, have concluded that, by trying to consolidate in one volume all the technical aspects of lighting for the various sections of the industry, we might help other generations to avoid many of the pitfalls that we experienced.

Safety requirements are becoming more stringent and in many cases deservedly so. Most of us involved in the industry are confronted more and more by masses of rules and regulations, usually written in such a way as to defy any professor of language studies. In this book we will attempt to translate the safety implications into an understandable form, so that people concerned with their implementation will have a clearer picture of the legislation. It is pointless to reinvent the wheel every time a problem emerges; the best way is to call upon the knowledge others have accumulated and take or remould those ideas and solutions. Hopefully, by setting down our thoughts, ideas and, most important of all, our experience – learnt the hard way – we will succeed in our aim.

Light reveals to us colours, shapes and textures of objects in our everyday lives. It also allows us to photograph, film and televise for the purpose of conveying visual information, and in the theatre to enable us to enjoy drama and music.

For most of our lives we take light for granted. It is hoped that this book will help towards the understanding of what light is, how it can be used and the instruments by which it can be moulded and shaped.

2   Theory of light

2.1 The eye

It is an incredible fact that we take for granted one of the most
sophisticated pieces of the anatomy. Even with the wonders of modern
technology scientists cannot come up with a piece of equipment that has to
include the following:

1.   Three dimensional optical system.
2.   High definition.
3.   Highly sophisticated colour sensitivity system.
4.   Auto focus.
5.   Auto iris.
6.   Automatic sensitivity.
7.   No signal-to-noise problems – no grain!
8.   High overload factor.
9.   Virtually no maintenance.

Luckily nature did, and from the time of man's arrival on earth, eyes were
essential to survival and – even more importantly for the advance of
civilization – for communication. Before the telegraphic, wireless and TV
systems were introduced in the late 19th and early 20th centuries, man
could only communicate directly through speech and additionally by
symbols, drawings and script.

A major problem with the human eye is that it can be fooled; it is not an
absolute measuring instrument such as a colour meter, but relies mainly on
comparative measurements to assess information. If we show a human
being, in a darkened room, a succession of similarly coloured lights with
intervals of darkness between, the subject is totally unaware of a change
over quite a wide range, for example from pale blue to a mid-blue.
However, two colours when shown side by side have only to vary by a small
amount and the difference is noticeable. As we can process much visual
information by using our superior intelligence, the human eye does not
have to be as good as that of many birds and animals.

When light enters the lens of the eye, it is received by the retina which
consists of millions of photoreceptors, packed into an area about 1.5
centimetres square. Human beings have two types of receptors called
'rods' and 'cones', because we live in two distinct worlds – night and day.

The cones, which number approximately seven million, are for the detailed full-colour examination of objects in bright light; the rods, which number approximately one hundred and thirty million, are for the examination of objects in low light conditions. Rods and cones are not dissimilar in their individual sensitivity; but to achieve a higher sensitivity several rods are coupled together, and this accounts for the eyes' loss of sharpness at night.

The eye can accept intensity levels that vary by a factor of more than 10^{12} (a million million) but our eyes' iris can only control over a range of 16:1. How is this?

In 1877 a German biologist, Franz Boll, examined a frog's eye taken from a dark closet in the laboratory. At the back of the eye he saw a reddish substance that quickly faded upon exposure to light. This phenomenon had been noticed by other scientists who generally dismissed it as a blood clot. Boll was dissatisfied with this theory and upon examination discovered that if the eye was returned to the dark and the experiment repeated, the reddish substance reappeared. Boll had discovered that a chemical change takes place in the eye when light enters it. In 1959 at the Johns Hopkins University, two scientists inserted a microscopic electrode into the brain of a cat and recorded the activity of a single nerve cell in the vision system of the brain. When the cat viewed a light flashing, electrical signals were emitted from the nerve cell. The connection between these two experiments is that light when passing into the eye creates a chemical reaction, and subsequently the chemical reaction is transferred into electrical energy. Shortly after Boll had realized the significance of the reddish substance, Wilhelm Kühne managed to extract some of the chemical from the rods in the frog's eye. This substance was called *Sehpurpur,* a German word meaning visual scarlet, but was incorrectly translated into English as *visual purple,* and even today is known as that. The chemical's correct name is Rhodopsin. A Rhodopsin molecule consists of two parts; a simple molecule called Retinal and a protein molecule called Opsin. Opsin is built from amino acids and its complex structure has not yet been fully catalogued. Different proteins are found in the cones and these determine the colour response. Incidentally, the Rhodopsin pigment is a close relative to the vitamin A of carrots. Earier in the present century researchers had found that vision in humans was harmed by vitamin A deficiency, and to some people this meant that by eating large quantities of carrots they would improve their vision. However, this is not the case and people on a good balanced diet will not have any problems. The excess vitamin A taken by an overdose of carrots is simply passed through the body: the greatest danger is turning a shade of red by consuming large quantities of the 'carotene' present in the humble carrot.

Rhodopsin absorbs all wavelengths of light and when it is subjected to high light input levels it bleaches out and thus loses some of its absorbency. The reduction of sensitivity in the rods means that the cone receptors will be used. These, being less sensitive, will pass lower signals to the brain thus producing a form of automatic gain control.

Owing to the complexity of connections between the rods and cones and the optic nerve, there are 150 million photoreceptors connected to about 1 million fibres in the optic nerve, with a much higher number of rods, in relation to the cones. As several rods work together into one nerve to increase low light sensitivity, our low light acuity of vision is poor. The cones with their lower density means signals are passed with higher resolution. Due to the cones' lower sensitivity, we all feel better doing fine work in high light levels when the cones are working efficiently. (See Figure 2.1(a), (b), (c).)

In 1825, Jan Evangelista Purkinje noticed that at twilight the flowers in his garden apparently changed colours in relation to each other as the illumination changed. As it became darker, red flowers became black, although at this point the green leaves were relatively unaffected. Purkinje had experienced the change from 'cone' vision during daylight to 'rod' vision at night. The 'rod' light receptors, although generally more sensitive than 'cones', have a lower response to light at long wavelengths, thus reds diminish rapidly at dark. The Purkinje effect states that there is a shift of maximum sensitivity towards blue at low light levels.

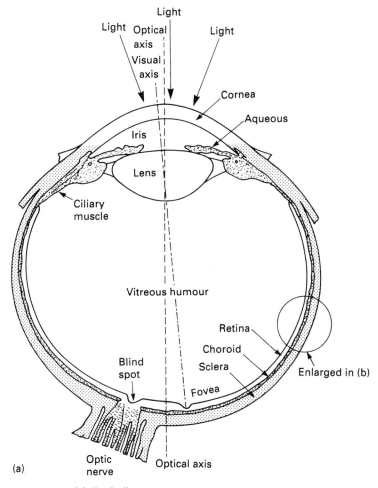

(a)

Figure 2.1   (a) Eyeball

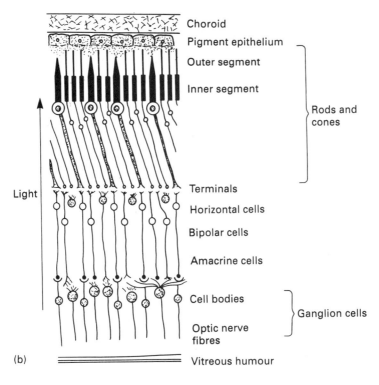

Choroid

Pigment epithelium

Outer segment

Inner segment

Rods and cones

Light

Terminals

Horizontal cells

Bipolar cells

Amacrine cells

Cell bodies

Ganglion cells

Optic nerve fibres

(b)

Vitreous humour

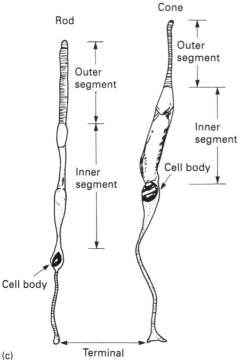

Cone

Rod

Outer segment

Outer segment

Inner segment

Inner segment

Cell body

Cell body

(c)   Terminal

Figure 2.1   (b) and (c) Rods and cones

As we go about our daily lives, the world is viewed under many different sources of illumination. The colour of noon daylight is much 'bluer' than the incandescent lights used in our homes. Fluorescent lighting as well as street lighting does not always provide good colour rendering. However, an apple held in our hand when we stand in any of these light sources appears to be the same colour, *irrespective* of the light source. It is as though our brain is programmed to recognize the object and adjust for the colour differences, and therefore our colour vision may not be totally dependent upon the eyes' input to the brain (see Figure 2.2).

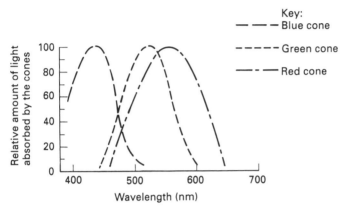

Figure 2.2   Sensitivity of eye receptors

The effect just described is known as 'colour constancy' and holds true for single sources of general illumination. What happens when we are able to see contrasting areas of coloured light at the same time? If we project a beam of white light onto a screen and encircle it with blue light the original beam will become yellow in appearance. Likewise if we encircle the beam with a red surround it will appear cyan. The original beam colour has not changed but we see it differently. Our eyes have seemingly adapted to the surround more than the reference white beam.

We can also have problems with image retention; possibly the most well-known demonstration of this effect is that of staring at a 'green heart shape' surrounded by a yellow border for about 20 seconds and then looking at a plain white surface. The after-image is that of a magenta heart in a blue border. The theory here is that the green of the heart bleached out and what is left are the 'red' and 'blue' receptors, hence magenta. However, image retention is the phenomenon which allows us to perceive the rapidly changing image on a television screen or cinema screen as one smoothly moving picture.

There have been so many theories over the centuries as to how the eyes' colour system works. Isaac Newton, when he published the first edition of his famous book *Opticks* in 1704, speculated about colour vision. One statement was incredibly accurate with a view to the future.

May not the harmony and discord of Colours arise from the proportions of the Vibrations propagated through the fibres of the optic Nerves into the Brain as the harmony and discord of Sounds arise from the proportions of the Vibrations of the Air? For some colours, if they be view'd together are agreeable to one another, as those of Gold and Indigo and other disagree.

In 1801 Thomas Young suggested that the eye contained three colour receptors. It was also reasoned that to provide the correct colour information signals the range of wavelengths for the *red, green* and *blue* receptors would have to overlap each other to some degree and it was only during the 20th century that scientists discovered the true response of the rods and cones to the colour of light.

A point worth making here, as it is relevant, is that the photoreceptors can only respond by changing their voltage, which gives no absolute information as to the colour of the stimulus that caused the change. For the eye to assess accurately the colour and pass the information to the brain, nerve cells from differing colour receptors must be stimulated so that the relative amounts of colour energy in the viewed scene can be assessed. Thus a stimulation of a *red receptor* and a *green receptor* will give a result between pale yellow and deep orange, depending upon the balance of the two receptors.

In more recent times evidence has emerged that in addition to the *red, green* and *blue* visual receptors, cells exist within the nervous system that respond to *red, yellow, green* and *blue* either in combination or opposition. This discovery tends to substantiate the theories of the 19th century physiologist Ewald Hering who proposed four fundamental colours – red, yellow, green and blue. The 'opponent colour theory' suggests that the four colours act in pairs – red/green and yellow/blue. Colour after-images (staring at our green heart is a good example) can be explained by bleaching of photo pigments coupled with some insensitivity in the eyes' complex nervous system. However, it is difficult to explain simultaneous contrast effects such as our circle of light surrounded by another colour particularly when we think of a white light beam turning yellow when viewed with a blue surround, without considering Hering's theory.

Most of the problems associated with the eye when it has a fault are generally corrected by the use of supplementary contact lenses or glasses. One severe problem that is associated with old age is the onset of cataracts on the eyeball and there is evidence that in India, operations on cataracts were made as early as 1000 BC. History tells us that the eye surgeons of the time were remarkably successful and charged very high fees for operations. We are also told, however, that if a wealthy man lost the sight of his eye during the operation, the surgeon's hand would be cut off! The surgeon was much luckier if it was only a slave undergoing the operation because he just had to replace him.

We have tried to show in this section that although the eye is a marvellous instrument, it is not perfect. There is much that we do not know about its operation although the evidence so far shows that there is much in common between the eye, TV cameras and film cameras. In fact, it has been suggested that the coding system for passing colour information in the human brain is very similar to that used in the vision chain of any TV station. What we are aware of as we go about our daily lives is an abundance of wonderful pictures in 3-D and colour that enrich the human spirit.

2.2 Electromagnetic spectrum

The narrow band of electromagnetic radiation which lies between ultraviolet and infra-red of wavelengths from 0.0004 mm (400 nm) to 0.0007 mm (700 nm) is detectable by the human eye and is known as light (see Figure 2.3).

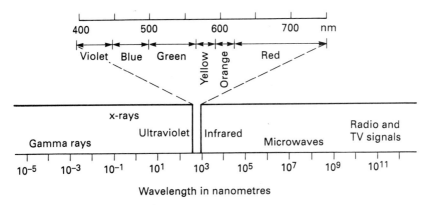

Figure 2.3   Electromagnetic spectrum

Heinrich Hertz in 1888 experimented with the transmission of electromagnetic waves at a frequency of approximately 100MHz generated by a spark-gap transmitter. Hertz was able to calculate the speed at which the electromagnetic waves travelled and found them to be exactly the same as the speed of light. He also, in the course of his experiments, observed wave reflection, wave refraction and wave interference. All of these are also well-known optical phenomena and thus Hertz concluded that lightwaves were another form of electromagnetic waves.

Hertz believed that his discovery of the properties of electromagnetic waves would not find any practical applications. He tragically died of cancer at the age of 37, approximately one year before Marconi demonstrated the first wireless transmission in 1895.

When an object is heated it radiates energy in the form of electromagnetic waves. These waves go from the radio wave end of the electromagnetic spectrum through the infra-red, the visible, the ultraviolet, x-ray and gamma ray. Ultraviolet (UV) is invisible to human beings, but unfortunately, in significant amounts is extremely harmful. Infra-red is also invisible and produces a sensation of heat, but fortunately with no adverse side effects. For most of the hot objects that we encounter on the planet earth the energy lies mainly in the infra-red region. A cooker hot plate may show no visible signs of heat, but when a hand is held over it, it feels warm; we are experiencing infra-red at about 500K. When the hot plate is turned up and reaches 1000K we see a slight glow coming from the element which is the onset of visible radiation: the plate also becomes noticeably hotter, showing that there is a increase in the amount of radiated energy. A good example of infra-red radiation is that from the black luminaires that are used in the entertainment industry: there is no visible sign of heat from the body of the luminaire, although we get a nasty burn if we touch it.

The tungsten filament in the lamps that we use radiates a white light around 3000K. To produce ultraviolet radiation in significant amounts, temperatures of 3500K and higher are required and most solid objects on earth melt by the time they reach this temperature. We generally produce temperatures around the 6000K mark by mercury vapour lamps, such as fluorescent, xenon and modern HMI lamps, and they all emit large amounts of ultraviolet radiation. When using modern discharge light sources, we have to be very much aware of the dangers connected with this type of illumination.

Ultraviolet radiation covers the range 4–400 nm and it begins at the short wavelength limit of visibility (violet) and extends to x-rays. It is divided into near (400–300 nm), far (300–200 nm) and extreme (below 200 nm). The near ultraviolet energy is known generally as 'blacklight'. The UV emitted is used to excite fluorescent pigments used in dyes, paints and other materials to produce effects for advertising and, more importantly to us, in the theatre and sometimes on television. The ultraviolet radiation in sunlight on the surface of the earth extends from about 300 nm to 390 nm and is generally our source of getting a suntan, with very long exposures causing cancer of the skin. At wavelengths shorter than this, UV becomes exceedingly dangerous to the human being. The reasons for this are that the radiation between 300 and 390 nm is little absorbed and is not so active on organisms. The radiation between 200 and 300 nm is well absorbed, produces damage to cells and the effect is nearly always permanent.

For the purposes of this book, we are concerned with the visible part of the spectrum and to a large extent the infra-red. The visible gives us the light by which we can illuminate for the purposes of entertainment, the infra-red gives us problems with heating and subsequently the ventilation, which will be discussed later in the book.

2.3 Colour perception

If we read any book on physics concerning light, it will inevitably discuss the principle of waves and particles. At the turn of the 20th century there was much discussion as to the physical properties of light, and in 1905 when Einstein demonstrated that light travelled quite happily in a vacuum, he proposed that light behaved like a wave and also like a particle. Most of the debate at that time centred around the theory of blackbodies and their radiation; the problem being that the observed experiments did not conform to the scientific predictions. Although the world owes Einstein and his colleagues an enormous debt for showing us the way with most of modern physics, we are ourselves, for the purposes of this book, not concerned with the basic physical theory of light itself – only the effects it has and how we can use those effects.

The early philosophers, such as Pythagoras and Euclid, debated the nature of light and how the eye responded to a viewed scene. Theories went from a projected image from the viewed object which entered the eye, to the possibility that sensing rays went from the eye to the subject, rather like radar and that these rays would pass information back to the eye. We now know that most objects do not radiate any lightwaves whatsoever, and only convert the incident light on them into the shape, colour and appearance that we see. The two sensations we are most concerned with are the objects, brightness and colour. It was probably very fortunate for most scholars of today that Isaac Newton, to escape the effects of the great plague of London during 1665 and 1666, retreated to the family farm in the countryside. It was during this period of time that he focused his attention on the nature of light and subsequently produced his classic book *Opticks*. Newton's experiments with colour were conducted by allowing sunlight to pass through a small hole in a darkened window. This beam of white light was passed through a glass prism and the emerging light spread out in a 'spectrum' of colours. The colours were red, orange, yellow, green, blue, indigo and violet. History tends to give Newton the credit for discovering the prism for this effect but this was not the case; it had been observed by scholars for many years. What Newton did was to take the original idea of splitting light via a prism and then use this to examine the colours coming through. By selecting one colour from the first prism and passing that colour through a second prism, he discovered that the second prism had no effect at all on the colour of the original light. He therefore concluded that colours were not the result of the prism changing the light but the fact that all normal white light contained the observed colours and the prism only acted to separate the colours. Having separated the colours out, Newton thought he should be able to return them back to the original white light source and by using an inverted prism after the first prism, he was able to recreate a white beam of light. Newton then experimented with coloured objects under the various sources of illumination and from these experiments discovered most of the concepts that enabled modern colour theory to evolve. For instance, he found that a red object would efficiently reflect red light but would appear very dark and nearly black when illuminated by lights of other colours. It was apparent to Newton that objects have colour because they reflect certain colours while absorbing the remainder of the spectrum. If we view the spectrum as split by a prism, as Newton did, we will notice that it does not contain all of the colours that we encounter in our everyday lives such as magenta or black and white.

Newton's theories caused a great stir in the world at large and one of the reasons for this was the fact that most human beings first learn about colour by painting. The lessons learnt from mixing the colours of paint are somewhat different to those from mixing the colours of light. It has to be realized that light is the source of all colour but pigments in paint are simply reflectors or absorbers of parts of the light that illuminates them. Most artists when asked for their primary colours will quote blue, yellow and red, whereas the scientist, on being asked the same question, will list red, green and blue. One interesting fact is that the scientist does not quote yellow as a prime colour. However, if a beam of red light and a beam of green light are superimposed the result is yellow. On the other hand, if we mix red and green paint we get rather a nasty looking browny-black colour. When using light, all spectral colours can be created by adding various component parts of the red, green and blue light and the system used is called 'addition', ultimately creating white. Pigments derive their colours by subtracting parts of the spectrum; therefore the system with pigments is called 'subtraction' and ultimately creates black.

The light from the sun and incandescent sources is generally white by nature and contains all the colours of the spectrum. However, as we will discover in other sections of the book, various sources produce light by exciting portions of the visible spectrum to gain a response from the eye; but because they do not contain all the colours of the spectrum some distortion of colour can take place.

If we ring a colleague in Australia from England and describe a red dress, she does have some idea of what we are talking about. A problem arises when we require our colleague to reproduce *exactly* the colour of the dress. How can we specify colour and its brightness accurately? One of the first attempts to define colour precisely was by an American called Albert Munsell in 1915, and his three-dimensional colour system is still in use today (see Figure 2.4 in colour plate section). The Munsell system enables three qualities to be quantified. These are:

Hue describes the basic colour such as red or blue;
Value (or brightness) refers to how light or dark the colour appears (it is a measure of the amount of reflected light);
Chroma (or saturation) refers to the intensity of colour; as a colour moves away from white it becomes more and more saturated.

However, the Munsell system is only as good as the illumination it is viewed in. We have all come across the problem of the piece of material that we are buying in the shop, or the suit that we have selected, which looks much better when we go to the doorway of the shop and examine it under daylight. We are also aware of how bad our skin looks under sodium street lighting. Coloured objects reflect light; the problem is that they do not reflect the entire spectrum of the light that falls on them, or the light that falls on them is deficient in some way. The effect that the source of light has on any object is known as the 'colour rendering'. In general, under normal illumination such as daylight, incandescent light, etc., there will be no problems; however, discharge lighting (which may be fluorescent, street lighting or the type that we would use in studios) will cause colour distortion by not having continuous spectral outputs. For instance, a green sample of cloth will look green only if there is green energy in the incident light. When we look in the manufacturer's data on lamps, we will invariably find in the sections on fluorescent, discharge, etc., reference to the *colour rendering index*.

In 1965 the Commission Internationale d'Eclairage (CIE) introduced a system to regulate the colour rendering index (Ra). The system measures eight colour samples taken from the Munsell system, illuminated with a test source, and this is compared with a reference illumination. The reference source has a value of 100, and due to the deficiencies in spectral output, the test source can at best equal or generally be less than the reference source and thus the Ra can never be greater than 100, and in most cases will be 90 or less (see Table 2.1).

Table 2.1   CIE general colour rendering index (Ra)

Reference source	Typical application
Greater than 90	Where accurate colour matching is required, e.g. colour print inspection.
80 to 90	Where accurate colour judgements are necessary and/or good colour rendering is required for reasons of appearance, e.g. shops and other commercial premises.
60 to 80	Where moderate colour rendering is required.
40 to 60	Where colour rendering is of little significance but marked distortion of colour is unacceptable.
20 to 40	Where colour rendering is of no importance and marked distortion of colour is acceptable.

Note: For film or TV use we would need an Ra index of at least 80.

Two approaches have been used to describe colour. The first uses standard colour samples such as the Munsell system against which materials can be compared. A second system is to analyse the light reflected from a surface and then assign a set of values which specify the colour. As we are now looking at reflected light we can use the primary colours of red, blue and green, giving a '*tri-stimulus*' to the eye. The first system to try to define the colour by its spectral components was that of Newton, but Newton used seven basic primaries derived from his prism observations where from any mix of the seven it was possible to produce a range of colours towards white. One of the problems with the Newtonian system was that it did not contain the entire range of colours, for instance lacking any reference to purple (see Figure 2.5).

To be able to compile a very accurate system of colour specification, it was necessary to have a deeper knowledge of colour mixing, which unfortunately Newton did not have. He was also incapable of measuring light with the great accuracies that are required for modern colour measurement (see Figure 2.6, colour plate section).

In 1931 it was decided by the Commission Internationale d'Eclairage to develop a more accurate colorimetric system. To comprehend the system that the CIE adopted, we have to understand how metamerism works. The spectral difference between sources can be quite considerable, as shown in Figure 2.7, where a stimulus consisting of continuous power throughout the visible spectrum is matched by three narrow bands of energy in the red,

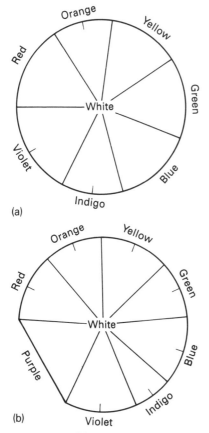

Figure 2.5   (a) Newton wheel. (b) Modified wheel by Harris

green and blue only. If we choose three primary sources of light which are derived from standard white light filtered by a red, a green and a blue filter, we can use these as standard sources for colour mixing. The CIE system is based upon using a standard observer who is seated in front of a white screen. On one half of the screen is projected some arbitrary light source; on the other half of the screen is projected a combination of our three primaries. The observer has to adjust the intensity of the three primaries until both sides of the screen match exactly in colour and brightness. Although the two halves of the screen now look the same, they do not necessarily have the same spectral composition. The amounts of the red, blue and green sources specify the colour that we are viewing but not the light itself. Those three numbers are unique to the colour observed.

The theory of colour matching is quite complex and the CIE set out to create a system that was relatively easy to use and understand.

Figure 2.8 shows the three primaries chosen by the CIE and these are called $\bar{x}$, $\bar{y}$ and $\bar{z}$; where $\bar{x}$ corresponds to the red primary, $\bar{y}$ to the green primary and $\bar{z}$ to the blue primary. The green primary curve ($\bar{y}$) shows the

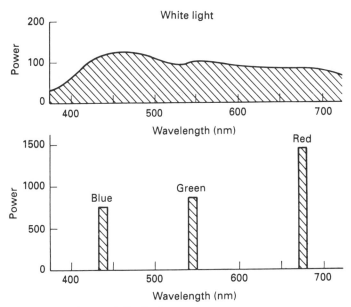

Figure 2.7 Spectral distribution

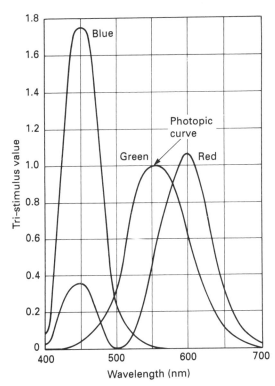

Figure 2.8 CIE primary functions

sensitivity of the human eye to light of different wavelengths and, as can be seen, the eye's sensitivity is at a maximum at around 550 nm but very poor towards the blue and red ends of the spectrum. By using the 'photopic curve', as it is known, as a 'multiplier' for any spectrum which is being analysed, we can calculate the apparent brightness. In other words, the source has much more energy than we are able to absorb.

The X, Y and Z values are called the tri-stimulus values of the spectrum and the relative amounts of each give the colour and brightness of the viewed scene. To find X, we have to multiply the spectrum as measured, by the x̄ curve and the result gives the energy required for the stimulus. We would also have to do the same for the Y and Z values. The values of X, Y and Z are able to specify the colour accurately. The trouble is, it is very difficult when given these values to imagine what the colour actually looks like. We need a method by which we have an instant reference to the colour itself. The easiest way of looking anything up is to have a visual presentation, and in this case it is the CIE chromaticity diagram. The diagram is another version of Newton's colour wheel system; thus as we did with the Newton system we can use the chromaticity diagram to analyse colours. Newton's original colour circle did not include purple, which is of course a combination of red and blue, but as can be seen from Figure 2.6 we do have a purple line. What has happened is we have plotted the spectrum locus on a graph which has an 'x' axis and a 'y' axis. The colour co-ordinates are derived from the following formula:

$$x = \frac{X}{X + Y + Z}$$

$$y = \frac{Y}{X + Y + Z}$$

$$z = \frac{Z}{X + Y + Z}$$

As the sum of $x + y + z$ will always equal 1, we only need two variables as the third can be determined from the other two. By convention, we use the co-ordinates x and y to describe the colour. It must be noted, however, that those co-ordinates only specify the hue and the saturation of the colour but *not* its brightness. To ascertain the brightness, we have to use the value of Y, the green tri-stimulus value (photopic curve). As we move from the periphery of the colour locus towards the centre of our diagram, saturation of colours diminishes until we reach white. The centre of the colour locus is positioned at the co-ordinates x = 0.33, y = 0.33, where the saturation has become zero. This point is known as 'equal energy white' or 'reference white' (colour temperature 9600K).

In the laboratory we can do a spectral analysis of a source and then by using the CIE values compute the amount of X, Y, Z to give the tri-stimulus values. However, this is not always convenient in the studio, on the stage or in the middle of the sports field, and conveniently for us Minolta developed a hand-held tri-stimulus meter which measures the values of the three primaries, does the computations and presents the figures for the co-ordinates and brightness very neatly on a little screen.

The CIE method enables us to do two things:

1.   To analyse the colour of a surface.
2.   To analyse the spectrum of a light source coming to a surface.

Most of our use of a colour meter is to measure the colour of the light source, be it normal or modified by filters, etc. If we are examining the colour of a surface, then we need to know the colour of the reference source to reduce the variables to manageable proportions. The CIE adopted three standard light sources and these are:

Source A: This is a source typical of an incandescent lamp operated at a colour temperature of 2856K.

Source B: This source is typical of noon sunlight and has a colour temperature of about 4870K.

Source C: This represents an overcast sky or average daylight and has a colour temperature of about 6700K.

Blackbody radiation

The scientists studying blackbody radiation discovered the following facts:

1.   The spectrum is continuous, just like the sun's, and includes all the visible colours together with the infra-red and ultraviolet spectra.
2.   When a graph is plotted of intensity versus wavelength, there is always a maximum intensity at only one wavelength.
3.   As the object becomes hotter, the wavelengths of maximum radiation become shorter.
4.   The hotter the object becomes, the greater the total amount of radiation from a given area.

Lacking the knowledge of today's scientists, their predecessors postulated the theory of a body absorbing all the radiation falling on it and to do that effectively it would have to be black, and hence the world was introduced to the term 'blackbody'. What the scientists did not know was that the blackbody was capable of radiation and although not commonly realized, every object radiates some light. The chair we sit on appears quite cool but in a room at 20°C, it is still 293° above zero Kelvin and according to the known laws of physics will radiate energy. Many modern surveillance systems actually look for radiated energy of low intensity. One good thing about blackbody radiation is that it starts in the very deep reds and goes to the very deep blues, passing through white in the process which, as human beings, we happily accept. When we depart from the blackbody curve and approach green or magenta we are psychologically disturbed.

Figure 2.9 shows blackbodies at 2000K, 3200K, 5600K and 6500K. In addition to the visible spectrum, many other wavelengths are also radiated; the more the temperature is raised, the more energy and subsequently light is radiated. The curves also show a shift towards the blue end of the spectrum as the energy becomes greater. Modern incandescent lamps are very close to the blackbody radiation curve and in general are given a colour temperature to signify the colour of their light output. Incandescent

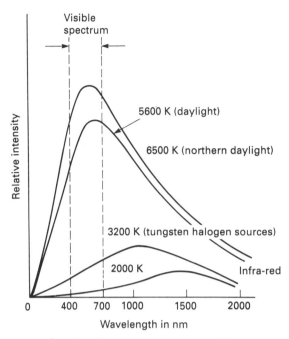

Figure 2.9   Continuous spectrum emitted by four typical blackbodies

lamps that we deal with have a colour temperature around the 3000K mark. The sun is around 5000K and light from the blue sky is generally from about 6000K upwards.

If we wish to measure purely colour temperature, we measure the relative amounts of red and blue of the blackbody curve of the source in question. When the source deviates from the blackbody curve we have to use a tri-stimulus meter so we can measure the green component.

Why is it that the discharge source is so different from that of the incandescent? Probably at some time in our lives we have thrown an object into a fire and then been amazed at the magnificent colours produced when it burns. The colours are unique to the substance. In 1752 a Scotsman, Thomas Melvill, studied the light from a flame through a prism and discovered that the spectrum was not continuous. Some parts of the observed spectrum were bright and other parts were dark. When Melvill experimented with different chemicals burning in the flame, he found the locations of the bright and dark areas changed. From the early 19th century onwards the spectroscope was developed to enable researchers to examine the various colours generated within light sources. Each chemical element has a unique set of wavelengths and thus bright lines within its spectrum, and these can be used just like 'fingerprints'. With the advent of electricity, research was carried out on the effect of voltage when applied to gases. During the latter part of the 19th century many different gases were studied and their element lines plotted, and it was discovered that some gases have thousands of lines and some have very few. Sodium in particular has only two lines in the yellow part of the spectrum, so close together that they appear as one and this is the characteristic of many street lights that are in use today. Neon, on the other hand, has very strong lines in the red and orange sectors of the spectrum.

Observing these bright line spectra was one thing, but to actually understand their generation was another. Ernest Rutherford, of atomic energy fame, was the first to postulate the theory of the planetary atomic structure. This theory suggests that the atom is mostly empty space, rather like our solar system, and that the individual parts of an atom orbit a nucleus. The scientific theory of the time, however, did not explain the existence of bright line spectra. In 1913, Niels Bohr, a Danish physicist, set out to explain how the bright line spectra evolved. His theory was that the electrons occupied defined orbits around the nucleus; these orbits were governed by the amount of energy an electron had as it orbited the nucleus. If the electron was given additional energy by some means, the electron could be made to move to one of the higher levels within the atom. As well as moving, the excited electron had also become unstable. To regain stability, the excited electron would have to fall back to the lower level from whence it came and in the process lose the energy again, in the form of light.

Bohr's experiments were generally confined to the energy levels of the relatively simple hydrogen atom, and thus provided details of the hydrogen spectrum. These experiments laid down some of the ground rules for further research, which in modern times has revealed more and more complexities of the atom. When we view sources made up of several lines of energy we do not see the individual lines because our eyes integrate all the energy and tend to mix the colours together. However, it may be that the energy is not in the visible spectrum at all and is produced in the ultraviolet region. This energy, while not directly visible, is able to produce visible light by exciting certain chemicals, and a good example of this is the fluorescent light. Fluorescent tubes are glass tubes coated internally with a phosphor. Phosphors are similar to atoms in their response to energy but produce bands of colours rather than individual line spectra. An electric current flows through the vaporized mercury in the fluorescent tube and in so doing excites the electrons. When the electrons fall back to the lower levels they release energy. Some of the energy generated is in the visible region of the spectrum but mostly it is in the ultraviolet and it is this ultraviolet energy that causes the phosphors to glow. It should be noted that higher energy sources can excite phosphors but lower energy sources are incapable; thus ultraviolet will cause the production of light but infra-red energy cannot. Fluorescent tubes tend to have much energy at the blue end of the spectrum as well as nasty spikes in the green, and to balance their colour, combinations of phosphors are used so that the integrated light output approaches that of normal incandescent lamps. Thus we hear terms like 'daylight', 'warm white', etc. which are descriptions of their inherent colour, but not always of their colour rendering properties.

The modern discharge sources such as the HMI, MSR, CSI, etc. operate from the principles discussed, usually with an electric arc exciting mercury vapour and rare earth gases in various forms to give blends of colour. If we observe from its cold state a discharge lamp slowly warming up to its final operating temperature, we will see the discrete bands of energy joining in at various levels to form the colours that make up the composite output.

2.4 Spectral output of sources

Although apparently the graphs, shown below, are very different to each other, the various light sources produce a sensation of white in the human eye. When a light source produces light at every wavelength in the visible spectrum and possibly energy either end of the visible spectrum, it is considered a continuous source. Four of the most common are reproduced in Figure 2.10.

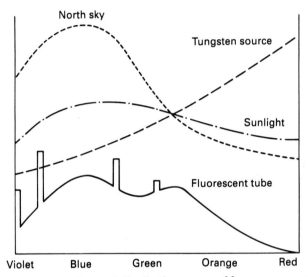

Figure 2.10   Spectral distribution curves of four common sources

Although these four sources appear white as far as we are concerned, when objects are viewed under the various types of illumination, we will get vastly differing results. As a yardstick, it would be nice to have a source that gave a perfect white, and such a source would not show any imbalance towards the red, the blue or the green of the spectrum, and would contain equal amounts of each. This source is called an 'equal energy source' and has been discussed in reference to the CIE system.

All blackbody sources are continuous radiation sources and although biased heavily either to the red or the blue, according to the temperature of the radiator, the colour distortion is at a minimum. The interesting thing about continuous sources is the fact that nature has provided sources of this type from time immemorial and all the light derived from hot objects, such as candles, oil lamps, and wood and coal fires, obey the laws of the blackbody radiator. It is only in recent times that sources of a different type have been developed for use by mankind; the reason being more light for the power consumed and is usually a consumer-led development by lamp manufacturers. Probably the most well known of these is the fluorescent tube. One advantage of using mercury discharge sources was that they provided high efficiencies of light output. In the

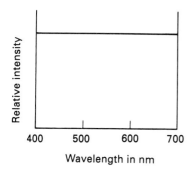

Figure 2.11   The equal energy spectrum

earlier days of discharge lamps, however, quantity was put very much
before quality. In the basic mercury discharge lamp, radiation is mainly
found in the blue, the green and the yellow sectors in very narrow band
spikes and obviously does not give a good colour response. Typical
examples of basic discharge lamps are those used in street lighting and
some forms of crude floodlighting, which tend to be either rather blue or
predominantly yellow. To improve the colour of the light source, it is
necessary to introduce elements such as tin, indium, sodium, lithium and
scandium. One of the problems with using some of these elements is that
they could react with the silica envelope and rapidly destroy the lamp. In
practice, by using metals in the form of their halide salts (hence the name
metal halide lamps) most of the problem is overcome. The list below gives
examples of the radiation that can be produced with the various elements:

Tin produces orange/red radiation
Scandium produces blue and green radiation
Sodium produces yellow radiation
Thallium produces green radiation
Lithium produces red radiation

By selecting the various metals and metal halides that can be used, we can
introduce more spectral spikes into the characteristic and eventually end
up with colour rendering of a very high order, such as those in HMI lamps
and MSR lamps.

2.5 Filters

We have discussed in other sections the need for the almost apparent
perfection of the white light that we use either for daylight matching or for
incandescent source matching; in this section we shall talk mainly about
distorting the colour of light.

The choice of colour to create the required effect or mood in theatre was
established from very early days by placing a coloured glass or silk in front
of the light source. In 1858 Covent Garden introduced overhead gas
battens running the width of the stage, and provided colour change by

stitching together two-foot-wide lengths of gauze coloured red, green and blue which could be pulled around the gas batten to produce the required colour. Alternative materials were silk, calico or tammy. A high price was paid for early experiments with lighting and the attempts to provide colour: theatres caught fire and many people died. It is therefore no wonder that the fire officers insist that all materials used as colour filter must pass the appropriate safety tests.

Early colour filter material was made of gelatine dyed to the required colour. This offered an enormous range, but suffered the problem of handling. As it dried out, it would become very brittle and virtually shatter and fall to pieces, and of course, presented a fire hazard. However, the use of gelatine filter persisted into the 1960s. The advent of electric lamps in the late 1890s provided another possibility for colouring the light by dipping the lamps into coloured lacquer. This provided an excellent choice of colours but, of course, it could not be changed once the lamp had been coated. With the introduction of the incandescent tungsten filament lamp in the early 1900s, the heat was to prove too much for the lacquer coating for anything other than low wattage sources. This led, in the early 1930s, to the introduction of a new colour material made from cellulose acetate by a complicated method of shaving thin sheets from a large block of the dyed material and polishing the sheet until it became a transparent colour filter. This type of filter has persisted until today but has lost popularity to the alternative plastic materials that can be coated with the appropriate colours on a continuous production method of manufacture. The main problem with cellulose acetate filter is that it becomes very soft when used with tungsten halogen lamps with their more efficient light output. These lamps will also burn a hole at the centre of the filter, bleach the colour out or turn it dark, depending on the pigments used in its manufacture.

Glass filters have always been used and are still in use today. However, after the initial euphoria over the fact that the glass filter does not fade or burn out, one soon finds that they are so restrictive that they are not a very practical solution. The colour restriction is caused by the glass manufacturer requiring the lighting filter stockist to order what is known in the glass industry as a 'melt', which can be about one tonne, but of course, it is all one colour and will probably supply his customers for years. Unfortunately any one particular melt cannot be guaranteed to match the next melt, and therefore some permanent applications, such as cyclorama backings that were thought to be ideal for glass filters, were faced with changing all of the filters when replacements were required, because the new colours stood out from the rest. An additional problem with glass filters is that they can shatter if unevenly heated, causing a safety problem when used in overhead luminaires.

The two main colour filters in use today are plastics, known as polyester and polycarbonate. Both are suitable for tungsten halogen luminaires and both have their attractions. Polyester is normally cheaper but does not last so long, and the polycarbonate tends to justify its price by the reduction in replacement costs and the time involved. Both materials are available in over 100 colours and hues and can even be used by adding colours in the same luminaire to create a special shade for the lighting director (LD) who cannot find the one he wants in the swatch book.

Many books have been written on the subject of the use of colour to create the right mood and setting – from joy to sadness, from shock to restful security. However tempting it is to pursue this course, we must confine our studies to producing the colours for the LD to use and the simple physics involved to achieve the desired effect. The LD has two variables to consider:

(a) the colour of the light;
(b) the colour of the subject.

He has total control of the first variable but the second is completely beyond his control and must be determined at an early stage of planning if he is to achieve the desired artistic effect. The correct colour of costumes and scenery must be used during the rehearsals when the colour filters are being chosen or disaster will result.

As human beings we tend to associate reds and yellows with bright and breezy situations, and blue with much more sombre occasions; red is also associated with daylight and blue with night. One only has to look at any old Hollywood movie – or for that matter a British movie – to see the use of unfiltered carbon arcs giving extremely blue night-time lighting for effect. A very well-known ex-BBC lighting director once opined that the only time to use a green filter in colour television was with a cello player, to enhance the rich colour of the wood. It is an interesting observation of how we associate colour with certain things in our lives.

Originally very few filters were produced for effects purposes, but over the years manufacturers have come to produce vast ranges of subtle colour filters. Most of these, we suggest, are to satisfy the individual foibles of the lighting practitioners and not necessarily the requirements of the viewer.

Other types of filter required in the lighting industry are the kind that either change the colour of the light source itself or change the colour of the viewed image as seen by television, film or photographic cameras. It must be said at this time that any filter which changes the nature of the light cannot necessarily be designated as a particular colour filter, a colour temperature changing filter or any other type. A filter essentially changes the colour of a light source and therefore could be used for any purpose where the resultant colour may be required. What is extremely important, for the purposes of this book, is how do we achieve good filtering and at the same time keep a high transmission level so that we do not waste large amounts of light. It also has to be remembered that a filter called 'Bright Rose' looks decidedly not 'Bright Rose' when put in front of a predominantly blue source. Most publications – and for that matter filter manufacturers – go into great realms of detail about *mired shifts*. It is our experience that most practitioners of the art of lighting tend to do things on a trial and error basis, the point being that mired values are only as good as the light sources themselves allow; in other words mired values applied to a known shift such as 5600K down to 3200K are somewhat changed if the source is not at 5600K to start with.

A good filter should only be interested in the visual energy, i.e. that from 400 nm to 700 nm. A perfect filter would only remove that portion of energy in which we are interested in a very precise way. However, filters cannot be made to this sort of tolerance and generally have some form of overlap and thus remove other bits of energy from the light beam.

When light falls on any material three things occur: some light will be reflected; if the material is translucent enough some light will pass through the material; and some of the light will be absorbed within the material. The absorbed light will be converted to heat energy. When the majority of the light is either reflected or transmitted or there is a combination of the two effects, the smaller quantity will be the heating effect. To illustrate this effect, white and other pale coloured materials usually reflect most of the incident light. For example, many people will wear light coloured clothing in the summer which reflects most of the energy in the sunlight, but we generally wear dark coloured clothing in the winter to keep us warm. The black telephone sitting in the sunlight on our desks has an extremely low reflectance and it also transmits little or no light. Consequently the telephone gets rather hot, which may be good news for the telephone company's replacement programme, but is not so good for the user.

When we wish to change the colour of a light source for effect or colour correction, we will invariably put some form of coloured filter in the light path. We cannot introduce a colour that is not present in the source. The colour of the emerging light from the filter depends upon the spectrum of the incident light striking the filter and on the characteristics of transmission of the filter itself. As well as the *colour* of the emergent light from a filter we will also be very much concerned with the *quantity of light* the filter lets through, otherwise known as the *transmission*. A filter works by subtracting selected portions of the spectrum away from the light source. If we start with the same amounts of red, green and blue light in the light source, and our filter takes away the green component, we are left with the red and blue which, when mixed together, give *magenta*. Thus our magenta filter can also be called a *minus green* filter. A yellow filter would allow the red and green portions of the spectrum through, taking away the blue; thus it can be called a *yellow* filter or a *minus blue*. A cyan filter allows the blue and green light through and stops the red portion of the spectrum; therefore a *cyan* filter is also a *minus red*.

So far, we have looked at removing one colour. If we remove two colours we can then produce our three primary *additive* mixing colours used for lighting; i.e. if we remove the red and blue components we are left with *green*. The removal of red and green gives *blue*; finally if we take away the blue and green we are left with *red*.

As will be realized, the filters we have just given as examples have the ability to subtract *light away from a portion of the visible spectrum*; it will also be obvious that we are looking at a *subtractive* light process. The amount of light transmitted by any of these filters will be determined by the density of colour of the filters which is determined in turn by the thickness of the colour layer.

By using combinations of the basic magenta, yellow and cyan filters which are often used in photographic processes, in various thicknesses, almost any colour can be produced. The alternatives given for red, green and blue show the two methods of arriving at the same result. For example,

Desired effect	Filters required
White	None
Black	Yellow, cyan, magenta
Red	Yellow, magenta or ($-$blue, $-$green)
Green	Yellow, cyan or ($-$blue, $-$red)
Blue	Cyan, magenta or ($-$red, $-$green)

*Note: In other words removing all the light from the source.

A fine example of the two principles of additive and subtractive colour was demonstrated by Adrian Samoiloff in the 1920s when he had a stage act of illusions created with coloured light and selectively coloured subjects, one of which was to make up the actor in red cosmetics and wearing a coat of black and blue/green stripes. The actor would first be illuminated using a red filter when he would appear to be a white man in a black coat, and when illuminated with a blue/green filter he appeared to be a black man in a striped coat. This effect can be very interesting by design but quite a disaster if created by accident.

When we use two filters to produce a result, what has happened is that the original incident light has been modified by the characteristics of the first filter and consequently the emergent light from the filter is modified by the characteristics of the second filter. The transmission has also been affected and working this out is relatively simple, because if half the light was removed by the first filter and half of this light passed through the second filter, we would have ended up with a quarter of the original light. By this simple example it can be seen that the transmission can be down to quite low percentages on some colours; particularly when we are using primary transmission colours. Colour filters for light sources are usually produced with specified colours in various densities to meet the needs of the LDs. Some luminaires used for colour effects, which have a single light source, have to use combinations of yellow, magenta and cyan filters to achieve their results. A close examination of some manufacturers' filters, particularly in the yellow range, will reveal that a medium yellow filter could be made up from two or more sheets of less dense yellow filters. Other than the need to remove portions of the visible spectrum for effects purposes, there is on occasions need to remove the ultraviolet and infra-red energy from the spectrum. For example, when filming in museums, special precautions have to be taken to remove much of the infra-red and UV portions of the spectrum from the light sources to avoid contaminating the colours on valuable paintings and *objets d'art*.

In general, the filters used for television, film and stage are essentially types of plastic with dyes in them. Other specialist filters can be produced and these are dichroic layers on sheets of glass. Dichroic filters work by having a very thin layer of a chemical deposited on a piece of glass. The thickness of the surface coating will be one quarter of the wavelength of the light concerned and is obviously extremely thin. The filter works by reflecting a selected wavelength within the spectrum and if a blue dichroic filter, such as the type used with small luminaires, is examined, it will be found that one surface reflects yellow in large amounts. Dichroic filters rely upon the light being perpendicular to the surface of the glass due to the need to keep a precise quarter wavelength for the selection of the colour to be reflected. Light incident from other angles will be affected in different ways; thus it is possible in practice to see a slight variation in colour over the width of a light beam when using dichroic filters. This problem could be solved by curving the filter surface so that all rays are normal to it.

When dichroic filters are mounted on toughened glass, they generally are much better able to withstand heat than conventional type filters. Manufacturers of dichroic filters are able to tailor the surface coatings very precisely to select portions of the electromagnetic spectrum, particularly with infra-red and UV where the division between the visible light and the harmful rays is very narrow. A good example of dichroics is the infra-red reflectors used on cold lamp sources in projector systems and in many of the low voltage sources used in shop displays and architectural lighting.

Colour temperature correction filters are those that change the balance between the red and blue portions of the spectrum only. To change a source from 3200K to 5600K means that the red end of the spectrum has to be diminished; therefore there is a higher balance of blue to red in the filter. To change a 5600K source to 3200K, an orange correction filter removes part of the blue from the light beam to achieve a correct red/blue balance.

We need to use coloured filters to correct the output of light sources in one of two ways. It may be that we have a 3200K source that requires to be raised to 5600K to be used with daylight sources. It could be that we are using a source of 5600K and this requires correction down to 3200K. A problem that exists with filters is that they cause a definite change and are dependent upon the light source for the resultant colour output. A blue filter placed in front of a 3200K lamp would create much less change than if it were used to filter a discharge source. As this is the case, we can hardly label a filter as a 2000K correction filter. Luckily for us, there is a way around the problem and we do this by using 'micro reciprocal degrees'. Suffice it to say that a filter will cause a constant shift in the reciprocal value of the colour temperature of the source. To make the maths easier, the reciprocal value is multiplied by one million, and thus 'mired' stands for 'MIcro REciprocal Degrees'. A colour temperature of 2000K is equivalent to 500 mireds and therefore 4000K equates to 250 mireds. A filter which changed the light from the source from 2000K to 4000K would produce a change of −250 mireds: this filter can be designed so that it always produces the change of −250 mireds, irrespective of the original source.

Note that filters which decrease the colour temperature of sources have positive values, but filters which increase the colour temperature have minus mired shifts.

If we look at some examples, they give a good idea how this system can be used in practice (see Table 2.2).

One type of filter that we require which would fail in its task if it changed the colour of the light in any way, is the neutral density filter. Its very name indicates its purpose; it has to be absolutely neutral and diminishes only the quantity of light and not the colour of light. It generally has two purposes, one of which is to diminish the amount of light entering the camera lens; or

Table 2.2   MIRED examples:

	MIREDS
1. 5600 K Source	178
Filter value	+ 72
Final mired value	250

Therefore *colour temperature* $= \dfrac{1 \times 10^6}{250} = \textbf{4000 K}$

2. 3200 K Source	312
Filter value	−72
Final mired value	240

Therefore *colour temperature* $= \dfrac{1 \times 10^6}{240} = \textbf{4167 K}$

3. 4000 K Source	250
Filter value	−72
Final mired value	178

Therefore *colour temperature* $= \dfrac{1 \times 10^6}{178} = \textbf{5600 K}$

Note that although the same filter has been used in examples (2) and (3), the colour temperature change in (2) is **967 K** and in (3) **1600 K**.

it can be used to filter the light coming through windows and other apertures to allow a balance between a mixture of natural light and artificial light on any scene.

All the foregoing comments have been made with regard to light that was basically white in content on entering the filter. If the light entering a filter was essentially magenta in colour and filtered by a green filter, the result would be no light, as the green light has already been removed and the green filter would just remove the red and blue components of the magenta. This is obviously an extreme case but can serve to illustrate the need to be careful when filtering light sources.

Colour filter comparison tables

One common request amongst filter users in film, TV and theatre, has been for a comparison table of various brands of filter to show that a filter is the same colour as another, or that it is a shade lighter or darker. The main reasons given for this request are:

(a) to select a filter of a different make;
(b) to select a filter of a lighter or darker tint;
(c) to reproduce an LD's lighting plot faithfully, anywhere in the world;
(d) to purchase replacements on the road;
(e) for rental companies, to provide the colours requested from their stock.

All colours offered by the brands included are represented in the tables (see Figure 2.12 in the colour plate section), irrespective of the fact that they are offered as an effects filter or a colour correction filter, thus making most colours available for effects use. The exceptions are a few odd colours that will not fit into the bands represented by the 70 colour references and additionally colours such as chocolate and, of course, the neutral density filters.

The authors have made all filter comparisons by using a 1000W 3200K light source and reading the 'xy' colour co-ordinates on a tri-stimulus meter. The filters were then mounted in order of colour and moved by eye for density so the results can be considered as a subjective opinion of the authors. Cinemoid (a product of Strand Lighting UK) has been included; although it was discontinued in 1987 it had been in use since the early 1930s and appears on many old lighting plots.

To read the tables

From the centre line of each of the 70 colour references, two lines have been drawn horizontally, representing the mid-position of that particular reference colour. Therefore all filter numbers that fall between these two lines are the same colour and density. Numbers that appear above the lines are lighter than the reference, and those that fall below the line are darker. Although the colour references are actual photographs of the colour filters, they will not portray an exact representation of that colour, because of the colour shift inherent in the photographic and printing processes. However, if a colour swatch book of any of the filter stockists mentioned is available, it is quite simple to look up any particular colour in the tables and then make comparisons with all of the other types. For example, if Cinemoid No. 32, which is a medium blue, is called up on an old lighting plot, the alternative filters that are a direct comparison are: Lee 165; Chris James 165; Rosco 67 and 851; Gamcolor 810; Arri 165; Strand 465; Gelatran 71.

All of the following filter stockists provide colour swatch books with information on each filter, giving it a name, its light transmission and a spectral distribution curve. The colour filter comparison tables only quote the manufacturer and their reference number. The range of filters covered are shown in Table 2.3 on page 31.

2.6 Conversion of light in film and TV cameras

Whether light is a wave or a particle, there is no escaping the fact that light is a form of energy, similar to heat, electrical, mechanical and nuclear. In nature energy changes from one form to another. The energy conversion we are most interested in is the conversion of light, either into chemical energy, such as in the eye or in the process of filming, or by the photons that are guided by a lens to the electronic receptors in our television cameras.

One only has to go to various viewers' homes and see the adjustments made to individual television sets to realize that opinions on what constitutes good colour vary quite considerably.

Table 2.3   Colour filter suppliers

Stockist	Name and intended use	Number series	Material
Lee Filters	Effects	100	Polyester
	Correction	200	Polyester
	Effects	HT100	Polycarbonate
Cinemoid	Effects	100	Cellulose acetate
Chris James	Effects	100	Polyester
	Correction	200	Polyester
	Effects	300	Polyester
Roscolab	Roscolux effects	100–300	Polycarbonate/polyester
	Supergel effects	100–300	Polycarbonate
	Cinecolor effects	600	Polyester
	Roscolene effects	800	Cellulose acetate
	Cinegel correction	3000	Polyester
Great American Market	Gamcolor effects	1000	Polyester
	Cinefilter correction	3000	Polyester
Colortran Inc.	Gelatran effects	100	Mylar
Strand Lighting	Chromagel effects	100–300	Polycarbonate
	Strand filter correction	200	Polyester
	Strand filter effects	400	Polyester
	Chromoid effects	100	Polycarbonate
Arri (GB)	Effects	100	Polyester
	Correction	200	Polyester
	Effects	300	Polyester

Before we progress further, perhaps it would be wise to declare the objectives that we would try to reach in the reproduction of colour in any scene. The main criterion in the reproduction of colour is that if we were able to look at the reproduced scene, side by side with the original, there would be very little difference between the two.

Modern 35 mm film emulsion can withstand enormous exposure latitudes and to some extent colour distortion. We, as professionals in the entertainment field, must have standards to adhere to and, as boring as it may seem, these usually involve a scientific measurement or some form of discipline in operational procedures. Whether we are going to produce negative film or reversal film the basic system is the exposure of three layers of emulsion to red, green and blue light. Those layers are inherently superimposed within the emulsion itself. It is of course possible to individually process the red, green and blue light arriving at the film by using three separate film stocks, and this was the basis of the old Technicolor system used from 1932 to 1955. One of the problems with using three different stocks for the red, green and blue components is that although it is easy to separate the constituent colours, the superimposition of the three images to reproduce the final image is somewhat difficult and requires a high degree of precision. Even with the Technicolor process, the final copy of film sent to the cinemas for projection was multilayer film stock. Although cameras have an iris exactly the same as the eye, we can only reduce the amount of light hitting the film, we cannot increase the light level above the largest opening in the iris of the lens. If we wish to have greater sensitivity, we have to change to a different type of film. As a general rule, the more sensitive film becomes, the greater is the granular structure. The reason for using larger grains in the film is that they stand a higher chance of being struck by the photons. This use of a larger grain structure is similar to the grouping of the rods in the human eye. In the case of the eye, and in the film, the sharpness of the image reduces with the need for greater sensitivity.

The exposure of film to light causes the photons to strike the silver halide crystals in the film emulsion and these will change according to the intensity of the light. Photographic emulsion is naturally sensitive to the blue part of the spectrum; to increase the sensitivity to the green and red layers sensitizing dyes have to be added to the emulsion. If we use the basic emulsion as the top layer in our system, it will be sensitive to the blue part of the spectrum and so we need no filter for the blue input from the lens. Because of the sensitivity of the other two layers to the blue, we reduce the blue going through the film by having a yellow filter immediately beneath the top layer. If the bottom layer is made sensitive only to red light we will not need a red filter. Between the yellow filter and the red emulsion is the green emulsion. As the blue light has been prevented from reaching this emulsion, which is sensitive only to the green part of the spectrum, we do not need a green filter. By constructing the film this way, we have effectively had three single exposures for the red, green and blue but all taken at the same time and in perfect register. Also by allowing the longest wavelengths to travel the furthest through the layers, we reduce the tendency to scatter, which causes lack of resolution.

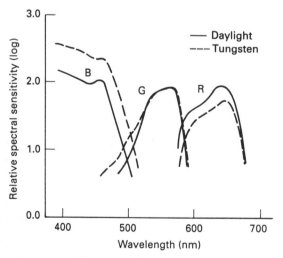

Figure 2.13 Film comparison. Courtesy of Fuji Film Co. Ltd.

The film is now processed so that cyan, magenta and yellow images are formed in the three layers. This is typical of negative film stock. To produce the positive from this stock, it is basically only necessary to photograph it with a similar type of negative, although in practice very sophisticated films can be used for the reversal process. Films can be balanced for artificial light or daylight and this is accomplished by the balance between the red and blue emulsion sensitivity. Figure 2.13 shows the difference between negative film for daylight and negative film for artificial light.

As can be seen, this film is composed of three emulsion layers being sensitive to red, green and blue light along with a protective layer, a yellow filter layer, an antihalation layer and other layers, all coated on a clear safety base. The other side of the base is coated with a black resin backing to provide such properties as antiscratch and antistatic. It also provides for lubrication so that its passage through the mechanical system is made easier. Different couplers are incorporated in the various emulsion layers and through post exposure processing, colour dyes and mask images are formed in the emulsion. The film contains an orange coloured mask which allows for correct colour rendition when prints are made through this negative material on a positive film (see Figure 2.14).

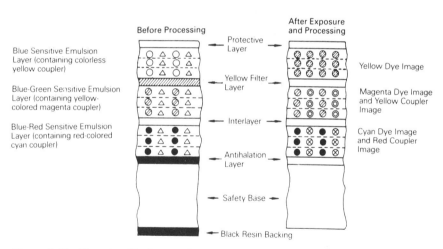

Figure 2.14 Negative film layers. Courtesy of Fuji Film Co. Ltd.

Television cameras have to analyse the light from a scene and the method is somewhat different to that used with film. The pickup devices themselves have the same colour sensitivity, and are therefore not adjusted for the individual red, green and blue components of the light. Secondly, there are no commercially available pickup sensors capable of producing the red, green and blue signals in a single device as required for the process of high quality broadcast colour television. A fundamental requirement for broadcast television standards is that three individual sensors have to be used together with colour filtering systems: thus the use of the three colour sensors and the consequent splitting of light that has to occur makes the colour camera optically very complex. Light falling on the three sensors must have a common entrance, i.e. each sensor must see exactly the same scene in order to avoid optical distortion. When processing the light through the optical system this has to be done with minimum loss, avoiding either excessive lighting levels in the studio, or producing noisy pictures by not having sufficient light to satisfy the sensitivity of the camera sensors. Most of the optical requirements with the systems for colour cameras can be met by using zoom lenses to create a single path from the viewed scene to the camera electronics.

Older style television cameras always used pickup tubes, which were mainly the lead oxide type and somewhat deficient at the red end of the spectrum, creating in the earlier days of colour television, noise in the 'reds', ultimately improved by clever electronic circuits that boosted the red signal. Eventually pickup tubes improved so that the red response was slightly better. Because tube systems use magnetic focusing, it was possible, quite often, when aberrations occurred, to correct these by adjusting the magnetic focusing system. The system still required that the red, green and blue images were in registration but this was relatively easy to accomplish in 'line up' by the use of the electronic system. Figure 2.15 shows a typical beam splitting system to derive the red, green and blue components.

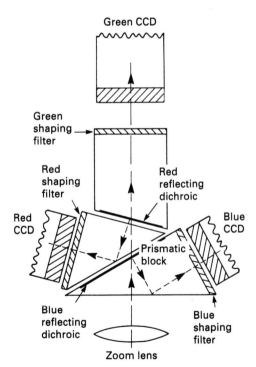

Figure 2.15   Splitter block

The arrival of 'charge coupled devices' (CCD) has somewhat changed the pickup system. CCDs have been introduced for several reasons, the main ones being that they are more robust, free from shock and vibration and have much better geometry than the old tube cameras; thus microphony has become a thing of the past. A major advantage of CCD systems is that they have very good sensitivity. Generally CCD cameras offer a half to one stop extra sensitivity compared with tube types. In terms of light levels in the studio, these are quite significant differences and allow the incident light level to be reduced from 1600 lux to about 800 lux with a consequent use of about half the electrical power. CCDs are immune to the influence of external magnetic fields. In some older type cameras, it was possible when the camera panned to see slight variations in the vision output caused by stray fields or even the earth's magnetic field.

What is a CCD? A charge coupled device is a solid-state chip covered in several hundred thousand photosensitive cells, all of this built onto a device roughly a centimetre square. Each photosensitive cell represents one piece of picture information (pixel). Like camera tubes, CCDs have the same colour sensitivity; therefore three devices and filters for the red, green and blue components have to be used. As the CCDs are built to an absolute, almost perfect, matrix, there is a lack of geometric distortion in pictures. The three chips have to be positioned extremely accurately so that the individual elements are aligned to an error of about half a pixel. If a registration accuracy of 0.05% is required, this means the alignment must be accurate to two thousandths of a millimetre, which can only be accomplished by the camera manufacturer. If we are aligning the chips on the prism block to this degree, it is not difficult to imagine that heat can pose a problem. Temperature differences within the optical block will obviously cause misregistration, due to different coefficients of thermal expansion. One advantage of this system is that having been aligned in the factory, the system will not drift out of tolerance. A further tremendous advantage of CCDs is that they have a superb colour response although a problem is that the peak sensitivity is in the infra-red region. This has to be corrected, otherwise we would have problems with the reds in the system, and an infra-red 'cut off filter' is fitted to the optical path to do just this. However, having looked at the two types of input system, either tube or CCD, at the end of the day all they do is produce small electrical signals which represent the red, green and blue components of the viewed scene. These signals are then processed within the camera control units and ultimately arrive in our homes as colour television.

3 Light measurements

3.1 Units, terminology and calculations

Man has always been dependent on light for his very existence but through his own ingenuity, he discovered how to extend the hours of daylight for his own purposes. The first artificial light was fire, so it was a natural progression into burning oil in a container with a lighted wick. In various parts of the world oil was extracted from available supplies of fish, nuts or vegetables, depending on the locality. Even the storm petrel was used because of its high content of oil by threading a wick through it to make a primitive type of candle. One wonders if this discovery came about by a barbecue that got out of control but there is no record of how many lux would be equal to one storm petrel! The more practical development of this idea was the rush candle, made by peeling all but the last layer of the outside leaves so that the soft absorbent centre could be dipped in tallow and dried. Obviously this was the prototype of the tallow candle as we know it; but not so in the hot countries, because tallow melts at 52°C. Eventually to measure and record light a unit was required that could be understood and repeated experimentally. This of course was the candle – but not any old candle. It had to be well defined so that it was repeatable (well, almost repeatable). It is quite laughable today to think of a world-wide standard measurement of light being dependent on the repeatability of a burning candle, but it is a fact and the specification for the standard candle defined the type of wick and the tallow mixture to be used: the dimensions were a ⅛″ wick and a candle of diameter 1⅛″.

Owing to the unreliability of a wax candle, it was replaced by a lamp burning vaporized pentane with an intensity equal to about 10 of the original candles. Eventually even this was considered inaccurate and in 1909 a filament lamp was adopted as the standard, which continued until 1948. To enable very accurate measurements to be made it was decided, at this time, to create a standard based upon the light emitted from a platinum radiator at 1773°C contained within a special vessel. The unit of luminous intensity, the candela, is defined as 'the luminous intensity, in the perpendicular direction, of a surface of 1/600,000 square metres of a blackbody, at the temperature of freezing platinum, under standard atmospheric pressure'. The luminous intensity of a lamp is defined as the light radiated from a source in a given direction, in candelas.

However, for our purposes, let us consider the light being emitted in

Figure 3.1, which shows a candle burning with a source brightness of one candela. The light is assumed to be distributed evenly in all directions, and the two areas shown are representing parts of the inner wall of two spheres, one at one foot from the source and the other at one metre from the source.

It can be seen that the smaller area closest to the source will be brighter than the larger area further away from the source. By definition, one foot candle is the amount of light falling on an area of one square foot at a distance of one foot from a source of one candela. The principle is the same for one lux being defined as the amount of light falling on an area of one square metre at a distance of one metre from a source of one candela. To find the relationship between foot candles and lux, it is necessary to relate the areas being illuminated in Figure 3.1. By converting the area of one

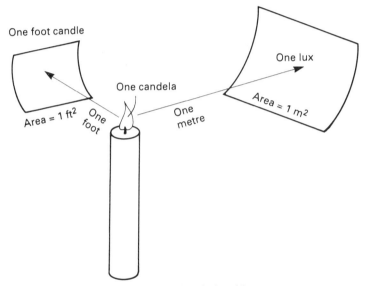

Figure 3.1   Candela/lux/footcandle relationship

square foot to square millimetres, we have 92,903 mm², and of course, one square metre is 1,000,000 mm². If we now divide the larger area by the smaller area we get a factor of 10.76 as shown in Figure 3.2, which is the conversion factor to use when relating foot candles to lux.

1 m² = 1,000,000 mm²
1 ft² = 92,903 mm²

∴ The conversion factor is $\dfrac{1,000,000}{92,903}$ = 10.76

$$\frac{lux}{10.76} = fc$$ or $$fc \times 10.76 = lux$$

Figure 3.2   Relationship of lux to footcandles

We explain the fall-off of light as the distance is increased in Section 3.2 and the cosine relationship in Section 3.4 with the trigonometry involved to determine the light distribution at various distances. However, the examples shown in Figure 3.3 bring together all these calculations in one place as a convenient reference.

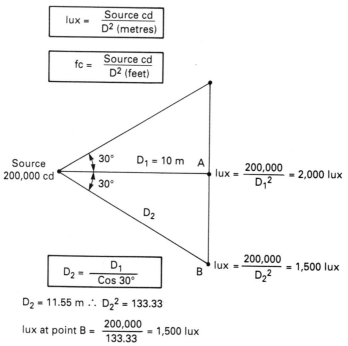

$$lux = \frac{Source\ cd}{D^2\ (metres)}$$

$$fc = \frac{Source\ cd}{D^2\ (feet)}$$

Source 200,000 cd

30°

30°

D_1 = 10 m   A

D_2

$$lux = \frac{200,000}{D_1^2} = 2,000\ lux$$

$$D_2 = \frac{D_1}{Cos\ 30°}$$

B

$$lux = \frac{200,000}{D_2^2} = 1,500\ lux$$

D_2 = 11.55 m ∴ D_2^2 = 133.33

$$lux\ at\ point\ B = \frac{200,000}{133.33} = 1,500\ lux$$

Figure 3.3   Examples of applied laws

3.2 Laws – square and inverse

Although there are many ways of reducing the light output of a luminaire, there is not one way of increasing it, and therefore our only interest is the reduction of light and the laws that it obeys.

If a diffusion filter or wire gauze is placed in front of a light source one would expect it to reduce the light output and it is equally obvious that if the material restricts half of the light, then the level will fall by 50%. It would appear by a similar rationale, that the light from a luminaire would fall off with distance and a common misunderstanding is that at double the distance one would expect to get half the light. This is not so. The light is governed by a simple formula called the 'inverse square law' which states that the light is falling off as the distance squared. Therefore if the distance from the light is doubled, the light will fall to one quarter. It is convenient that when the distance is halved, one will get four times the light, and when it is doubled one will get a quarter of the light. Let us consider more difficult distances other than the mentioned convenient ones.

If the light reading is taken at a given distance, say 10 m, and has a value of 1000 lux, we can determine the light intensity from the luminaire simply by multiplying the lux reading by the distance squared, i.e. 1000 lux × 10^2 = 100,000 candelas. We now have a constant value for the intensity of the luminaire and it is expressed in candelas. As we arrived at the candela value by multiplying a lux reading by the distance squared, it is equally true that we can divide the candela value by any distance squared and obtain the lux reading at the new distance.

3.3 Polar diagrams and their interpretation

We can determine two main important facts about the light output of a luminaire from its polar plot, the intensity of the light and its coverage. All lighting manufacturers use the same system to produce their catalogue information, so it is worth investigating the method of the test to help to understand the results. Whilst light meters are used to read the light arriving at the subject and so provide us with the actual information to work with, it is quite impossible to assess a luminaire against the manufacturer's catalogue information in the same way, because of the variables that must be catered for before a light output comparison can be made.

The supply voltage must be stabilized at the design voltage of the lamp; a 5% reduction at 240V will result in an approximate light loss of 15%. The lamp used for the test will have been calibrated by the manufacturer that made it, who also supplies a laboratory report, showing the exact voltage

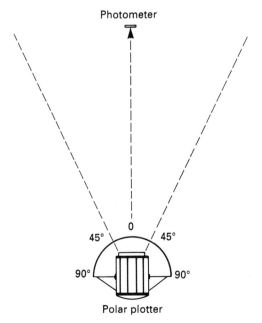

Figure 3.4 Method of producing a polar diagram

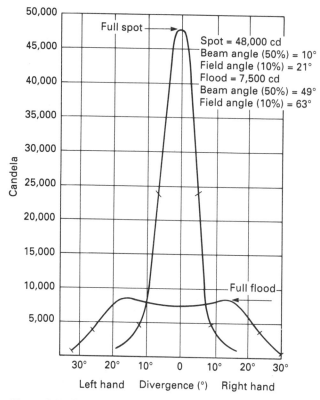

Figure 3.5   Fresnel polar distribution

to run the lamp at to achieve the stated wattage and colour temperature. This sample lamp is kept by the luminaire manufacturer as his standard for all tests. (See Figures 3.4 and 3.5.)

When assessing a polar diagram, determine if the manufacturer's light readings were taken with a wire guard in place, because a 25 mm wire guard will reduce the total light by about 8% – a ploy often used to enhance a product's specification. When making a polar curve, the luminaire must be checked to see that the reflector is centralized and that the lamp filament is in line with the centre of the reflector. Assuming that lenses and reflectors are clean, then a meaningful test can be made. With the light cell set at the same height as the centre of the luminaire, two methods of test are available to us; a polar test or a flat wall test.

The flat wall test is made by moving the cell across a screen at a set distance from the light and recording readings at regular intervals. However, this method is far from accurate because of the distance measurements and the angle of the cell to the light, so the accepted method is a polar test, where the light is rotated and the cell remains stationary. Then, if flat wall information is required, it can be produced mathematically by simple trigonometry and the inverse square law. The tests are conducted in a darkened room and care must be taken to see that no reflected light from walls or ceiling reaches the light cell. The readings can be taken at any distance; however, a very short distance will require very accurate measurements to be made, because any error in the distance will be magnified by the effect of the inverse square law, so that a slight change in distance can produce a large change in the light level.

Typically, luminaires up to 1 kW are measured at 5 m, 1 kW–5 kW at 8 m, and 10 kW at 10 m, but this is only a guide because the test can be made at any chosen distance. The polar plotter is made up of a stand or platform that will allow the luminaire to rotate. A semicircular scale is placed under the luminaire, equally divided in degrees, and this scale is locked off to the luminaire, so that it rotates with it. A pointer is fixed to the bottom of the support structure so that it remains static. The test can now be made by aligning the centre of the scale with the pointer and positioning the centre of the light output beam onto the cell. This setting-up procedure is usually easier to achieve by first setting the focus to the spot position. The luminaire can now be rotated and readings taken at regular intervals. A typical method is to take readings at every degree for the spot position, and every 2.5 degrees for the full flood position. The centre reading starts at zero degrees and the readings are taken left and right of centre. Having taken the readings and plotted them on a graph, similar to the one illustrated by the Fresnel polar diagram, it is normal to place a mark at the point on the curve that corresponds to 50% of the centre brightness and another mark at 10%. These are known as the 'beam angle' and the 'field angle' respectively. The significance of the 50% beam angle is that if two lights are required to overlap and provide an even reading across the two distributions they must overlap at the 50% mark to produce 100% to match the centre reading. The 10% mark is normally considered to be the total angle of the light, in view of the fact that any light outside of this reading is of little use.

The readings are taken in lux at a given distance, but are normally quoted in candelas. This is arrived at by multiplying the lux reading by the distance squared from the light to the cell. It is more useful to display the information in candelas because the light level in lux at any distance can be easily calculated by dividing the candela reading by the required distance squared. In this way the manufacturer makes up the typical light output readings in lux at various distances that are used in the catalogue data sheets. Then with a little trigonometry, the diameter can be predicted, given the output angle of the light and the distance. The shape of the flood position in the Fresnel distribution illustrated will produce an even reading across a line 90° to the source. Because the readings are higher either side of the centre, this will compensate for the greater distance that the light is projected to reach that part of the distribution.

3.4 Types of meter

When the incident light falling on a cell is normal (at 90°) to the plane of the cell, the light cell will correctly measure the incident light. If, however, the light reaches the cell at any angle other than normal, the amount of light to be measured will change. This variation in light is in direct relation to the angle the light enters the cell, and the light diminishes as the cosine of the angle to the normal; this is known as 'Lambert's cosine law'. Thus, in theory, light that enters the cell from the side, in other words 90° to the normal, would be 'zero' on a cosine-corrected meter. This variation comes about because the light has to cover a greater area when striking from any angle other than normal.

The best example of the spread of light is to consider the follow spot used in a theatre. When normal to a surface it produces a round beam of light. When pointed at an angle to the stage, to cover the artist, the beam is now spread in an elongated shape. The amount of light in the beam has not changed, but the area covered has increased; thus the illumination per unit area has diminished. Obviously, if the beam is elongated more and more as the light approaches from the side, the area covered by the light beam becomes infinite. Thus the amount of light per unit area becomes less and less and approaches zero.

With very shallow angles to normal, the variations are not significant, but as the angles become greater and approach anything from 45° to 90° quite large variations in light level can occur. This is particularly so when considering outside broadcast lighting and the floodlighting industry have had problems with this phenomenon for many years. Just to give an example, the cosine of 30° = 0.866, the cosine of 45° = 0.77, the cosine of 60° = 0.5, the cosine of 75° = 0.259, the cosine of 90° = zero.

As well as changing in one plane, the light can change in two planes at the same time. The light in the horizontal plane can come in at an angle as

T-1

Figure 3.6   Incident light meter
Courtesy of Minolta (UK) Ltd

well as from the vertical plane, so both our 'x' and 'y' co-ordinates can vary. If this is the case, we have variations of the cosine law from two directions and this is normally called the 'cosine cubed law'. How does this affect us practically? In our measurement of light, it is essential that we use a cosine corrected cell which gives readings that are correct and take into account the angle of the light incident on the meter. It is also important that the meter would be facing the direction of the most interest visually, i.e. along the path that the camera would look at the scene (see Figure 3.6).

Incident light meters

Photographic meters, either the built-in type as with most modern 35 mm cameras, or a hand-held meter, measure the reflected light from the scene which is going to reach the film. As the film has a certain sensitivity, either the stop and/or the speed of the shutter have to be adjusted so that the correct quantity of light reaches the emulsion, so that well-exposed pictures are produced. Of course, nowadays most cameras do everything automatically. The basis of reflected light measurements is an 18% reflectance value which produces an average brightness standard of measurements for film and TV cameras. At this point it must be stated that we are only measuring the amount of light, not the colour of the source, as long as the meter responds faithfully to all visible wavelengths. If we have a red card that reflects 18% of the light striking it or we have a green card with the same reflectance, they will appear to be the equivalent as far as a camera is concerned because we have not taken any account of the colour involved. We have all been caught out by taking pictures of snow scenes or pictures in very dark areas when the average brightness cannot equate the scenic values very accurately to the 18% reflectance.

A better way of measuring the amount of light is by taking incident light readings which are not influenced by the subject matter itself. If we measure incident light, it is then up to the operator to adjust the equipment being used to give a balanced exposure on the scene itself. A good modern incident light meter should be capable of measuring the luminance in either lux or foot candles. In addition, it is much better if the meter has a digital readout so the figures are accurately displayed. The spectral response must match within fairly close limits the CIE photopic luminosity curve which gives the correct assessment of colour balance for incident light readings. (See Figure 3.7(a), (b).)

William Thomson (later to become Lord Kelvin) was an eminent physicist of his day (1824–1907), and responsible for establishing the Kelvin scale used for colour temperature measurement. Kelvin was faced, when experimenting, with two scales on which temperature could be measured – the fahrenheit system and the Celsius or, as it is more commonly called, the Centigrade system. Both of these were in use for standard temperature readings and both suffered the same problem, namely that the scale did not start at the lowest point of a temperature range and could produce negative values.

In their time the scales might have seemed adequate and to represent the Centigrade scale starting at zero, this being the freezing point of water,

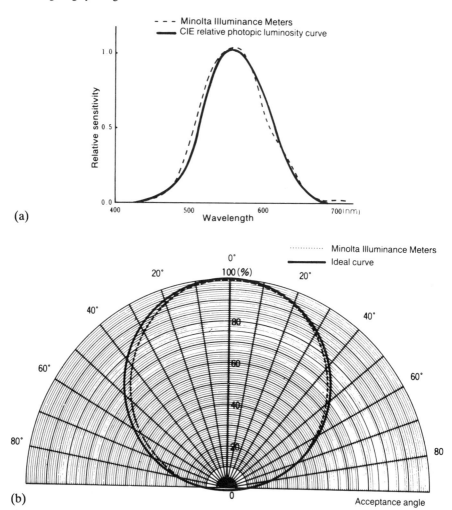

Figure 3.7   (a) Incident light meter – spectral response. (b) Incident light meter – acceptance angle characteristics
Courtesy of Minolta (UK) Ltd

seemed a good idea. Unfortunately, water freezes at different temperatures at different altitudes and various degrees of purity and, quite frankly, has no relevance at all; it could just as easily have been any other substance.

Kelvin decided that both temperature scales were unsuitable for scientific measurements. He had no argument with the Centigrade scale; it was its starting point that caused the problem. Being not only a prominent physicist but also a brilliant mathematician, he calculated the theoretical point of absolute zero as being −273° on the Centigrade scale; At this point no material can be further lowered in temperature. This then was his starting point – to set zero on the Kelvin scale at −273 degrees Centigrade, thus from zero upwards getting only positive values.

Since the Kelvin scale is a Centigrade scale displaced from its zero by 273 degrees, a tungsten filament which is glowing and radiating a colour that is 3000 Kelvin is burning at a temperature of 2727° Centigrade. (See Table 3.1.)

Table 3.1 Kelvin colour temperature of typical light sources

Kelvins	Light sources
9000–11,000	Bright sunlight with blue sky
6000	Electronic flash
5800	HI carbon arc and average daylight
5600	Film and TV discharge lamp (correlated colour temperature
3400	Tungsten halogen film lamp and photofloods
3200	Tungsten halogen film and TV lamp
3000	Tungsten halogen theatre lamp
2600	100 W household lamp
2000	Oil lamp
1925	Candle light
770	The eye starts to see the darkest reds
660	The eye starts to perceive a filament changing colour
0	Absolute zero

The Kelvin colour temperature scale can only be used when measuring a source that emits energy in a continuous spectrum and approximates to a blackbody radiator such as a tungsten filament, or the ultimate in light sources, the sun. What this means is that a lamp with a 2700K colour temperature produces approximately the same spectrum of light as a blackbody at 2700K. (Most hot objects do not follow Planck's blackbody radiation law: only perfectly black objects do.) If we examine the visible spectrum portion of the blackbody curves given it will be seen that the curves are continuous over the visible wavelengths. As the object becomes hotter, it is noticeable that the amounts of red energy and blue energy are varying in relation to each other. If we could have a meter which measured the ratio of the red/blue balance, we would then have a reasonably close approximation to blackbody temperatures. In fact, the older style of colour temperature meters made throughout the world generally worked on the fact that they employed a red and blue filter to measure the relative amounts of each and thus find the corresponding colour temperature.

The colour of light emitted from a discharge lamp cannot be expressed in Kelvins because the spectral output in the lamp is not continuous but dependent on the gases and rare earths used in its manufacture to introduce the required additional colours which help to create the colour of the source; and the compounds used emit colours in only comparatively narrow bands. In photographic and television cameras the film stock and the colour receptors are responsive to the amounts of red, green and blue in the light, but unfortunately due to the spiky nature of the colour

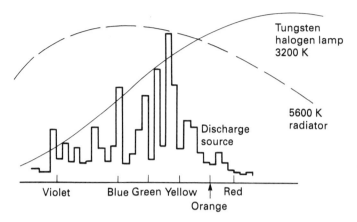

Figure 3.8   Comparison of discharge and incandescent sources

distribution from a discharge lamp a standard colour meter that measures only the red/blue balance of a source will give erroneous readings because it is not measuring the total spectral output. (See Figure 3.8.)

Tri-stimulus colour meter

The world of the theatre will rely upon the LDs setting the lights to give the maximum visual effect and although a meter might be useful, we strongly suspect it would be extraneous to the emotional feelings conveyed by the lighting to the audience and would ignore the fact that the eye is self-adjusting and has a built-in time lag in its response. Therefore a meter cannot take into account the previous light level which will influence the *apparent brightness* of the scene. In film and television, however, we do need accurate measurements of incident light onto subjects; we need an accurate measure of colour temperature if we are using sources that approximate to the blackbody curve; and we also need to be able to measure colour accurately of any type so that errors are avoided when operating discharge sources in either film or television. A tri-stimulus meter is really a clever little hand-held computer. It contains three photo cells which are filtered to detect the primary stimulus values of blue, green and red light under an opal diffuser. This diffuser is specially made to take account of the direction of light and therefore inherently calculates the cosine angle of incident light. The incident light level can be derived from the output of the green photo cell as this relates to the photopic curve. It would appear that only the blue and red photo cells would be required to give a colour temperature reading; a meter of this type will generally compute the colour temperature from all the receptors. One wonderful advantage of using meters such as this, is that one can accurately measure by using the 'x' and 'y' co-ordinates to ascertain colour shifts by reference to a CIE spectral diagram. Any of the readings will be assigned a 'K' output reading signifying colour temperature but, of course, in several

Figure 3.9   Tri-stimulus colour meter
Courtesy of Minolta (UK) Ltd

cases this will be correlated and always have to be referred back to the 'x y'
co-ordinates to get some accurate representation from the CIE diagram.
Meters such as this, although relatively expensive compared with a basic
incident light meter, are invaluable and in fact, indispensable in the
professional entertainment industry.

4 Light sources

4.1 Tungsten sources

The incandescent filament lamp was the original backbone of the electrical manufacturing industry as we know it today. In the 1930s all the large electrical companies owed their existence to the common household bulb because it was domestic lighting that created the demand for generators to supply the electricity to homes which had no other use for an electrical supply system. Following this, the motors in domestic appliances became the slaves of the generators. More importantly, the bulb sales provided the money for all the electrical development in the early days. The original bulbs were very expensive. From 1883 to 1900 the price was 25p while an engineer's salary was £1.50 per week, so in todays' terms, 16% of an engineer's weekly salary would seem extortionate for a common household bulb. In 1840 Joseph Wilson Swan conducted an experiment in the open air of burning a thin filament made of carbon. It lasted a few seconds and was the first of his experiments. In 1845 Mr Starr patented an idea in England of producing light by causing a carbon filament to glow in a vacuum. However, this idea could not be pursued for the time being and had to wait for Hermann Sprengel to invent an efficient vacuum pump to enable the bulbs to be exhausted of air. The development of the incandescent filament lamp was long and tedious; Swan finally completed his design and was able to demonstrate it in Newcastle in 1879.

Also during 1879 Thomas Edison was working along the same lines in America and was astute enough to take out a British patent for a carbon filament burning in a vacuum. The following four years were largely taken up by a legal battle between Edison and Swan over the rights to the idea with the only winners being the patent lawyers, for in 1883 they called off the fight and joined forces, registering the Edison and Swan United Electric Light Company. The manufacture of the carbon filament, which incidentally has the reverse characteristic to tungsten inasmuch as its resistance decreases as it heats, was manufactured until 1906 when the tungsten filament was first produced for domestic sales. This enabled the bulb manufacturers to greatly increase the light output from the filament by lacing it around supports and coiling it back upon itself to maintain a high temperature by the close proximity of the filament coils to each other. The filament could also run at comparatively high colour temperatures in view of the fact that the melting point of tungsten is 3410°C.

A common household 240 V 100 W bulb has 1147 mm of wire in the filament. Therefore the next development was the coiled filament where the wire is returned and coiled again on itself; this was a great advance in reducing the size of the source. Various improvements were introduced in the following years, one of which was the use of nitrogen and argon in the lamp to retard evaporation of the filament and thereby prolong its life.

The next significant development in lamps occurred during the late 1950s and when it became commercially available in 1960 was known as the quartz iodine lamp, later to be renamed tungsten halogen with its benefit of the tungsten halogen cycle. (*See under* Tungsten halogen cycle, below.) Other advances were made by including internal reflectors inside the envelope of the lamp and in some instances a dichroic coating which not only reflected the light forwards but permitted the infra-red end of the spectrum to pass through the reflector, thereby reducing the heat in the beam. (*See* Figure 4.1.)

Figure 4.1 Tungsten halogen lamps

Tungsten halogen lamps can be divided into two groups of manufacture – synthetic silica quartz and hard glass. In the case of the synthetic silica quartz, the walls are extremely strong and have a high melting point thus allowing a small envelope which permits a comparatively high internal pressure. This has the effect of doubling the life in comparison with hard glass. The hard glass envelope is thinner and much larger but still maintains the tungsten halogen cycle. At half the life one is not disappointed to find that it is approximately half the price, thus the cost per hour of life is approximately the same. Therefore the choice is purely a high initial capital investment with the synthetic silica quartz lamps with reduced maintenance replacements against the low initial cost of the hard glass. (*See* Figure 4.2.)

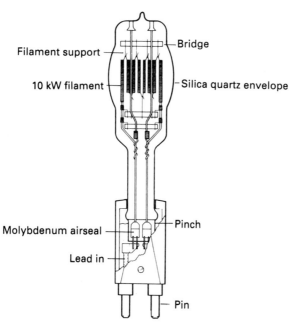

Filament support

Bridge

10 kW filament

Silica quartz envelope

Molybdenum airseal

Pinch

Lead in

Pin

Figure 4.2   Silica quartz tungsten halogen lamp

The electric lamp is a heat generator from which we can get a little light. This would appear to be an odd statement until one compares the efficiency. The conversion of total electrical energy produces 90% heat at the luminaire and 10% light. The light energy is transmitted through the air which is also absorbing heat from the beam and the remainder of the heat is absorbed by the subject being illuminated – a very important fact when considering ventilation requirements for a building.

The temperature of the lamp is one of the manufacturer's main design considerations, with the need to operate at relatively high temperatures, bearing in mind the melting point of tungsten which is approximately 3400°C. The high efficiency 3400 K (3127°C) lamps are obviously burning very near their melting point and therefore only give approximately 20 hours life. The lamp designer has to concern himself not only with the correct temperatures to keep the tungsten halogen cycle working, but also the filament design to achieve the exact colour temperatures required. He also has the problem of maintaining the lamp's seal temperatures below a maximum of 350°C for long life lamps and 400°C for short life lamps. This is because the leadout of the filament through the silica quartz envelope is made by a thin foil of molybdenum. The expansion of molybdenum and quartz are not quite the same; therefore as the temperature increases the difference increases and above 400°C the seal between them would become porous and the molybdenum would oxidize. When lamps are used in a design with inadequate ventilation, the end of life can be seal failure rather than filament failure. At the other end of the scale, if the source is force cooled by a fan reducing its wall to 250°C the tungsten halogen cycle is affected.

Filament vibration can sometimes cause a sound problem. With a sinusoidal voltage applied to the lamp, the current produces a shock on the filament every half cycle. The vibration of the filament can set up a sympathetic vibration in the luminaire and – particularly in the case of scoops – the sound as well as the light is beamed down on the microphone. The lamp manufacturers tried to reduce this effect by clamping the filament supports onto the filament in a positive manner using non-magnetic wires and calculating the spacing of the supports to try to dampen the vibration. This problem was slight in the case of auto transformers and resistance dimmers, but with the chopped waveform principle of dimming the situation is much worse. This is because the current is rapidly switched on every half cycle and does not increase slowly as it would in a sinusoidal waveform. The worse position for vibration is at half power when the dimmer is firing at a 90° angle. Manufacturers of high quality dimmers use a choke in the output to dampen this effect. It is an interesting experiment to observe the filament movement with various firing angles by taking a standard lens and positioning it at its focal length from the filament projecting the image onto a screen; the filament can be focused and the movement observed.

The effect of inrush current on the filament is described in Chapter 8. The cause of the inrush current on the initial switch on a cold filament is that tungsten has a comparatively low resistance in its cold state. The current initially reaches a very high value but as soon as the filament heats, its resistance increases and the current soon falls. To generalize, the inrush current can be from 10 to 17 times the normal running current, depending on the filament size and the impedance of the circuit, but only lasts for approximately 0.2 to 0.8 seconds. This can become a problem in determining the type of fuse for a circuit and the current rating of miniature circuit breakers.

The effect of varying voltage

All lamps are designed for one specific voltage. The manufacturer decides the following criteria: operating voltage, colour temperature, life, current and the wattage which is a product of the current and voltage. The performance of a light source is tested in an integrating sphere, where the total luminous efficacy is measured and then expressed in the manufacturer's data as 'lumens per watt'. The higher the lumens per watt, the higher the lamp temperature and consequently the colour temperature.

If any parameters are changed, all the other values must change because they are all inter-related. The easiest way to understand this is to take the case of varying the voltage to the lamp. If the voltage is reduced, the flow of current will reduce, and as the wattage is a function of 'volts × amps', the wattage will reduce. Because the filament is now burning at a lower temperature, the colour of the light will change and will move towards the red end of the spectrum; and the good news is that the life will be extended.

It is apparent by now that it is very difficult to calculate the outcome of a voltage change because all of the values that could be used for a formula are variables with no constant to latch onto. Even the resistance of the filament increases when it is heated. Therefore, when we reduce the voltage, and thus the heat of the filament, the resistance will decrease.

It is, however, possible by the use of the graph (Figure 4.3) to read off all the changes that take place with varying voltage by starting with a complete set of known values. Fortunately every lamp manufacturer provides the relevant information which is peculiar to his product so it is necessary first to determine the make and type number of the lamp. A typical example would be type: CP-40 (ANSI code FKJ) 240 V, 1000 W, 3200 K, 26 lumens per watt, thus giving a total of 26,000 lumens and a life of 200 hours.

It will be seen in Figure 4.3 that the horizontal scale refers to percentage change of the applied voltage and the vertical scale shows the resultant change by percentage of the stated manufacturer's values.

Do remember to convert any value into a percentage of the manufacturer's stated value. For example, taking the CP-40 1000 W lamp quoted earlier, we have a rated voltage of 240. If the voltage is reduced to, say, 205 V, a reduction of 35 in 240 equals 14.6% (say 15%). Referring to the horizontal scale of the graph, percentage change of the applied voltage, a reduction of 15% gives a value of 85% voltage. Move vertically up the 85% line and read off the following values:

Light output	60% of 26,000 lumens	=	15,600 lumens
Watts	77% of 1000 watts	=	770 watts
Current (A)	92% of 4.17 amps	=	3.84 amps
Colour Temp.	94% of 3200 K	=	3008 K
Life (Est.)	300% of 200 hours	=	600 hours

In the case of life, it was necessary to project the life curve above the graph and estimate that it would meet the vertical line at approximately 300%. When the life value is changed considerably, it cannot be estimated with great accuracy; however the principle gives a good indication of the life that one would expect. The example quoted is the result of running the lamp at position 7.5 on the lighting control console, if it has a square law fader characteristic. (See Chapter 8, Dimming and Control).

The electrical supply system in the United Kingdom is normally very good. However, the supply authorities are very generous with themselves

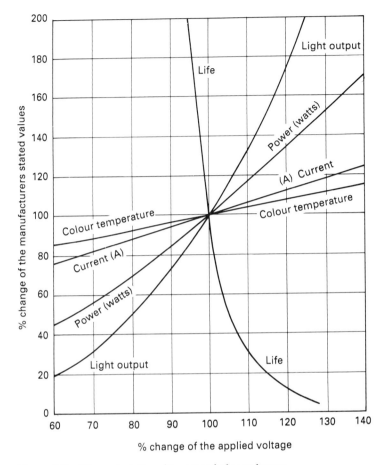

Figure 4.3   Characteristics of tungsten halogen lamps

in allowing a maximum variation of ± 6% voltage in 240 V. *This represents 225.6 V to 254.4 V.* Referring to Figure 4.3, 254.4 V equals 106% voltage, which would result in a life of 50%, so don't always blame the lamp manufacturer for poor life performance – it might not be his fault.

The tungsten halogen cycle

When a tungsten filament is burning at a comparatively high temperature, tungsten atoms leave the filament and normally attach themselves to the inside surface of the lamp envelope. This is most noticeable in the household bulb, which becomes quite black by the end of its life. Theatre and studio lamps, before tungsten halogen designs became available, had the same problem resulting in the reduction of both light and colour temperature throughout their life. The chemical principle of including a halogen gas in the lamp to reduce blackening was well known for many years before it became practical to produce a lamp to accommodate it. The first lamps to appear on the market in the early 1960s used a quartz envelope and an iodine filling. This had the desired effect but unfortunately the iodine had a slight pink colour when hot and changed the colour of the light. The new development was called 'quartz iodine' but in fact most of the halogen gases would work in the same way. Unfortunately most of these gases radiated a colour when heated or were quite obnoxious towards the tungsten filament, eating it away before it reached old age. Some halogens would even attack the filament when it was on the shelf, resulting in a very short life instead of an extended one. Over the next five years, the manufacturing techniques improved, enabling the lamp manufacturers to use bromine in place of iodine and a synthetic hard glass in place of pure quartz. In general, the more reactive the halide, the more effective is the halogen cycle. So in theory, fluorine, the most reactive, should be the best but it is so reactive that it even attacks the glass or quartz. Therefore iodine, bromine and chlorine are the only ones in use for halogen lamps.

Although this was a great technological breakthrough because the bromine did not add a colour to the light, and the new material for the envelope was cheaper than pure quartz, it produced havoc with the lamp manufacturers' marketing departments that had spent years promoting quartz iodine only to have the name changed because the product no longer used quartz or iodine. The safe way out was apparent: because all lamps would use a tungsten filament and a halogen gas filling, the name 'tungsten halogen' was agreed upon, resulting in years more publicity and a confused public.

The tungsten halogen cycle is simple in principle. Atoms of tungsten evaporate from the filament and combine with atoms of bromine which then circulate together, eventually returning to the filament and separating, leaving the tungsten atoms on the filament and releasing the bromine atoms to circulate and repeat the procedure. In principle, an everlasting lamp – but fortunately for lamp manufacturers, it does not work quite like that, because the tungsten emits uniformly along the filament, but the returning atoms prefer to select the cooler parts of the filament, and therefore the thinner parts of the filament, which are also the hottest, get thinner and the thicker parts get thicker. However, the advantages are enormous:

1. A greatly extended life.
2. A constant light output throughout life.
3. A constant colour temperature throughout life.
4. A smaller envelope means that compact luminaires can be designed.
5. Reduced maintenance costs in time spent replacing lamps.
6. In general, a higher light output is achieved (higher lumens/watt).

To simply explain the tungsten halogen cycle, a lamp is designed so that the wall of the envelope is moved close to the filament to maintain it at a high temperature. The evaporating tungsten atoms leaving the filament soon cool down below 1400°C. In this state, they can combine with the halogen atoms and circulate until they find the temperature that is below 250°C that would enable them to separate. This eventuality has been designed out of the lamp by moving the envelope close to the filament to maintain it at a high temperature, say 350°C, at which temperature the compound will not separate. So the tungsten and halogen atoms circulate until they find a temperature above 1400°C (which is obviously the filament) permitting the compound to separate and deposit the tungsten atoms back onto the filament.

It would appear that because the tungsten halogen compound separates at temperatures above 1400°C and below 250°C, a problem would occur when dimming a lamp to a low light level, subsequently reducing the wall temperature to below 250°C. This, however, does not cause a problem in practice, because the evaporation from the filament is substantially reduced at lower temperatures and the small amount of deposit that does occur is rapidly removed when the lamp is restored to full voltage.

One aspect of the tungsten halogen sources to be considered is that of ultraviolet radiation. Synthetic quartz will pass ultraviolet rays and can cause a slight sunburn. For instance, if the skin is exposed continuously for four to five hours with a light level of 2000 lux, a slight reddening of the skin will take place with a 3200 K lamp. At half this level, 1000 lux, the time would be double. The problem applies particularly to lamps running in open reflector luminaires. If, however, the lamps are operating behind a lens which is normally manufactured from borosilicate glass, the problem does not exist because borosilicate glass is a good UV filter.

Construction

Lamps for entertainment, in the main, have compact filaments to produce the smallest size source for the optical systems employed, with the exception of floods and softlights, where an elongated filament is a distinct advantage when trying to evenly illuminate a large reflector.

4.2 Discharge sources

If we accept that the sun was the first light source with a nuclear fusion reaction in its core which is approximately 14,000,000 K and an outer surface temperature of 5800 K, then an electrical discharge was certainly the second.

Benjamin Franklin, the American statesman and scientist who helped in the forming of the American Constitution, also found time to invent the Franklin stove and bifocal spectacles. In 1745, or thereabouts, he demonstrated how to electrocute oneself by flying a kite in a thunderstorm. That part of the experiment did not work: however, the real object of the experiment did. Franklin was so convinced that lightning was caused by an electrical discharge that he submitted himself to the risk of electrocution by pointing his finger at a metal ring attached to the end of a silk line that was holding the kite and demonstrated that a spark jumped from the metal ring to his finger. This experiment proved that light was generated from an electrical discharge and that Benjamin Franklin became the inventor of the lightning rod (which is in fact true).

The same type of discharge phenomenon could be seen on the tall masted sailing ships of the day when in a storm a greenish glow appeared around the top of the mast and was known by sailors as 'St Elmo's fire'.

Sir Humphry Davy (the inventor of the miners' safety lamp), demonstrated an electrical arc between two rods of carbon in 1810. To maintain an arc the two rods were continuously adjusted at the same rate as they were being burnt away, which was a hot, dirty job, bearing in mind that carbon vaporizes at 3382°C. These experiments employed Alessandro Volta's type of battery that used alternate plates of zinc and silver. This demonstration took place at the Royal Institution in London and required 2000 battery cells to provide the voltage and current required to maintain the arc.

In 1816 a further development was taking place with experiments by Thomas Drummond, when he demonstrated a bright white light by directing jets of burning oxygen and hydrogen onto a block of calcium (quicklime) thus heating it to incandescence. However, this form of lighting had to wait until 1837 before it was first used in the theatre and was in widespread use by 1860. Because the light was difficult to operate, requiring a man in constant attendance adjusting the block of calcium as it burned and to adjust the flow of gas from the two cylinders of oxygen and hydrogen, the lights were used mainly from the auditorium as open-faced lanterns and were immediately named 'limelights'. Hence the expression 'in the limelight' means being at the focal point on the stage.

In those days, a follow spot operator most likely had the same instructions as today – when in doubt, follow the money!

Battery operated carbon arc lights first appeared for entertainment when they were used at the Paris Opera. They were also used for floodlighting in the Place de la Concorde in 1830 and later at the Royal Exchange in London.

The early work by Humphry Davy in his experiments with carbon arcs laid the ground for the film industry to develop a succession of arc lights from 1900 through to 1965. In the early 1900s the film industry blossomed in Hollywood and all the studios had their own generators to run the lighting. Because carbons arcs require a direct current (dc) to maintain an arc and a voltage in the range 40 V to 85 V between the carbons, the generators were made to produce 115 V dc so that a resistance ballast could be conveniently connected in series with the supply to limit the current flow and maintain the arc volts.

The size of the luminaires was rated by the current that was drawn by the carbons, e.g. 40 A, 60 A, 150 A, 225 A and 300 A. For comparison, today's discharge lamps have a range which includes 575 W, 1.2 kW, 2.5 kW, 4 kW, 6 kW, 8 kW, 12 kW, 16 kW and 20 kW.

The 'Brute', an extremely powerful 225 A Fresnel spotlight, was developed in 1950 with geared drive to feed the carbons as they burnt away and to rotate the positive carbon at the same time. The 'Brutes', which were regarded with great affection, have today been replaced by discharge sources but comparisons are still being made between the old and the new.

The light readings published by Mole Richardson (England) when they introduced the 'Brute' in 1953 make interesting reading:

At full flood, over a throw of 35 ft (10.67 m) the light level was 1000 footcandles (10,760 lux) with a beam width of 25 ft (7.62 m)
Or
At full flood over the longer distance of 60 ft (18.29 m) the light level was 340 footcandles (3661 lux) with a beam width of 43 ft (13.1 m).

Which rather proves that trying to balance the shadow areas in daylight shooting requires a lot of light!

A 300 A water cooled follow spot was developed for the film *Red Shoes* and was used in the rental department of Mole Richardson for many years. However, the 300 A 'Super Brute' developed in 1963 was not successful because the extra light did not warrant the increased current, i.e. only three 'Super Brutes' could run from a 1000 A generator, whereas four standard 'Brutes' could be supplied.

Like many inventions, discharge lighting could not be used commercially to any great extent until the electric dynamo was invented by Michael Faraday in 1831 to provide a continuous source of electricity. The first commercial generator was produced by Woolrich of Birmingham and was used for electro-plating in 1844.

The first practical discharge lamps were the cold cathode carbon dioxide 'Moore' tubes of 1895. Light was produced by the activity caused when fast moving electrons collided with molecules of gas. To accelerate electrons in the early lamps, the applied voltage was in the order of 2000–10,000 V at high frequency. Cold cathode tubes contain gas at low pressure, about 100th of an atmosphere. The colour of the light is dependent on the gases used. Carbon dioxide emits a very white light of very low intensity. Neon, first isolated in 1898, produces a red light and was used extensively in advertising displays from 1922.

The hot cathode lamp was a much better commercial proposition because it could operate at mains voltage. This was made possible by using metallic substances such as 'thoriated tungsten' which, when heated to incandescence, produced a high level of electronic activity in the tube. By 1932 the hot cathode lamp led to the development of the high pressure sodium and mercury lamps with their much higher efficiency and these lamps are still in use in today's street lighting.

In all types of discharge lamps an arc is struck between two electrodes in an envelope containing an inert gas or vapour. A choke or electronic ballast is used in the ac supply to limit the flow of current after the arc has been established. Striking the arc is usually achieved by applying a high voltage (5000–15,000 V) across the electrodes to break down the resistance between them so that the gases or vapours inside the lamp may start conducting. At this point the ballast takes over and regulates the flow of current. This starting-up procedure normally takes about one to two minutes until the heat in the lamp vaporizes the metallic elements which emit their characteristic colours, but if the lamp is switched off it will require to cool down before it can be restruck. The cooling time can take from two to five minutes to allow the internal pressure of the lamp to reduce to a level where conduction can occur. Alternatively, lamps are designed to be 'hot restrike', in which case a voltage of approximately

40,000 V is applied to overcome the high internal pressure and provide instantaneous starting when the lamp is hot.

Discharge lamps are made using mercury, halides, rare earths and gases; often containing a mixture of many types of chemicals. There are some 40 metal halides to choose from and each manufacturer has his own 'brew'. Iodides of sodium produce mainly yellow light; mercury emits blue/green light in the visible parts of the spectrum and a great quantity of invisible radiation in the ultraviolet wavelengths. Thallium is used because it emits mainly green light. (Figure 4.4.)

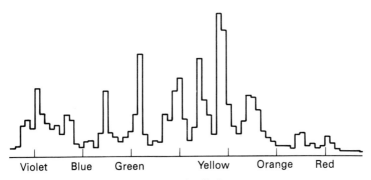

Figure 4.4   Spectral distribution of a discharge source

There are many types of discharge lamps, each with its own reference code, although many have similar characteristics. We will only consider here the lamps that will be useful in entertainment, being those that approximate to the daylight or have a correlated colour temperature approaching 3400 K. As the lamp manufacturing companies develop a new design of lamp, they register the reference as a trade name so other manufacturers are obliged to make up their reference for a similar development.

The following sources require an ac supply:

HMI	Hydrargyrum (Latin for mercury). Medium arc length. Iodides, 95 lumens per watt, 5600 K. Made by Osram, Germany.
HMI/SE	Single-ended version of the HMI. 95 lumens per watt, 5600 K. Made by Osram, Germany.
MSR	Medium source rare earth, single ended, 95 lumens per watt, 5600 K. Made by Philips, Holland.
MEI	Metal earth iodide, 95 lumens per watt, 5600 K. Made by Osram, England.
GEMI	General Electric metal iodide, 95 lumens per watt, 5600 K. Made by General Electric, USA.
CID	Compact iodide daylight, 70–80 lumens per watt, 5500 K. Made by Thorn UK.

CSI	Compact source iodide, 90 lumens per watt, 4000 K. Made by Thorn UK.
SN	Tin halide, 60 lumens per watt, 5500 K. Made by Philips, Holland.
DAYMAX	Mercury halide source, 95 lumens per watt, 5600 K. Made by ICL, USA.
BRITE ARC	Mercury halide source, 95 lumens per watt. Made by Sylvania, USA.

The following source is fed from a dc supply:

EMI	Xenon, 40 lumens per watt, 6000 K. Made by Thorn UK.

Although lamp manufacturers quote a colour temperature of the light in Kelvins, this is only an approximation to the nearest point on the blackbody curve. The total output from a lamp is made up of many separate colours from any number of the halides and gases employed to achieve the correct colour balance in the red, green and blue parts of the spectrum to match the response requirements for colour films and TV cameras.

To generalize, most of the modern developments in daylight balanced lamps have an efficacy of about 95 lumens per watt. It is useful at this point to make comparisons with the studio incandescent tungsten halogen lamp of 3200 K that has an efficacy of 26 lumens per watt. This means that the discharge lamp has approximately four times the light output of the tungsten halogen lamp for the same wattage or, an alternative comparison is, that for the same light output the discharge lamp is running at 25% of the tungsten halogen 'lamp watts' – an important fact when considering the heating effect in the luminaire and the air conditioning installation in a studio.

We make the point of saying 'lamp watts' because the current drawn from the mains is much higher than would be expected. This is because the current and voltage are not in phase and can have a 'power factor' as low as 0.6. If a choke ballast is used it is a winding on an iron core which makes the current lag behind the voltage, whereas an electronic square wave high frequency ballast can make the current lead the voltage by about the same amount.

A typical example is a 2.5 kW discharge lamp compared with a 2.5 kW incandescent lamp. From a 240 V supply, the tungsten halogen lamp would draw 10.42 A; in the case of a discharge lamp supplied from an inductive ballast with a power factor of 0.6, the current drawn from the supply is 17.36 A (W = VI cos ϕ, where cos ϕ is the cosine of the angle of lead or lag of the current). This is obviously an important consideration in supply requirements. The current apparently lost between the resistive load and the inductive load is known as the 'wattless' current.

Discharge lamps are generally made of a synthetic quartz material which permits very high operating pressures within the lamp when it is hot; therefore caution must be taken when relamping to ensure that the lamp has cooled down before the luminaire is opened. The operator must avoid handling the envelope even when the lamp is cool to prevent grease from the skin contaminating the quartz envelope. Care has to be taken when inserting a lamp into its holder because exerting pressure on the envelope can cause a fracture at its joint to the base.

The discharge lamp emits large quantities of radiation in the ultraviolet wavelengths which pass straight through the quartz envelope; it is therefore most dangerous to be directly exposed to the lamp. It must always be housed or have a lens or protective glass in front of it. It is fortunate that all standard borosilicate Fresnel lenses have the characteristic of absorbing UV but if the luminaire is open faced the safety glass provided must also be capable of absorbing the UV radiation. Because of the UV radiation, safety standards require that a switch is fitted to the lens door to automatically extinguish the lamp to prevent hazards to the operators and artistes by opening the luminaire while the lamp is on. Alternatively the lens door must be securely fastened by fixing screws or bolts.

The end of life of an incandescent lamp is very obvious; however this is not the case with a discharge lamp. Normally the end of life will be caused by the electrodes burning back during their life, creating a larger gap. The effect of this is a poor starting characteristic requiring many attempts to get the lamp to run continuously after the initial high voltage spark is applied. Therefore inconsistent starting is an indication of the end of life.

Discharge lamps provide a comparatively small light source. This is certainly welcomed by luminaire manufacturers, enabling them to make efficient optical systems. Another bonus is that the total light output of a discharge lamp is comparatively constant throughout its life. However, many lamps suffer devitrification of the quartz during life which is not visible to the eye but has the effect when the lamp is running hot of diffusing the inside surface and making the apparent source size that of its envelope. This is most noticeable in ellipsoidal spotlights and follow spots where the initial light output can be *double* that of the light performance halfway through the lamp's life. The effect of the apparently enlarged source size due to devitrification does not significantly affect focusing Fresnels.

Light flicker is caused by the lighting following the mains frequency from zero to a maximum value and back down to zero again. This causes a flicker at twice mains frequency when the source is current regulated by a choke. However, the problems can be overcome by the use of an electronic square wave ballast which operates at higher frequencies – 400Hz is quite common! By using very fast switching times between the positive and negative half cycles the light output 'OFF' period is very small compared with the 'ON' period; consequently the light output appears to be constant.

One other advantage of the electronic ballast is that it is possible with the correct selection of the discharge lamp to obtain a degree of dimming. However, dimming can only be performed over a comparatively small range – typically 50% of the light output – before the arc becomes unstable.

One major problem that can occur during dimming is a colour shift: it is wise therefore to do tests before relying on dimming a discharge lamp. Another problem, when using electronic ballasts, it that the chopped waveform presented to the electrodes induces an audible noise in the arc as well as in the ballast. Although the noise in the ballast can be isolated by running it in a remote position, care should be taken when positioning the luminaire to determine if the noise is being directed towards any microphones in use.

Other types of interference can be present in an electronic ballast. The output from the ballast can produce:

(a) Voltage spikes which can be sent back down the supply line and hence onto the mains, which in turn can affect other electronic equipment connected to the same supply.
(b) Radio interference transmitted down the supply cable to the luminaire which is picked up by microphone cables in close proximity, causing audible hum on the sound output.

Both of these problems can be prevented by the addition of high quality filters in the ballast unit.

5 Luminaires

5.1 Optical design theory

The Fresnel and plano-convex lenses

In 1748 George Louis Leclerc de Buffon originated the idea of dividing a plano-convex lens into separate concentric rings in order to reduce the weight significantly. In 1820 the idea was adopted by Augustin Jean Fresnel (pronounced 'Frenel') to overcome a real problem in lighthouses. Before this date the only way of controlling the light distribution from a lighthouse was with mirrors.

At that time it was impossible to mould large conventional lenses of the size required for a lighthouse because the glass could not be gathered in sufficiently large 'gobs' quickly enough to fill a mould of the size required. The problem was that the method of handling the molten glass during this period was by using a rod which collected relatively small 'gobs' of glass which were cut off and dropped into the mould. It would also have been quite useless, even if the process had succeeded, because the lens would have been so thick that its weight would have prevented its use in a lighthouse optical system.

Fresnel adapted de Buffon's idea to make a one-piece moulding of the separate concentric rings which could be pressed in a mould of large diameter but maintaining a thin cross-section to reduce its weight. In this way, very short focal length lenses could be produced which would normally require a very thick cross-section. Therefore, a Fresnel lens can be considered to be equivalent to a standard plano-convex lens of the same focal length.

In Figure 5.1 the plano-convex lens is superimposed on the equivalent Fresnel lens showing that the same curvature of the plano-convex lens can be achieved by moving sections of the surface down to the same plane. The sketch is an over-simplification of a Fresnel lens design, but it is sufficient to show the principle.

The focal length of either lens is the point behind the lens where an object in front of the lens will be focused. The focal point can be found by focusing a bright object such as the sun onto a surface and measuring the distance from the lens to the image when it is in sharp focus, in the same way that all young boys ignite a piece of paper by focusing the sun's rays onto it with a lens.

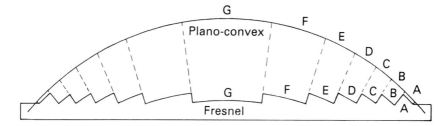

Figure 5.1   Fresnel/plano-convex lens comparison

If a light source is placed at the focal point of a lens, the reverse procedure would be expected, thereby producing an image of the filament when it is projected onto a screen. This is the position of the source when a Fresnel or plano-convex luminaire is focused to the full spot position. The sharpness of the filament image is smeared over by adding a slight diffusion to the rear surface of the lens. As the source is moved forward the beam will increase in angle and achieve full flood in its most forward position. The two luminaires that employ the above lenses are obviously the Fresnel and the plano-convex. Other luminaires that employ the plano-convex lens are the profile projector (ellipsoidal as it is known in the USA), follow spots and effects projectors.

Figure 5.2 shows a simple solid cone which is responsible for all the reflector shapes that would be required for any type of luminaire. It can be seen that by cutting through the cone, along the lines indicated, five basic shapes are generated. We will employ some of them in the following reflector designs.

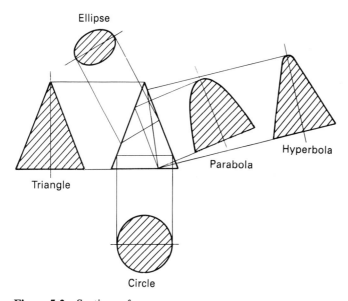

Figure 5.2   Sections of a cone

The circular true radius reflector is used extensively in luminaires such as Fresnels and PCs and, in fact, any design that requires a single small source of light. It can be seen from Figure 5.3(a) and Figure 5.3(b) that all the light falling onto the reflector is returned to its place of origin where it joins the rest of the light. Although this reflector provides the single source requirement, it is very inefficient because it is quite useless to extend the reflector to collect more light if the resultant redirected rays cannot be directed onto the lens. The reflector is therefore designed with the source in the full flood position which is nearest to the lens by drawing the two outer extremes of collection from the lens through the source and then

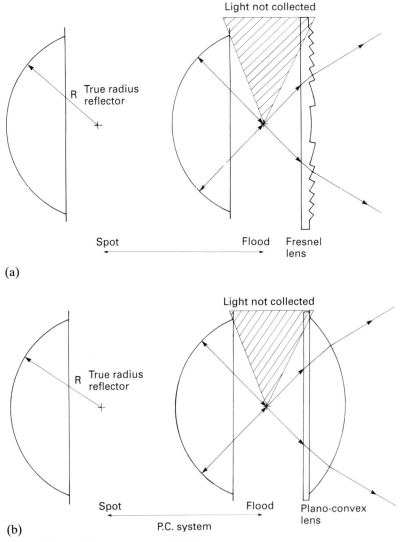

Figure 5.3   (a) Fresnel system. (b) PC system

projecting them on to determine the maximum diameter that is required for the reflector. Any true radius reflector with its centre at the source will suit the design, so the resultant size and radius can be determined by the luminaire size and the cooling requirements. Figure 5.3 also shows the gross inefficiency of this type of reflector which does not collect the light shown in the shaded areas. This system is even more wasteful in the spot

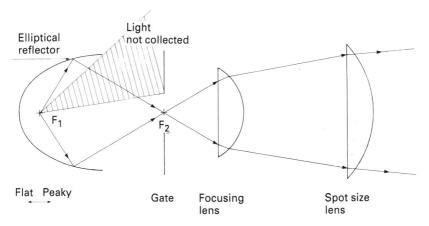

Figure 5.4   Elliptical reflector used in a profile projector

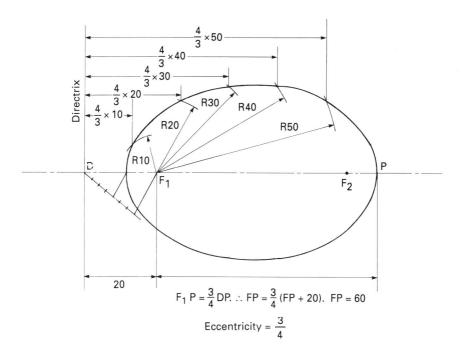

$$F_1 P = \frac{3}{4} DP. \therefore FP = \frac{3}{4}(FP + 20). \quad FP = 60$$

$$\text{Eccentricity} = \frac{3}{4}$$

Figure 5.5   Construction of an ellipse

position, which is rather ironic because most lighting men think that the high intensity spot is the more efficient position of focus, but it is obvious from the diagram that a lot more light goes through the lens in the flood position. A good point to remember when using colour filter is that the most arduous position for the filter is when the luminaire is in full flood with the added heat of the lamp being very close to the lens and therefore close to the filter.

Figure 5.4 shows an elliptical reflector in its most common application in a profile projector. With the source placed at F1 the reflected light is directed to F2. This reflector system is comparatively efficient compared with the true radius reflector but it still suffers the losses shown in the shadowed areas. It is pointless making the reflector larger to collect more light if the resultant increase in collection cannot be directed onto the first lens at an angle that can be redirected by the lens. Some designers have used an annular reflector to redirect the wasted light back through the gate: however, the steep angle of collection and redirection normally provides only 15% more efficiency at a much higher cost. The first design requirement must be the light output angles. Once these have been fixed, the correct lens combinations can be determined and their relative positions drawn in. The gate diameter can now be positioned and the light ray lines drawn from the lenses to the reflector. Having satisfied these design requirements, any size of elliptical reflector can be used, with the choice varying from a long thin shape to one that appears to be almost a circle. They will all obey the same reflector reflective law. This can be easily demonstrated with a piece of string and two drawing pins where the pins will be F1 and F2 and the string will represent the light ray. This form of design provides a wonderful range of ellipsoidal sizes to be considered but would no doubt cause great hilarity in the tool room where the finished

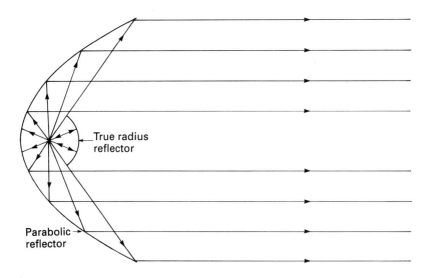

Figure 5.6   Parabolic reflector used in a beam light

reflector tool is made. We would therefore recommend the method of construction shown in Figure 5.5 on page 65.

The parabolic reflector is normally used as the name implies, in applications where a near parallel beam of light is required. The searchlight is a good example where the discharge source is mounted along the optical centre line facing the reflector. In this way a very efficient collection is achieved because all the light from the source is reflected in the output beam. The diagram shows a typical design for a beam light where the forward light from the source is redirected back through the source by a true radius reflector which can be part of the lamp's envelope which has been silvered or a separate reflector mounted in front of the source. Greater efficiency can be gained by the use of low voltage lamps that provide higher lumens per watt and a small source size; typically 12/24/48 V lamps are used. The only problem is, of course, that the mains electricity must be reduced by some form of transformer generally supplied from a solid state power supply circuit.

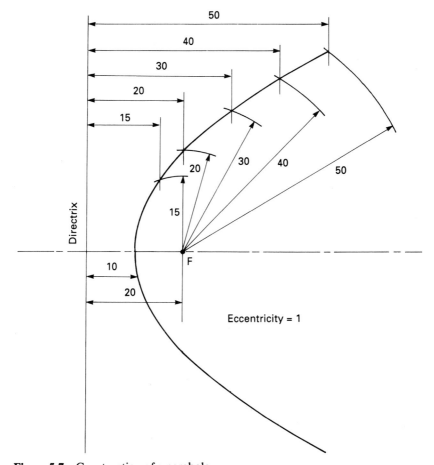

Figure 5.7 Construction of a parabola

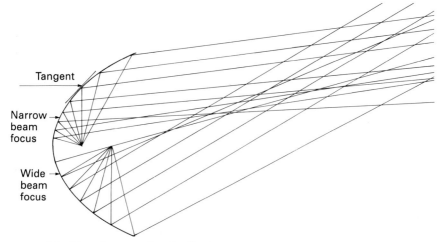

Figure 5.8   Focusing open-faced reflector

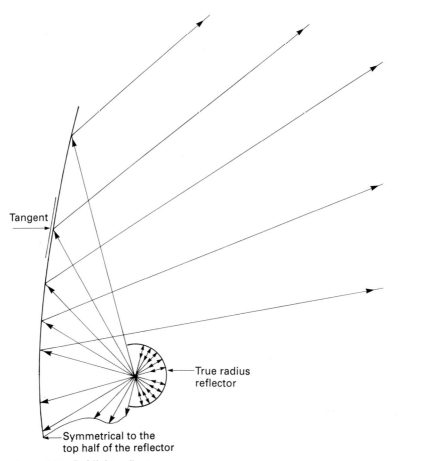

Figure 5.9   Softlight reflector

The type of open-faced luminaire shown in Figure 5.8 achieves a degree of focusing by moving the source along the optical centre line of the reflector. The direct light from the source will not change, but the reflected light can be superimposed onto the centre of the distribution, producing a higher lighting level. This reflector design is arrived at by tracing the required rays back to the reflector where a tangent can be drawn between the angle from the source and the required ray. In this way a series of tangents can be formed into an approximation of the required curve.

The reflector shown in Figure 5.9 is constructed in the same manner as the open-faced reflector by ray tracing. However, if the light output is to render a soft shadow the small source must be covered up so that it does not produce a conflicting shadow which would appear as a well-defined hard shadow from the source, followed by a secondary soft shadow from the larger reflector. As the softness of shadow is a direct function of the size of the reflector, it is desirable to have the largest reflector surface area that can be achieved. Additionally, a light stippling of the reflector will help to diffuse the light. Sometimes matt white paint is used; however, this deteriorates with age and becomes yellow, resulting in a reduction in the colour temperature. The reflector placed in front of the source is normally a true radius reflector so that the light rays from it can be ignored because they will be incorporated with the other rays produced by the source.

The cyclorama reflector shown in Figure 5.10 is made by ray tracing in the same manner as the open-faced reflector, but in this case an

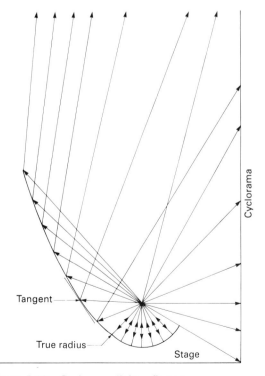

Figure 5.10 Cyclorama light reflector

asymmetric distribution is required to provide as much light as possible to the top of the cyclorama. It is quite common with this design to make the bottom of the reflector a true radius drawn around to the point of cut-off at the bottom of the cyclorama. In this way, the only light falling on the bottom of the cyclorama is the direct light from the source. The amount of reflected light is increased as the distribution extends up the cyclorama in an attempt to cancel out the fall off of light through the inverse square law. It is not, however, possible to achieve a constant lux reading up the cyclorama because the light level at the bottom of the cyc will always be determined by the direct light from the source leaving insufficient reflected light available to match it; so the next best type of distribution is one that falls off evenly at a constant rate without dark or light bands which would draw attention to the change.

5.2 Reflection and refraction

Reflection

We are so accustomed to the reflection of light that we would not normally stop to consider that our very existence depends upon it; for every item that we see is reflecting light to our eyes so that we can form an image of it. When we think of a reflector, we visualize a bright shiny surface. However, every solid that is exposed to light is a reflector, otherwise we could not see it. The laws of reflection are the same for all bright plane surfaces, as shown in Figure 5.11; however, if the surface is diffused, this will have the effect of scattering the light.

If we consider a bright, shiny surface with a light ray falling onto it we can see that the ray is reflected off the surface at the same angle as it approaches it. That is, if the angle is measured from a line drawn at a

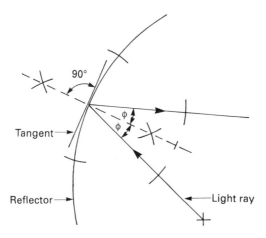

Figure 5.11   Reflection

Figure 5.12   Refraction in water

tangent to that part of the reflector. This rule remains true for any shape of reflector; and as the angle of reflection becomes less as the ray approaches 90° to the surface (at which point the angle onto the reflector is the same as the angle off the surface) the light ray is returned to its place of origin. This explains why a flash from a camera will over-expose any part of the subject that is exactly 90° to the camera. A simple simile can be applied to estimate where the reflected light will be directed, because it behaves in the same manner as a billiard ball striking a cushion where the angle off the cushion is the same as the approach angle.

Refraction

The most obvious demonstration of refraction is shown in Figure 5.12, where a stick is placed into the water at an angle. If this is viewed from the side the stick appears to change direction. This displacement of the image accounts for the difficulty in trying to pinpoint the position of an object under water, such as a fish. We can therefore say that refraction causes a light beam to change direction when striking or leaving a surface of a transparent material.

Figure 5.13 shows a piece of glass with a light ray entering from the left-hand side. At the point of entry, the ray is refracted down towards the norm, this being a line at 90° to the surface. The ray does not change direction through the glass, no matter how thick it might be, but it does change direction on leaving the surface of the glass on the right-hand side, adopting the same angle of refraction as it had when approaching the other side, but now it is displaced.

Figure 5.13 also shows an overlay of the refraction in the sheet of glass with a front surface of a lens superimposed onto it. The dotted line shows the original refraction of the light ray, which is now also influenced by the

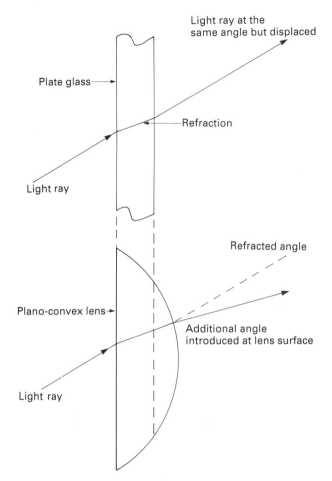

Figure 5.13   Refraction in glass

curvature of the lens. So, it can be stated that the direction of a light beam passing through a plano-convex lens is changed, firstly by the refraction and secondly by the angle of the surface at the point of departure. The reason for refraction occurring in the first place comes about by the difference in optical density of the two substances; in this case that of air and glass. Each is assigned a refractive index which relates to the speed with which light can pass through it. The refractive index of a vacuum is 1.0 at which light travels at 186,280 miles per second, so all other transparent substances have a refractive index greater than 1.0. Glass is typically 1.5 to 1.9, showing its higher optical density, with the resultant lowering of the speed of light through it, and a refractive index of 2.0 would halve the speed of light.

   Air is so near to the value of a vacuum that we can ignore the difference and treat air as having a refractive index of 1.0. Given the wavelength of the ray of light, the refractive index of the glass, and the angle of approach, the resultant displacement of the light ray can be calculated.

5.3 Centre of gravity (C of G) design considerations

Every luminaire is suspended by a yoke, stirrup or fork. All are names describing the same supports that are used in film, TV and theatre; the function remains the same, that is to provide a means of support that will enable the luminaire to rotate (pan) and to tilt. It is the tilt movement that requires to be mounted in the C of G of the luminaire. Whilst every luminaire has a means of locking the tilt movement, or in the case of a pole operated unit gears are provided to hold it steady in tilt, it is necessary to position the yoke at the C of G to prevent judder. In the case of pole

Figure 5.14   How to find the centre of gravity

operation, if the luminaire is out of balance it will be difficult to rotate the pole in one direction and judder will result in the other direction caused by the gears alternately releasing the load and stopping it again. In the case of the manually operated luminaire, an out of balance light causes two main problems: one, when the tilt lock is released the out of balance weight takes charge and rotates the luminaire very quickly, normally trapping your fingers between the housing and the yoke. The annoyance caused by an out of balance luminaire is seen when rigging lights onto a bar in a theatre which has already been fully rigged and all beams directed and set. Then an additional unit is added – the worst case being an out of balance profile. The influence of the weight of the large lenses mounted at some distance from the C of G produces a moment about the mounting hook clamp which tends to rotate the bar causing all of the other lights that have been previously set to tilt downwards, much to the annoyance of the electrician who has to reset them all. Having established the desirability of having luminaires in balance, sometimes a compromise is required because the C of G might come in line with the gate or some other obstruction. However, the first step for the manufacturers is to find the C of G, which can be simply achieved by experiment.

First of all one must position the variables that can occur to represent mid position when in operation. In the case of the Fresnel, the barndoors should be open, the lamp must be inserted in the lampholder and the focus in the mid position. In the case of a profile, the lenses should be placed in a mid position. From Figure 5.14 it can be seen that the luminaire is being suspended from two corners on opposite sides with a plumb bob weight positioned in the centre of the support bar mounted in line with the two support strings. Two marks are made behind the plumb line and a straight line is drawn between them. The luminaire is now rotated approximately 90° to the next two corners and the experiment is repeated. Where the two lines cross is the 'C of G'.

5.4 Ventilation

The importance of adequate ventilation in a luminaire cannot be overstated. An overheated lamp will give a short life, the internal electrical system and lampholder will deteriorate and the housing will become dangerously hot. The rules to achieve good ventilation are simple but are so often ignored. A common mistake is to believe that lots of holes in the housing will introduce a lot of airflow through it. In fact, the opposite may be true. A splendid example is a kiln, where a chimney is erected with hot air rising through it, creating a partial vacuum behind it, sucking the air into the kiln at the place where it is required to fuel the fire. The same is true for luminaires and an air path is worked out bearing in mind the working angles of the unit to determine the inlet and outlet path. One system is to have an inlet – scoop or mouth – positioned so that internal baffles can direct the air across the base of the lamp and then between the lamp and reflector and ultimately through an escape chimney.

This system works well to maintain the correct lamp temperature; however other means are required to cool the housing. If a wall cavity is provided by placing internal baffles in the housing, a separate ventilating system can be adopted to keep the outer skin cool. By providing separate inlet vent holes between the two skins, the air can be accelerated through the cavity by positioning the outlet slots adjacent to the chimney outlet; the hot air rising through the chimney creates an air rush around it, sucking the air up through the two skins. A third ventilating system will be required around the lens and colour filter (see Figure 5.15).

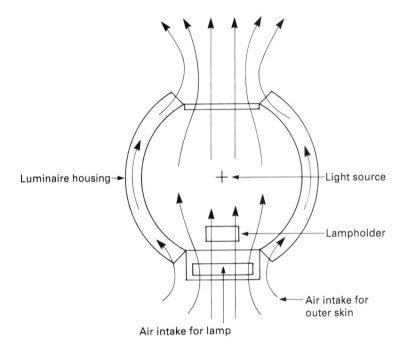

Figure 5.15   Luminaire ventilation air path

5.5 The carbon arc

Most high efficiency carbons produce about 46 lumens per watt, which is double the efficacy of a tungsten halogen lamp and half the efficacy of a discharge lamp. All of the light is emitted from the centre of the positive carbon; the positive is constructed by an outer shell made from compressed carbon with a core injected under high pressure made of various rare earths and carbon. This enables the manufacturer to create the correct mix for maximum efficiency and the required colour temperature. This construction also provides a hollow in the centre of the core which is containing the crater – that is the centre of the light output. It is necessary with most carbon arc luminaires to have an operator present to keep a constant distance between the two carbons and this is known as trimming the carbons. The correct burning position can be seen from Figure 5.16, where the tail flame is held in the vertical at the correct angle. If the positive or negative carbons are allowed to overfeed and become out of

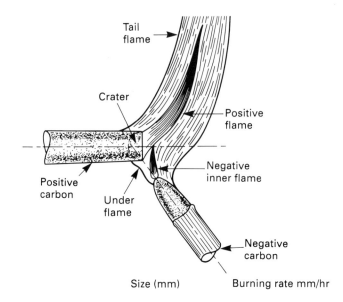

Amps	Arc volts dc	Size (mm)		Burning rate mm/hr	
		Positive	Negative	Positive	Negative
225	72	16	13.5	430	70
150	65	16	11	230	64
120	53	13.6	10	240	64
60	52	9	7	330	80
40	50	8	7	100	76

Figure 5.16   Carbon burning characteristics

alignment, the tail flame will become unstable and create a flicker and ultimately the carbons will set up a squealing noise. One simple method of setting up a carbon arc when cold is to take a spent end of a positive carbon and use it as a gauge by placing it between the tip of the negative and the front edge of the positive carbon. In this way a reasonable running condition will result when the carbon is struck – that is the negative is raised up until it touches the positive and then allowed to drop immediately an arc is struck. As soon as the arc has been established the gap can be adjusted by eye through the coloured glass of the viewing port. The running speeds are normally adjusted by a motor drive which feeds the positive and negative carbons towards each other at a predetermined rate which can be varied by a potentiometer. The negative carbon does not rotate; however the positive carbon is rotated continuously to prevent the outer shell of the carbon burning away at the top and allowing the crater to spill out. Carbons always operate from a direct current which can be derived from generators or from a transformer rectifier unit working from ac mains.

If carbons are used in a confined space, adequate ventilation must be provided to extract the fumes and the large quantities of ozone which are produced. Arcs normally work with a controlling ballast in series with the supply to them; the ballast will provide high voltage to initiate the arc and then become self-regulating as the arc starts to draw current through the ballast increasing its resistance and reducing the voltage. Arcs have mainly been replaced by the higher efficiency HMI sources which do not require adjustment during operation and can therefore be remote controlled. However, the arc still lives on with some nostalgia amongst the old hands.

5.6 Luminaire types

The entertainment lighting industry should have its own dictionary of names and descriptions to guide potential users through their catalogues. Every manufacturer has contributed to the proliferation of pet names for their products, so what is basically the same luminaire can have many names. Originally it was fun no doubt to build up a vocabulary that could only be understood by the lighting fraternity, thus adding mystique to the art. Some examples are shown in Figure 5.17:

'Brute' – an enormous 225A arc.
'Basher' – a 500 W bulb in a reinforced pudding basin.
'Skypan' – an enormous dustbin lid with a 5 kW lamp at its centre.
'Northlight' – a bounced softlight from a corrugated reflector.
'Pup' – a small focusing Fresnel.
'Inkie Dinkie' – a miniature focusing Fresnel.
'Scoop' – in essence a loud hailer megaphone with a 1 kW lamp at its centre.

The list is endless and not one of the names describes the use of the luminaire and each manufacturer uses a different name for a similar type. To expose the mystique, we will place every luminaire in the entertainment business into only eleven groups; each group can be subdivided when reading a lighting catalogue into Wattage, Voltage, Beam Angle, Incandescent or Discharge Source, Manual or Pole Operated Controls, followed by the finer points which separate one make from another. The eleven basic types are:

1. Fresnel
2. PC
3. Profile
4. Follow spots
5. Floodlight
6. Softlight
7. Focusing reflector light
8. Beam light
9. Sealed beam
10. Cyclorama/backing light
11. Effects

We will now break down the eleven groups, describing their use and optical systems.

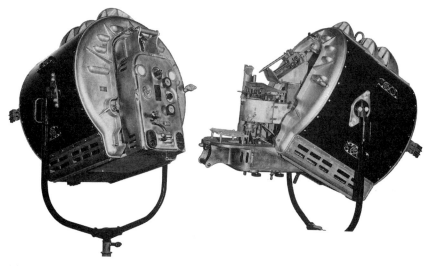

(a) 225A Brute

(b) Basher

Figure 5.17

(c) 5 kW Skypan

Figure 5.17 *continued*

(d) 5 kW Northlite

Figure 5.17 *continued*

(e) 1 kW Fresnel (Pup)

Figure 5.17   *continued*

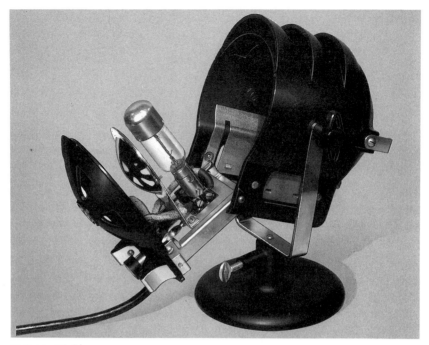

(f) Inkie Dinkie

(g) 1 kW Scoop

Figure 5.17   *continued*

1. Fresnel

This luminaire employs a Fresnel lens and circular reflector with the source placed at the centre of radius of the reflector. To focus the light the source and reflector are moved together. The spot position of focus is when the source is at the focal point of the lens, and maximum flood is achieved when the source is nearest to the lens. The variable beam is typically 8–65° and provides a soft edge keylight used as the main illumination on the artiste or subject in TV, film and photography and for large area illumination in theatre. One disturbing fault with the Fresnel is that light is scattered from the top of the risers on each zone of the lens, which can cause a problem of spill light.

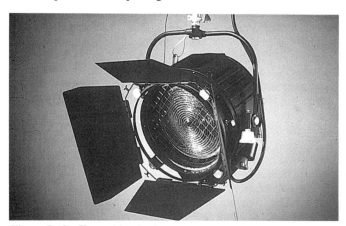

Figure 5.18   Fresnel luminaire

2. Plano-convex

The PC uses a plano-convex lens and circular reflector and is similar to the Fresnel in construction and performance. It is used mainly in theatre and has a beam appearance of an out-of-focus profile. In performing a similar

Figure 5.19   PC luminaire

role to the Fresnel the question is often asked: 'Why do we require both types?' The main reason is that it has a well-defined soft edge to the beam and does not produce spill light that would otherwise fall onto parts of the set or backing and cause problems. The disadvantages, however, are that the filament tends to image itself in full spot and any plano-convex lens has the problem of producing a dark hole in the centre of the beam between the full flood and the full spot positions. Some manufacturers provide a diffusion on the rear surface of the lens to reduce both problems.

3.   Profile (Ellipsoidal USA)

Europeans refer to this luminaire as a profile, describing its ability to project an outline of a cutout image placed in the gate; whereas in the USA it is referred to as an ellipsoidal, which describes the type of reflector employed. The unit uses one or more plano-convex lenses and an ellipsoidal reflector, with the source positioned at the first point of focus of the reflector. The beam size and focus of a zoom type can be varied by moving the inter-relationship of the two lenses and the beam can be modified to provide a hot centre or an even field by fore and aft movement of the source in the reflector. Normally the most rear position of the source in the reflector provides the most even beam and produces the sharpest images of the gate, shutter blades and gobos. To obtain an efficient zoom, the beam angles are normally restricted to 2:1, i.e. 16° to 32° or thereabouts. On wide angle, the edge of the beam is often ringed in a halo of blue halation which can be removed by placing a reducing cutout circle between the lenses at the expense of the luminance efficiency. Typical beam angles are 5° to 45°. The beam shape can be modified by four beam shaping shutters or an iris diaphragm which can be focused from a sharp definition to a soft edge. This luminaire is the workhorse of the theatre used mainly as a keylight for the artiste, or as a silhouette projector. For

Figure 5.20   Profile spot

TV and photography it is used as a gobo projector for backgrounds. The beam is a clear-cut, well-defined illumination that can be focused to provide a sharp image, or the focus can be backed off to provide a soft edge without emitting spill light. The main disadvantage is that the housing is very long, particularly on narrow angle units, and can prove a problem in restricted rigging space and adjacent flying scenery can sway and knock them out of position.

4.   Follow spots

The optics for the follow spot are the same as the profile projector and the unit only varies from the above by the following characteristics. The gate area is much more elaborate then the profile; it omits the four beam shaping shutters and replaces them by two horizontal blades, one in the top of the gate and one underneath the gate. A single lever operates both blades in unison, producing a variable parallel slot of light known as 'Chinese'. The blades can close the gate completely, giving a blackout known as a 'douser'. In addition to the iris diaphragm for spot size and gobo projection, a dimmer iris is often provided by placing it in the light path but keeping it well out of focus. This has the effect of dimming the light without changing the colour temperature or the shape of the spot – a desirable feature for normal control and very useful when balancing the light on stage from two spots at different distances. A cruder, simple way of achieving this effect in profiles, as well as follow spots, is to put a barndoor from a Fresnel into the colour runners and move all four blades

Figure 5.21   CSI follow spot

inwards to dim the output. Some follow spots provide a mechanical coupling between the two lenses to produce a zoom effect of automatically maintaining focus when changing distance. The main advantage of a follow spot is the ability to focus constant attention onto a moving artiste; however, the disadvantage of a low angle follow spot without other illumination is a complete lack of modelling and atmosphere for anything other than the 'sock it to them' approach.

5.   Floodlight
From Figure 5.22 it can be seen that the floodlight produces a very wide angle illumination which is unfortunately totally uncontrollable. The beam will not provide a cut off if a barndoor is used because of the large area of the source and reflected light, and therefore spills onto everything in front of it. It is hardly ever used in television, except for house or working lights, and in the theatre it is limited in use to large areas of colour wash. Another disadvantage is that the shadows cast from this type of luminaire give a confused rendering. The shadow from the filament is very hard in the vertical plane and softer in the horizontal if a linear lamp is used. Add to this the secondary shadow of the light from the reflector which appears softer than the shadow from the source and the resultant illumination is beyond control. The advantages are a very wide angle and high efficiency because most of the light is projected out of the housing. The units are usually low cost.

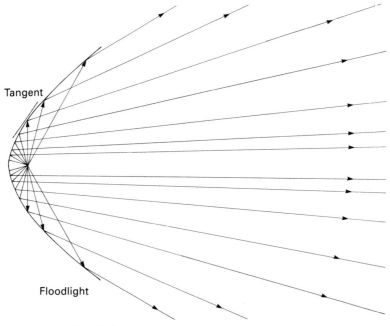

Figure 5.22   Floodlight

6. Softlight

The name Softlight refers to the shadow definition and implies that the edge of the shadow bleeds away without a defined edge to it. The ultimate soft light is the bounced light from the North sky which is so large in comparison to man that the light approaches from a very large angle so that we appear to have no shadow at all. There is therefore no such thing as a small softlight and the term is open to abuse. We do know, however, that the larger the reflector the softer the shadow so the design of a softlight is always a compromise between the largest that can be reasonably achieved and the size that can be tolerated in a studio (see also Figure 5.9). Softlights are mainly used in photography and television as a fill light to lift the shadow areas created by the key light to an acceptable level to get the required response from the film stock or television camera. It is desirable to achieve this without creating more shadows on the subject. The main disadvantage is light spilling onto backings or cycloramas which can be partly controlled by an egg crate louvre placed in the front of the luminaire which restricts the light output to an angle of 90° vertical, 120° horizontal. The terms 'soft' and 'hard' are comparative and do not define the shadow created by the light. Mr Neenan tackled the problem by defining the shadow and produced a test whereby a cross is placed in front of a backing and the light is measured in the shadow area and the lighted area. The two are expressed as a ratio, known as 'the Neenan factor'. Although this method of test works, the industry has not adopted it, still preferring to put up a hand in front of a backing, and, after much consideration, declaring the shadow to be good, bad or indifferent.

Figure 5.23 Softlight

7. Focusing reflector light

There are many types and wattage of focusing reflector lights but the most famous is the 'Redhead'. The name describes the colour of the housing, but of course the French have their own way of expressing themselves and call it a 'Mandarin' referring to its segmented shape. The unit is mainly used in television and photography and is particularly useful in interview situations because of its comparatively high light output from a small unit and the ability to focus the beam. This focusing is achieved by moving the lamp fore and aft in the reflector which provides two superimposed beams, one from the direct output of the source, and the other from the reflector (see also Figure 5.8). When the lamp is moved into the spot position the reflector provides the increased intensity in the centre of the beam while the overall total light output angle remains practically the same because of the direct illumination from the filament. Two problems with all open-faced lights are hard shadows and the need to provide a safety glass or mesh to catch the quartz from the envelope in the event of the lamp shattering. The standards require that particles of quartz 3 mm or more in size are arrested.

Figure 5.24   Redhead focusing reflector light

8. Beam light

This luminaire employs a parabolic reflector with the source placed at its centre of focus (see also Figure 5.6). With an ideal point source, the optical system would produce a parallel beam of light, the same diameter as that of the reflector. However, if a true radius reflector is placed in front of the source, it prevents the light from the source from leaving the housing in a direct line, and thus reflects all the light that falls onto it back to the source and hence through the filament to the parabolic reflector. In real life, the size of the source has the effect of slightly spreading the beam and typical beam angles are 4° to 8°. A slight amount of focus can be achieved by moving the source fore and aft in the reflector and this will provide a few degrees change in the beam. This optical system has been used for many years in lighthouses and searchlights where in the latter, a positive carbon

Figure 5.25   Beam light

is mounted along the centre axis of the reflector with its light emitting crater facing the reflector. This type of luminaire was originally used by necessity in large opera houses and the big 'Germanic type' theatres, because of its high efficiency and narrow beam required when lights were positioned a long distance from the stage.

The main disadvantages of a beam light are that the beam angle cannot be increased to any great extent by focusing and that most efficient luminaires use a low voltage lamp to make use of its small source size and high light output (lumens per Watt) therefore requiring a transformer in the mains supply line. The main advantages are a very narrow beam for long throw applications, a high efficiency and very little spill light.

9. Sealed beam

The sealed beam lamp employs the same optics as the beam light but replaces the front reflector with a moulded lens which has the effect of controlling the beam to a predetermined angle. Because the lamp is completely sealed, it can be run at a high pressure and consequently provides a high efficiency. The lamp manufacturers offer a choice of five beam angles by lamp selection; each lamp has a different lens moulded onto the front in quite the same manner as the car headlamp. The most popular lamp in entertainment is the Par 64 and as with all Par lamps, the number is the diameter expressed in eighths of an inch; therefore a Par 64 is eight inches in diameter or 204 mm. The beam is usually oval and typical beam angles are (9°H 12°W) (10°H 14°W) (11°H 24°W) (21°H 57°W) (70°H 70°W) for 240 V lamps. Beam angles and efficiency vary with voltage, particularly when comparing 240 V lamps with 120 V versions. The most common application of this lamp is the Parcan, used extensively on road shows for its high light output, small size, low cost and light weight. It is the only luminaire that comes to mind that costs less than the lamp that is used in it. Increasingly the sealed beam lamps are being used in theatre and television, supporting the argument that lighting for theatre, TV and film is coming closer together.

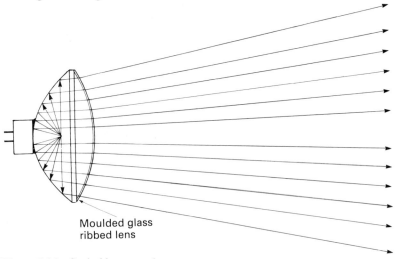

Moulded glass
ribbed lens

Figure 5.26   Sealed beam optics

10. Cyclorama/backing light

By following the ray diagram (see also Figure 5.10) it can be seen that the lower part of the reflector is a true radius about the source. This has the effect of returning all of the light that falls onto it back to the filament and through the envelope to the main part of the reflector. The main part of the reflector is designed to direct as much light as it can towards the top of the distribution and to only light the bottom part of the cyclorama with direct light from the filament. With the inverse square law working against the designer, it is always a problem to get enough light to the top of the cyclorama, so it is realized that a cyclorama or backing cannot be evenly lit from the top or bottom only. It is necessary to light from both positions if an even effect is required. If only top or bottom lighting is used, then the fall off of the light should be designed to be a continuous reduction without any dark or bright bars. In this way, the change is not exaggerated. The choice of linear tungsten halogen lamps is important because of the ring supports that hold the filament in the centre of the envelope. These cause shadows which will appear as five or six fanned out dark bars, projecting up the cyc, and can be overcome with the use of frosted lamps. When assessing the light distribution of cyclorama lights, it is not possible to get a true result by observing only one unit, because the lights are designed to have a wide horizontal angle of distribution, typically 45° each side of centre. It is necessary to light three units spaced at the recommended distance from the cyclorama and positioned at the correct distance apart, this being when the overlapping lighting gives an even horizontal coverage. Under these conditions it is possible to assess the vertical distribution on either side of the centre unit. Polar diagrams are not normally produced for cyc lights because they have no practical application, so it is normal for manufacturers to set up three lights as described above, and take readings progressively up the cyclorama and to show this information graphically. When setting cyc lights, it is a good guide to remember that it is the distance from the cyclorama that determines the coverage; also a small change in distance will create a large change in light level opposite the luminaire and almost no change at all at the top of the distribution. This is because the distance in the vertical direction has hardly changed.

A starting point to set up cyc lights is to place the groundrow 1m from the cyc to the back of the fixture and to have each recurring colour at 1.2m centres, this being the average design criterion. However, having said that this is a good starting point, you will always be compromised by the demands of the set and often return to the action to find that your cyc lights have been pushed so close to the backing that the lighting result looks like a series of bright blobs – nothing like the dawn you visualized.

Cyclorama lights are made in the following configurations:

Single and double units;
Four lights in line and the same configuration with hinges between each compartment for bending around corners;
Four-way unit mounted in domino formation.

All types of units allow for up to four colours before the first colour is repeated to provide colour mixing or four particular choices of colour, but

Figure 5.27   Cyclorama lights

don't forget to include a clear compartment if you are using a red/green/blue colour mix to desaturate the colours. Also remember that the dimmer setting is just as important as the colour that has been chosen.

The design of colour frame can have 'tiger teeth' along the edge to break up the shadows created by the linear lamp filament being in line with the inside edge of the colour frame. This can be important in television when lighting the cyclorama from the top and allowing it to spill out onto the floor. The main disadvantage of cyclorama lighting systems is that they eat up dimmer circuits at an alarming rate, so it is necessary to investigate distribution systems that can be patched from acting area lights to the cyclorama when required, and the possibility of using a nine-way plug and socket system at 4 × 5 kW per circuit; the cyc lights can then be daisy-chained to work in parallel. The space taken by the luminaire is always difficult to find in operation, and the TV lighting barrel system presents a particular problem of trying to rig the lights on the side of the cyclorama that is presented with the ends of the barrels without tying up every barrel for this purpose – a point often overlooked when designing a studio lighting barrel system.

11.   Effects light

Effects projectors normally employ a true radius reflector or an elliptical design similar to the reflector used in a profile projector. Figure 5.28 shows an elliptical reflector with its increased efficiency when compared with the true radius type. The first element is normally a heat absorbing glass that has the effect of reducing the heat passing through it by about 80%, with a light loss of approximately 20%. This special glass requires an airflow over its surface to dissipate the heat collected. An alternative heat filter is a glass with a dichroic coating which reflects the heat from the surface of the coating back into the luminaire. This type of filter is slightly more efficient than heat absorbing glass but care must be taken to ensure that the source is not overheated.

The condenser lens – as the name implies – helps to direct diverging rays of light through the gate. It can be a conventional plano-convex lens or, to provide a slightly diffused output and a weight saving, a Fresnel lens is often employed. The gate is designed to accept a conventional photographic slide or a large piece of glass with the scene to be projected painted onto it. It is therefore possible to make a photographic slide of the actual backing required from the correct position to give the proper perspective and then project it onto a white backing. In the same way, an effects projector can be used to project a scene onto a backing for the scenic artist to sketch in the outline with the correct perspective before painting it. An alternative accessory is a rotating disk positioned on the front of the projector with the appropriate effect painted onto the rotating glass, i.e. rain, fire, snow, etc. In this way a moving effect can be created at variable speed. A choice of objective lenses is made available to give the coverage required at the appropriate distance. Disadvantages are the high

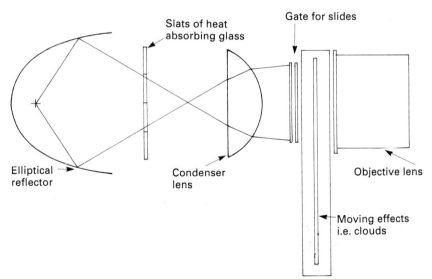

Figure 5.28   Effects optics

cost of the projectors and high effects costs, and comparatively low light output levels that cannot compete with high lighting levels on the set. A very steady mount is required, as any vibration will produce judder in the output beam and ruin the effect, particularly if the building being used is old and somewhat unstable.

5.7 Special designs

Multipurpose luminaire

This luminaire is basically a focusing Fresnel mounted back to back with a softlight and was developed for television in 1961.

The reason for the development was a requirement to mount luminaires at regular intervals all over the studio at approximately 2m centres, known as a saturated lighting system, where in this way a light can be found anywhere near the required place, pulled along its barrel and positioned. The luminaire is then rotated, offering the choice of Fresnel key light or softlight. A switch is then selected to divert the electrical supply to the chosen light, and a second switch used to provide a choice of power. This is achieved by using four tungsten halogen linear lamps in the soft end, and a twin filament, 4-pin lamp in the Fresnel end.

This arrangement is intended to cover 80% of the requirements of the LD, with the remainder being mounted for each show. The additions include 1kW Fresnels, profiles or specials as required. To add more

Figure 5.29   (a) Multipurpose luminaire. (b) Twister

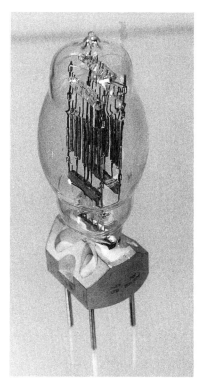

Figure 5.30   Four pin twin filament lamp

flexibility to the system, the multipurpose luminaires are mounted onto pantographs to provide a degree of independent height adjustment. The BBC adopted this form of luminaire in all their major studios, claiming very fast turn round time, increasing the output from the studio. Leaving the lights permanently rigged substantially reduced the damage normally caused when lights are continuously rigged and de-rigged.

Battery hand lamps

These are mainly used for news gathering on outside locations, so they are completely self-powered from their own battery. The most popular batteries for size to weight ratio are nickel-cadmium or zinc. A typical luminaire has an open-faced reflector, containing a tungsten halogen lamp, the largest of which is normally 250 W at 30 V. A degree of focusing is obtained by moving the lamp in the reflector. More recently 200 W discharge lamps have been used to enable high light outputs to be achieved. The battery unit will also contain high frequency ac convertors for the lamp supply.

This is quite an efficient luminaire, making use of the increased efficiency of the low voltage tungsten halogen lamp. The batteries, however, do require special care in operation, because if they are left connected to the light and allowed to run down to zero volts, it is possible for all the other cells to reverse into the weakest cell and thereby ruin the

Figure 5.31   Hand lamp and battery

battery. Nickel-cadmium batteries that are not in regular use should be discharged and recharged at least every two weeks. This keeps them in good condition as they are designed to work regularly.

5.8 Assessment of luminaires

The LD's assessment of a luminaire is how well can he achieve his lighting requirements with this instrument, which is quite understandable from his point of view. The electrician who has to rig and set it has quite different criteria and the maintenance engineer has his own particular problems to keep it in good repair. The LD's assessment is quite straightforward and can be seen by demonstration; it is also well documented by the lighting manufacturer with polar diagrams for the light output.

We shall therefore turn our attention to the mechanical assessment that will affect the reliability and practical needs of the user. It is most interesting to watch the experienced practical user at any exhibition. He will walk up to a luminaire and in minutes run through a set routine of things to try, gained by years of disappointment and annoyance with things that can go wrong and just do not work in the way that they should. His checklist leaves the manufacturer in no doubt that he is demonstrating his product to a discerning user.

Luminaire checklist

Mechanical construction

Check on the general mechanical construction particularly with a view to maintaining the luminaire in the future. Examine the quality of the finish on the body of the luminaire together with the paintwork involved.

Electrical construction

Ensure that all wiring used on the luminaire is adequate for the working temperatures to be encountered. Check that all metal parts are adequately earthed to the main earth terminal. Ensure that the switches and wiring are adequately rated for the current to be used within the device. Check that the input cables are adequately terminated and accessible for test purposes or for replacement and maintenance.

Dimensions and weight

Examine the overall dimensions in all planes with particular reference to the space occupied by the luminaire when panning and tilting. Check the weight of the basic luminaire plus the weight of any accessories to be used.

Pan and tilt

Unlock the tilt lock knob and see if the unit is in the centre of gravity. Not only does the luminaire take charge and trap your fingers if it is not in balance but it will also put a pressure on the locking mechanism that can result in the luminaire drooping after it has been set; so the second test is to lock the tilt mechanism and try to force the luminaire downwards, making it slip in the yoke. If the unit is pole operated, try the tilt and pan for backplay in the drive mechanism. In the case of the tilt, an out of balance luminaire will result in a jerky movement in one direction and a heavy load in the opposite direction; this is caused by the load alternately taking charge and then being arrested by the gears. Backplay in the pan movement will result in a horizontal wandering movement after the light has been set. Check that the carcase rotates in the yoke assembly correctly, particularly with open barn doors. When pan and tilt pole operation is fitted, ensure that they can be over-ridden by manual adjustments.

Focus

Here we are looking for a smooth movement, best tested at, say, 45° down. This will show up judder, if it exists, or sticking, followed by a sudden movement, both of which cause lamp failure due to the fact that the lamp must be on to focus it when the vibration on the hot filament can cause it to rupture. Check for 'end stops' on lamp holder movement within the luminaire body.

Note: Check the amount of torque required for operating the focus and the pan and tilt controls because if it is too stiff this will cause problems in practice.

Optical tests

Plot a polar diagram and note the peak intensity of the luminaire. Check the beam angles, both vertical and horizontal at the extremes of focus. Check the quality of the light, both vertically and horizontally at the extremes of focusing, thus ensuring a subjective check for striations and evenness. Ensure there are no light leaks from the luminaire so that light emits outside the main beam and causes problems in operation. Check for evenness of colour distribution in the light output beam, particularly with discharge sources. Check for the efficiency of the luminaire in converting the power into useful light output.

Temperatures

In the luminaire's normal working modes, e.g. depressed to 45°: Check that the pinch temperatures on the lamps are not in excess of the manufacturer's stated values. Check the cable gland input working temperatures to ensure cables are not getting too hot. Check all external surfaces to ensure that the luminaire is not going to be too hot in practice.

Shutter blades

Profile shutters have always been a problem, mainly because they are in the hottest part of the beam and will normally run at a temperature that makes them glow red, so adequate insulation on the operating handle is essential. The most common complaint, however, is the shutter blades that slide down in the guides when they get hot, so try it after the other tests have been done to make sure that you maintain a positive movement on the blade at high temperature.

Profile edge focus

Most manufacturers demonstrate a profile projector in a sharp focus position, demonstrating its ability to project a well-defined image. Adjust the lens movement to the minimum and maximum angles to determine if the edge is sharp over the whole range and at the same time observe the edge for colour fringing. It is most important with the profile that it can be soft focused, so determine there is sufficient lens movement at both ends of travel to achieve a soft edge.

Barndoors

The main point to observe is that the flaps stay put with sufficient friction to sustain the top flap when it is hot. A floppy barndoor flap is the lighting man's cross. Check that smooth rotation can be achieved by poking it with a pole (quite a common practice). Light leaks can be assessed by half closing the two small flaps and then bringing the large flaps in to touch them. A well-defined 'letter box' shape should be produced at this point; observe any spill light that comes out of any slot between the sides of the short flap and the large flap. This is a good time to see if spill light comes out between the back of the barndoor and the front of the housing. One easy way to check for spill light is to pass your hand around the area of concern, which will soon pick up any unwanted light.

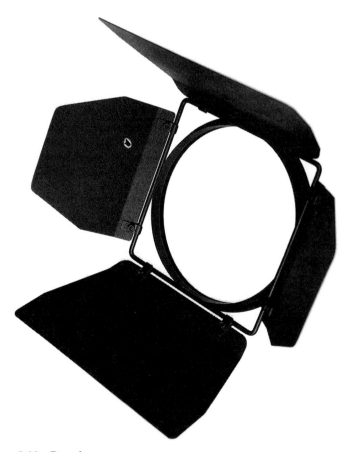

Figure 5.32   Barndoor

Safety requirements

The following items should be checked. Has the luminaire had a drop test done, and if so, was a certificate issued? If so, this should be provided. Luminaires are also generally supplied with safety bonds or chains and these should come with certificates or specifications indicating their suitability for use with the item of equipment. Have adequate safety precautions been taken against an exploding lamp and the loss of minute pieces of glass? Have precautions been taken with regard to lens breakage and the possibility of large pieces of glass leaving the luminaire? Ensure that the most important bolts and screws which attach items that may become dislodged from the luminaires are adequate for the purpose intended. Are supplementary safety bonds provided for any detachable accessories, such as colour frames, barndoors, etc. or how are the barndoors retained in normal practice? Check for any sharp edges or dangerous protrusions which in practice may give problems for the operators. (See also Chapter 16, section 16.4: Safety checklists and inspections.)

Burning angle

It is a requirement to state the permitted burning angle of the luminaire. This is normally found on the product label and will give the permitted angles above and below the horizontal. This limitation can be imposed by either the luminaire's cooling system or the lamp manufacturer.

Spares

Ask to see the spares list (some manufacturers do not automatically provide one); this could save a lot of trouble identifying spare parts in the future. Check on the availability of spares and what components are used and where are they sourced.

Lamps

Determine if the type of lamp used is made by more than one manufacturer or if not, is it going to be readily available in your area? One common problem with lamps is arcing at the pins. Check the clamping arrangements for any lamps in use. In addition, check for the ease of operation when fastening and unfastening lamps in their holders.

General

A general inspection should examine the ease of stacking for storage purposes. Where is the attached luminaire cable stored when not in use? Check for ease of handling when being carried and rigged.

6   Lighting suspension systems

6.1 Suspension and why it is needed

In theatres and studios, the majority of lighting is placed at a reasonable height above the acting area. The reasons for this are quite simply that we do not wish the acting area to be full of equipment, especially as in a TV studio the floor is also cluttered with cameras and booms. In this chapter we will look at the various ways that operators can suspend equipment above the acting area accurately and quickly, together with a high degree of safety.

In 1803 Frederick Winsor demonstrated on stage a coal burning apparatus for the generation of coal gas. The light consisted of a model of Cupid with a lighted torch in one hand whilst holding onto the gas pipe that was suspended from the ceiling with the other hand. Of course, a lighting suspension system for candles and later for oil lamps had been used on the stage for many years. Winsor went on to greater things and was responsible for the installation of gas lights for the King's birthday in 1807 on the walls at St James's Park and Carlton House.

You might well ask what relevance this anecdote has to lighting suspension in view of the fact that the lights were fixed to the walls? Winsor ran a supply pipe from his house in Pall Mall where he had installed coal gas generating equipment several hundred yards over gardens and along the walls. The relevance is that he chose 1.5 inch bore pipe for his supply system. He could hardly know that this size of pipe would become the standard size to be used in theatres because the gas supply system for London was not introduced until 1812 with the forming of the Gas Light and Coke Company and the first gas street lighting was installed on Westminster Bridge in 1813. Theatre followed in 1817 when the London Lyceum introduced gas lighting over the whole stage but the overhead gas batten had to wait in design until 1865 when it was introduced and consisted of a 1.5 inch bore gas pipe with rat tail burners mounted along its length every few inches across the whole width of the stage. The pipe was suspended from steel ropes and fed by flexible hoses from the sides of the stage.

As far as we can research, this was the introduction of the 1.5 inch gas pipe for lighting suspension which has remained the standard for the industry to this day. As we are no longer concerned with the nominal bore of the pipe but only its outside diameter when we are suspending lights, it is interesting to note that the 48 mm diameter, the standard for the industry, is in fact the outside diameter of a 1.5 inch gas pipe = $1\frac{29}{32}$ inches. It is obvious by now that theatres used the redundant gas pipes that they had to hang their new-found electric lanterns when electricity was introduced at the London Savoy theatre in 1881.

The film industry, which had progressed from glasshouses that tracked in a circle so that the sun provided a constant key light, to studios that were lit by electricity, tended to use single lights suspended by hemp ropes from blocks and tackles mounted on steel beams in the roof. When more lights were used, a platform with hand rails (called a 'boat') was suspended from two or more blocks and tackles above the studio so that the lights, which were quite often arcs or required adjustment due to the absence of pole operation, could be attended by the studio electricians (*see* Figure 6.1). In some film studios the use of long barrels to suspend lights was being introduced. It is worthwhile stating here that the film and photographic industry tends to work from the studio floor 'up', as opposed to the theatre and TV industries which work from the ceiling 'down'.

Figure 6.1   Film studio 'boats'

In 1936, when the BBC started television transmission, all the lighting equipment came from theatre and film manufacturers, mainly using the rigging techniques of the film industry, such as hemp ropes and blocks and tackles.

By 1956 the BBC had introduced a motorized hoisting system for lighting, comprising a unit with a motorized gearbox and wire ropes to suspend a 2.4 m long, 48 mm diameter barrel (Figure 6.2).

Figure 6.2   Motorized barrel

With the introduction of commercial television in 1955 a new type of suspension system had been designed; this consisted of an overhead walkover grid at high level with slots, running the length of the studio, into which telescopic suspension units were placed and winched down to the required height from the grid. (Figure 6.3 (a) and (b) and Figure 6.4.)

Starting from this date, an argument ensued and persists to this day of the merits and disadvantages of motorized barrels versus single point suspension. The motorized barrel protagonist will insist that the saturated lighting rig with two or three lights on each barrel provides enough choice of lighting positions and can be rigged from the studio floor at the same time as other trades are working on the set in comparative safety; whereas a single point suspension installation requires men to be above the grid for rigging. The lighting director, working in a single point suspension studio, will argue that he can be more precise and can place the luminaire of his choice at the point in space where he wants it, with independent height control of every luminaire. No doubt the argument will continue.

Before we get immersed in the detail of each system, it would be useful to have an idea of what each type of suspension offers.

6.2 Grids

The dictionary defines a 'grid' as a grating, a gridiron, a framework. It is also described as the 'framework above a theatre stage from which scenery

Figure 6.3   (a) Monopole grid (viewed from above)

and lights may be suspended'. The original theatre grids were usually wooden platforms suspended from the roof structure, providing a working level for men to walk over. The floor, which was slatted, offered a means by which ropes or scenery could be suspended. Additionally, the lighting bars were suspended from this platform (Figure 6.5).

Modern theatres now use steel grids where the slots are 63.5 mm (2.5 inches) wide and generally made of rectangular steel tube. The distance between the various slots is dictated by the spacing of the counterweight fly bars used for scenery, together with the lighting bars, which may be either the counterweight type or motorized.

In television, the term 'grid' usually describes the roof structure that supports the lighting systems installed, and these can be from the very simple fixed barrel rigs down to the highly sophisticated monopole grids. The television industry tended to follow the example of the theatre, due to

Figure 6.3   (b) Monopole grid (viewed from below)

the need to suspend lights and scenery. The film industry has traditionally always built scenery from the studio floor upwards and any rigging is done by using ropes and blocks and tackles, suspended from RSJs at high level. In a television studio, where motorized units are installed, the basic need to walk to the units installed at high level can be met by walkways adjacent to the units. However, some organizations have made the entire area at high level completely free to walk over, thus allowing unrestricted access to almost any point above the acting area. Monopole grids do require access by staff to move the units. One of the problems associated with walkover grids is that of safety: obviously, no object must fall from the grid with personnel working on the studio floor, and to this end either pocketless overalls are worn by staff or any items that can be used at high level are usually attached to devices to prevent them falling through the grid slots. Arguments ensue all the time as to the viability of walkover grids, bearing in mind modern safety legislation, and most studios installed these days, generally provide maintenance access only.

The alternative to this safety problem is to allow only those staff working at high level to remain in the studio, having cleared the acting area of all other staff. Unfortunately this is time consuming and raises the operational costs.

The most basic design of grid from which we can hang a light consists of 48 mm diameter metal barrels suspended above the acting area. The height will generally be fixed although the use of spring pantographs or drop arms can be advantageous. When the lighting requires adjustment, steps or ladders have to be used to provide access to rig and de-rig the luminaires. If

Figure 6.4   Monopoles

the position of the luminaires is correct then pole operated controls enable adjustments to be made quickly without much disturbance to the rehearsals. Power sockets are usually distributed in a uniform manner just above the fixed barrels.

   To give more flexibility, at a low installation cost, a roller barrel system is often used. This allows barrels, about 2m long, to run along a set of parallel tracks mounted at high level in the studio. It is usually the practice

Figure 6.5   Theatre grid. Courtesy of A. S. Green and Company (Lancashire) Limited

Figure 6.6   Roller barrel system

with this type of installation to mount the trunking with the power sockets attached, between the trackways. As this requires the minimum of space, the trackways can be installed very close to each other, subsequently allowing the luminaires to be positioned with a high degree of accuracy. It is essential that the moving barrel units are provided with trolleys designed so that they run smoothly along the trackways when pushed or pulled at any point on the barrel unit. There is nothing more annoying to the operator than pushing a roller barrel along the trackway only to see it jam

Figure 6.7   Spring pantograph

and then having to waste time and effort in moving the unit once again. It is often advantageous to fit a brake to the barrels so that they maintain their set positions in the studio. The barrels must be installed so that they cannot be removed from the trackways without the use of tools, otherwise a hazardous situation can occur. This system, which allows very good positioning in the horizontal plane, still suffers the drawback that unless additional equipment is provided, the height of the luminaires is fixed. Also, when the barrels move over a reasonable distance, some plugging and unplugging will have to take place due to the fixed socket arrangement. It is normal practice with the roller barrel system to suspend each luminaire from the barrels by a roller trolley; therefore movement in

Figure 6.8   Motorized pantograph

two planes is achieved. To make the system even more flexible, the luminaire can be suspended by a variable pantograph from the barrel trolley, giving a high degree of flexibility in three planes.

A system of suspension that has achieved a reasonable degree of success is the use of pantographs, mounted on roller trolleys and moving on long single trackways. This gives extremely good height flexibility and, when the trackways are positioned as near to each other as possible, also offers a very good coverage over the acting area; the spacings between the trackways are dictated by the maximum size of luminaires used in the installation. Generally, the system uses spring pantographs where the height can be easily adjusted. Horizontal movement is accomplished by dragging or pushing the pantograph top trolley unit along the trackway. The major drawback of the system is that special safety precautions have to be taken when changing luminaires on spring pantographs. The power feeds to the individual pantograph units are often provided by a catenary cable system, rather like those used for overhead cranes. A modern advance, favoured by large broadcasting organizations, is to use motorized pantographs where the height is adjusted by motor-driven wire ropes and the horizontal movement accomplished by a motor-drive onto the trackways. Catenary feeder cables for both the control system and the power system are essential. The system can be easily adapted for remote control and has the great advantage of overcoming the safety problems connected with spring pantographs and is very quick and easy to use.

The above systems have mainly allowed only one luminaire to move at a time. When we wish to move more lights at the same time, the systems

Figure 6.9   Self-climbing barrel

become mechanically more complex. The most basic of these systems is to use a long barrel with the adjustment of height made by a counterweight system. In the theatre, these consist of very long barrels up to 10 m long, slung from several wire ropes. The lights are all at the same height and the weight on the barrel can be considerable when the power cables are attached. The counterweight system allows for the weight of the barrel, plus all the luminaires and cables mounted on it, to be balanced by a selection of special iron weights and provides an easy method of raising and lowering barrels with heavy loads. Counterweight barrels are mainly used in the theatre; although they have been used in some television studios, they could not provide the flexibility of other systems for this application.

An advance on the counterweight systems is the provision of motorized barrels. The motor unit can be separate from the barrel unit or, in the case of self-climbers, integral to the barrel unit.

The barrel itself is over 2 m long and enables several luminaires to be placed side by side along the bar. Power is provided by fixed sockets, mounted on trunking along the barrel so that the luminaires can be easily plugged into the lighting supply. The adjustment of height is totally flexible and the system inherently safe by its design. It is very easy to operate from a remote control.

Finally, we come to probably the most accurate lighting positioning system of all. The monopole grid, although expensive to instal, allows monopoles to be positioned about 600 mm from each other in adjacent tracks and individually to be placed anywhere along the trackways. The height of the monopoles is adjusted either by personnel at grid level, using portable drive tools, or by remotely controlled integral drive motors. The main drawback of monopoles is that a reduction in the number of units used in a studio for economic reasons means more physical movement of the units themselves and this requires riggers working over the acting area, which, with modern safety legislation, dictates that special arrangements have to be made. It is difficult to move the units in the grid area if they are permanently cabled so the electrical system has to be designed to cater for multi-positional use, allowing the units to be connected as necessary (Figure 6.10).

When discussing more sophisticated lighting suspension systems, there are certain items that are common to either monopoles, motorized barrels or motorized pantographs. If we cover the ground rules for the component parts, the understanding of the complete pieces of equipment becomes easier.

It is difficult to state which items have the most importance due to the reliance upon one another for the satisfactory operation of particular items of equipment. However, to stick our necks out, we plump for the electric motors first as without these we have to resort to muscle power.

The motor unit

Most modern barrel winch units today employ three-phase electric motors of about 1–1.5 kW rating: they also have a combined gearbox. The gearbox will have reduction gears so that the barrel unit moves up and down at a reasonable speed, which is usually 8–10 m per minute. The gearbox is

Figure 6.10   Electrical distribution

selected so that when maximum weight is applied to the barrel and the electrical system is 'off', the unit will not move, thus providing a self-sustaining system of gearing. To prevent the barrel unit over-running when being raised or lowered, an integral electrical braking system is installed on the high speed side of the gearbox. This brake is normally applied and only released when the motor is activated. Monopole motor units may use three-phase, single-phase or dc drive motors. Because a monopole has a maximum lifting capacity of only about 60 kg compared with a barrel of about 150 kg, the motors are generally smaller. It is easy to reverse a three-phase motor but single-phase motors have to have special drive circuits to allow forward and reverse operation. If dc motors are used, although they allow very easy control, they may present problems by becoming generators and supplying harmful voltage back into any control circuits. With any of the systems using motor drive units, it is essential that some form of manual drive is available in the event of electrical failure of the system.

Wire rope winding drums

There are two basic types of winding drum, the first being the scroll drum where the wire rope is wound on side by side in much the same way as a cotton reel. Due to the length of wire rope, together with the need to keep a low torque on the motor, the drums are usually reasonably small in diameter (200 mm approx.) and, as only one turn of rope is used, around 250 mm wide. It is important that the drum width is held as small as possible so that the horizontal angle where the wire rope meets the drum is kept within certain limits. Usually a groove is formed in the winding drum so the rope follows the correct path. A big advantage of the scroll drum system is that the speed of the barrel unit remains constant when being raised and lowered.

The other type of winding drum is the pile wind and this works rather like a large yo-yo. The rope is piled singly, several layers thick upon itself between two substantial metal plates. This means that as the effective diameter of the drum is changing as the rope piles the barrel unit's speed of travel varies from its highest point to its lowest. A problem for the designers of pile drum systems is that the torque is not constant and the system has to cater for the worst case, which is when the barrel is at its highest point where the pile drum provides maximum speed with reduced lifting ability. This means that larger motors have to be used on pile wind winches than will be used on scroll drum winches of similar lifting capacity. The system also suffers from the tendency for the ropes to be easily damaged if the mechanical design is not of the highest quality, particularly if the retaining plates on the pile drum are weak. With both scroll and pile wind drums the wire ropes have to be very positively anchored to the drum and two clamps are used for each rope. To ensure a margin of safety, a minimum of two turns of rope must be left on either type of drum when the barrel is at its lowest operating point.

It is preferable on self-climbing winches to use scroll drums because, by keeping to a low torque, it will also enable the motor to be smaller – with obvious benefits. Obviously, with a self-climber, having the motor unit positioned approximately in the middle of the bar, with scroll drums either side, means that the unit will be wide and this might prove to be a problem. In practice, however, this does not appear to be the case. As an alternative it is possible to use scroll drums positioned so that they lay in the same direction as the barrel, but if this is done, precautions have to be taken to make certain that the unit, when winding up and down, stays in the same vertical plane. Also, there is the danger that the motor unit sticks out to one side and causes an out-of-balance condition. It is normal with self-climbing winches to use four wire ropes to enable a better balance to be achieved and to meet current safety standards.

Diverter pulleys

Diverter pulleys, which are generally made from steel for strength and durability, consist of a grooved wheel running on bearings. When the wire rope leaves the winding drum it has to be guided via the diverter pulleys to the correct position. The diverter pulleys are grooved and it is important that the wire rope fits snugly in that groove. The diameter of the pulley is also important due to the wire rope having a minimum quoted bending radius so that damage to the rope is avoided. Current regulations call for a diameter not less than 20 times the rope's thickness. The pulleys must run on properly lubricated bearings, due to the high mechanical loads involved, and also so that noise is kept to a minimum. As a general guide, each diverter pulley in the system will reduce the lifting capacity by between 2% and 5%, dependent on the type of bearings used.

Wire ropes

Barrel winches normally have two ropes, each capable of supporting at least *six* times the total applied load. Self-climbing winches generally have four wire ropes for suspension; however the rule for the breaking strain of the ropes remains at *six* times total load for each rope.

Monopoles and motorized pantographs which could be operated by a single wire rope have to be provided with twin lifting ropes for safety. Each single rope must support the total load of the monopole or pantograph in the event of failure of either of the two ropes. The minimum breaking strength of each rope must be able to cope with at least *six* times the Safe Working Load (SWL) plus the weight of the suspension tubes and electrical cables. In the event of a single rope failure free-fall, via the rope compensator system, should be no greater than 12.7 mm. It is extremely important that in practice wire ropes do not become frayed and damaged. If a wire rope gets nicked or crushed, it is vital that the rope is changed.

Motor control and safety system

Various functions on the motor unit have to be made automatic to avoid either damaging the equipment, or, more importantly, injuring staff. The functions are as follows:

Figure 6.11   (a) Top and bottom limit switches

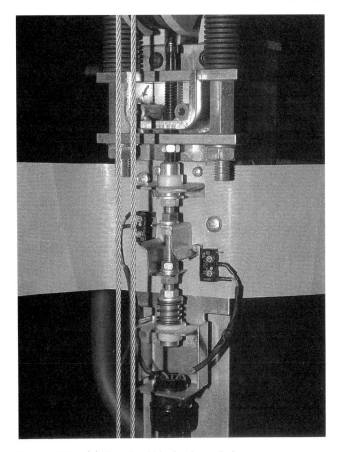

Figure 6.11   (b) Overload/slack wire switches

Limit switches
Limit switches generally consist of a striker which is driven along a finely threaded shaft towards a microswitch that activates a relay and switches 'off' the power to the motor. Rotational movement of the strikers is prevented by a retaining bar which is placed in slots on the strikers themselves. To adjust the strikers, the bar is simply raised and the striker is screwed along the thread to the preset position desired and then the retaining bar is replaced. The threaded shaft which activates the strikers is driven from one end of the main drive motor usually by a belt or chain drive.

Top limit
This is the switch which will automatically disconnect the motor supply when the lifting assembly is raised to its highest set point. To avoid straining the motor gearbox, the diverters, wire ropes, etc., if the unit tries to drive itself to a dead stop, in the event of the top limit switch failing,

current European standards require a second top limit switch situated just after the normal top limit. This system is generally used where an automatic overload cutout is not provided. If an automatic overload system is provided, another solution under the European standards is to have a mechanical buffer which the barrel unit will hit before it reaches its highest point just after top limit, thus activating the automatic overload system to trip causing the unit to stop. Either of these solutions has to prevent an overload to the unit of more than 1.4 times, thereby ensuring no permanent mechanical damage.

Bottom limit
A switch which will automatically disconnect the motor supply when the lifting assembly is lowered to its lowest set point, which is usually 1m above floor level. In the event of failure of the bottom limit switch, and if the ropes keep unwinding, the slack rope switch will operate.

Slack rope (sometimes called underload)
If any of the wire ropes which suspend the units are allowed to slacken, usually by meeting an obstruction on the descent, a dangerous situation arises. If the unit does not automatically stop it may: (a) tangle its own ropes causing permanent damage to them; (b) suddenly fall free under its unbalanced weight.

Obviously (b) is the more hazardous and to prevent any danger sensors are usually fitted to each individual wire rope which operate rapidly as soon as any slackness occurs. Slack rope sensors invariably consist of a striking mechanism attached to a spring under compression and a short distance away from a microswitch. When the ropes slacken, the spring expands and forces the microswitch to operate.

Overload
Although not specified under current European regulations, a sensing system should be provided so that if a load greater than the SWL is applied to the barrel unit, the motor supply will automatically shut off. The European tolerance for overload is 40% but some organizations ask for closer limits of about 20–25%. Overload rope sensors usually consist of spring-biased pivoted diverter pulleys. Normally the spring keeps the diverter pulley assembly from striking the microswitch. On overload the spring compresses and the microswitch operates. Obviously the springs have to be selected to cater for the designated load of the particular unit.

In the case of standard winches or self-climbers, the overload condition is dependent on the position of the load applied to the barrel. Some units are designed to assess the overload as if it were positioned in the centre of the barrel. Thus 100 kg will present a load of 50 kg on each rope, in the case of a two-rope system. If each rope were designed to sense a 100 kg overload, the system would not work; if, however, the ropes were designed for 50 kg each, the system would work correctly. The main problem would arise when a load of 100 kg is off centre, thus presenting an overload condition to one rope most of the time. Most modern winch systems should attempt to use a design where the load is added, totalling the correct SWL irrespective of the load's position on the bar. Both overload and slack rope systems are usually designed to reset automatically once the problem has been cured.

All of these sensors are fed to a purpose-built electrical control box which contains the contactors for the raise and lower motor functions together with the control circuits for top and bottom limits, overload and slack wire rope sensors. Local control for raise and lower should be provided for ease of maintenance. The system accepts remote control signals from elsewhere in the operational area.

Labels and warnings

Each unit has to be provided with labels to indicate clearly operational functions used by the staff. In addition, warning labels must be provided to ensure staff safety. A reasonably comprehensive list is given below.

1. Unit number.
2. Lighting supply cable identification.
3. Lighting power socket identification.
4. Each control must be labelled, i.e. Raise, Lower, Local control, Remote control, Supply On/Off.
5. Warning labels must be provided to indicate the mechanical loading and the electrical loading.
6. Any safety hazards connected with the operation of the equipment.

The barrel suspension unit

The length of the barrel is dictated by the needs of the installation. The unit, which would be capable of lifting loads up to 150 kg, is fitted with brackets so that the wire ropes from the winding drums may be attached. In line with the rest of the equipment connected with a winch the attachment brackets must have a sufficient safety factor and this is normally six times the applied SWL. The barrel, which may be steel or aluminium, will bend when loaded with lighting equipment and it is important that the barrel does not deflect more than recommended amounts. Therefore the barrel supports must also be capable of some deflection without permanent damage. The wire ropes must be attached to the brackets by correctly locked-off shackles so that they will not loosen in operational use. The ends of the wire ropes where the shackles pass through must be permanently formed into eyelets by correctly splicing the ropes. A trunking is usually fitted above the barrel itself for the termination of the power feeder cables and these cables go directly to sockets mounted on the front face of the trunking, with the trunking mounted approximately 300 mm above the barrel. Many configurations of sockets are used according to the electrical standards of the user country. In the UK most companies have now settled for 240 V 32 A BS 4343 sockets. This allows the connection of 5 kW lights and falls in well with the practice of using 5 kW dimmers. The BS 4343 16 A socket is also used for lower powered luminaires and sub-circuits. Many British theatres still use the old 15 A plugs and sockets.

Power cables and their support systems

The power cables for the lighting socket outlets are fed from high level down to the trunking on the barrel unit. Over the years, many systems have been used but the two most popular are the 'curly cable' and 'flip flop'. The first system uses cables formed into a coil which is wrapped around the wire ropes. The cables, which are suspended from the high level structure adjacent to the winch units, tend to act like elongated springs. Either one or more of the wire ropes can be used and the curly cables are generally multicore. Due to the weight of the cables, there is a tendency for the coils to compress immediately above the barrel unit. The flip flop system, on the other hand, allows the cable to fold in a uniform and controlled manner. Each section of the fold is about 1 m long; the cables can be unsupported where each fold is determined by a mechanical clip or a device to form a radius. Although more costly, a system of lightweight support trays can be used as a definite route so that the cables fold almost perfectly. Plastic trays, although on the surface seemingly ideal for the job, will probably distort in the heat from luminaires hung from the barrel, especially at the lower end of the flip flops just above the luminaires. Precautions have to be taken so that the trays will pivot at grid level to avoid damage if a barrel assembly is moved sideways. The cable system should never be allowed to become straight in its maximum travel, thereby avoiding the sections of cable tray from attempting to fold in the opposite direction to normal.

6.3 Pantographs

Pantographs allow luminaires to have their operating height adjusted over a specific range. Manual pantographs come as two distinct types, either spring balanced or manually wound with wire ropes. The ones most used in practice are those which are spring balanced: the reason for this being that once the springs are adjusted to balance the weight of the luminaire on the pantograph, very little effort is required to raise and lower the luminaire and this system is extremely quick in studio use. The main problem with spring pantographs is that adjusting the springs is extremely hazardous if not carried out by trained staff. Wind-up pantographs, on the other hand, have little or no safety problems, but the disadvantage of this type is that they are slow in operational use due to the gearing via a pole operated system. Manual pantographs come with either two springs, four springs or six springs; and the number of springs has some bearing on the adjustment range for the luminaires. Obviously with more springs, a finer range of adjustment can be achieved. Spring balanced pantographs generally have a range from approximately 1.8 m to 4.5 m. The stabilizing framework for pantographs can either be twin cross-armed devices or a single cross-armed device. Spring pantographs are always twin cross-armed devices. The pantographs are usually fitted with cable clips, either side along the cross-armed devices, to allow for cable routing from the trolley, where the unit is usually mounted on the barrel, down to a socket outlet at the base of the pantograph which can either be free or permanently fixed adjacent to the luminaire spigot holder. As pantographs are an additional load for the grid, they are generally made from aluminium. Due to the range of springs that can be fitted to them, pantographs come in various weight ranges; therefore during the studio installation, it is important to know the weight of the luminaires to be used.

The original motorized pantographs had one motor for lifting to ease the problems associated with spring and manually wound pantographs. However, without a traversing motor, it means that the operators had to drag quite heavy units along the trackways.

Modern motorized pantographs are mostly fitted with two motor units, one for lifting and one for traversing on its associated trackways. All the electrical cables are terminated in a box at the top of the unit. A socket outlet is provided adjacent to the luminaire attachment point. The unit is designed to occupy as little height as possible when fully raised to the grid. The pantograph must be capable of operating with any load between zero and its SWL plus the weight of all permanently attached components such as the stabilizing framework, the electrical sockets, cables and cable supports. The luminaires are usually attached to the bottom of the pantograph by means of a female 28.58 mm (1 ⅛ inch) spigot holder or a 'C' clamp over a mini barrel. Normally they are designed for a SWL of approximately 40 kg.

The speed of operation is extremely important with the 'raise and lower' being approximately 8–10 m per minute. The pantograph's traverse speed must be slower than 15 m per minute. At speeds faster than this the unit is inclined to jerk, and the luminaire may oscillate in travel. Bearing in mind that the pantograph unit should be as compact as possible, the usual operating height range is around 7 m owing to the length of wire rope needed and the subsequent effect on the size of the winding drums. The two motors are normally powered from an ac single-phase supply. The unit for raising and lowering the luminaire will be approximately 600 W and the unit for traversing will be about 100 W. Brakes are required to stop the unit over-running and these should operate on the high speed side of the motor gearbox units. The brake is applied automatically whenever the motor supply is switched off or interrupted and electromagnetically released when the motor supply is on. The gearbox, as usual, should be self-sustaining. For the purposes of maintenance the electric motors, gearboxes, brakes (if fitted), wire rope winding drums, travel and load limit switches, must be accessible and easily replaced in the event of faults occurring. Provision must be made so that the units can be wound by hand in the event of failure of the electrical equipment or in order to facilitate maintenance. In a similar manner to monopoles, two wire ropes have to be fitted to meet current safety standards, and the twin drums will be either pile wind or scroll. The suspension system using the wire ropes on a pantograph is the same as that used on a monopole and to compensate for the differential in rope lengths a toggle bar is used for the rope attachment at the base of the unit. The pantograph should be fitted with slack rope and overload sensing systems; it must also incorporate vertical travel limits to stop the pantograph at preset positions at the top and bottom of travel. The traversing system consists of an electric motor, a gearbox and a friction drive system formed as an integral unit. The pantograph is propelled along the trackway by a friction wheel or similar drive. The drivewheel is normally permanently engaged but must have a method of easily uncoupling it and manually traversing the pantograph in an emergency. These types of pantographs rely upon remote electrical control. A termination box has to be provided and fitted close to the motor unit assembly. This box will accept the remote control supply system, together with a main luminaire supply for the particular unit. All of these signals will be supplied through a catenary cable feeder system. The remote control system has to provide 'raise', 'lower', 'traverse left and traverse right' signals. To keep the complexity of the electrical system on the pantograph system to a minimum, it is preferable to remote the control relays and use mains drives direct to the motors. The unit should also be provided with local electrical control where the traverse and vertical control of the unit is accomplished by standard pole operation cups pinned to the shafts of biased rotary switches. Pantograph movement is obtained by turning the switches either left or right. It is obviously impossible in practice to have a left and right traverse, as it is dependent on the position of the operator in the studio, so the directions are called 'red' and 'white' and appropriate marker boards fitted to the studio walls. The indicators for red and white direction and raise and lower must be clearly visible from the studio floor.

6.4 Counterweight bars

The counterweight bar shown in Figure 6.12 is the primary means of support for everything above stage in the theatre. The bars are adapted to lift scenery, lighting, drapes and practicals. The only special adaptation for

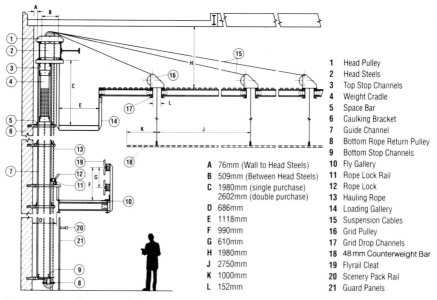

1	Head Pulley	
2	Head Steels	
3	Top Stop Channels	
4	Weight Cradle	
5	Space Bar	
6	Caulking Bracket	
7	Guide Channel	
8	Bottom Rope Return Pulley	
9	Bottom Stop Channels	

A	76mm (Wall to Head Steels)	10	Fly Gallery
B	509mm (Between Head Steels)	11	Rope Lock Rail
C	1980mm (single purchase)	12	Rope Lock
	2602mm (double purchase)	13	Hauling Rope
D	686mm	14	Loading Gallery
E	1118mm	15	Suspension Cables
F	990mm	16	Grid Pulley
G	610mm	17	Grid Drop Channels
H	1980mm	18	48 mm Counterweight Bar
J	2750mm	19	Flyrail Cleat
K	1000mm	20	Scenery Pack Rail
L	152mm	21	Guard Panels

Figure 6.12   Counterweight system

the lighting bar is the provision of a distribution system of sockets running along its length with a terminal box at one end of the barrel supplied from a hanging multicore cable system known as 'tripe'. The support cables or ropes travel via diverter pulleys to the side of the stage where they are connected to a counterweight box. The box is loaded with cast iron weights until it balances the intended load. At this point very little effort is required to raise and lower the bar, a function carried out by the flyman on the fly gallery. When the bar has been adjusted to the required position, a clamping device is applied to the ropes to hold them firmly in place. The rope brake is designed to hold with only a small out-of-balance load. This prevents a dangerous condition when either the barrel is overloaded or luminaires are removed by mistake, i.e. the rope starts to slip with about 25 kg out-of-balance load. The counterweight bar appears to satisfy all the rigging needs of the theatre. It does, however, present a problem inasmuch as the counterweight box is normally 2 m high, which represents a loss of height by the time it reaches stage level. To make maximum use of height in the fly tower, the scenery should go immediately next to the grid, when it clears the sight lines. However, to achieve this the roof would require to be 2 m higher or, as is more commonly the practice, the floor of the stage is cut away at the wall allowing the counterweight boxes to travel through the stage into the understage void. Although this system works very well for theatre, its adaptation into television studios does not permit the counterweight system to travel through the studio floor. Therefore, when contemplating such a rigging system for lighting in a television studio the height of the weight box and the ultimate height of the lighting bar must be considered. However, the main disadvantage of this suspension system in television studios is that even if the bars are made half the width of the studio with counterweights on both sides, the bars are still much too long to provide accurate lighting positions for other than one or two luminaires, in view of the fact that all the other lights on the bar are in a compromise height position. The exceptions to this statement are a row of top cyclorama lights at the side of the studio presenting a continuous length of barrel and banks of floodlights.

6.5 Motorized barrel winches

Standard barrel winch unit

The main drive unit which can be mounted at high level in the studio on a side gallery or at floor level, consists of a substantial framework to which is attached the electrical motor drive unit, gearbox, wire rope winding drums and the wire rope diverter pulleys. The barrel unit, together with its associated lighting power sockets, mounted on an integral trunking system, is suspended from high level by wire ropes which may be taken to the drive unit by additional diverter pulley systems. The associated electrical control box can be positioned adjacent to the unit or away from the unit in purpose made cabinets. However, a remote control unit would require more individual mains cables to connect it to the winch in the studio area.

The design of winches should provide for the lightest weight of support framework commensurate with minimum mechanical distortion. Any framework distortion may give problems with the mechanical sensing systems for 'slack rope' and 'overload': it also may give problems with the pile or scroll drums. The physical size and weight of the unit is extremely important as this will have considerable impact on the support structure.

A problem that always exists with conventional barrel winches is that of access to the motor units, usually solved by either walkways adjacent to the units or 'walkover' grids.

Self-climbing winch unit

In essence a self-climbing barrel winch is an upside down standard winch with the motor gearbox mounted above the barrel on the same assembly.

The main problem with self-climbing winches is that in addition to lifting the normal SWL, they have to lift their own weight; and bearing in mind that the weight of the unit is usually similar to that of the SWL, it would not be inconceivable that a self-climber would have to be rated to lift something like 250 kg from the studio floor. This means that the power of the motors will be more on self-climbing units, particularly so if pile wind drums are used, hence the motor gearbox becomes heavier, which poses a design problem. The self-contained unit consists of a motor and gearbox, wire rope winding drums, diverter pulleys and the sensing system for top and bottom limits, slack rope and overload. The unit is secured and suspended by the steel wire lifting ropes from the underside of a suitable ceiling or grid structure. All lighting and control circuits are fed from the ceiling or grid structure via flip flop or curly cables. The barrel, which is usually 2.25 m long, and capable of lifting loads up to 120 kg, is suspended from the main housing which contains the motor gearbox unit, etc. With self climbers it is normal to integrate the lighting power sockets into the main housing instead of supplying a separate trunking system.

A major advantage of self-climbers is that they do not require complex grid systems and are much less time consuming to install. Generally any maintenance can be carried out at studio floor level.

6.6 Monopoles

A monopole or 'a single suspension unit' is a means by which a luminaire can be raised or lowered by a wire rope winding system with stability being maintained by metal tubes which are telescopic and slide within each other. Because of the self-sustaining gearboxes employed, it would be a very tiresome business to manually wind a luminaire from studio floor level to grid level. Therefore, the units are generally operated by powered drive systems.

A manual monopole will normally be operated by a portable tool which can be driven by compressed air or electricity. Alternatively, the unit may be operated by a purpose designed integral electric motor gearbox unit and is designated a 'motorized monopole'. Both types of monopole are mechanically much the same. The SWL of monopoles is approximately 45 kg with some specially designed units capable of loads up to 60 kg. Due to handling problems at high level, it is important that the weight of each unit does not exceed 80 kg and preferably should be a lot less. Each monopole generally consists of seven or eight interlocking steel tubes, manufactured for a working height range of 10 m, and all the tubes have to be made to close dimensional tolerances and straightness. The telescopic sections should be provided with interlocking retaining tabs which prevent the monopole twisting too much in operational use. Each tube locks into the one above to restrict rotational movement of the individual tubes to within ± 2.5°. It should be noted that the telescopic sections are only to give stability and are not load carrying. The tube sets are always made longer than the wire ropes at their maximum extension and it is extremely important that the tubes do not stick at any point. If the tubes do stick at high level and then suddenly become free, the energy transferred to the rope suspension system will probably be sufficient to cause considerable damage. Due to safety considerations, each monopole must be fitted with twin wire ropes and these can be contained within twin scroll or wire rope pile drums. The twin cables must be independently terminated on the winding drum assemblies and to a compensator attachment (to allow for differential in the length of the ropes) which should be fitted to the base of the telescopic tube assembly. All the wire rope terminations must have provision for a visual inspection at regular intervals to meet current safety standards. The gearbox on both motorized monopoles and manual monopoles must be self-sustaining. Where integral electric drive motors are used, they are usually a special single-phase type, but dc motors are also used. Due to the lower SWL of monopoles together with their lower self-weight, less powerful motors can be used.

In the case of monopoles with integral drive motors, electromechanically operated overload and slack wire rope devices should be incorporated into the units, together with top and bottom travel limit switches. In the case of manual monopoles, which employ drive tools, it is obviously important to have some form of torque limitation on the drive system, otherwise undue stress will be applied to the wire ropes and pile drums. The motor control units, which are generally mounted at the top of the monopole, normally require an ac supply. The control units should also provide a local or remote control facility which can be selected. Remote control circuits are usually by low voltage dc. The local control can either be an 'up' or 'down' button or a centre biased 'raise' and 'lower' switch. In an emergency, or in the event of system power failure, the gearbox should have a spindle drive facility for the unit to be operated by hand or by suitable portable drive tools.

The monopoles have to be provided with a trolley which is purpose made to suit the grid slot system in use and have to meet such safety standards as required by the installation and to the operator's satisfaction. Normally these trolleys are fitted with eight wheels to mount on the grid slots. The trolley should be braked, and can be fitted additionally with a lifting mechanism for ease of rotation for direction changes when using transfer slots.

A spigot holder has to be provided at the lower end of monopole tube sets, to take a standard 28.58 mm (1 ⅛th inch) spigot as normally fitted to luminaires. For many years, the electrical supply cable to the luminaires

Figure 6.13   Spigot holder

suspended from monopoles was dropped from high level with a female socket attached so that the luminaire could be plugged in at low level. In recent years, some manufacturers have provided luminaire supply cables which are made in preformed coils and wrapped around the telescopic sections with a socket fixed adjacent to the spigot holder and in this way a much neater system has evolved. The supply socket would obviously need to meet the requirements of the particular studio and country where the installation occurs.

6.7 System controls

It is no good installing motorized units in a theatre or studio without having some form of control. The simplest form of control is two wires that go to a unit, and say, 'go up' and 'go down'. However, doing this one at a time is very time consuming. It is far better to have a certain number of units that can move up at the same time as another set can come down. In the case of the winch systems, the 'up/down' commands are the only ones needed. Unfortunately, if we are using motorized pantographs, or for that matter, motorized monopoles with a traversing system that requires control, then the system becomes more complex.

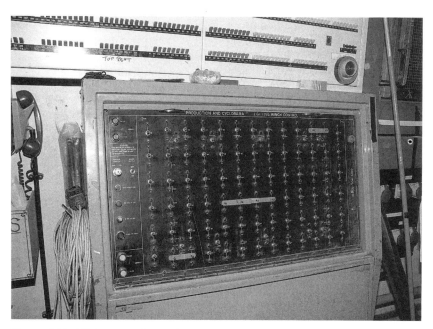

Figure 6.14   Hoist control console

Let us now consider how we can control a fairly simple unit going up and down. It is obviously more economical if from the control console to each unit we use the minimum of copper wire, and to achieve this we use low power relays driving mains contactors. In the case of three-phase drive motors, we use subsidiary relays to drive the 'up' and 'down' contactors. Present day systems employ 24 V relays. The mains power for the motors can be derived from a ring main going from unit to unit; if the power requirements of each motor are fairly small, then a reasonable size ring main will allow several units to be used at once, and most studios aim to control 20 units at any one time. This avoids a surge on the electrical supply caused by the motors all starting at the same time and prevents a large dynamic load being applied to the grid. For either standard barrel winches or self-climbing winches where the installation is fixed, the electrical control system is relatively straightforward. If, however, there is a need to control monopoles from the studio floor, to reduce the amount of operational work at grid level, the monopoles would have to be provided with either extremely long electrical cables coming from the motors or a multiplicity of control points at grid level.

The most common consoles used today are equipped with a 'green' and 'amber' group control system, where each winch is capable of being routed either to the 'green' or 'amber' control. Therefore some units can be switched to green control, giving up/down commands, and other units can be switched to the amber, also giving up/down commands. The amber and green controls are completely independent of each other, so that some winches can be going up while others are coming down. Where winch units are coupled together for operational reasons, some clear indication of this state must be made on the appropriate console. In the past this was often achieved by bits of sticky tape, or pieces of perspex coupling the switches together; in modern consoles this can be accomplished by electronically interlocking the system. The limitation placed on the number of winches to be used at any one time is occasioned by the dynamic mechanical load applied to the grid structures when the motors start. Some recent advances in the control of suspension units in studios include using microprocessor control with alphanumeric keyboards and VDUs to display the information. With some intelligence built into the system it is therefore possible to have sophisticated selection whereby units that are coupled together are easily recognized by the system and the studio should generally become more safe.

The large control consoles, which are mainly banks of switches, are usually positioned on a convenient wall in the operational area; but there are occasions when it is impossible to see what is happening when operating from the console, and therefore remote control units are often used to allow the operator to walk to the area being lit and so have good sight lines to the equipment being moved. Originally these remote controls were by wire back to a point adjacent to the main console. Recent developments include radio and infra-red transmitted control systems.

Remote control of monopole systems has never been developed to any degree, whereas motorized pantograph systems have become quite complex. The motorized pantograph requires control of 'up' and 'down' and its traversing motion. Units in use at the BBC in their regional studios control on/off information of the luminaires as well, this control being accomplished by a small portable hand-held radio controller that can be carried about in the studio and used by the LD or senior electrician. The system is used for a rigging aid and not for total control of the luminaires. It does have the advantage that one man can move and adjust lights with relative speed. Control of motorized pantograph units is generally done from a base system, which sends mains signals to the motorized pantograph units, thus avoiding too many relays and subsidiary circuits within the units mounted at high level.

7 Lighting the subject

Introduction

Evidence exists that from about 15,000 BC oil lamps were being used for lighting and for many centuries this continued as the sole means of artificial light. In the 18th century candles were used more and more and the oil lamp underwent a significant improvement by burning the wick in a tubular glass chimney to give a brighter light source. In 1765 at the Lonsdale coal mines near Whitehaven, surplus coal gas was piped into the mine offices to be used as a source of light and from this point in time gas lighting was gradually introduced, eventually being supplanted by the electric lamp.

The theatrical staging of drama and verse has been going on for several thousand years. In the beginning, it was staged during daylight hours to take advantage of natural light and, although difficult to date, no doubt the Greeks and Romans used oil lamps to illuminate their theatrical work. Early light sources were generally floodlights with little or no finesse. As taste became more refined, so did the lighting. If we go into modern theatres or studios the majority of lighting is placed at a good height above the acting area. The reason for this is quite simply that we do not wish the acting area to be full of equipment. This holds true for most lighting equipment, but in a TV studio the floor is also cluttered with cameras and booms, etc. As members of the human race we are conditioned that light is above us and at an average of about 45° to any standing object on earth. This fact lays down the most important ground rule for the artificial lighting of any scene. Artists throughout the ages have appreciated the light sources available to them. The sun provides a wonderful key light with warm rich colours and the blue sky provides a soft light of cool brilliance. When artists such as Rembrandt worked their time was mainly dictated by the weather conditions and the time of day. Eventually, people could not keep to this discipline and therefore had to control light and thus the lighting industry as we know it was born.

In our everyday lives as human beings, we go around in illumination that can vary from the minimum amount on a moonlit night to a maximum of an overhead sun in the Sahara desert. Other than a psychological difference, we are not much disturbed by the differences between gloomy, grey overcast days and the intense blue skies of winter when the atmosphere is at its clearest. We are not bothered by little or no shadow detail, and on other occasions we see no problems with the intense black shadows created by sunlight. We do become disturbed, however, by green light applied to the human skin; we also become rather unnerved by lighting when it comes from below subjects and not from above. We are conditioned by living on the planet earth by the basic form of lighting which consists of a mixture of sunlight and light from the blue sky; and our experience of lighting is conditioned by the fact that in our everyday lives we perceive fairly well-balanced light, due to the sun and the sky.

In the absence of light from the sky, such as on the moon, we see extremely contrasting pictures due to one light source only, namely the sun. We feel much better when we are bathed in warm sunlight and not standing in the cool of a grey day. Some of this is caused by the generation of vitamins by sunlight, but mostly it is psychological. It is interesting to note that we also feel better on a sunny day in the middle of a cold winter. Red and yellow give us a lovely cosy feeling, and this is probably occasioned by our mental stimulation with the association of the sun. It is a strange fact that as colour temperature increases towards the blue end of the spectrum, we do not necessarily feel warmer and we actually associate blue with cool conditions. Green has a refreshing quality, which is probably occasioned by the response of the eye which is at its peak with the green portion of the spectrum. We view black as a very sombre colour and associate it with the macabre. We generally associate white with coolness and a feeling of something that is quite unspoilt; but it is interesting to note how disturbed we are by snow when it has become muddied, as the thaw sets in. From this short list of examples, it must become obvious that we can associate colours with a sense of stimulation of appreciation within the viewed scene, and many of the effects used in artificial lighting are based upon these feelings.

To the untrained eye, lighting, whether it is hanging in the theatre or in the television studio, or on a film set, looks somewhat similar. However, closer inspection reveals that the luminaires used in the theatre are somewhat different to those used for film and television. There really is not any need to have such a wide disparity in the types of luminaires used, and in recent times we find that stage lighting designers have adopted many of the lights of television and film for the stage, such as the high powered discharge sources. Many of the sources used on stage, and for that matter in the pop world, are now being used more and more in television. Why is this? Light in its basic form consists of sunlight and skylight, as we have already noted, and these can be analysed as a form of extremely hard light that gives very well defined shadows with the sky giving us very soft diffused lighting without any apparent shadows. The reason that the light behaves in different ways is that the sun is a very small source in comparison to the subjects it illuminates, hence it produces the hard shadows, whereas the sky is an extremely large source in area and thus produces our shadowless lighting.

Although on the surface, the aims of lighting for the theatre, film and television are extremely similar, because of the way we view the scene, the techniques are different. In the theatre, we view a wide scene with action accentuated by the use of the basic lighting, colour and lighting effects. When sitting in the theatre, unless we use some binoculars, we do not see the subjects in close up. In television and film, we are looking for most of the time at subject matter in very tight close ups. The use of colour for film and television helps to obscure many of the problems of good modelling on subjects and it is surprising how much bad lighting the human eye will tolerate by the use of colour.

Most of the lighting conventions used in the film and television industry emerged from the earlier days of film when all the material was shot in black and white. It was obviously extremely important to give a sense of depth to pictures and when one sees some of the original extremely old movies that were made without the use of enhanced artificial light and shot purely by daylight, the results are somewhat flat and uninteresting. During the late 1920s and early 1930s increasing use was made of high powered light sources in the film industry and these enabled the lighting cameramen to achieve better results than previously. Hollywood discovered that a key light placed at the correct angle could enhance the artiste greatly. Thus we had 'Paramount' lighting where a hard key light was fairly low and straight onto the face, which enhanced the beauty of ladies with high cheekbones, Marlene Deitrich being one supreme example. The film makers also learnt from portrait painters and noted that a more interesting result could be given when the key light was not straight to the face, but taken to the side, and thus had a type of lighting known as 'Rembrandt' portraiture. Probably the pinnacle of black and white film lighting is *Citizen Kane*, with its highly dramatic portraiture and extremely imaginative use of shadows and highlights. The advent of colour film, with its lower contrast range, meant that the lighting cameramen had to control the lights to a narrower band of illumination, using colour more imaginatively to obtain contrast.

The major difference between the theatre and film and television is that within the theatre lights are focused onto the scene of action at much sharper vertical angles than they would be for the film and television studio. Why is this? In the theatre, the stage area is relatively small and as well as the need to suspend lights above the production, there is the need for many items of scenery to be flown in and out. Consequently, space is at a premium in the theatre. As we have already noted, we are attempting to make the audience concentrate on certain areas of the stage to highlight the enjoyment. Invariably this is accomplished by lighting small areas which create the mood and atmosphere for the viewing audience. For drama, realistic approaches are usually adopted, where colouring is natural and the use of filtered lights restricted to scenery and effects. Lighting for music, opera and ballet will be accomplished by much broader sweeps of lighting, as most of these types of production have a wider vista from the point of view of the audience. It is probably due to the needs discussed that the theatre traditionally uses small, fairly hard spotlights together with flood luminaires capable of giving broad washes of illumination. On the whole, the subjects will always be lit by profile lights of some description with fill light supplied by luminaires of a similar type; thus hard lighting is used the majority of time on the artistes. In the theatre, the light levels used are conventionally dictated by those that are comfortable for viewing by human beings, and therefore there is not the need for high light levels as there is in the film and television industry; and in fact, light levels might not be necessarily much higher than those in some homes. This gives the theatre an immense advantage over the film and television industry when using extremely subtle effects.

Whereas the theatre has to be lit for the entire viewed scene, the film and television industry is lit 'piecemeal' in a different way. Traditionally, the film industry has always shot from one camera position at any one time; therefore the lighting is only adjusted for that camera position. When the camera position is moved, the lighting is readjusted to suit the new position. This has two distinct advantages, one of which is that only one film camera is needed, and secondly not too many lights are required. Obviously this is much more applicable to drama than it would be to musicals, when broad vistas would have to be lit at the same time irrespective of the varying camera positions. A problem that exists with this technique is that continuity has to be watched very carefully: for example, sunlight, if not accurately noted, could vary in its direction within a room.

Higher light levels were required in the film industry, dictated by the sensitivity of the film stock in use at the time. The areas involved with productions could be quite large, and there was a necessity to use luminaires which, when the beams overlapped, produced a much more natural effect than the spotlights used in the theatre. The use of the close up occasioned the need for much better lighting on the artistes and parts of the setting. The mere fact that the close up can dwell on an area for considerable periods of time necessitates a greater attention to detail. The best example of this would be the joins where sets are built and scenery flats overlap.

The basic lighting set-up for actors on the stage is two lights – one from either side of the actor's face and both predominantly from a front position, so that reasonable modelling is achieved. As in television and film techniques, a back light enhances the look of the scene. A problem that exists in the theatre much more than in television and film, due to the slightly more confined space, is the need to watch where the shadows are projected from the artistes and also from the scenery. A particular interesting type of lighting is that for ballet and sometimes for effect, where lights are focused from either side of the stage very low down and straight across. For ballet it enhances the legs of the dancers; in drama it has a dramatic effect when people walk in and out of the light beam. Strong side light also brings out the subject from the background, giving them a white outline and a 'cartoon' like clarity. This latter technique has been used most successfully on the European stage with the use of discharge lamps as the sources; but it must be noted that very few light sources were used during some of these productions.

7.1 Basic lighting

Basic lighting, be it for the theatre, film or television, has very similar fundamental requirements, and the main forms of illumination used are as follows:

1. **The key light**
Why is it called the key? The luminaire used provides the principal light on the scene and tends to be the key to the whole picture. It establishes the

mood and character and generally is capable of producing acceptable results when used on its own. However, it makes no contribution towards the depth of the picture. Key lights for film and TV tend to be used at a vertical angle of 30° to the subject but can be within the range of 20–45°, although the lower angle can produce disturbing glare to the actors. In the theatre they are generally steeper. The key light can be used over a horizontal angle of incidence within 45° either side of the normal to the subject. As a general rule 30° vertical and 30° horizontal displacement gives extremely satisfactory results for visual close ups.

2.   The back light

A back light is needed so that the separation and depth is enhanced. The positioning of back lights is extremely critical and they should not be placed too steeply in the vertical plane otherwise they may spill over onto the subject's face and create rather disturbing effects. Back lights can be varied much more than a key light for their angle of incidence and many good effects are produced by taking them to extremes. The back light usually is in a ratio of 1:1 with the key light, but if increased produces a much more dramatic effect. In film and TV single back lights are usually effective on the subject but quite often twin back lights are advocated for a subject with long hair.

3.   Fill light

Why do we require fill light? When viewed with the eye, a subject lit with a key and back light will look perfectly all right. However, due to the restrictive contrast ranges used for film and television, the results would look somewhat contrasty when viewed via either the cinema screen or the television screen; therefore fill light is used to reduce the contrast by diminishing the shadow areas. As a guide, the lighting level of the fill light is about 50% of that of the key. One point that should be noted is that having made a shadow with one light, there is no way that the shadow can be removed or diminished to any great degree by the addition of more and more fill light. Fill light is often a soft source because we are used to the sky being our fill light. However, if we use hard light in a controlled manner, which is the technique of the theatre industry, then we can still achieve a pleasing result. Whereas, in the theatre, double shadows might not be quite so apparent on the human face, they are extremely apparent in close up in the film and television media.

7.2 Choice of light sources and luminaires

What type of luminaires are we going to use in the film and television industry? Because of the need for broad lighting techniques, luminaires with much softer edges are employed; therefore the Fresnel spotlight becomes more useful with its soft edge to the light beam which allows an integration of light sources for a much smoother result. In the film studio, a 2 kW Fresnel is a relatively low-powered luminaire; 5 kW and 10 kW tungsten luminaires are more the norm. The need of the film industry for extremely high light levels, particularly when colour was introduced with the old Technicolor process, etc., necessitated high intensity carbon arc

LIGHTING PLOT A:

The Key

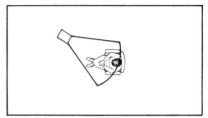

LIGHTING PLOT B:

Single backlight

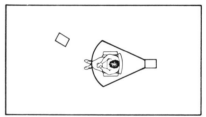

LIGHTING PLOT C:

Twin backlight

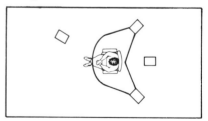

Figure 7.1   Basic lighting. Courtesy of Strand Lighting Limited

LIGHTING PLOT D:

Fill light (soft light from front)

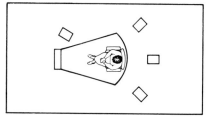

LIGHTING PLOT E:

Fill light (Soft light at 45° to subject)

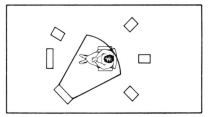

LIGHTING PLOT F:

Fill light (soft light from side)

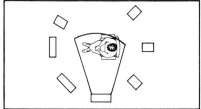

Figure 7.1   *continued*

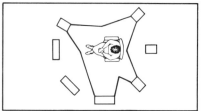

LIGHTING
PLOT G:

All lights
built up

CAMERA 1

CAMERA 2

CAMERA 3

Figure 7.1   *continued*

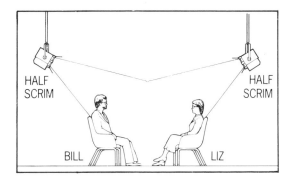

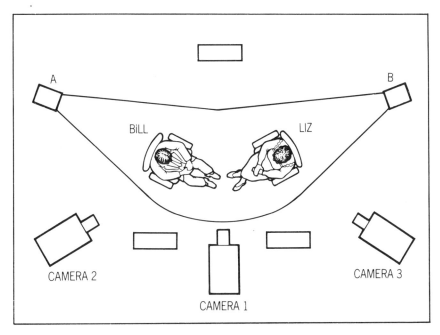

LIGHTING PLOT H
Bill's key is Liz's backlight: Liz's key is Bill's backlight.

Figure 7.1 *continued*

sources, culminating in huge things like the 'Brute' with a power of 225 A. In more recent times, the carbon arc has been superseded by discharge luminaires such as the HMI and MSR sources. For fixed lighting, there is much to commend the discharge lighting sources; they provide a very good quality light output with high brightness, very high efficiency and very low wastage of heat, compared with their tungsten counterparts. However, they have the disadvantage that they can only be dimmed over a restricted range, and thus do not allow for complex lighting effects changes when fading up and fading down is required.

The methods of positioning lights vary considerably between the theatre, the film and television industries. There is obviously no need to hide the lights in the television studio or the film studio, but in the theatre, the majority of lights have to be tucked out of the audience's viewing line so that they do not become distracting. In the theatre, the main lighting positions will be over the stage, at the front of house and to the sides of the stage. The stage lights will be suspended from bars, capable of being raised and lowered over the stage area, and these bars will be interspersed between the scenery flying bars. These lights are the most important ones that have to be obscured from the audience as they would be directly in their sight line. Consequently the position of the lights in relation to people towards the front of the stalls is extremely critical and thus forces the lights generally upwards, vertically away from the stage area. The front of house lights, which are above the audience, are not so noticeable and do not need to be obscured; however, from a consideration for theatre decor, it is nice if they are not too noticeable. To each side of the stage will be ladders or vertical bars for rigging selected luminaires for additional effect and use, particularly so for low-angled cross lighting.

Luminaires used for stage productions include floodlights, which may be straightforward flood units, or special cyclorama lighting units for illuminating backcloths, etc. These units can be provided as single sources or in groups of three or four so that colour mixing can take place. Small Fresnel spotlights are used where a good smooth spread is desired and are often used in theatres in the round; they are also useful as back lights on many productions, particularly with musicals. The profile spotlight is the most used light in the theatre because it enables precise control of the beam, the size of which is controlled by an iris diaphragm. Modern profile spots are also fitted with metal shutters for producing hard flat edges to the beam, and special shapes can be introduced into the projector gate of a profile spot. The edge of the light beam can be made either fairly soft or very hard by adjusting the lens. Many modern profile spots in use have zoom optics which allow a great deal of flexibility when rigging and lighting in the areas concerned. Recently the use of Parcans has become more and more widespread, but a problem with the Parcan is that it is fairly uncontrolled inasmuch as the beam width is dictated by the type of lamp used. However, they have one advantage – they are cheap to purchase, fairly easy to maintain and allow a multiplicity of effects at not too high a cost. Many productions on the West End stage and further afield now use small motorized luminaires where pan and tilt are controlled from a remote position; therefore a smaller number of luminaires may be required because of the ability to reposition the direction of the light beam within the course of the production.

The introduction of sophisticated colour changing mechanisms has also allowed the number of lights in the theatre to be reduced considerably. In the theatre, remote controlled luminaires and colour changes must of course be as quiet as possible, to avoid disrupting the audience's enjoyment of the play or musical.

Lighting in the film industry tends to be from the floor upwards: and because of the rehearse/shoot techniques of the industry, a production is generally filmed shot by shot, not necessarily in a logical sequence and put together in the editing room. To make the lighting as flexible as possible, it is obviously more useful to have lights on adjustable stands which can be moved to new positions very quickly by the electricians on the set, rather then having the lights suspended from the ceiling which are likely to be fixed and their removal time consuming when changes are required. For the suspension of lighting units in film studios, the simplest form is to have a block and tackle with the capability of running along a steel RSJ mounted at roof level. Thus a single point suspension can be used which can be pulled across or along the studio. One drawback to this system is that to introduce any new light at any position often requires shifting other lights which causes further rigging problems. Another technique is to suspend long platforms with handrails either side, called 'boats', where several luminaires can be rigged on the rails and manipulated by electricians manually. Although access to the luminaires is obviously better, changing the position of the boats in the studio is a time consuming process, and probably only pays dividends when luminaires are set up for considerable periods of time on a major production. Film lighting does not rely upon dimmers to balance the lights themselves. Lighting intensity is adjusted by spotting and flooding luminaires and by the careful selection of the power output of luminaires and, if necessary, scrims and neutral density filters can be used to achieve technical balance. The main reason for this technique being used is that film stock is generally balanced for 3200 K or for 5600 K daylight. Although the film stock concerned will have some small latitude of colour response to the lights concerned, the industry has always gone along with the fact that the lights should be relatively fixed in relation to the 3200 K or 5600 K standards. When filming, it is obviously essential that the majority of the luminaires used will be of the same type, i.e. either tungsten or discharge sources. If not, there will be a requirement to filter either one or both of the sources themselves. For many years, tungsten was the main source of most illumination in film studios, with carbon arcs being used when higher power was required. These days, it is possible to see discharge lighting being used solely as the general source of illumination, due to its greater efficiency and reduced generation of waste heat.

7.3 Problems in practice

Television lighting, which evolved from film lighting, relied on the tried and tested methods used by the film makers for many years, and many of the original television studios were, in fact, converted film studios. As television became more and more sophisticated and the need for a greater productivity arose, the studios had to become more efficient with their output being raised so that the need for additional studios was avoided. During the 1960s it was possible that a day's filming would yield two minutes of finished material, whereas in television the need was to produce 30 minutes from each day of production. The basic luminaires used in television, after the Second World War, were Fresnel spotlights in 1 kW, 2 kW, 5 kW and 10 kW versions together with a miscellany of soft lights such as Scoops, Tenlites, Hewitt Banks, etc.

In Europe during the 1950s tremendous strides were made in modernizing television studios; the greatest of these was the adoption of motorized rigging systems, such as the monopole and motorized barrel winch. This enabled a small team of electricians to service a studio rapidly and effectively and – most important of all – safely. Subsequently the monopole system was employed where fairly accurate rigging was required, but not used on a saturated basis, working on the principle that lights could be moved to suit during the rigging periods. The solution reached by the BBC for monochrome TV during the 1960s was to equip all its main production studios with motorized barrel winches utilizing 2 kW Fresnel luminaires and Tenlites for soft sources. The advent of colour saw a different technique evolve. The single Fresnels and soft lights were replaced with the multipurpose luminaire, which is a combination of a soft light and a hard light. This tended to be somewhat of a compromise as a soft source because of its small physical size and compact reflectors, but it was a fairly good Fresnel spot light. By having the complete area covered with the multipurpose units, a saturated lighting system was evolved where the need to rig and de-rig luminaires was obviated to a large degree; and during the 1970s the BBC achieved extremely high productivity in its studios, based at that time on multicamera shooting techniques. The multipurpose luminaires were generally fitted with a 2.5 kW/5 kW lamp in the Fresnel half and 4 × 1250 W linear lamps in the soft half. This allowed the luminaires to be either in a 2.5 kW mode or a 5 kW mode and enabled the operators to control the light level and colour temperature over various distances of 'throw' within the studio. A later development provided one filament at 1.25 kW with the other at 2.5 kW, thus enabling a range of one-third, two-thirds or full power; giving a much better control of light intensity within the limits of colour temperature.

With the spread of colour TV in the UK, experiments took place to ascertain the parameters that could be used to maintain good colour balance for the pictures, but allowing some form of control on the lighting itself, and it was found that a tolerance of 200 K either side of 3000 K was reasonable; thus the cameras were lined up for this colour of incident light. The light level requirement was given by the sensitivity of the colour cameras working between f2.8 and f4.0. The dimmers used in television studios normally have a square law light output, which means that the square of the fader setting from 1 to 10 gives the percentage light output, i.e. level 6 = 36%. It is normal when commencing operations in the studio to align the channel controllers to position '7' which means that the dimmer would supply current to operate the lamp at 49% of its light output; its colour temperature at this point is approximately 3000 K. As we have an acceptable variation of ±200 K, it allows the fader lever to go down to '5' with a 25% light output, and when faded up to 'full' to have 100% light output; thus we have two stops variation in the light level. This system offers a wide variation in the intensity of light and allows a great deal of control so that we may balance the light sources. However, it requires that all luminaires are fed from dimmers; thus there is a need for very large dimmer installations if saturated lighting systems are used.

It is possible to reduce the number of dimmers by using a power patching system, but this is often time consuming and not always convenient when in a rehearse/record situation. Also, a patch system costs almost the same as a dimmer installation.

In both the film and television industries, if we adopt the principle that the key light has to be at somewhere between 45° and 30° in the vertical angle to the subject, the height of the luminaires will be dictated by the intensity of light required on the subject and subsequently the power output of any luminaire used. In television, with a 2.5 kW lamp at position '7' on the dimmer, this approximates to around 4 m above floor level. In the film studio it could be that the distance above the floor is increased using higher powered luminaires. This fact has implications from the point of view of luminaire positions in relation to the scenery.

Where are we actually going to rig luminaires?

In the theatre, the majority of luminaires tend to be suspended from the bars and around the edges of the acting area. In the film and television industry, other than using luminaires hanging from the grid or working from stands at floor level, there is a need to mount lights on the scenery flats themselves and to conceal luminaires within the sets for effect. On all these occasions, the size of the luminaire has a great bearing on rigging in the studio or theatre. Luckily, in the theatre, where many luminaires are used, they are relatively small, the only drawback being that the profile spot is rather a long device and therefore when panning around requires quite a large operating circle. Although small compact luminaires can be used for both film and television, the majority are fairly big and require a large operating space. Therefore, rigging is often at a premium. Although the multipurpose luminaire is very useful from many points of view, it is very inconvenient when trying to tuck it into the corner of sets as it requires quite a large space. Although the BBC perseveres with the multipurpose luminaire, the majority of other users of lighting systems utilize the 2 kW, 5 kW and 10 kW beloved of the film and television industry. Associated with these will be specially designed soft sources, invariably larger in area than those provided by the multipurpose and in general much more effective.

It should be remembered that the light sources themselves are only the tools of the trade, and as one famous British lighting director said of one of his well-known colleagues: 'That man could obtain good pictures using candles mounted in milk bottles'. Lights themselves are only a means to an end and even the most modern lighting devices still cannot produce good pictures when used by incapable hands.

7.4 Lighting for high definition television

In the early 1950s, television studios were lit in the same manner as film studios, although using multicamera techniques. The old Photicon cameras used at f1.9 required very high light levels, probably in the order of 4–5000 lux. This was needed to reduce the severe spurious shading signals with high velocity camera tubes. Very rapidly, in the mid-1950s, with the introduction of the Image-Orthicon camera, the light levels dropped so that a 4.5 inch Image-Orthicon used at f5.6 required an incident light level of 600 lux. The introduction of colour television in 1967 saw light levels rise to 1600 lux with camera stops of approximately f2.8 and the light levels at present in studios are anywhere between 600–1100 lux.

Due to the need to maintain a satisfactory 'signal to noise' ratio in the HDTV systems, where the amplification of the input signal is already at a maximum, a higher light input level is required. High definition camera manufacturers make claims that their cameras are reasonably sensitive and, as far as we can ascertain, the basic light level required for the same lens aperture is about 50% more than for conventional colour TV cameras. Experimental work done by broadcasting organizations with a European standard high definition television system used incident light levels of 1900 lux at f2.8. If we assume that at the present state of the art with high definition television systems the lighting requirement is twice that used at present in studios, what would be the problems associated with this increase of light?

Tungsten halogen luminaires used with the existing systems are generally between 2 kW and 5 kW. Tungsten lamps are not the most efficient devices and with about 90% heat loss represent a big heating problem in the studio with a subsequent need for sophisticated air conditioning systems. If the light level is doubled by changing to lamps of a higher wattage, the power input to the luminaires is increased by a factor of two, thus creating more problems for the air conditioning system; and the subsequent increase in plant size would probably not be possible in existing installations. Higher powered general purpose tungsten luminaires are available for both soft and hard sources; however, effects lighting used in studios is only just adequate and it is suggested that this is a problem area where higher light levels are required. At the present time the basic dimmer size is 5 kW but with an increase in light levels would probably have to become a 10 kW module. The resulting increase in lamp current presents more problems, particularly for the power intake to the studio, and it is more than likely that the existing power supplied would be totally inadequate. Also, it is possible that the protection devices used in the system would have to be uprated due to potentially greater fault currents. The higher current flowing in the cables from the dimmers to the light sources would be a source of increased electromagnetic interference, and therefore the circuits would have to be carefully installed to prevent problems. Some of these problems can be easily overcome in a new studio installation, but what happens if we wish to convert existing studios? In an existing studio the four main problems are:

1. The possibility of a fixed power intake.
2. Plant size already determined and incapable of expansion.
3. The types of luminaires in use would have to change.
4. The dimmer installation and its associated power switchgear and wiring would have to be modified, and in fact, probably replaced.

Television studios use tungsten halogen lighting because it provides good colour rendition, stable light output and the ability to be controlled very easily – this latter factor being by far the most important. As we need a higher light level, one solution might be to move our tungsten sources nearer to the action and if we position our source 2.83 m away instead of 4 m (our typical distance for a key light), we would double the light level. Unfortunately, the nearer the light source, the more dramatic are the changes of intensity within the light beam, so it would be extremely difficult to cater for normal movement of the artistes. Another solution would be to keep all the dimmer outputs at 'full' where we could only reduce the light level and subsequently not have flexible control of the light output and colour temperature.

It might seem that a better answer to the lighting of HDTV is to use the discharge source. Here we have a light source which has an efficacy of four times that of a tungsten lamp, of good colour rendition and fairly compact in size, and it would appear to be the solution for many of the problems. It should be borne in mind, though, that many discharge sources do not have a good power factor and require more current than an equivalent tungsten source. Television studios require light sources to be faded up and down. Unfortunately, the discharge source does not lend itself to this operation, and the only possibility would be to put mechanical dimming shutters on the discharge source: however, the speed of operation would probably not be high enough for the lighting director when required for effects lighting.

Another hazard is that discharge lights make rather peculiar noises when being switched on and the fact that they have a finite warm-up period will force the user to keep them ticking over. Imagine, also, how much noise would be generated with 50 mechanical shutters being operated simultaneously. From a practical point of view, there are many discharge spotlights available but very few effective discharge soft lights and, of course, the compact size of the source does not lend itself to the design of soft lights. Present European TV standards are based on 50 Hz repetition rates; if a high definition television system based on 1250 lines, 50 Hz were adopted, then a conventional discharge source ballast system should pose no operational problems, as the TV system is inherently locked to the mains frequency. However, what would happen if a high definition television system which operated at 1125 lines, 60 Hz were adopted? If such a system were implemented we would have to use discharge lighting that produced no flicker, and the control units for these can produce more electromagnetic interference and are much more expensive than conventional ballasts.

The present use of high definition television is generally confined to televising or recording special productions. Thus HDTV uses either the production and lighting techniques as practised by the film industry, or on other occasions outside broadcast techniques with special lighting. The existing HDTV cameras still use Plumbicon tubes for their receptors but with the advent of CCD (charge coupled devices) sensors it is more than likely that the sensitivity of the cameras will increase, thus allowing light levels similar to those used in today's TV systems.

8 Dimming and control

Introduction

If we go back in history to the development of lighting control systems we find that most of the use of devices for controlling lighting was to fade lights up and down. To actually hold the light level at a point somewhere between 'zero' and 'full' to achieve a lighting balance is a practice that has only become more normal with the advent of electricity. It was more than likely that the Greeks could fade down the intensity of their oil lamps by adjusting the length of the wick, although extremely difficult with floating wicks. When candles are used for illumination, they give a somewhat interesting light output which is a slow fade as the wick becomes shorter with the height of the molten wax rising, to a sharp increase of light when the wax runs down the side of the candle. One problem that existed with candles and oil lamps was the fact that the source of illumination on a breezy night was not too steady.

A major advance for the illumination of theatres was the introduction of gas lighting, which in its early days suffered from many problems, the major one being that of safety. As the gas systems became more advanced, control of portions of the lighting was achieved by small control taps and stopcocks placed in strategic pipework so that sections of the lighting could be switched off while other sections were switched on. Another problem with gas lighting is that it requires ignition to achieve incandescence and it was very inconvenient to light each gas jet individually. Several methods were used to enable the gas jets to be controlled; the most favoured one ultimately was a system where either a pilot light was employed or the actual gas jet was never completely extinguished. As far as we can research, no form of intermediate light level was provided by gas lighting, purely the ability to ignite groups of lights while possibly turning off other groups within the auditorium and in the stage area. The biggest step forward in the control of lighting in general was made by Richard D'Oyley Carte at the Savoy theatre, which opened in 1881 and was to be used specifically for performances of Gilbert and Sullivan light operas. From the outset D'Oyley Carte was determined to have the new electric lighting in his theatre to give much better illumination for the performances. He was also shrewd enough in the earlier days to have a gas system installed in addition to the new electrical power. Due to teething troubles, the official première on 6 October had to be delayed until Saturday 8 October. At that performance the stage was lit by gas and it was not until Wednesday 28 December that the entire theatre was lit by electricity. We quote from a publication of the time and it is interesting to note that the idea of controlling light was first mentioned.

> An interesting experiment was made at a performance of *Patience* yesterday afternoon, when the stage was for the first time lit up by the electric light, which has been used in the auditorium ever since the opening of the Savoy theatre. The success of the new mode of illumination was complete and its importance for the development of scenic art can scarcely be over rated. The light was perfectly steady throughout the performance and the effect was pictorially superior to gas, the colours of the dresses, an important element in the aesthetic opera, appearing as true and distinct as by daylight. The Swan incandescent lamps were used, the aid of gas light being entirely dispensed with. The ordinary electric apparatus has the great drawback for stage representations that the flames (sic) cannot be lowered or increased at will, there being no medium between full light and total darkness. This difficulty has here been successfully overcome by interpolating in the circuit . . . what in technical language is called a resistance. This resistance consists of open spiral coils of iron wire . . .

The above quote was from the Daily News, 29th December 1881. In early 1882 a technical observer commented in *Engineering*:

> The most interesting feature however, from a scientific point of view, of this most interesting installation, is the method by which the lights in all parts of the establishment are under control. For any series of lights can in an instant be turned up to their full power or gradually lowered to a dull red heat as easily as if they were gas by the simple turning of a small handle. There are six of these regulating handles corresponding to the number of the machines and circuits arranged side by side against the wall of a little room or rather closet on the left side of the stage, and each of these handles is a six-way switch which by throwing into its corresponding magnet circuit greater or less resistance (increasing or decreasing it in six stages) the strength of the current passing through the lamps is lessened or increased by as many grades.

We find it most interesting that the machinery for controlling the lights was placed 'in a little room or closet', which rather sets the scene for the years that followed in which we are now always confronted with small dimmer rooms and control areas, be it in the theatre, in television, film or any other entertainment media.

8.1 Theory of dimmers

A dimming device is one that reduces the flow of energy from a source to a destination and the source we are concerned with is electricity. As has been noted, the original control of the flow of electricity was by resistance which consisted of varying the length of iron wire introduced into circuits. Another form of resistance dimming was by varying the distance between two electrodes in a saline solution. The dimmers themselves looked rather like large portions of underground glazed drainage pipe, containing a solution of salt water, with a fixed electrode within the cylinder and a movable electrode usually lowered in and out of the solution, by a wire or piece of rope. It is interesting to note that 'salt pot' dimmer installations were in use in London, at the Garrick theatre until 1958 and the Savoy theatre until 1960. The major disadvantage of resistance dimmers is that the introduction of the additional resistance causes power to be wasted. In an attempt to reduce the power wasting situation and also to give better control of systems, Strand Electric, during the 1950s, introduced the auto transformer dimmer. Whereas a normal transformer has a primary winding and a secondary winding to transform the voltage across it, the auto transformer is made with one winding where part of the winding is common to the primary and secondary circuit. By varying a tapping point on the secondary side of the transformer we can vary the voltage applied to the load. Auto transformers have a lower resistance loss in their windings, and the efficiency is generally higher than in a transformer with two windings. A big advantage of the auto transformer dimmer is that it has a superb output law for the smooth control of any lights connected to it: the law of a dimmer being the relationship between the input setting and the light output from the luminaire. Other than auto transformer dimmers, saturable reactor dimmers were used to control lighting systems. These worked by having an iron cored coil in series with the ac fed lamp. By applying dc control signals the saturation of the coil could be adjusted and hence the impedance to the flow of current was also adjusted. The main disadvantage of saturable reactor dimmers was that they were extremely heavy, which had major implications in dimmer rooms; and the biggest problem of all was that the law of the dimmer varied considerably according to the wattage of the luminaires supplied. One big advantage of a saturable reactor dimmer was that the small dc control signals could be supplied from a remote point. Both the resistance dimming systems and auto transformer systems generally depended upon complex mechanical drive arrangements being provided to achieve any form of control.

The greatest advance in lighting control came about during the mid-1960s with the introduction of the 'thyristor' silicon controlled rectifier (SCR). Because the thyristor is a uni-directional device, two have to be used for the control of ac supplies for lighting systems so that we control the positive and negative half cycles of the ac supply. A close cousin of the thyristor is the 'triac'. Whereas the thyristor is uni-directional, the triac is a bi-directional device, and by applying a signal to the gate, we can obtain full wave control of ac power. There are several advantages of using solid state devices such as the SCR and triac: the power loss is exceedingly small; they are very easily controlled; and, most importantly, they are independent of the load across them. In the 'good old days' it was not unknown to connect, for example, two 1 kW luminaires across the output of a 2 kW auto transformer dimmer: one the real load and the other a dummy so that the dimmer output was fully loaded, thus ensuring the law of the dimmer. The major drawback to solid state switching devices is that the period of time from its 'off' state to its 'on' state is extremely small, in fact of the order of microseconds, and it is this switching cycle that gives problems in practice. All the other types of dimmers that have been mentioned – such as resistance, auto transformer and saturable reactor – work on the principle of diminishing or increasing the sine wave with virtually no distortion. The thyristor dimmer output, as can be seen from Figure 8.1, chops the waveform into discrete quantities.

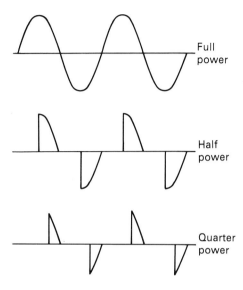

Figure 8.1   Thyristor waveform diagrams

A typical analogue control thyristor dimmer works as follows. The input control signal, which usually has a maximum of 10 V dc and can be either positive or negative (according to the manufacturer), is varied at the control console. The amount of dc voltage between 0 V and 10 V reaching the dimmer is compared internally on the dimmer control circuit and, according to that comparison, the dimmers are switched on at some time during the positive and negative half cycles. Thyristors automatically switch off when they pass through the zero point of the mains cycle; therefore a signal has to be applied to the thyristors controlling the positive and negative portions of the input mains every half cycle to enable them to conduct continuously. If, for instance, we are working on a linear system, and '5' on the fader literally means 50% power output from the dimmer, the thyristors would conduct at the 90° point, which is halfway between the start of the half cycle and the completion of the half cycle. Solid state devices such as the thyristor depend on a flow of current to keep them activated, which is somewhat similar to the action of the holding current in the coil of a magnetic relay. Thyristors require a well-defined minimum current to maintain a conducting state. When the current drops below this minimum level, which is known as the 'holding current', the thyristor will stop conduction and become effectively an open circuit. It is therefore essential that a minimum current has to flow in the thyristor circuits so that they are stable.

In the earlier days of thyristors it was felt practical that one short pulse applied at the nominated switch-on point in the half cycle would be sufficient to keep them conducting for the remainder of the half cycle and in most practical situations this was true. It was found in practice, however, that dimmers used for tungsten lighting became unstable with small electrical loads. Several methods were employed to overcome this problem, one of which was to keep a continual stream of pulses into the thyristor gate during the nominated conduction periods of the negative and positive half cycles, so that there was no tendency to switch off. Another method was by applying a switching signal which consisted of a constant dc signal to the thyristor gate during the nominated conduction period, so that during the half cycle there was always a voltage present to ensure that the thyristor fired for the selected period of time.

When lamps switch on, the current flowing through a cold filament may be up to 15 times greater than the normal current. Thus a 5 kW studio Fresnel spotlight with a normal steady state current of around 21 A on a 240 V supply, would have a cold inrush current of anything up to 300 A. This obviously must have some effect on a thyristor being used as the dimmer; the main problem being that to cater for the short-term high current, the thyristor has to be rated at a greater current level than would normally be expected.

A problem associated with thyristors is that as the output power of thyristors increases the gate requires a higher current flow, and to ensure high sensitivity of input for large current devices a subsidiary thyristor may be used to fire the gate circuit. The reason for this that the small primary thyristor will require a very small current at its gate to conduct and its output, which will be several times greater than the input current, will quite adequately fire a higher powered thyristor. Most of the discussion taking place here relates to the practice of using two 'back to back' thyristors, rather than any use of triacs, which tend to be used only in lower quality dimmers. In recent times, it has become possible to obtain solid state devices which incorporate the two thyristors and some of the associated firing circuitry, all in one encapsulated package.

8.2 Problems in practice

Since the inception of modern electronic dimmers using thyristors, etc. all manufacturers have been trying to solve the problem of the chopped waveform and the associated electromagnetic interference. Several ideas have emerged from manufacturers to reduce that interference to manageable levels: unfortunately at the lower price end of the dimmer market, the interference is only just contained to the general level set by the standards authority of the countries concerned, and is usually not good enough for professional installations where microphone cables and video cables are used. At the upper end of the market, manufacturers – at a cost – will make dimmers with very low interference levels from the point of view of audio and video circuits. Some strange ideas have also emerged from manufacturers; a notable one was to control the dimmer over one complete cycle rather than over the half cycle generally adopted. Although this method produced lower interference, the fact that at certain points in the dimming cycle we could have, for instance, one complete half cycle in operation with the other half cycle completely obliterated, produced high levels of direct current within the system. This ultimately caused the manufacturers some concern when problems arose within dimmer racks themselves. One operational hazard that occurred by this application of control was that if the lights were all approximately at the same level, there was a huge imbalance on the input three-phase supply system. If this imbalance does occur, it may be that the control system itself eventually gives problems, because the zero point of the mains is wandering, and therefore the dimmers do not know their switch-on points accurately. In practice the effect is that one set of lights may be faded up and down in one area of the studio, and at the same time it may be possible to see odd lights appearing when they are not, in theory, being controlled in other areas. This can be rather disconcerting!

Most thyristor dimmers are operated at about 80% of their full output and this is enough to guarantee that we will always have a rapidly rising current waveform which is the switch-on point of the negative and positive half cycles. We hope our readers will appreciate, without our going into complicated mathematics, that any waveform approaching a square wave is made up of a multiplicity of other waveforms, varying from waveforms at fairly low frequencies to those at extremely high frequencies, and it is the generation of these high frequency waveforms that gives us problems.

If we examine the effects of the lower frequency waveforms, we find that these can cause sympathetic vibrations to be set up in lamp filaments every half cycle, and if by some terrible coincidence we approach the resonance of the filament itself, we can have quite loud acoustic noises coming from the luminaires, manifested as a high pitched buzzing – colloquially known as 'lamp sing'.

It would seem on initial inspection that to get around the problem of the wave shape output of solid state dimmers is almost impossible However, this is not the case in practice, and a very simple trick is employed. By introducing into the circuit a choke, which consists of a coil of wire wound on a fairly heavy iron core, the rise time of the leading edge of the waveform (the switch-on point) is slowed down and if we effect a change from the normal two or three microseconds switch-on time to around one millisecond, then we have overcome most of the problems. A method of measuring the amount of noise generated is required and the generally accepted standard for assessing interference from dimmers was that introduced by the BBC during the late 1960s, which even today still holds true. Various groups of people had experimented with measuring the amount of interference generated and the experiments included specific lengths of wire laid adjacent to the dimmer power cables. Special coils were also used mounted adjacent to power carrying conductors, to assess the electromagnetic radiation. One of the problems with these methods is that they are much too flexible and have too many variables, i.e. length of cables used, the position of the cables in relation to each other, and how we equate the current flowing with the interference received. Before making any measurements or standards it was necessary to establish the levels of noise that would cause problems in practice. In general, within controlled studio conditions, very few problems occur with the vision circuits – only on the audio.

The basis for the measurements to avoid audio problems was as follows. On the assumption that when a microphone is working at −70 dBs, its normal operating point, quite considerable amplification has to take place before the audio signal is processed. It was found at that time that sound desks had a signal-to-noise ratio of about 50 dBs, so a figure in excess of this had to be aimed at to avoid deterioration in the quality of sound.

It is easy to keep the dimmer power cables away from the audio and vision circuits in the permanent installation, but it is extremely difficult where many flexible cables are used. At the time these experiments were taking place Star Quad microphone cable, with very superior interference rejection properties, came into use. This enabled quite reasonable levels of interference to be tolerated and thus the dimmer manufacturers were not presented with quite the problem that they originally envisaged.

It should be noted that Star Quad cables have varied over the years, and the introduction of a thinner type of cable with lower rejection limits caused some concern during the early 1980s but does not seem to have proved to be a problem in practice. To measure the interference accurately, it was decided that the best way would be to wire some form of measuring device into the circuit so that as many variables as possible were removed.

A dimmer, when conducting at any level under maximum, will generate on its output a string of interference pulses. These pulses are at a maximum amplitude when the dimmer is at 90° conduction. It was essential that the test circuit when placed into the power feeds disturbed these as little as possible so avoiding erroneous readings.

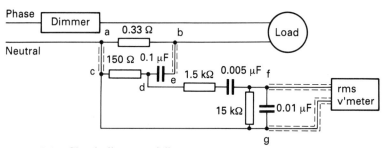

Figure 8.2   Circuit diagram of dimmer test system

Ultimately the circuit as shown in Figure 8.2 was adopted as the most effective method of measuring the interference in dimmer circuits. Two main points have to be observed when making these measurements:

1. As any noise generated by a waveform is proportional to its energy content, a method of measuring the root-mean-square (rms) value has to be used.
2. As the test is to assess electrical interference which becomes audible, a method of weighting the reading to the ear's response must be incorporated.

The measurement of rms is relatively straightforward as several test meters made by reputable manufacturers are available. Point (2) is covered by the circuit which electrically gives a similar response to the ear. Having decided upon a measuring technique, it was relatively easy to set the levels of permissible interference in the studio.

The measuring circuits have to be adequately encased within metal boxes so that external electric fields are minimized and no stray voltages are present on the meter readings. One other extremely important point is that the source impedance of the electrical supply to the test dimmer and load should be as low as possible because the interference readings may be artificially lowered on high impedance sources.

Having set up the test rig the sequence to be followed is:

1. Normal supply volts are applied to the dimmer.
2. The control level and hence the 'switch-on' point of the thyristors is varied to give a maximum reading on the meter, and this generally occurs at a firing angle of 90° with maximum rated load.

Test results

To meet acceptable levels, the rms meter readings must not exceed 15 millivolts rms for 2.5 kW or 5 kW dimmers, and must not exceed 30 millivolts rms for 10 kW dimmers.

The figures given are for the interference limits in 240 V dimmer circuits. Both 120 V and 240 V systems generate interference, the problem with 120 V supplies being that the current for any given wattage is double that of a 240 V system. As the interference is proportional to the amount of current, this will mean taking extra precautions on 120 V installations.

If the power cables going from the dimmer room to any of the luminaires run very close to other cables, then electrical induction takes place and the 'rubbish' voltage from the dimmers is transferred to all other forms of wiring. This might not be so bad if the wiring is the normal mains system around the premises, but it is obviously extremely bad if it is the vision or audio circuits that are affected. Of course, one of the unfortunate side effects of using a large choke in the output is that the choke itself can cause acoustic interference, and present day dimmer rooms can become quite noisy places, sometimes even causing problems in installation.

8.3 Dimmer types

Dimmers come in various shapes and sizes, the most popular being 2.5 kW, 5 kW and 10 kW. Smaller dimmers are available but these are generally used for the amateur stage and for small location lighting packs.

Dimmers are available in two distinct types; those which are 'wired-in' and those which have 'plug-in' dimmer modules. Wired-in dimmers are usually permanently installed inside some form of container, be it a small portable crate or a reasonably large metal enclosure rather like a filing cabinet. The majority of dimmers in use are of the wired-in type. Plug-in dimmers are often used where failure of particular dimmer modules causes problems with regard to the progress of rehearsals, transmissions and any live performance.

Plug-in dimmers

A plug-in dimmer consists of a chassis, which these days may be metal or plastic, on which is mounted the control circuit, made as a removable pcb, the output power devices, which could be either individual thyristors or an integrated circuit power block. Filtering chokes are generally mounted on this chassis, although in some systems the choke is mounted separately within the dimmer cabinet. When using plug-in dimmers, it is important that some distinction is made electrically and/or mechanically in the interchangeability of units within a dimmer rack; this is to avoid making the mistake of putting a low powered dimmer on a high powered source.

Figure 8.3   Plug-in dimmer

One major problem that occurs with plug-in dimmers is that of safety. It is obviously important when removing a dimmer module, which may be approximately the size of a shoe box, from a dimmer rack, that operator access to any live terminals is prevented, thus avoiding any electrical shock hazards.

Wired-in dimmers

This type of dimmer system is usually supplied with master printed circuit boards, with the control circuits on it for each of the individual dimmers. The power thyristors or integrated circuit power blocks are normally

Figure 8.4   Wired-in dimmers

separate from the mother board; and although a dimmer rack may contain a large number of dimmers, it is important that the printed circuit boards control only small numbers of dimmers to avoid the possibility of failure. One master control circuit board failing could be disastrous if it is controlling 30 or more dimmers. Control circuits that are common to about six dimmers are preferable.

High density wired-in dimmers are mounted in cabinets where access is only possible by the use of a key or tool to open the door so that safety is maintained. Small six-way dimmer packs, which are very common in practice, usually have to be dismantled by removing screws and covers to gain access for maintenance.

Dimmer technical parameters

1. Dimmer stability

To avoid fluctuations in the light output of the luminaires when controlled
by dimmers, it is important that the dimmers are relatively independent of
the input voltage variations. Most good quality dimmers made today are
supplied with 'feedback loops' so that the dimmer output is maintained
within certain limits (usually 10:1). However, it should be borne in mind
that a dimmer only works from the nominated output mains voltage
downwards. Unless supplied with special transformers and control
circuitry, it is not practical to have a dimmer which boosts the output; for
example, if the dimmer is rated at 240 V output and the mains input is only
210 V it is impossible to make the output any higher than 210 V.

In practice, dimmer loads vary considerably and any type of dimmer may
be required to work with loads of small power (e.g. our old friend the 60 W
practical lamp). It is obviously essential that the dimmer should remain
stable on such occasions and not go into any form of variation of output
caused by, say, internal oscillation. Dimmers are also abused by the
operators and more than likely they will have isolating transformers
plugged into them or many other inductive loads. On these occasions, it is
essential that the dimmer does not lose its stability or, for that matter, draw
excessive current which might destroy the output thyristors.

2. Direct current component

If the output power thyristors or integrated circuit power pack does not
have a balanced output, the imbalance will be seen as a small direct current
component in the output. It is essential that this direct current is kept to an
extremely low level so that it does not cause problems to any of the
connected loads or to the mains supply to the dimmer room. The electricity
supply authorities are not too happy with dc on their ac distribution
system!

3. Interference suppression

All dimmers have to meet normal electromagnetic spectrum interference
regulations of the country concerned. Additionally, the dimmers must
reduce the high frequencies present in the output waveform which would
cause problems with the sound and vision circuits in any installation. On 1
January 1992 an EEC directive came into force for the control of
electromagnetic interference from all types of apparatus.

4. Dimmer response

It is obviously important when controlling dimmers that the application of
a control signal will produce a known response; in practice dimmers are
required to respond instantly to any change of the control signal, the only
limitation being the lag within the lamp filaments themselves.

A problem that exists with the larger light sources, such as the 5 kW and
10 kW, is that of 'thermal shock', due to the large inrush currents. Modern
digital techniques can vary the 'turn on' time to allow a build-up of power
over several cycles of the mains when the channel is switched to 'full' thus
'fading' the lamp up, although it appears to be 'instant'.

5. Control input

Until recently dimmers have always been controlled by analogue dc control signals, i.e. the application of a small control voltage from 0–10 V dc will produce the changes within the dimmer itself. Several disadvantages exist with analogue control signals; first and foremost is that each dimmer has to have one input control wire, and thus if a control system of 240 ways is driving 240 dimmers, 240 control wires have to be used, together with one or more common wires. Recently the application of digital control signals to dimming systems has become wider spread. Digital control inputs are generally decoded on special cards situated within the dimmer pack and the control signal is conveyed either by co-ax cables or twisted pairs. All the dimmer control signals are fed down one cable, the usual limitation being the digital control system itself, and this seems to settle at blocks of 512 channels, so two cables are needed when we exceed this number of channels.

6. Dimmer law

A dimmer will obviously respond in some way to the control signal – that response will be dictated by the needs of the operators. It may be that a rapid fade up is required over the lower portion of the control channel with a slower progression over the upper portion of the control channel; or the operator requires very little light change from the luminaire over the lower portion of the fader characteristic with a large variation when the channel is raised towards its maximum. Dimmers have been made with built-in 'laws' to cater for various tastes in the theatre, film and television industry for many years. However, in recent times, with the more sophisticated control provided by modern lighting consoles, it is possible to use 'linear' dimmers where the law shaping is done by variations on the input control signals. With digital control, it is possible to set the 'law' of the dimmers precisely to the operators' requirements by adjusting the 'dimmer programme'.

Square law dimming

The square of the fader setting gives the percentage light output, e.g. fader at '6' equals light output of 36% (see Table 8.1).

Table 8.1   Fader setting for light output

Fader	Light output %	CT (K)	Output volts %	240	120	Current %	Power %
10	100	3200	100	240	120	100	100
9	81	3120	93	224	112	96	89
8	64	3040	88	211	106	93	82
7	49	2960	81	194	97	88	72
6	36	2860	74	178	89	85	63
5	25	2750	66	158	79	78	52
4	16	2600	59	142	71	73	43
3	9	2400	51	122	61	67	34
2	4	2200	39	94	47	59	23
1	1	–	23	55	27	46	11
0	0	–	0	0	0	0	0

In practice if we fade on an American system at 120 V or a British system at 240 V, we see little or no difference to the operation of the lighting system. However, if we choose to do comparisons of the parameters concerned, it is important that we remember that each volt of variation within an American dimming system will produce a change of 10 K, whereas on a British system at 240 V, each volt change produces a difference of 5 K. This is because of the relationship of Kelvins to the current and, as we all know, the American system is approximately twice the current of the British.

8.4 Fusing and sub-fusing

How do we protect our dimmers?

The first thing that would come to mind is the good old fuse! The problem with fuses is that, believe it or not, they take a finite time to operate. If a solid state device is rated at, say, 40 A, it quite happily carries a current of 40 A indefinitely and, over short periods of time, it will carry currents in excess of 40 A quite safely; however a high current for long periods of time will be fatal – for the fuse. The reason for failure of thyristors is that the semiconductor junctions within the device overheat and ultimately break down; thus if we overload the device well in excess of its normal current rating for any length of time we will destroy the thyristor. Therefore our first consideration when selecting a fuse is that it should adequately protect the thyristor circuitry. Additionally, the fuse must be capable of handling the cold current surge of the lamps without failing. Fuses operate extremely rapidly when a very high current is applied; or it might be a low current for a longer period of time. The time can be over the range from a few milliseconds to several thousands of seconds. It is therefore not possible to give the operating time for any specific fuse when the operating time is dependent on the value of the currents involved.

Before we go any further it would perhaps be better to introduce a new friend and this is a term I^2t. This refers to the time/current characteristic and is a quantity consisting of the time period combined with the square of the instantaneous current passing through a fuse between the instant when the circuit fault commences and the instant of the fuse rupturing. I^2t is often described as the 'let-through energy'. Both thyristor manufacturers and fuse manufacturers publish I^2t curves for their devices, and the manufacturers of dimmers simply have to compare these curves to select the correct type of fuse to protect the devices used. It is therefore essential to observe the manufacturers' choice of fuses for their equipment. Thyristors and triacs will also be damaged if an over voltage is applied in the reverse direction to the normal current flow and in most cases will only tolerate twice the peak value of the steady state voltage. Fuses to protect thyristors and other solid state devices in dimmers should meet the requirements of IEC 269-4 and BS 88 part 4. Fuses for 2.5 kW 240 V circuits usually are 10 A rating and those for 5 kW 240 V circuits are rated at 20 A. Any fuses used should be generally available and not specially made.

One problem that can occur with dimmer installations is that a 5 kW dimmer may be used to feed a practical light on a set and this practical light may only be a 60 W lamp fed via some lighting flex. In this case, the 20 A fuse would be well over the approved rating for the flex feeding the individual lamp; therefore some form of sub-fusing must be in place. This sub-fusing must be inserted at a point in the electric circuit so that it adequately protects the wiring concerned.

8.5 Dimmer rooms and switchgear

If we are designing from scratch, we can obviously make allowance for some area within an installation which would house the dimmers, their racks and the associated switchgear to control those racks. In practice however, any broom cupboard seems to be the solution to the dimmer room.

Figure 8.5   Modern dimmer room

What do we require from a well-designed dimmer room? First and foremost it is space. Secondly, the room has to be either self-ventilating or provided with proper means of ventilation. If we have a large area that can be used for the dimmers, it is possible to install dimmer racks containing a small number of dimmers per rack. Modern practice, however, because most areas allocated for dimmers are small, is the use of high density racks. These may be up to 192 dimmers per rack. The physical number in the rack does not necessarily create a problem, but the weight of the racks on the floor area does. The other possible source of concern is that by using one rack with many dimmers in it, controlled from only one piece of switchgear, any form of breakdown in the main supply would be quite disastrous on any transmissions, rehearsals or live performances. As a general rule, it is better to spread the eggs over more than one basket. Although this requires more pieces of switchgear, because each dimmer rack must be provided with a means of isolation, independent of all the other racks, it is much more expedient from an operational point of view and also from a maintenance point of view. Another snag that occurs with high density dimmer racks is that all the output power cables going to the stage or studio area have to be terminated somewhere within the dimmer rack itself; and the greater the density usually the greater the problem of termination. If we allow for a waste heat generation of approximately 100 W per 5 kW of dimmer power, it can be appreciated that in a high density rack quite high heat loads are generated. Thus the dimmer racks usually have to be force cooled by fans mounted within the racks, and in fact at one installation seen by the authors in America, the degree of cooling required in a room with several high density racks was so great that it was difficult to close the dimmer room door against the gale!

Dimmer racks will be designed for either single-phase input or three-phase input and this could be either by cables or some form of busbars. The dimmer rack itself should preferably be no higher than 1.8 m so that access to the rack is feasible without the use of steps or with the operators having to over-reach, which in itself is dangerous. It is obviously easy to have the control and power connections made when there is access from the front of the rack together with access from the rear. If rear access is required, allowance must be made for additional space within a dimmer room as the rear access would no doubt have an opening door and a clearance of at least 600 mm must be provided. Many modern dimmer racks have front access only but the problem of front access is that all the input and output terminals must be accessible and this often involves the manufacturers in some conflicts of interest with regard to space within the rack. Where small dimmer racks such as six-way packs are used, the problems are not so acute, although each of these racks would have to be provided with a small isolator adjacent to the racks for safety reasons. Dimmer racks have to be clearly marked because there will be several circuits within a rack, all with fuses or mcbs. The dimmer racks must also have indicators which show that power is supplied to the rack, and each individual dimmer should have some form of indicator to show that it is live. It is important that any form of earth leakage should be detected, although this is not usually provided on small dimmer racks. It is preferable that some kind of overheat detection is supplied within larger racks and this can be for two purposes: to detect firstly the generation of fire, and secondly the generation of additional heat which may be caused by fan failure within the racks. Although not a great danger within the premises, it may be that the failure of the fans causes the individual dimmers to fail by becoming excessively hot, subsequently causing the semiconductor devices to fail.

It is acknowledged that all dimmer racks have to meet high electrical and mechanical safety standards. Any form of electrical apparatus built within a rack or chassis system must meet the requirements of the country of manufacture and also the country in which it is to be used. Several years ago, when one of the authors was working for a major British broadcasting organization, a problem occurred with safety in a studio. One of Britain's better loved lighting directors was leaning back on a microphone boom platform in a studio admiring his work, when at the same time he reached forward to adjust a Northlite from a well-known equipment hire company. Unfortunately, the hired equipment had not been checked correctly and did not have an earth wire connected. At the same time a live wire had become dislodged and had touched the chassis of the offending piece of equipment, thus the luminaire had become live. The lighting director therefore received quite a severe shock between one arm adjusting the luminaire and the other arm resting on the microphone boom platform, which was connected to a very good earth. Fortunately the resulting shock was not fatal. At that time, it was considered by the broadcasting organization concerned whether or not to introduce earth leakage circuit breakers on all forms of lighting equipment, and although this was eventually done on distribution systems for outside broadcasts, it has not been employed within studio premises.

On the surface it would seem a very good idea to employ a residual current device (RCD) (formerly known as an earth leakage circuit breaker) with a very low sensitivity (30 mA/40 ms) on the output of each dimmer which would ensure that any operator coming into contact with either of the live wires, i.e. the phase or the neutral, would be safe. Evidence exists that would indicate that any RCD must be carefully chosen so that it operates almost independently of the dimmer output voltage levels. A point to be watched is that RCD manufacturers do not necessarily endorse the use of their products when used with dimmed, chopped waveforms. To quote from a paper given by a member of Strand Lighting at a safety conference: 'Finally there is a risk that increased use of RCDs may lead to complacency regarding the safe use of electricity. The use of RCDs is an additional safeguard and in no way forms a substitute for good electrical practice whether in the field of installation, operation or equipment maintenance'.

It is no good having a nice looking dimmer rack where, when faults occur, access for maintenance is a nightmare. It is particularly galling to any operator to find that to change the simplest of components requires minutes and sometimes hours removing screws, nuts, washers, panels, etc. often cutting one's hand in the process, accompanied by the usual quietly mouthed expletives. For ease of maintenance it is obviously essential to have good technical information which gives circuit diagrams, constructional details of the cabinets, and so on, and a complete set of instructions of how to go about maintaining the equipment itself, all of which must be totally unambiguous. Much modern equipment, however, is quite sophisticated and any maintenance, other than first line, would probably have to be carried out by the manufacturer, but this usually entails extra expense when calling upon a service engineer from the manufacturer concerned.

8.6 Control systems

In the days of resistance and salt pot dimmers, control of lighting was slow and cumbersome. The cues were accomplished by the electricians on the stage or in the studio coupling sections of rope and levers and wires together to make several dimmers move in unison for effect, and even to move one dimmer was a considerable task, the main problem being that the LD was not in control of the actual lighting system at all.

Eventually Strand Lighting introduced systems that allowed control of the dimmers by driving from a mechanical shaft system, electrical controllers that allowed the amount of current fed to the luminaires to be varied. The most famous of these were the auto transformer dimmers

Figure 8.6   Shaft driven dimmers

which were driven by an up/down clutching system driven by a variable speed shaft drive arrangement. The system worked on the principle that when the fader lever on the console was adjusted it changed the electrical parameters of a 'Wheatstone bridge' circuit, thus engaging the appropriate up or down clutch to follow the direction of the fader lever. These systems were relatively slow in operation and produced relatively good fades but not as swift as those accomplished today. These earlier systems generally were 'two preset' which allowed two states for each dimmer, according to which of the preset channel controllers were in use. The consoles were provided with master controls for over-riding the preset states, so that fades could be accomplished with groups of lamps.

One of the drawbacks with systems such as these was that there were no systems which memorized the on/off state of the channels so that groups of channels could not be switched on and off at will. Strand Lighting came up with an ideal solution for the time by using the technology from the organ builders and pictures of old control boards look like the consoles of cinema organs. The system of memory was extremely simple inasmuch as a small flexible contact pin was allowed to engage in a movable bar with contacts arranged as small notches along the bar, thus offering low voltage control of the particular channel, and upon selection of the appropriate notch bar would bring into play the group of channels. As can be well imagined, to have many memories meant that the system required a multiplicity of contact pins and several notch bars; thus this type of console was usually limited to about 40 memories on the red preset and 40 memories on the blue preset. It was not uncommon in the early days of memory systems that the operators had to re-plot major portions of the action to take advantage of the memory grouping facilities.

One problem associated with memory control in those days was that if you did not release your foot at the correct moment off the 'presetter' pedal on the console, you were in great danger of having a random selection of pins in the notch bars, which caused rather a lot of soul searching by the operator concerned.

One of the biggest steps forward was the introduction of solid state dimmers, which allowed voltage control of the dimmer directly from a console rather than control via the electromechanical system. As has already been noted, the saturable reactor system allowed direct control, but unfortunately again the memory systems were extremely primitive when using this system.

What are the bases of operation that any lighting console must provide for? Although many modern lighting consoles are rather daunting in appearance, they still have to provide the following basic functions.

1. To be able to set the channels and hence the dimmers anywhere from zero to full light output.
2. The ability to switch a channel on or off at any level of its fader setting.
3. To group channels together.
4. To mix either individual channels or groups of channels together.
5. The ability to over-ride channels by 'Master' or 'Group' faders and by master switching.
6. The ability to collect the channel information which would be its fader setting and/or its on/off condition, either as individual channels or in groups or combinations of groups, and consequently store in some form of memory system.
7. To be able to rehearse complicated fade sequences involving groups of channels or memories in a timed sequence and subsequently record this information.
8. To be able to recall settings, change them and re-record the result.
9. To replay the information stored in memory either manually or automatically in a sequence to suit the action.

Lighting consoles come as three distinct varieties, the first being the manual system, where each channel is individually fed from a fader; the second system is that of an 'enhanced' manual system where several faders are employed together with a very simple memory control so that the channel settings can be memorized and replayed and some or all of the faders re-used for other purposes; the third type is the fully automated control system where channel selection is invariably by a keypad: there are only one or two channel faders employed and these may exist in the form of a wheel rather than the traditional lever. The control console will have a memory system where anything is possible, and effects systems are built in.

Manual control systems

Generally, in a manual system each channel is directly fed from a fader; thus a simple 60-way system uses 60 faders. If the system is two preset, this means that two faders are provided per channel with the ability of using two preset master faders, to fade between either one of their preselected states; the highest of the selected states taking precedence when the two masters are fully on.

For example, channel X is set at '7' on the red preset and '5' on the green preset. With the red master 'up' and the green channel 'down', channel X is set to '7'; when the red master is 'down' and the green master is 'up', the channel is set at '5'. When the red master is at 'full', raising the green master to full will not change the state of the channel; as the red channel is the highest, the output will always be '7'. This gives simple twin-state (or preset) mixing. The state of each channel can be easily set on the lighting console and an over-riding master facility is available. For simple productions and the control of lighting of many types, this console is more than sufficient and is very fast in operation, as channels are very easily accessed. Most manual systems these days have a control where the cross fade is dipless, i.e. there is a small amount of electronic control which provides for a smooth fade progression between the two presets.

Figure 8.7   Manual control boards

One of the drawbacks of manual systems is that one cannot have more than two states of each channel with two preset systems, because otherwise the fader lever has to be reset.

The second type of manual system which has been slightly enhanced enables the faders to be used more flexibly. It is possible to set up a lighting state using the channel faders and then memorize this selected state, which then frees the fader levers for another totally different condition. The rest of the system operates in a manner similar to those on manual control systems and is only dictated by the extras provided by the equipment manufacturer.

Automated control systems

We finally come to the all singing, all dancing, memory control systems that exist today. Generally the system will have one or two channel controllers, each one of these with the ability to control any channel. It will also be quite possible that memories and groups may be introduced into the main system via the channel controller. Consoles of this type work on the principle that we select a channel on the controller, the level is set and stored away and we then move onto the next channel to be controlled. Thus systematically, one by one, we assign levels to the lights concerned, either on stage or in the studio. As the channels are switched on and the levels are set, we slowly build up the lighting within the scene. At the end of this period, it is possible, by using the memory system, to store all the channels at their various levels for future use. One advantage of this system is that if the same lights are used for a further piece of action within the scene, the lighting director can set completely independent levels from those already memorized without ever considering the information stored away: the control system does it all for him. To replay the scenes that have been memorized, they are usually recalled from the memory system by the

Figure 8.8   State of the art control system

selection of the appropriate buttons and subsequently played back via the master controllers which enable either cuts or fades to progress. Additionally, memories may be added or subtracted and multiple effects can be combined before being introduced into the lighting output.

A major problem that exists with consoles of this type is the tendency of manufacturers to fall into several traps, and these are as follows:

(a)   To use buttons to accomplish several operations which, to say the least, can be confusing when the console is operated at speed.

(b)   There is a tendency by manufacturers, because of the competition within the industry, to provide every 'bell and whistle' possible within their control system, the main reason being that they do not want their product to look deficient in any way.

(c)   The problem of trying to have one console to be everything to everyman. There is a conflict of interests between the television industry and its requirements, the theatre industry and its requirements, and the 'pop' industry and its requirements. It is very difficult to have a hybrid lighting console to bridge the gap, and invariably we end up with the horse so designed that it turns out to be a camel!

When talking to operators, we generally find that most prefer a fader per channel; the trouble is that being human beings, we always like all the little frilly extras that exist on any piece of equipment. One of the difficulties that now exists is how fast the operator can respond when a problem occurs. While everything is going well it looks fine, but in an emergency is it really necessary that the operator needs a science degree to be able to understand and operate many modern lighting consoles?

Advantages, however, do exist with modern consoles, inasmuch that effects can be immediately accomplished without much of a problem. Most modern consoles have integral soft patching systems, which allow the control of many dimmers usually via a smaller number of control channels. They also have the ability to shape the input control characteristic of the dimmers themselves; thus different shaped characteristics can be provided for lamps that respond rapidly when switched on, such as 1 kW profile spot luminaires, compared with the 5 kW and 10 kWs which have a much slower response time. It is now possible, within complicated fades, to tailor the curve of each individual light to gain a most harmonious result.

If we buy a console from a manufacturer together with that manufacturer's dimmers, no doubt they will nicely work together. However, this is not always the case when we would desire to buy dimmers from one source and a lighting console from another. It is absolutely essential that the console talks intelligently to the dimming system. In the days when systems used analogue dc control signals, this was more than likely possible, although over the years manufacturers all had their subtle variations, around a 10 V dc theme. With the advent of digital control systems, it is obviously important that the digital signal is recognized by the dimmer units, and to date several different types of protocol have been used and suggested by manufacturers. It is advisable when purchasing dimmers to check the compatibility of digital information.

A survey undertaken in 1990 listed 73 memory systems on the UK market, each one being different to the other. Confronted with such a number of systems, it would be somewhat presumptuous of the authors to recommend or suggest any one particular system for use by the customer. It is essential that anybody purchasing a control system makes himself aware of all the quirks and foibles of the system and associated dimmers necessary for his installation.

Remote control

Although the lighting console is 'remote' from the dimmers in most installations, the term 'remote control' usually refers to additional methods of control other than the main console. Two types of remote control of dimmers are required, the first being a fairly simple type which generally consists of switching dimmers off and on only, and which is used for rigging purposes by the electricians within the installation concerned. This might be a large panel mounted on the wall in a studio and often called 'an electricians' panel' (Figure 8.9) or it might be a small hand-held controller.

The second type, which is the LDs control, is required to be virtually an extension of a complete working console, thus enabling the LD to sit either in the stalls or conveniently stand within the studio and plot his lights at first hand (Figure 8.10). Designers' controls generally will give access to all the channels and memory system.

To contain costs in smaller installations, it should be possible to have one lighting console with the ability to interface with the dimmers from two or more control input points.

Remote control may be by 'wired' input, or by infra-red signals from the hand-held controllers to receivers in the area concerned.

Figure 8.9   Electrician's panel

Figure 8.10 LD's remote controller

Back-up systems

If the power input to the installation fails the dimmers will not work and of course we have lost the ability to control them. If, however, the main lighting console fails, what would we expect to be able to do? In years gone by pin matrix systems were used, which allowed several channels to be control patched to master faders, offering a fairly crude form of back-up system in the event of the main console failing. The main problem was that it only permitted large numbers of channels to be grouped together and faded up and down, and was almost a return to the original control systems seen during the age of gas lighting for the theatre. Possibly the best form of back-up system is where we virtually duplicate all the console facilities, and in fact, in some systems, this is actually done, although obviously at some premium.

The biggest loss of facilities is when the memory system itself fails, because of the reliance upon the memory system to store all the channel information. In general, back-up systems are not really used with manual control and enhanced manual control systems, but only used with the more sophisticated consoles. Obviously where a lever per channel is the operating method, the actual memory system is the fader itself. The most advanced back-up systems in use today allow for a monitoring of the main system and recording constantly all the channel levels to update the system in event of failure. If the back-up system allows for the selection of the memories together with some grouping and the ability to fade up and down from its master faders, then it is unlikely that the audience will notice any major differences.

Recent developments

Consoles have probably reached the height of development at the present time, although we have strong doubts as to whether designers will contain themselves and refain from introducting more 'bells and whistles'. There are, however, some interesting developments within dimmers. In the past, a signal went from the lighting console to the dimmer rack and only by observing the luminaires, together with hard wired indicator warning systems, did the operator know the state of the studio or stage. Although in recent years multiplex digital control signals to the dimmer room have been employed, they still had to be decoded and converted to local dc control signals within the dimmer racks. Recently, however, dimmers have been introduced where the digital signals are taken directly to the dimmer modules. This now allows much greater control of the individual dimmers, making it possible to programme the maximum output voltage of the dimmers to a high degree of accuracy. However, it should be noted that we still cannot make up volts; when the input voltage of the system falls below the set levels we can only go to the input voltage level, i.e. if the dimmer has been set for an output voltage of 240 and the input voltage falls to 230, we will still only get 230 V. From the console we can programme the dimmer laws with great ease, and in addition to built-in 'square', 'S' and 'linear' laws, it is also possible for the user to programme his own curves. Rather than having to remember that a certain key light is Channel 123, it is possible to use a five-character alphanumeric name. The dimmers are clever enough to report back to the operator various problems: these are *no load present; no output volts present; there is an excess of dc in the system; there is no control available and the units have exceeded their normal temperatures.* Whether or not we need this intelligence in every studio or stage installation is for the operators of the systems themselves to decide. The inescapable fact, however, is that it is now extremely easy for the manufacturers to control the entire system.

In conclusion, we make the following observations. Manual consoles invariably feed back visual information either by the setting of a fader lever or the button push as to what has been happening. The more sophisticated consoles use VDUs, where in general, it is essential they keep working, because when they fail, it is almost impossible to understand what the lighting console itself is actually doing. Recently, the BBC has gone back to square one, and reintroduced an updated version of the late lamented Thorn Q-file with very simple readout facilities built into the actual console itself such as illuminated buttons which show channels and memories selected. It is also equipped with servo operated channel fader levers which faithfully mimic the set channel levels. From an operational point of view it is very easy to see what is happening without recourse to a VDU.

Perhaps the time has now come when the major manufacturers and the users should review where we've got to and say, enough is enough, let's go back to something we can all understand.

9 Operational procedures

9.1 How to rig pantographs and monopoles

Pantographs

Pantographs, both manually and electrically controlled, are normally mounted onto roller barrel trolleys or heavy duty 'C' section track. The method of mounting when using this track is to slide the pantograph unit into the track from one end making sure that the end stops are replaced in both ends of the track. When mounting pantographs onto a barrel roller trolley, the trolley is placed over the barrel so that the support wheels may traverse along the barrel. Safety bolts or blocks are then fitted to the trolley under the barrel to prevent the trolley lifting off the barrel. Having mounted and secured the pantograph, the mains cable should be inspected to determine that none of the loops attached to the side of the pantograph can be trapped between the cross links which will act like a pair of scissors when the pantograph is opened and closed.

Load adjustment of spring pantographs is made by moving the position of the end of the spring up and down the outside rungs by use of hook plates attached to the end of each spring. This is a dangerous adjustment and must be performed to the manufacturer's instructions to ensure that the spring is not released when it is moved from one rung to another.

When balancing the load it is a good practice to equalize the position of diagonally opposite springs to prevent the pantograph twisting. The lower down the outside rungs that the end of the springs are attached increases the balanced load. To load a luminaire onto a spring pantograph it is necessary either to climb up to the top position with the light, which makes it difficult to adjust the springs for the applied load, or follow the much preferred practice of tying a piece of rope to the base of the pantograph and pulling it down to floor level, where a sandbag or other convenient weight can then be attached whilst the luminaire is being fitted to the base. The springs may now be adjusted until a perfect balance is achieved and the rope can be released. Extreme caution must be taken when unloading a spring pantograph to make sure that the reverse procedure is adopted to that of the mounting procedure, preferably with the rope, so that the pantograph is allowed to slowly close as the rope is played out. We have seen the results of a pantograph being released at floor level, allowing it to fly up to the top without a load. The effect is quite dramatic and very dangerous. Springs become detached and links are broken, showering debris on those below with a real danger of the whole frame structure falling on the person responsible for letting go of it.

Motorized pantographs are much easier to mount because they are lowered by a motor and can be loaded at floor level; however, the same procedure is required as in the case of the spring pantograph with regards to mounting and the path of the cables. If electrical traverse is provided, extra care is needed to ensure sufficient length of trailing cable and its safe routing.

Monopoles

Because of their weight monopoles are difficult to handle, requiring at least two men and, in the case of the motorized monopole with its mains cable, three men to rig them. If it is practical, it is a better proposition to use a small hoist or tackle to get them up to grid level and then the most simple monopole may be lowered into the appropriate slot from above, having made sure that the grid end stops are in position. With more sophisticated grids, a transfer trolley is provided so that the monopole can be loaded into the trolley from the top gallery, pushed along to the appropriate slot, and then positioned in the grid.

When the monopole has been placed in the grid slot, it is necessary to guide the mains cable through the cable guide ring that holds it in the centre of the slot. This is to prevent the cable being trapped by the wheels of the trolley. Monopoles are placed in the vertical and lateral position by motor drives in the case of the fully motorized unit, but for the manually operated monopole these functions can only be performed from above the grid. Under no circumstances should the monopole be pulled along the slot from below by pulling the tubes. This will damage or break the tubes or at least distort them, causing them to stick and bind when being lowered.

A good practice when installing monopoles is to determine the type of plug or connector being used at the luminaire end of the supply cable. Many types of 5 kW plug will not go through the standard grid slot of 2.5 inches (62.5 mm) and therefore must be fed through the end of the grid slot. This small observation before installation could save hours of shunting and moving monopoles around the grid when it comes to connecting up.

9.2 Loading barrel winches

Barrel winches come in a variety of types: they may be suspended by a counterweight system; they could be a standard winch unit where the motor is mounted at grid level; or they may be a self-climber where the motor unit is integral to the barrel. Two features common to any type of barrel suspension is that they have well-defined safe working loads (SWL); and being fairly long devices, occupy a large space in the grid system.

In the theatre, where barrels may be around 5 m long, it is purely a matter for the electricians to rig luminaires as dictated by the LD on the particular production, bearing in mind the physical space required by each unit; and when all the units are hung, to check that the SWL has not been exceeded. Another aspect of rigging barrels in a theatre is to allow sufficient space for the scenery that has to be flown in and out during a production so that the lights miss scenery flats and cloths. The majority of luminaires rigged will be at the same height. If large effects lighting units are being used, note should be taken of the extra space required. It may be that the addition of some units to the normal rig will exceed the SWL of the bar; therefore some compromise has to be reached with the final positions of the luminaires so the weight load is evenly distributed between the bars. With the advent of motorized lighting units which replace two or three standard luminaires, it may be that the density of rig is not so high, giving more flexibility to the LD and the electricians concerned.

Generally with counterweight systems, it is almost impossible to overload them as the counterweight bucket usually contains only sufficient weights to balance the SWL on the bar. The overload warning system heard is probably the grunts and groans from the 'sparks' using the system!

Owing to the need to fly scenery between the lighting bar rows, cross barrel systems from one lighting bar to another are virtually unheard of in the theatre. Other than the fact they would impede the scenery, there would be no point in attempting to get the subtle variations in the angle of throw from the luminaires within a theatre as the distance between the suspension barrels is never very great.

Motorized barrel units, as used in television studios, pose different problems. Because of the larger lights used in television, the spacing between barrels is fairly wide and this, together with the end-to-end spacing of the barrels, poses problems for the positioning of the luminaires. The position of the lighting has to be reasonably accurate and is dictated by the layout of the sets within the production area and the requirements of the LD to cover the action correctly. Many studios use a standard rig of luminaires which may be fastened directly to the barrel unit, or attached via a short spring pantograph so flexibility in height is provided. Where luminaires and pantographs are supplied as combinations, there is usually very little spare weight capacity on the bars; thus when additional equipment is required to be rigged to the bar, it may take the bar over its SWL limit. This poses real problems for the LD because he now has to make up his mind whether to lose a luminaire or use another type of light. It may be possible to de-rig a pantograph leaving its luminaire in place, although with long barrel units it is preferable to keep the pantographs to allow flexibility between the luminaires attached to the bar. Another problem is that even if the bar is capable of taking the extra luminaire weight, it might be that the unit is too large to fit in the available space. At this point, the LD could use a short drop arm on the luminaire required so that it hangs just below the space occupied by the luminaires already present on the bar; although this may restrict the up/down movement of the luminaires on the pantographs.

What happens when the barrel units do not provide the LD with his desired position for the luminaire? The only thing to do is to supply a temporary barrel that bridges two of the normal barrels. The two major problems with using cross barrels is that they tether two units together, inhibiting flexibility, and the ends of the cross barrel attached to the standard barrel units impose extra weight. This load will be in proportion to the length of the cross-bar between the attachment points and the point loads on the cross bar. For example, 50 kg in the centre of a cross barrel between two standard barrel units will present a load of 25 kg to each barrel unit. At the other end of the scale, if the point load of 50 kg were to be positioned at one of the attachment points, most of the 50 kg would be present at that point. It can be seen, therefore, that as the load moves along the bar, it moves proportionately between the two attachment points on the barrels.

The above example illustrates that it is not just simply a matter of putting a cross bar between two units. When using cross bars what happens when only one bar is raised and the other bar does not move? The bar that is moving in an upward direction will eventually take the total weight of the cross bar and attempt to pull it with itself. Just after this point in travel the cross bar will attempt to start raising the other winch barrel. Unless very good overload sensors are provided, it might be that the whole cross barrel structure is raised and eventually becomes dangerous because the luminaires are not hanging normally by the barrel clamping arrangement provided but have rotational stress applied. It may be that these exceed the mechanical tolerances as designed.

Conversely, the lowering of one of the main bars eventually means that one end of the cross bar becomes lower and lower and then will start to drag the other supporting bar into the moving unit. Once again, additional torque may be introduced into mechanical sections of the units. This case highlights the need for good overload protection but it is quite possible in practice that none of the loads on either the two original bars or the cross bar exceeded the system specifications, only when the units were moved. It is therefore extremely important that any cross bar is clearly marked so that the electricians operating the winch control console will not raise or lower one bar without the other.

The situation cited above involved two bars, with one cross bar attached, but in a long experience in studios we have seen several cross bars across several barrel units all at the same time, together with cross bars on cross bars, and one shudders to think of the complications this causes in practice.

The same rules apply to studios that employ self-climbing units but unfortunately, an additional hazard exists. When using cross barrels in self-climbing studios, not only will the cross barrel attempt to lift the safe working load, it eventually starts to lift the entire load of the barrel unit, and although it might not progress to a great height, it could get sufficiently high to suddenly swing free and act like a giant pendulum, which would be extremely dangerous, to say the least.

In recent times, broadcasting organizations using motorized barrel systems have examined more sophisticated control of their winch systems to prevent problems such as these occurring. Two methods can be employed: one is to *remove from any form of control* the two bar units with a cross barrel attached once they have been positioned; alternatively ensure that any movement of one of the normal bars will *guarantee the other bar moves in unison*, thus maintaining the *status quo* for the cross barrel.

Luminaires rigged directly to a bar require a safety bond from the luminaire that passes over the barrel. If, however, a pantograph is used to

Figure 9.1   Cross barrels

support a luminaire a different technique must be employed. A bond is required between the top of the pantograph unit, which will probably be a wheeled trolley, and this must pass over the main barrel. At the base of the pantograph, where the luminaire is attached, either by a spud directly into a spigot holder or by a 'C' clamp onto a spade fixing at the base of the pantograph, the luminaire safety bond must pass over the permanently attached bottom section of the pantograph unit.

When using bars that are, say, 2.4 m long, it is important that the roller trolleys used for the luminaires' horizontal adjustment do not entangle the cables from the lighting power sockets adjacent to the bar supplying the luminaires. Various methods have been employed over the years to prevent this happening; one of the most successful is to have a small subsidiary bar adjacent to the main bar with small runners attached so that the power cable is conveyed along out of harm's way rather like the power feeds used with gantry cranes. Another important point to watch when rigging bars is to ensure that the cable does not droop from the socket across the heat outlet at the top of the luminaire and thus either get too hot or melt completely. This may seem rather obvious, but unfortunately in practice happens too often and the cables do become very brittle and thus pose a safety hazard.

Many modern winch systems are fitted with a local barrel switch which enables the electrician, when rigging, to move the barrel up and down by using his operating pole in the cup of the operating switch. This allows very fine adjustments, which are only limited by the length of the pole used, and improves the productivity during the rigging period. The normal procedure for rigging bars in studios is to bring sections of the barrel system down to the studio floor level so the electricians can remove luminaires where necessary, introduce new luminaires, change filters and fit any other equipment as desired by the LD. This operation is usually done in groups of about 20 bars, this being the maximum amount that the winch system caters for at any one time and, by coincidence, is usually two rows across a production studio of about $800\,\text{m}^2$. While the rigging is taking place, it will usually involve a team of two electricians on the bars, one electrician fetching and carrying and another based near the winch console to move the bars up and down when requested. It is obviously extremely important that the communication between these men is good to ensure the correct weights are applied to bars, cross barrels are carefully noted and when the bars are moved they do not foul items of scenery and technical equipment. Additionally, on those occasions when temporary a circuit such as a $10\,\text{kW}$ feeder is draped across several bars for convenience, this must also be noted to prevent accidents, as this fairly large cable acts like a soft cross barrel.

Other than additional luminaires or positions for luminaires which require cross barrels, there is also a need to provide facilities for slung video monitors and column loudspeakers in a standard lighting rig. In installations where permanent audience areas are allocated, although the seating may not always be *in situ*, it is customary to feed specified bars with sound and vision facilities. Sometimes special bars are provided to be used only for vision and sound audience facilities. However, if we have to rig a large video monitor onto a barrel, we will invariably have to move some of the existing equipment due to the weight of the monitor. If the equipment to be removed is a short spring pantograph supporting a luminaire, it is essential that the spring pantograph is collapsed before removing the luminaire. Alternatively, it may be possible to remove the pantograph and luminaire as one combined unit in absolute safety.

Having removed any lighting equipment, it is essential that it is transported safely to a secure area for storage, thus ensuring that no damage occurs.

9.3 Rigging luminares

The first consideration when rigging luminaires must be safety. Any light mounted above people is a potential hazard. Each suspension device will have a maximum safe working load and this must be observed. Further, each luminaire is required to have its own safety bond made off around the primary means of support and the luminaire to arrest it in the event of it falling. The accessories, such as barndoors and colour frames, also require their own safety retention device to prevent them becoming dislodged during movement. Having established that these requirements have been met, the electricians can mount the luminaire onto its support. In addition to the safety bond, a safety pin is provided and this should be inserted into the top of the spigot when it has been passed through the spigot holder. The electrician connecting the luminaire to the supply is responsible for visually examining the cable and connector to establish that they are electrically safe before plugging the luminaire into its socket. The choice of luminaire is normally dictated by the lighting plot which will show the electrician the type of unit, its wattage and the colour of any filter to be used. A space is usually left on the lighting plot for the electrician to complete the circuit number used in the event that one has not already been allocated. It is normal practice to open the luminaire and determine that the correct size lamp has been fitted and then switch the luminaire on, focus it and direct it to the approximate position as indicated on the lighting plot. These disciplines can save an enormous amount of time during rehearsals when in all probability, to get to a luminaire over sets and obstacles, it will be necessary to use tall steps or a portable tower. There will be occasions when it will be impossible to reach the luminaire after rigging is complete and rehearsals have commenced.

9.4 The use of practical and set dressing lights

In addition to the suspended production lighting, there will be a need for luminaires mounted on floor stands around the sets, together with small luminaires on special clamps attached to the top of scenery flats for local lighting in the sets. There will also be a requirement to have 'practical' lights. These will be similar to those found in any normal house or business premises and consist of table lamps, fluorescent fittings, wall mounted units and pendant fittings hanging from a ceiling. The use of these fittings is to give a realistic effect to the scene. However, the general lighting effect will not be provided by the practical lamps but by the main lighting being used cleverly by the LD to supplement the effect of, say, a 100 W bulb.

We have to be careful with this 100 W practical lamp, because it will no doubt be fed by relatively small electrical flex so that it looks right as far as the viewer is concerned, but unfortunately in practice the circuit may not have the correct back-up protection if anything goes wrong. It has already been noted in the section on dimming that it is very important to select the correct fuse for the circuit involved. If we take the standard studio or stage set-up, the 240 V dimmers will be fused at about 10 A or 20 A, or possibly even more on some occasions. The problem that occurs when the practical is plugged into a lighting power outlet is that the cable size has reduced considerably with the use of flex for the practical and we must insert a subsidiary fuse at this point where the cable sizes change. If the practical is supplied from a wall outlet and the flex has to progress several metres across the acting area this also constitutes a source of danger. Our best bet is to ensure that we get as near to the practical as possible with well rated cable and then introduce an additional fuse at this point so that only a short piece of flex is used. The best method is to use special extension leads, but whereas the normal lead will just have a socket at the end of it, the special leads for practicals will have fuses fitted adjacent to the final socket. Obviously for convenience when two practicals have to be used together in a room, the extension cables should be supplied with parallel sockets, each one of these fitted with a small local fuse. Thus, the 20 A fuse used with a 240 V 5 kW dimmer will protect the cable all the way down to the sub distribution outlet. This can then be sub-fused at 5 A to supply the final piece of flex and the subsequent 100 W lamp.

Other than practical lamps, it is possible that some of the lights used on the scenery flats are also low wattage sources. These luminaires may be supplied from within the premises or are hired pieces of equipment, but in most cases they will be supplied with small mains leads fitted. Once again, we have to ensure that they are only plugged into a circuit that is correctly protected by a subsidiary fuse rather than directly plugged into the main lighting circuits.

With set dressing lights, which are often supplied from overhead sockets, it may be more convenient to have an adaptor unit with a plug that goes into a bar outlet, is sub-fused at that point and provides a smaller connector on its output. As an example, a 32 A BS 4343 plug may be used to go into the 32 A socket on the bar but the outlet from the adaptor unit would be a 16 A BS 4343 socket supplied via a fuse fitted in the adaptor.

Having said that we need to protect the circuits by the choice of the correct fuses, we must also ensure any cables feeding either set or practical lights are routed in such a manner that they are protected from mechanical damage at all times. This will require special covers over cables at floor level together with a careful choice of route through the scenery labyrinth.

On occasions, there may be a need to use an isolating transformer to give a higher degree of protection to some of the circuits appearing at floor level. Generally these will be those circuits used for musical instruments and, of course, these will not be dimmed circuits. However, it is important to be sure that at any time any load such as a transformer or motor, when plugged into the system, is going to work correctly with the dimmers installed in that system. Some items of equipment that may be provided from hired-in items may not be of the same voltage as the supply system in the premises and it would be somewhat disastrous to put a 120 V hired-in device across the output of a 240 V dimmer.

The main lessons to be learnt are:

- Check every point of detail at any time with regard to the disposition of small pieces of lighting equipment within sets.
- Check particularly on their ability to handle current and that they are suitable for the system voltage.
- Finally, it is no good having protected a 100 W lamp with a small fuse to have the cable draped across a corner of the set in such a way that the first person going that way trips over and breaks a leg!

10 Stage and studio technical design

Introduction

Before discussing modern installations, it is well worth glancing through the installation details of the Savoy theatre in 1882 when Richard D'Oyly Carte revolutionized the illumination of entertainment.

> . . . installation was entrusted to Messrs Siemens Brothers & Co., who appointed one of their electrical staff, Mr C Koppler, to carry out the work on their behalf. The theatre is lighted by no less than 1158 Swan lights of the improved form recently introduced by Mr CH Gimingham of the Swan Electric Light Company, who have adopted it as their most improved pattern. Of these 1158 electric lights, the auditorium is lighted by 114 lamps attached in groups of three, supported on very elegant three-fold brackets projecting from different tiers and balconies, each lamp being enclosed within a ground or opaloid shade, by which arrangement a most soft and pleasing light is produced.
>
> Two hundred and twenty lamps are employed for the illumination of the numerous dressing rooms, corridors and passages belonging to the theatre, while no less than 824 Swan lamps are employed for the lighting of the stage. The stage lights are distributed as follows:

6 rows of 100 lamps each above the stage	600
1 row of 60 lamps each above the stage	60
4 rows of 14 lamps each fixed upright	56
2 rows of 18 lamps each above the stage	36
5 rows of 10 lamps each ground lights	50
2 rows of 11 lamps each above the stage	22
	824

> And in addition to the above-mentioned lights within the theatre, there are eight pilot lights within the engine-room, which serve the purpose of illuminating the machinery; and as they are in the same circuit of the lights in the theatre, they indicate to the engineer in charge of the machines, by the changing of their illuminating power, when the lights on the stage are turned up or down.
>
> The lamps are at present worked in parallel circuits in six groups, five of which comprise two hundred lamps each, and the fifth embraces one hundred

and sixty-six lamps. The current of each group is produced by one of Messrs Siemens Brothers' W_1 alternate current machines the field magnets of which are excited by a separate dynamo-electric machine of the Siemens type, known as D_7 and which is in general form similar to that shown. The machines and engines are fixed in a shed erected on a piece of waste land adjacent to the Victorian Embankment, the current being conveyed to the theatre by means of insulated cable laid beneath the soil.

The most interesting feature however, from a scientific point of view, of this most interesting installation is the method by which the lights in all parts of the establishment are under control, for any series of lights can in an instant be turned up to their full power or gradually lowered to a dull red heat as easily as if they were gas lamps, by the simple turning of a small handle. There are six of these regulating handles – corresponding to the number of the machines and circuits – arranged side by side against the wall of a little room or rather closet on the left of the stage, and each of these handles is a six-way switch which, by throwing into its corresponding magnet circuit greater or less resistance (increasing or decreasing it in six stages), the strength of the current passing through the lamps is lessened or increased by as many grades.

. . . we would also point out that it is part of the Swan system as is that of Mr Edison, to make use of little fusible safety shunts at various places in the circuits, so that if from any cause there occurs any liability for the conductors to become overheated the current is instantly interrupted. . . .

The installation of lighting systems has a major impact on safety. It introduces large mechanical loads to structures. Heavyweight devices are hung over areas which may be populated by the public, artistes or technicians. The lighting system introduces electricity to many areas and, particularly when this is on flexible leads feeding equipment, can be a source of danger. The majority of electrical wiring in areas concerned with the entertainment industry will be used for the lighting system and associated with it will be large power supplies. Most of the heat generated in the building will probably come from the lights being used. If we do not install the electrical system concerned with lighting correctly, it can cause fire hazards and also it has to be handled properly. The electrical and mechanical systems installed can maim or even kill if we fool with them. Therefore, there is a necessity to install lighting systems as safely as humanly possible.

Lighting systems for the theatre have to be integrated with the scenery flying system; there is also a fundamental requirement that from an aesthetic point of view and for the comfort of the audience, lighting should be as unobtrusive as possible. The theatre has not really changed its method of lighting for many years; thus there is a recognizable pattern to the installation of lighting systems in the theatre and this is generally adhered to. This is not to say that the theatre is behind with new ideas, but most of these are in the types of luminaires used in the theatre. We therefore apologize at this stage (if you'll pardon the pun) and state that the majority of the discussion in this chapter will mainly concern the television industry. There will be spin-offs for the film industry and stage, but the greatest area of development in recent years has been in the television industry, initially caused by being last in the entertainment arena, and subsequently television programme makers seem to have larger budgets with which to install capital plant and thus experiment with new ideas.

May we make a plea to all architects to contact a reliable lighting consultant before deciding on the shape and size of any place of entertainment. We have both experienced the problem of being called in at a late stage in construction and being presented with a *fait accompli*, having no regard for the technical requirements.

10.1 Project team

Before discussing the technical aspects of installing lighting systems we need to have a team of people who will be intimately involved with the planning and construction of such systems. Normally, on large installations, a 'project team' would be formed consisting of senior key personnel. These would comprise the **architect** who will be responsible for the overall planning of the building installation and its associated services. His major concern will be the construction of a pleasing building or conversion of an existing building, together with the correct installation of any technical plant. He will be aided in his work by a **quantity surveyor**, who will cost the work and thus enable the architect to make decisions with regard to the budget. One of the main concerns of the architect will be the size of the structure required to support lighting systems together with the weights involved. To solve the structural problems that will arise, a **structural engineer** will work very closely with the architect, and it is his calculations that will decide the structure of the building. The lighting produces tremendous heat loads in a structure and obviously from the point of view of audience or artistes' comfort, these loads have to be successfully dealt with. The person concerned with this aspect of the installation will be an **air conditioning engineer**. One of his main problems will be that to move the vast quantities of hot air requires large amounts of plant which have to be housed somewhere in or on the building; the other problem being that the air conditioning itself can generate noise. This brings us to another valuable member of the team – the **acoustic engineer/architect** whose responsibility will be to ensure good acoustics for either the audience in the theatre or for the reception of sound in film and television studios. Major concerns to him will be the shape of the building and the noise generated by equipment, such as air conditioning, etc. and how this can be adequately dealt with. Finally, we have two people who will work extremely closely together, one of which is the **lighting consultant**, designing the lighting system and responsible for the technical aspects of lifting equipment such as motorized bars, cyclorama support systems, the dimmers and the provision of lights themselves. The other important member of this two-man team will be the **electrical engineer** concerned with the installation. One of his prime functions will be to interpret the needs of the lighting consultant for the wiring, the lighting power sockets and the power supplies needed for the lighting in the building. In addition, he will be concerned with the electrical supply for the air conditioning system and the general lighting in the premises, together with normal power sockets around the building. He will also be involved with fire detection and emergency lighting systems for either audience, technical staff or artistes.

Items to be considered by the project team are as follows.

1. **Building construction**
   (a) Floor
   (b) Walls
   (c) Ceiling or roof structure
   (d) Access to studio
   (e) Ancillary and control areas
2. **Studio size**
   (a) Length
   (b) Width
   (c) Grid height
   (d) Overall height
3. **Ventilation**
   (a) Position in studio
   (b) Capability
4. **Power system**
   (a) Method of supply, i.e. single or three phase, 'Star' or 'Delta'
   (b) Voltage and current rating of incoming supply
5. **Lighting requirement**
   (a) Type of cameras
   (b) Light levels required
6. **Studio requirements**
   (a) Scenic design facilities
   (b) Main lighting
   (c) Cyc lighting
   (d) Effects lighting
   (e) Special facilities, e.g. remote control of lighting power
7. **Control and dimming requirements**
   (a) Type of lighting control console
   (b) Location of lighting console
   (c) Number of dimmers
   (d) Location of dimmers
   (e) Provision of power and switchgear for dimmers
   (f) Provision of remote control consoles for winch systems and lighting.
8. **Special requirements**
   (a) Provision of movable scenery
   (b) Switching of lighting in remote areas; or, remote control of the system from two or more points.
9. **Provisions for safety**
   (a) Smoke detectors/sprinklers
   (b) Local authority requirements
   (c) Users' requirements

10.2 Safety requirements

As the requirements of safety have become more onerous in the theatre, film and television industries with the introduction of the Health and Safety at Work Act 1974 and the Electricity at Work Regulations 1989, these now have a major influence on the installations themselves. Therefore, it would probably be sensible to discuss this first, so that we can see how they influence the decisions ultimately made by the project team.

If we go back in the history of the theatre, which was the major area of entertainment for many years, we find that there have been several tragic accidents, and most of these were caused by fire. Fire in the entertainment industry usually comes from the acting area itself, often caused by the use of wooden scenery together with the close proximity of various types of light. In years gone by, naked flames were quite common, but in more recent times the use of small electronically driven candle effects has been introduced, thus reducing the amount of naked flames in use. One shudders to think before the introduction of such devices what the modern version of *Phantom of the Opera* would have looked like with all naked flames. On a stage any fire within the area created by the proscenium arch and the rear of stage will funnel towards the fly tower itself, causing a venturi effect, which creates a powerful upward draught, enhancing the heat generated.

If we have a standard stage, which has a proscenium arch, it is relatively easy to have a safety curtain to drop down at the front of the stage thereby providing an immense barrier between the audience and the stage. Over the stage would be provided a water sprinkling system which would be activated by any heat over the normal design levels. Many modern theatres do not necessarily provide the standard proscenium arch, but they do have stages that protrude into the auditorium, and if this is the case, the safety standards on the stage area have to be much higher owing to the close proximity of the public during a performance. One of the problems in any premises with a fire is that there is a tendency for people to panic in such conditions. It is relatively easy to train the permanent staff manning a building, and for that matter the artistes concerned with the production, in the most safe way to exit from the area of work. It becomes much more difficult with the public because of the inability to train them in the direction of where to go safely when a fire breaks out. Thus, there is a need for clearly marked 'exits', correctly defined passageways for staff, artistes and audience to evacuate a building. Although sprinkler systems are commonly used in the theatre because they can extinguish fires very effectively, they are somewhat of a hazard in the film and television industry as generally much more lighting will be involved together with a lot of technical equipment. There is obviously a desire, if a fire breaks out, not to damage too much of the existing technical plant. To this end, smoke detectors and 'rate of temperature rise' detectors have been used in more recent years to warn the local staff of problems, and these can also be coupled via the telephone network to the local fire department.

With any planned development of any premises, either existing or proposed, it is most important to involve the local fire authority at an early stage so that they are consulted on what should take place within the building. Having discussed the general entertainment area itself, such as the stage or studio, there is also a requirement that all the adjacent areas have to be safe as well, such as dressing rooms, control rooms, dimmer rooms, and so on. A good example of applied safety is that of a dimmer room which may have a door opening into the active area itself, and which will require another access door, generally at the opposite end of the room so that operators can evacuate away from areas of potential hazard. In film and television studios, there is a need to have defined fire lanes within the studio active area, so that people can exit safely from an area of great potential danger. Most modern television studios are built with a marked fire lane, which has to remain clear of any obstructions, around the perimeter. They also have to be equipped with a certain number of exits according to size. In television and film studios, acoustic barriers are often formed by having twin doors through a small lobby from the corridors adjacent to studios to the studio area itself. It is obviously important that these allow a safe exit. The various Codes of Practice which have to be adhered to and which will probably be the main concern of the architect, are laid down in British Standards and by various Acts of Parliament.

An area of great concern for safety is the mechanical structure formed above the acting area. This will usually weigh several tonnes and will be bolted and have pieces of moving machinery sitting on the structure itself. Thus, other than the static load of the weight of the equipment, we have the dynamic loads when the motors and lifting gear are operated, lifting scenery and luminaires from the acting area. Devices rigged to the mechanical structure such as the luminaires, pantographs, technical fittings of any description and scenery equipment, all pose areas of potential danger. Almost on a par with the mechanical problems are the electrical problems. Although it is not very likely that an electrical socket will suddenly work free and fall to the studio floor in normal operation, it is quite possible that any malfunction of the electrical system can cause fire. It is also important from the operator's point of view that the electrical system is installed to all known regulations so that the highest safety standards are maintained.

10.3 Green field sites and the refurbishment of existing premises

The architect may have been given a brief for a 'green field' site, which means building new premises from scratch, or the refurbishment of existing premises. In the first case, that of new premises, the architect obviously starts with a blank piece of paper and can incorporate many new ideas and suggestions. If, however, it is the refurbishment of existing premises, he is constrained by what he can do within the building, the limits being caused by the physical structure of the building and the loads that would be acceptable to that structure, how much space there is for the development or how extra space can be created within the development. Unfortunately for the poor architect every interested technical person has an input which usually conflicts with the rest of the team. For example, it might be that the lighting consultant, to meet the needs of his client, requires to make the area as large as possible, together with extremely high lighting and thus electrical loads, which will all cause problems for the air conditioning man and the electrical engineer. With all these changes to the structure and shape, the poor acoustics specialist starts to tear his hair out with all the extra work that this is going to entail. The structural engineer, at this point, probably has his eyes firmly fixed on the ceiling thinking of all the terrible calculations he has to make so that the architect can be satisfied that the building won't fall down.

Having said this, of course, most project teams work extremely harmoniously and usually generate a good team spirit. At this stage it is clear that a great deal of compromise will have to be reached on the installation itself. Thus, where do we start?

In an existing installation, the size of the studio or, for that matter, stage area, will be fixed, and very seldom will it be changed. It might be that new mechanical devices are incorporated in the new installation or the electrical installation is changed, but generally the size and height of the area is fixed. This is probably a good thing from the architect's point of view because it places quite logical constraints on what can happen within the area chosen for development. It may be that the existing lighting grid structure remains unchanged, the only alterations being changing the luminaires supplied to the premises themselves. If this is the case, the constraints already laid down by the lifting capacity of the equipment installed will dictate the type of luminaires purchased. If, however, some of the facilities are to be changed so that greater lifting capacity can be used, this will have a knock-on effect on the structural engineer's calculations, due to the devices imposing greater loads on the structure. It is quite conceivable that although the weight of the equipment does not increase, the power required for the equipment is higher; thus the electrical engineer will have to update his power system and the ventilation engineer will probably have a potential problem with the existing air conditioning plant. The room used to house the dimmers, if such a room exists, which was probably quite adequate, possibly now becomes inadequate by an increase in the number of dimmers required. All of this presupposes that the lighting consultant can actually do what he wants. Unfortunately, in any modern system, we also have to handle scenery, and this places constraints on the disposition of lighting bars in a system; it also dictates the spacing between lighting bars or trackways. The size of the luminaires involved will also dictate spacings in the grid. A modern controversy that reigns quite a lot these days is where do we put control rooms? In the theatre, control rooms with a window having a clear view of the stage are obviously desired for those staff operating sound systems and the lighting control console. In television there is not an overwhelming need to see in the studio as the pictures from the cameras will tell the operating staff what is happening. There is, however, a need for rapid access for the LD and people concerned with the production from the control rooms to the studio and to this end many studios built today have control rooms at floor level. In the theatre, and also for film or television, a walkover grid is highly desirable for the ease of suspending items of equipment from the grid itself. One of the major problems of walkover grids is that the building is required to be higher, or in a fixed building the proposed grid is forced to be lower. In an existing building the walls may not be capable of taking additional loads

Figure 2.12 is a colour filter comparison table. The data, organised by manufacturer / product line and by the five colour swatch series (Series 1 = lightest → Series 5 = darkest), reads as follows:

Manufacturer	Type	Series no.	Series 1	Series 2	Series 3	Series 4	Series 5
Lee	effects	100			174	196	161
Lee	correction	200		202		201	
	HT 100 effects						
Cinemoid	effects	100	67				61
Chris James	Effects	100			174		161
Chris James	correction	200	218 203	202		201	
Chris James	effects	300					
Roscolux	effects	300 / 100	62	60 61	63	64	65
Supergel	effects	300 / 100		61	63	64	65
Cinecolor	effects	600	649	648	647 650	651 655	654
Roscolene	effects	800					
Cinegel	correction	3000	3216 3208	3206	3204	3202	
Cromagel	effects	300 / 100			61	64	65
Chromoid	effects	100		167		161	145
Strand	correction	200	218 203	202		201	
Strand	effects	400				474	461
Gamcolor	effects	1000	870 885	830 820	842	860 888 880 882 / 840	815
Gamcolor Cinefilter	correction	3000				1526	
Arri	effects	100			174		161
Arri	correction	200	218 203	202		201	
Arri	effects	300					
Gelatran	effects	100			72	65	69

Figure 2.12 Colour filter comparison table

Gel/filter colour cross-reference chart

Number series	Lee effects 100	Lee correction 200	HT 100 effects	Cinemoid effects 100	Chris James Effects 100	Chris James correction 200	Chris James effects 300	Roscolux effects 300/100	Supergel effects 300/100	Cinecolor effects 600	Roscolene effects 800	Cinegel correction 3000	Cromagel effects 300/100	Chromoid effects 100	Strand correction 200	Strand effects 400	Gamcolor effects 1000	Cinefilter correction 3000	Arri effects 100	Arri correction 200	Arri effects 300	Gelatran effects 100
																	847 848					
	165			32	165			67	67		851					465	810		165			71
								68	68	656			68	91								
								78	78		856		78	86								
	132		132		132		357	81 84	81 84				81	92		432	910		132		357	66
	197		197 079	63			361	80 79	79	653 657	857 861		79	119			835				361	64
	119		119	19	119			82	82				82	163		419	845		119			
								85	85		862		85	93								
	195		195				363	74	74	661	863		74	140			850				363	
								83									890 915					
	120		120	20	120			383	383		866					420	905		120			60
	181		181		181			385	385							481			181			61

Number series: five grey colour swatches (S1 = lightest → S5 = darkest)

Manufacturer / Product	Series	S1	S2	S3	S4	S5
Lee	effects 100	117	144	143	118, 14	141
Lee	correction 200					
Lee	HT 100 effects				118, 183	141
Cinemoid	effects 100	45, 17	40, 86	43	18	41, 62
Chris James	Effects 100	117	144	143	118, 183	141
Chris James	correction 200					
Chris James	effects 300	349	350	353	360	
Rosco — Roscolux	effects 300/100	66				69, 76, 77
Rosco — Supergel	effects 300/100	66				69, 76
Rosco — Cinecolor	effects 600				658	659
Rosco — Roscolene	effects 800	848		853, 850		859
Rosco — Cinegel	correction 3000					
Cromagel	effects 300/100	66				69, 76
Strand — Chromoid	effects 100	117				141, 162
Strand	correction 200					
Strand	effects 400	417	444	443	418, 483	441
Gamcolor — Gamcolor	effects 1000	790	780, 730	770, 760	740, 750	
Gamcolor — Cinefilter	correction 3000					
Arri	effects 100	117	144	143	118, 183	141
Arri	correction 200					
Arri	effects 300	349	350	353	360	
Gelatran	effects 100				76	

Cross-reference chart of lighting filters by number series. The "Number series" row is represented by five colour swatches (Colour 1–Colour 5).

Series	Colour 1	Colour 2	Colour 3	Colour 4	Colour 5
Lee 100 effects				115	116
Lee 200 correction	242	241			
HT 100 effects				115	116
Cinemoid 100 effects					
Chris James 100 Effects				115	116
Chris James 200 correction	219				
Chris James 300 effects					
Roacolux 100 / 300 effects	92	93	70, 72, 71, 73	15, 354	16, 95
Supergel 100 / 300 effects			70, 72, 71, 73		95
Cinecolor 600 effects	673	677, 676, 675	652	613	
Roscolene 800 effects			849, 855, 854		877
Cinegel 3000 correction					
Cromagel 100 / 300 effects			70, 72, 73		95
Chromoid 100 effects			87, 144	115	116
Strand 200 correction	219				
Strand 400 effects				415	416
Gamcolor 1000 effects	680, 685	720	725	710, 690	
Cinefilter 3000 correction					
Arri 100 effects				115	116
Arri 200 correction	219				
Arri 300 effects					
Gelatran 100 effects				36	

The following reproduces a cross-reference chart of gel/filter "Number series" (shown as five grey swatches, from lightest to darkest) across several manufacturers. The table has been transposed for legibility: each manufacturer series is a row, and the five number-series swatches are columns (Swatch 1 = lightest … Swatch 5 = darkest).

Manufacturer	Series	No.	Swatch 1	Swatch 2	Swatch 3	Swatch 4	Swatch 5
Gelatran	effects	100		47			
Arri	effects	300			378	371	
Arri	correction	200	213				
Arri	effects	100	138	121	122	124	139
Gamcolor	Cinefilter correction	3000					
Gamcolor	Gamcolor effects	1000	520, 535	540	570	660	655, 650
Strand	Strand effects	400	438	421	422	424	439
Strand	Strand correction	200	213				
Strand	Chromoid effects	100	151	121	122	123	94, 124
Strand	Cromagel effects	300/100	96	86	89	389, 94	90
Rosco	Cinegel correction	3000	3317, 3316, 3315, 3304				
Rosco	Roscolene effects	800			878	871	874
Rosco	Cinecolor effects	600	669, 671, 642		672		674
Rosco	Supergel effects	300/100	96, 388	86	89	389, 94	90
Rosco	Roscolux effects	300/100	87, 96, 88	51	388, 86	89, 389, 94	90, 91
Chris James	effects	300			378	371	
Chris James	correction	200	213				
Chris James	Effects	100	138	121	122	124	139
Cinemoid	Cinemoid effects	100	77, 38	21	22	23, 24	39
HT	effects	100		121	122	124	139
Lee	correction	200	213	243			
Lee	effects	100	138	121	122	124	139

Filter number cross-reference chart (colours shown as grey swatches in the "Number series" column):

Number series	Lee 100 effects	Lee 200 correction	HT 100 effects	Cinemoid 100 effects	Chris James 100 Effects	Chris James 200 correction	Chris James 300 effects	Roscolux 300/100 effects	Supergel 300/100 effects	Cinecolor 600 effects	Roscolene 800 effects	Cinegel 3000 correction	Cromagel 300/100 effects	Chromoid 100 effects	Strand 200 correction	Strand 400 effects	Gamcolor 1000 effects	Cinefilter 3000 correction	Arri 100 effects	Arri 200 correction	Arri 300 effects	Gelatran 100 effects
swatch 1 (grey)										642							980					
swatch 2 (light grey)							340	54	54				54	172		436					340	
swatch 3 (medium grey)	136			36	136			52	52		840		52	136		470	970		136			
swatch 4 (dark grey)	170				170		339	47/48	48	638	838/839		48	126		469	990		170		339	
swatch 5 (black)	126			26	126			49	49				49	96		426	995		126			81

Number series	Gelatran 100 effects	Arri 300 effects	Arri 200 correction	Arri 100 effects	Gamcolor Cinefilter 3000 correction	Gamcolor 1000 effects	Strand 400 effects	Strand 200 correction	Strand Chromoid 100 effects	Strand Cromagel 300/100 effects	Cinegel 3000 correction	Rosco Roscolene 800 effects	Rosco Cinecolor 600 effects	Supergel 300/100 effects	Roscolux 300/100 effects	Chris James 300 effects	Chris James 200 correction	Chris James 100 Effects	Cinemoid 100 effects	HT 100 effects	Lee 200 correction	Lee 100 effects
Swatch 1						920			89	53				53	53				71			
Swatch 2		342		137			437		171	55		841		55	55	342		137	42			137
Swatch 3		344		142		940 / 960	442					844	641	356	356	344		142				142
Swatch 4	88	343		180		950	480		137 / 88	57 / 58		842 / 843	639 / 644	57 / 58	57 / 58	343		180	058			194 / 180
Swatch 5	62					948 / 925 / 945 / 930			170	56		846	645	358 / 56	358 / 56 / 59				25			

Number series	Lee 100 effects	Lee 200 correction	Lee HT 100 effects	Lee Cinemoid 100 effects	Chris James 100 Effects	Chris James 200 correction	Chris James 300 effects	Rosco Roscolux 100 / 300 effects	Rosco Supergel 100 / 300 effects	Rosco Cinecolor 600 effects	Rosco Roscolene 800 effects	Rosco Cinegel 3000 correction	Strand Cromagel 100 / 300 effects	Strand Chromoid 100 effects	Strand 200 correction	Strand 400 effects	Gamcolor 1000 effects	Gamcolor Cinefilter 3000 correction	Arri 100 effects	Arri 200 correction	Arri 300 effects	Arri Gelatran 100 effects
	154			53	154											454			154			
	153				153											453			153			
	109			9	109			36 34	36	626	825 826 834		36	110		409	190		109			15
	107		026	7	107			26	26	621			26	106		407	195		107			08
								31	31													
	166				166						832					466	180		166			
	148			48	148											448			148			09
	113			13	113			42		620						413	220		113			

Gel / lighting filter colour cross-reference chart (colour swatch samples shown in the "Number series" column).

Number series	Gelatran effects 100	Arri effects 300	Arri correction 200	Arri effects 100	Gamcolor Cinefilter correction 3000	Gamcolor effects 1000	Strand effects 400	Strand correction 200	Chromoid effects 100	Cromagel effects 300/100	Cinegel correction 3000	Roscolene effects 800	Cinecolor effects 600	Supergel effects 300/100	Roscolux effects 300/100	Chris James effects 300	Chris James correction 200	Chris James Effects 100	Cinemoid effects 100	HT 100 effects	Lee correction 200	Lee effects 100
						108, 107, 106, 155					3318, 3314, 3313		622									
													624	33	33						247	
				110		105	410		108	38	3308		625	38	38, 37			110	10			110
														337	337							
	05					160			90	35			627	35	35							192
	04					170						827										
				111			411		112	43			631	43	43, 44			111	11			111
	63	328				150, 130	412					828				328						
				128		110	428							339	339			128				128
	13	332				120	449		111, 113	45, 46		837		45, 46	45, 46	332			12	046		
						140						836										

Number series	Lee effects 100	Lee correction 200	Lee HT 100 effects	Cinemoid effects 100	Chris James Effects 100	Chris James correction 200	Chris James effects 300	Roscolux effects 300/100	Supergel effects 300/100	Cinecolor effects 600	Roscolene effects 800	Cinegel correction 3000	Cromagel effects 300/100	Chromoid effects 100	Strand correction 200	Strand effects 400	Gamcolor effects 1000	Cinefilter correction 3000	Arri effects 100	Arri correction 200	Arri effects 300	Gelatran effects 100
(swatch 1)	157			57	157											457			157			17
(swatch 2)	193, 166			66																		
(swatch 3)	164		019	64	164			32, 40, 41, 24, 25, 19	32, 40, 24, 25, 19	632	819, 818		32, 40, 24, 25, 19	157, 178, 95, 164, 135		464	280		164			
(swatch 4)	182				182											482	270		182			
(swatch 5)	106		026, 027	6, 14	106		321	27	27		821, 823		27	114		406	235, 245, 250		106		321	08

Manufacturer	Type	No.	1	2	3	4	5	6	7	8
Number series										
Gelatran	effects	100								
Arri	effects	300					308			
Arri	correction	200	223	206				205		204
Arri	effects	100				103				
Gamcolor	Cinefilter correction	3000						1549	1570	
Gamcolor	Gamcolor effects	1000	363		440		365	360	385	
Strand	Strand effects	400			459	403				
Strand	Strand correction	200	223	206				205		204
Strand	Chromoid effects	100					103		98	
Strand	Cromagel effects	300 100					13		09	
Rosco	Cinegel correction	3000	3410	3409			3408			3407
Rosco	Roscolene effects	800			805					
Rosco	Cinecolor effects	600				605	608		613	
Rosco	Supergel effects	300 100					13		09	
Rosco	Roscolux effects	300 100				08	13		09 16	
Chris James	effects	300					308			
Chris James	correction	200	223	206				205		204
Chris James	Effects	100			159	103				
Chris James	Cinemoid effects	100	73				3			
Lee	HT 100 effects									
Lee	correction	200		206	212			205		204
Lee	effects	100			159	103				

Number series cross‑reference chart (table rotated 90° on the page). The five tints shown under "Number series" correspond to the five swatch columns; the numbers below are the equivalent filter references for each manufacturer/series. Column positions (1–7) read left‑to‑right across the chart.

Manufacturer	Series	1	2	3	4	5	6	7
Lee	effects 100			101	104	102	179	105
Lee	correction 200							
HT 100	effects			010			015	020
Cinemoid	effects 100	50		1	4	49 2	46	33
Chris James	Effects 100	156		101	104	102	179	105
Chris James	correction 200	212						
Chris James	effects 300				306	309		315
Rosco	Roscolux effects 300/100	06 07	12 10	312	15	11	14	20
Rosco	Supergel effects 300/100	06 07	10	312	15	11	14	20
Rosco	Cinecolor effects 600	604	609					
Rosco	Roscolene effects 800	804			806 810	809 807		
Rosco	Cinegel correction 3000							
Strand	Cromagel effects 300/100	06 07	10		15	11	14	20
Strand	Chromoid effects 100	159 150		101	146	149	102	97
Strand	Strand correction 200	212						
Strand	Strand effects 400	456		401	404	402	479	405
Gamcolor	Gamcolor effects 1000	510	470	460 480 450		420		350
Gamcolor	Cinefilter correction 3000	1560						
Arri	effects 100	156		101	104	102	179	105
Arri	correction 200	212						
Arri	effects 300				306	309		315
Gelatran	effects 100				41		36	

Gel / colour-filter cross-reference chart (Number series by manufacturer)

Manufacturer	Product / Number series	Codes (listed)
Lee	100 effects	162, 152, 151, 176
Lee	200 correction	
Lee	HT 100 effects	
Chris James	Cinemoid 100 effects	52, 51, 75, 78
Chris James	100 Effects	162, 152, 151, 176
Chris James	200 correction	237
Chris James	300 effects	303
Rosco	Roscolux 100/300 effects	02, 304, 05 / 305, 04 / 03, 01, 30
Rosco	Supergel 100/300 effects	05, 04 / 03, 01, 30
Rosco	Cinecolor 600 effects	602, 603, 617
Rosco	Roscolene 800 effects	802
Rosco	Cinegel 3000 correction	
Strand	Cromagel 100/300 effects	05, 03, 01, 30
Strand	Chromoid 100 effects	154, 152, 175, 176
Strand	Strand 200 correction	237
Strand	Strand 400 effects	462, 452, 451, 476
Gamcolor	Gamcolor 1000 effects	364, 340, 325, 305, 260, 320
Gamcolor	Cinefilter 3000 correction	1552, 1575
Arri	100 effects	162, 152, 151, 176
Arri	200 correction	237
Arri	300 effects	303
Gelatran	100 effects	18, 06

Gel filter cross-reference chart (rotated table). Colours are represented by the five grey swatch columns in the "Number series" row.

Manufacturer	Product / type	Series	Swatch 1	Swatch 2	Swatch 3	Swatch 4	Swatch 5
Gelatran	effects	100		30		20	22
Arri	effects	300		311	313	317	
Arri	correction	200	236				
Arri	effects	100		147	134	158	
Gamcolor	Cinefilter correction	3000	1546	1565			
Gamcolor	Gamcolor effects	1000		375	343	335 345	315 290
Strand	Strand effects	400		447	434	458	135
Strand	Strand correction	200	236				
Strand	Chromoid effects	100				134 158	
Strand	Cromagel effects	300 / 100				21 23	
Rosco	Cinegel correction	3000		3401			
Rosco	Roscolene effects	800		811	813	815 817	
Rosco	Cinecolor effects	600		614 612 610		611 615 618	619
Rosco	Supergel effects	300 / 100				21 23	22
Rosco	Roscolux effects	300 / 100		18	17 321	21 23	22
Chris James	effects	300		311	313	317	
Chris James	correction	200	236				
Chris James	Effects	100		147	134	158	
	Cinemoid effects	100		47	34	5 58	35
	HT 100 effects					021	022
Lee	correction	200	236				
Lee	effects	100		147	134	158	135

Figure 2.4   Munsell system

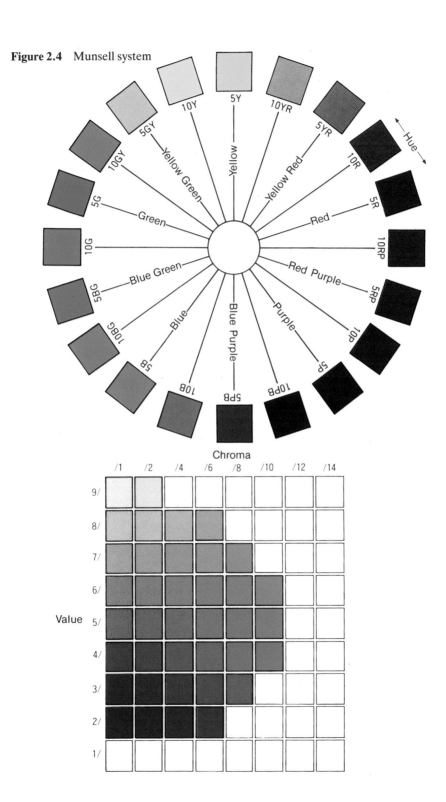

Figure 2.6 CIE chromaticity diagram

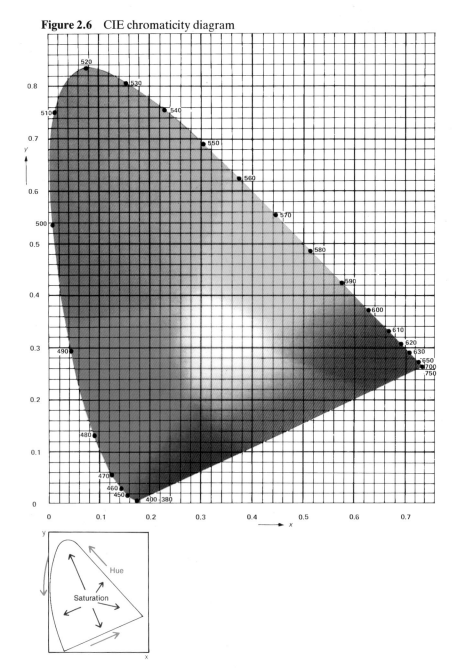

and any new equipment installed require either building alterations to the walls themselves so that the loads become spread or that structures are employed that use the floor area as support. If we are building from scratch on a green field site most of the problems can be taken care of, hopefully with the ingenuity of the architect and the structural engineer. The main requirement in a green field site would be that of the acting area and its associated facilities. There is always a need for large theatre stages, but commonsense has to prevail and generally the architect, having been briefed by the client as to what the requirements are, has to do his best within the budget to meet the planned objectives.

If we were starting from scratch in the film industry, which at this point in time is extremely doubtful, we would be building studios with very large acting areas, i.e. around $1500 \, m^2$ to $3000 \, m^2$. In the film industry, the feeling generally is that a small production can fit into a large studio area but not the other way around. This might appear to be the case for the TV industry as well but because the studios have defined purposes within television, such as small news areas, small presentation areas, medium sized news and current affairs studios or large multipurpose production studios, there are finite limits to areas required. Most of these are established by custom and practice within the industry itself. Another aspect of developments of this type is that film studios tend to be large areas not permanently equipped with technical equipment and are usually provided as large free standing structures.

Television studios are generally integrated into production centres, which may vary from fairly small to very large, such as the BBC Television Centre in London. By integrating a series of box-like structures into a building, the design of the building is greatly influenced. In television there is a need for many adjacent areas to a studio such as make-up and wardrobe facilities, dimmer room, production, lighting, vision and sound control rooms. The disposition of all these areas has a bearing on access ways and vantage points to the studio. In the theatre there is not the need for so many technical rooms as the production is controlled from the stage area. Most of the support areas have to be close to the stage so that artistes are provided with good access to dressing rooms and quick-change areas. A requirement of theatre productions is to have complex mechanical stage lifting arrangements, possibly integrated with orchestral facilities. All of these will have to be considered by the architect so as to integrate the whole system to a meaningful production area and the following sections give the various parameters that need to be observed so that the various requirements of the building are met.

10.4 Building construction and how it can be influenced

Problems in theatre lighting

In the theatre, the height of the grid which will be used for both scenery and lighting will be dictated by the height of the fly tower. Fly towers are used to take scenery from the stage to a safe parking space above the stage area. The height of the fly tower is generally dictated by the audience's sight line from the front seats of the auditorium; thus when the scenery is suspended it should be out of sight and not obtrusive to the audience viewing. As a general guide, the height of the grid is between two and a half and three times the height of the proscenium opening.

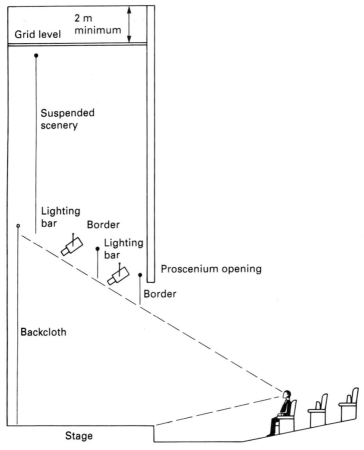

Figure 10.1   Audience sight lines

A practical spacing for the counterweighted barrels used in theatres is around 200–250 mm. This is generally dictated by the requirements for flying cloths and scenery. As counterweight bars may be used for both scenery and lighting, it should be noted that there are practical limitations to the distance between the suspension lines used on the bars themselves. For lightly loaded bars it might be possible to get away with a span of four metres between suspension points but with heavier loaded bars several lines have to be attached to each bar and these would be at around three metre intervals. Unfortunately, although several suspension lines may be used, if heavy point loads are applied to a bar this will cause distortion, and it is preferable to use bars formed as trusses in these circumstances. Several forms of power assistance have been used on counterweight bars in the theatre but in general bars are manually operated. Due to the beam spread of the lights used above the stage it is possible, by using a drawing showing the side elevation, to calculate the coverage of the lights on the stage itself (Figure 10.2). This will then dictate the position and rows of units required to light the whole stage area effectively. If this is the case, it might be that some of the bars could be motor driven and these would be extremely useful for the lighting units themselves.

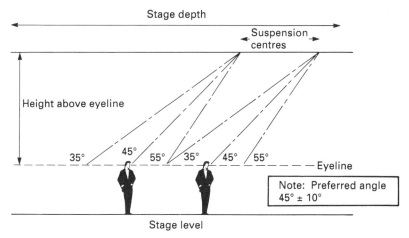

Figure 10.2   Positioning stage luminaires

In addition to the lights above the stage, the front of house lights also have to be considered, and the best solution for this type of lighting is to use lighting bridges across the auditorium which hopefully will be concealed but sometimes can be in view of the audience without being too distracting due to their height above the paying customers.

Wall slots for lighting positions will have to be provided in the sides of the auditorium but where these slots are not available in existing theatres, it will be necessary to rig some vertical scaffolding bars to support the lighting units.

In all the cases discussed, we must have access to the lighting units, so that they can be focused, pointed in the right direction, have their colour filters changed and at times be maintained. It is generally impossible to provide access to reach the bar units above the stage area; thus most of the lighting will be adjusted either with bars at low level or with the aid of 'tall-a-scopes' so that the electricians can adjust the units *in situ*. This is a case where pole operation will probably be justified on the grounds of speed of adjustments during rehearsals. As the front of house luminaires are rigged from a lighting bridge over the auditorium it will be easy for the electricians to reach these units. Luminaires at the side of the auditorium pointing towards the stage also require access and, in new installations, this is usually possible to achieve by having one or two access platforms at reasonable heights. In existing premises, where the equivalent of temporary scaffolding has to be rigged, it is probably a climbing job for the electricians to do most of the adjustments.

Where access is required, such as in the grid and from any of the lighting bridges, sufficient head room must be allowed for the electricians to work in safety. A head clearance height of 2.5 m is usually sufficient.

To sum up then, in the theatre the lighting is usually an adjunct in the design to the scenery system itself. The requirements for power, dimmers and luminaires are somewhat similar to all other systems. The specialist architects who work on theatre design have many years of experience in this field and thus they are aware of many of the pitfalls of modern stage design.

Film and TV studios

If we turn now to the construction of film and television studios, the decisions are somewhat dictated by the needs of the set designer and not by the needs of the audience as in the theatre. In the case of the film industry, it can be said that 'big is beautiful'. Large-scale studios often have wide vista shots taking place, which dictate the height of any cycloramas used. A studio 32m long will require cycs at least 9.5m high and probably higher. If we allow a clearance above the cyc sight line so that luminaires do not intrude, we additionally need at least 1.5m clearance from the top of the cycs to the grid. If, for instance, boats are used in the studio, then even more clearance is required above the cyc line and this would imply an extra 2.5m, thus allowing operators to work at this level without hitting their heads on the grid structure. Film studios are not traditionally equipped with walkover grids, but they do require access at high level, even if it is only walkways to allow access for rigging and de-rigging of the block and tackle units to suspend lines for scenery and luminaires. There is obviously also a need to reach the electrical distribution system at this level where luminaires are being used or power feeds have been dropped from the grid down to lights which may be suspended on block and tackle or some other lifting device.

Attempts have been made in the past to provide some form of mechanized system similar to that used in the television industry. The most famous of these was the installation of a monopole system in two studios at Pinewood in England. The BBC also experimented with the use of motorized barrels at its facility at the old Ealing film studios in London. For most of the time, however, the film industry is content to go on in the same way that it has practised lighting for many years. Thus the prime requirements of the film studio are suspension trackways at fairly frequent intervals down a studio so that lifting equipment may be attached where and when desired. Owing to the sheer physical size and subsequent weight of the luminaires used in the film industry over many years, the grid structures have had to be reasonably robust to take the weights of the equipment: however, saturated lighting, with its well distributed weight load, is not generally used in the industry, one of its main requirements being high point loadings caused by several large, high intensity lights in one small area of the grid structure.

With the construction of a new film studio, it might be that we would have to integrate its use for either film or video shooting. Much of the economy of the film industry these days is based upon the shooting of pop videos and commercials for television. Film studios are fairly simple in their nature, being rather large 'box-like' structures immune to outside noise if designed as sound stages, and constructed in such a way that almost any production can be fitted in them with the provision of high cycloramas. The actual lighting arrangements are extremely basic, with the occasional use of dimmer units for some control on productions. The one big advance that has helped in the film studio is the introduction of discharge lighting taking away the need for the large carbon arcs. These units, with their highly efficient output, require much less power from the electrical system.

Talking about power in systems reminds us that some film stages may still have dc voltage feeders, although in most cases these are being converted to ac systems. Generally there is no need to provide permanent dimmer rooms adjacent to film studios, although if new studios did evolve for dual purpose film/vision systems, then a provision should be made so that fairly large dimmer installations could be added at a later date in the studio's life. The general requirement in film studios is for large power distribution cabinets, placed at regular intervals around the studio, from which can be taken all the temporary feeds to the lighting units themselves. Whereas in TV studios highly sophisticated air conditioning systems are used, the film industry is still fairly basic in its requirements. Due to the nature of filming, which may be a rehearsal period and then a 'take' with long extended intervals between, it is easy to allow the premises to cool over periods of time. However, it must be said, in modern television studios the use of rehearse/record techniques using a few sets at a time diminishes the requirement for the large air conditioning systems at present employed.

The need to contain costs within the television industry is paramount and it is strongly suspected that other than refurbishing existing studios, very few new studios will now be constructed, either in Europe or America. What may be required is the conversion of some premises for studio use and this is highlighted by the case of the Greenwood theatre in London, converted from a theatre for use as a multipurpose television studio in 1979 by the BBC. It is interesting to examine this installation to see some of the problems that arise during the conversion process. The Greenwood theatre when acquired for use by the BBC was some four years old, and therefore all its facilities were very modern and the basic structure was very good. The stage area was reasonably generous and it had a section of the stage capable of being raised and lowered on jacks, thus allowing part of the stage to be converted for use as an orchestral pit. To maximize its use for television the stage was extended by removing some of the audience seating. This stage extension was built from wood and had to be capable of taking loads up to $488 \, \text{kg/m}^2$ ($100 \, \text{lbs/ft}^2$). Thus it was possible for cameras and sets to be on the audience side of the proscenium, which transgressed the normal fire curtain arrangements.

Other than the stage area to the rear of the proscenium opening, there was now a requirement to light 'television style' over the extension to the stage and also above the audience itself. The requirement over the stage extension was met by providing seven additional bars, each 7 m long and spaced at approximately 1.7 m intervals; the bars were arranged for coverage from front to back of the theatre and not across the area. Four bars were installed above the audience, each approximately 6 m long to give frontal coverage to the stage, and these were installed across the auditorium. The weight of the new bars did not pose any problems with the structure itself being a very modern installation.

Major problems emerged from the conversion of the Greenwood theatre for television use; these were concerned with the provision of heavier television lights, using the existing counterweight bars, above the stage area as opposed to the normal fairly lightweight luminaires of less power used by the theatre industry. As the theatre was going to be used for three

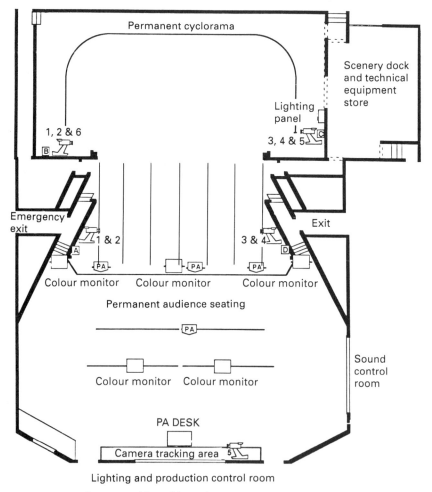

Figure 10.3   Greenwood barrel layout

standard productions per week it was relatively easy to come up with standard lighting plots to cover these and thus choose the luminaires necessary for illumination. The final choice was to use 2.5/5 kW Fresnel luminaires of fairly lightweight construction, produced by Ianiro of Italy, together with standard 2.5/5 kW softlights, also produced by Ianiro. To make life easier on a day-to-day basis, and because the installation was possibly only for a period of two years, it was decided to wire the supply to all the bars in flexible cables, with free socket outlets at the end of each power feed. The majority of wiring was to provide 5 kW circuits although a few 10 kW circuits were used.

So that the lighting rig could be serviced relatively easily by electricians from tall step ladders on the stage itself, all the cables were fed from the fly gallery across to the bars on loops of cable so that they could be raised and lowered without having to disconnect any of the wiring, similar in principle to the 'tripe' cabling used in theatres. The wiring was taken along the bars and dropped off at regular intervals to suit the disposition of the luminaires. The problem arose when calculations revealed that the weight of the cables attached to the bars, plus the weight of the TV luminaires, would exceed the existing fly bar safe working load. To reduce the load per bar, it was decided to operate pairs of bars for the lighting system so that one bar had all the luminaires fitted and its adjacent bar carried the cables; thus the load was fairly well spread. To avoid any errors in operation, the two bars were tethered together by wire bonds. The counterweight buckets were also incapable of taking any more standard cast iron weights to enable these lighting bars to be balanced easily, and therefore special lead weights were manufactured and introduced onto the buckets to enable balance to be achieved.

The theatre had 30 fly bars installed and of these eight were used for luminaires and cables. Three twin barrels were used for the main lighting over the stage. Additionally, two single barrels less densely loaded, were used at the rear of the stage for back lights and effects. One bar was used for the house tabs and 11 other bars were used for either drapes or scenery to be used on the three productions in the theatre.

Having surmounted the loading problems on the bars, it appeared that there might be a problem with the heat generated by the new luminaires over the stage area and going into the fly tower, where a sprinkler system was installed. Experiments took place over many hours with maximum lighting load (we might add with the sprinkler system drained down!) to ascertain whether the sprinkler heads would rupture and thus cause a problem in practice. Luckily the experiments proved that the existing sprinkler system was capable of handling the 200kW of lighting over the stage area. The original theatre dimmers were installed at the side of the theatre with electrical feeds going to the stage area, but due to the need for heavier cables and the consequent cost, it was felt that the television system should have its dimmers nearer the grid so that the cables had a shorter route and consequently 120 dimmers were installed on the fly gallery on the opposite side to the counterweight system. These dimmers, in low density racks of 20 to reduce floor weight loading, unfortunately caused problems as the fans forcing air through the dimmers created acoustic noise which was picked up by the microphones on stage. As the dimmers were contained in racks with a lot of space, it was felt that the solid state devices in them could run at slightly higher temperatures than normal. Thus, the fuses for the fan units were removed and over several days experiments took place to ascertain the temperature of the dimmers. Luckily, they performed satisfactorily with no problems and in fact, to this date, have been running over 11 years. This may be a case for lower density dimmer racks on some occasions. Please note!

Although the Greenwood was converted for a forecast period of two years' temporary occupation to ease the BBC's studio usage at that time, the premises are still in use today and although not now owned by the BBC are operated by an independent production house.

Let us now turn our attention to the design of lighting systems for television studios and how those designs will influence the building construction. Most television studios use a complex grid which in itself poses installation problems; but prior to that is the need to ascertain the height of the grid and clearance above for services and personnel. There have been cases over the years where the management and accountants were convinced by the arguments put forward by architects saying that for each 300 mm of additional height in a studio enormous additional costs were incurred. Thus certain studios were limited in height, only to find the programme makers were forever complaining about the limitations imposed in these studios. As a starting point it is extremely important to get the height of the studio correct and the following system gives the method of calculation. It is relatively easy to decide upon the acting area that is required and consequently the floor dimensions. However, an important parameter that can only be ascertained by examination of the camera viewing angles is that of the cyc height and its subsequent effect on wide shots in a studio.

Cyclorama heights

Camera viewing aspect ratio = 4:3. Assuming a 36° lens is used this gives a vertical angle of shot = 27°.

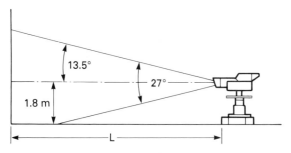

Figure 10.4   Cyclorama heights

Note: By knowing the aspect ratio and horizontal angle of view, the vertical angle can always be derived.

Assume a lens height of 1.8 m above floor level. Cyclorama height = (L × tan 13.5°) + 1.8 m. Cyclorama heights (in metres) for studios with different maximum floor area dimensions (in metres) are shown in Table 10.1.

Table 10.1   Studio dimensions and cyclorama heights

Max studio dimension	Cyc. height	Max studio dimension	Cyc. height
6	3.2	20	6.6
8	3.7	22	7.1
10	4.2	24	7.6
12	4.7	26	8.0
14	5.2	28	8.5
16	5.6	30	9.0
18	6.1	32	9.5

To see how the studio height has been influenced by the choice of the cyclorama height the following example is given:

Studio dimensions	= 30 m × 24 m
Cyclorama height for 30 m	= 9 m
Height allowance above the top of the cyc for luminaires and pantographs from the suspension system	= 2 m
Therefore the grid height	= 11 m
Allowance above the grid for maintenance	= 2.5 m
Allowance for air conditioning and services above the grid maintenance area	= 2.5 m
Total studio height	= 11 + 2.5 + 2.5 = 16 m

The example quoted is for a conventional studio with a barrel grid. The figures still hold for monopole grids, but if no access is required above the grid, or ventilation is provided such that access is not impeded, then the total height could be reduced.

In the smaller studios little or no access is required at high level, the only space requirements generally being for the air conditioning equipment and electrical services.

10.5 Structural loads

Monopole installations

Monopole grids consist of continuous longitudinal trackways at very regular intervals usually engineered from steel, because they will wear so much better than lighter weight materials such as aluminium. At right angles to the main trackways, again at regular intervals, are the changeover tracks to enable monopoles to be wheeled from one track to another.

The method of construction of a monopole grid is to have a series of oblong platforms, made from steel with aluminium decking infill, individually suspended from the under side of the primary steels which will generally be used to support the roof of the studio. The long sides of the platforms form the main trackways and the short sides are the cross over tracks.

In the monopole system the mechanical loads on the structure can move around the grid; in comparison, a barrel grid, because of the design of the system, spreads the structural load fairly evenly. If we take as an example a monopole capable of lifting 60 kg, it will have a self-weight of approximately the same amount; thus its total overall weight will be 120 kg. Therefore the point loading on the grid is 120 kg every time one of these units is used. The next problem arises when considering how many units per linear run we could use, and for television it is quite possible that a high density of monopoles have to be provided and allowance made for the units to work almost next to each other, although it is doubtful that more than about 20 would be used in any one cluster. For the structural engineer concerned, the problem is that these large lumps of metal can move around the structure and appear almost anywhere. Therefore a monopole grid has to be extremely strong and thus tends to be quite heavy. All this creates loading problems for the structural engineer and the architect to incorporate into their design. To give some idea of possible loadings in a studio it may be that 120 motorized monopoles are used in a studio of some 600 m^2. This represents a load, just for positioning the lights, of 14.4 tonnes. If there is a need to cluster the light sources, for example, 16 lights formed into a square would occupy approximately 4 m × 4 m and present a load of 1.92 tonnes to that area, which, of course, is a high point loading.

Another problem arises inasmuch that if we started all the units up at the same time, the dynamic load on that portion of the grid would be considerable and we certainly would not want it springing and oscillating every time we moved equipment. Therefore, it has to be reasonably rigid, and this requirement also dictates the need for fairly beefy grid structures. In addition to the basic grid, there is a need for loading platforms adjacent to the grid for rigging monopoles into the trackways. Possibly suspended just below grid level around the studio are walkways, used for access to power feeds and specially rigged peripheral luminaires. Approximately 1 m from the edge of the studio there will be a permanent cyc track. Trap doors have to be provided for lifting equipment into the grid area, either built into the grid itself or at the side of the studio. Owing to the highly flexible nature of monopole grids they only require a certain basic amount of luminaires because these can be moved around to suit the production. Figures for luminaire requirements are given in the next section.

Barrel installations

Many American studios are equipped with counterweight barrel systems where the length of the bar may be around 4–5 m. Studios are generally equipped with a reasonable density of this type of barrel. The nice thing about counterweight bars from the structural man's point of view is that the load on the grid is usually the basic SWL of the bar itself and most of the weight is contained within the counterweight system, usually mounted on the studio walls. Some barrel studios have been constructed with bar units in the studio area with the support wires taken via diverter pulleys to the edge of the studio where the motor units are mounted on the walls. In most modern barrel studios where the scenery handling facilities are integrated into the grid structure the motor winding units for the scenery lifting system are mounted on the side walls of the studio. Most of the problems for the structural engineer with grid designs arise with the heavy motorized barrel units which may be of the standard type with motors mounted at grid level or self-climbing units with integral motors. Even if the system uses self-climbing units, the total weight presented to the grid structure at any point is approximately the same.

Most barrel studios are constructed with the bar units approximately 1.5 m apart with an end-to-end spacing of approximately 1 m. Thus, having been given the studio area which does not include the fire lane, it is relatively easy to work out how many bar units will be employed. To take account of cyclorama tracks which are radiused at the corners of the studio short bar units may be employed in the four corners of the studio.

In a monopole grid, because the slots provided at grid level are very similar to those in the theatre, it is relatively easy to drop spot lines for holding scenery up or suspending scenery pieces. In barrel studios, it is important that provision is made for the use of scenery and many modern studios have specially installed scenery winching systems, which run in between the main bars themselves. It is fairly obvious that the easiest installation for scene winches is in the same orientation as the bars. Going crosswise across the bar system could pose considerable problems. Motorized barrel winch units, when they are of the standard type, are usually supported lengthways along twin structural members.

In a studio of some considerable span these members have to be supported at frequent intervals to take account of the load; thus several upright members between the grid and the primary steels have to be used and consequently the studio is not totally unobstructed. This point must be brought to mind when designing walkover grids so that access is reasonable. A typical barrel winch unit will weigh approximately 150 kg, with a lifting capacity of almost the same amount, so the total load on the grid from any one winch unit may be around 300 kg. The encouraging thing from the point of view of the structural engineer and architect is that these loads are fixed in position in the grid. The weights given here assume the use of bar units approximately 2.5 to 3.0 m long. If we use shorter units the relative weights are somewhat similar from the point of view of the structural man; i.e. a shorter bar unit may have only half the lifting capacity of a long unit and its motor unit, mounted at the grid, may be only around 75% of a big unit but we will use twice as many bars in the studio. Thus the total load on the grid is approximately the same.

Most studios fitted with barrel systems operate with a high density of lighting. It may be in the BBC style of multipurpose luminaires rigged permanently to the barrels, or rather like some of the studios in New York,

Figure 10.5   Winch unit mounted in grid

where many 2 kW and 1 kW luminaires are rigged per barrel, just for ease of general operation.

To avoid dynamic loading problems on the grid in many of the studios that use motorized devices it is more likely that some restriction is placed on the amount of units used at any one time

The smaller studio

Smaller studios such as those using motorized or spring pantographs will have long trackways where, rather like the monopole studio, the loads can be grouped in areas. The weight of equipment in these studios is significantly less than motorized barrel and monopole systems. However, due to the nature of operations in studios of this type, their load is fairly well spread throughout the structure and, of course, can be contained by loading notices which prohibit too much clustering within the studio area. Perhaps only about 40 luminaires may be used together with 40 suspension points so this does not present the problems that exist in a large studio. Small roller barrel grids can also present a moving load to the main structure, although by not using motorized units, the weight on the structure is considerably less. In the larger studios such as those used with monopoles and motorized barrels which may have their motor units mounted at grid level, or be the self-climbing type, special metal structures have to be arranged, usually by the structural engineer in consultation with the architect, so that the rather heavy lighting grid system can be installed safely. This may require the use of special large beams being incorporated into the structure at high level. It must also be remembered that other than a lighting grid, air conditioning requirements exist and there will be a lot of additional weight from the power wiring system, etc. In the smaller studios it may be that special attachments can be made to, for example, a concrete roof going over the studio which can be made sufficiently strong by the astute use of reinforcing rod. The saving grace in a smaller studio is that the spans are not so great.

So far we have discussed the installation of grid systems and their subsequent structural loading, on the assumption that we are in a new building and can influence the design. What happens if we require to put a lighting system in existing premises? First of all it is important to come up with the lighting scheme itself, which can then be presented with all its facts and figures to the architect and structural engineer concerned. They will obviously be able either to accept the scheme as it stands for the new design, or it may be that they are able to modify the building in some way to accept the new design. Therefore it is back to the poor old lighting consultant to come up with an idea to be contained within the parameters set by the architect and structural engineer. It is quite possible that the idea could be acceptable but with some change to the structure itself, such as spreading the loadings between the walls and the roof, not just using the roof itself. It may be that the roof structure cannot accept any load other than the one existing; therefore all the new installation would have to be supported from the side walls or from a structure built up from the floor level. The first of these requires that the walls are strong enough, and the second that the floor is also strong enough. Any one of these solutions may be acceptable and it might even be a combination of any of them or all three. It must be remembered, when discussing the structural arrangements with the architect and structural engineer, that these figures have to include for all the lights, all the rigging system, all the power system and any ancillaries that may be added at any time.

In addition to the structural loads presented by the lighting system in the studio, the structural engineer will also be concerned with the size of plant installed in areas adjacent to the studio. Generally, the weight of the switchgear will be spread out in a fairly uniform fashion. The input power cables to the switchgear and the cables from the switchgear to the dimmer racks will also be fairly well distributed throughout the area. Most of the problem will be concerned with the weight of the dimmer racks where in a large installation the structural engineer may be confronted with a room with up to 20 or 30 dimmer racks. The biggest concern at the present time is the use of high density dimmer racks containing anything up to 108 dimmers. Whereas a small rack containing 30 dimmers may be around 200 kg, a large high density rack may weigh anything up to 1000 kg. Dimensions of dimmer racks vary considerably and, as an example, a lightweight rack of 200 kg from one manufacturer has base dimensions of 905 mm × 510 mm whereas another is a high density rack weighing 900 kg with base dimensions of 850 mm × 600 mm. The latter rack obviously gives floor loading problems, being a large weight over a small area. It would seem at first sight that the best solution to any of the loading problems in dimmer rooms is to keep the weights of the racks low and use more racks so that the loadings are well spread. However, the size of the room dictates how many racks may be used and the economics of the situation is that more racks generally put up the cost. In a new building, the structural engineer would obviously cater for the high floor loading at the planning stage; in existing buildings, however, special precautions will have to be taken, or it may be that additional building work is required.

In practice, over many years of experience, it is very seldom that we have found buildings to be so bad that they would preclude some form of solution being adopted albeit possibly far removed from the original concept.

10.6 Studio requirements

The influence on the structure caused by the lighting grid has nothing to do with the amount of luminaires to be provided. Grids are there to hang lights, almost anywhere, using whatever quantities of luminaires that may be available. The basic requirement in any television studio is for a certain amount of light to satisfy the technical requirements of the cameras. This quantity of light will be determined by the average reflectivity of scenery together with the exposure time of the camera coupled with the aperture of the lens in use. Without going into the background as to why, suffice it to say that at the present time, a figure of 650 watts of lighting per square metre is considered adequate for the majority of general purpose requirements in television. Watts per square metre give the power required so that the acting area can be adequately lit. As the use of CCD cameras becomes more widespread, it is possible that the light levels may be reduced.

Although the figure of $650 \, W/m^2$ is satisfactory for most basic purposes, it must be understood that additional requirements, such as cyc and effects lighting, will impose an additional burden. A colour mixing system used on cycloramas will probably require loads of anything up to 2000 W per metre of linear run; thus a 40 m cyclorama cloth might require anything up to 80 kW to be provided for adequate effects purposes. It is therefore suggested that a slightly higher estimating figure of around $800 \, W/m^2$ is used on any studio above about $250 \, m^2$. An important fact in the choice of luminaires is the size of the studio. Studios up to about $100 \, m^2$ will generally work quite happily with a 2 kW as the highest power luminaire required; however, above this size of studio, luminaires will probably settle at 2 kW, 5 kW or 2.5/5 kW. These powers, of course, are related to working distances involved between the lights themselves and the subjects.

Whatever estimating figure we use for the power requirements for a studio, be it 650 W per square metre, or 800 W per square metre, it is obviously relatively easy to work out the power requirement by taking the active area in square metres and multiplying it by the appropriate wattage figure. In the case of monopole studios and the smaller pantograph type studios it is highly probable that the power requirements of the supply system will match the available total wattage of the luminaires used. However, in the case of saturated lighting grids, the total power of the luminaires installed will probably exceed the power available by a factor of

50m²
Minimum power required: 32.5 kW
8 × 2 kW Fresnel spots
10 × 1 kW Fresnel spots
8 × 1.25 kW softlights
4 × 1 kW profile spots
4 × floor stands

Cyc:
12 × 625 W single compartment top
units

150m²
Minimum power required: 97.5 kW
24 × 2 kW Fresnel spots
10 × 1 kW Fresnel spots

or
34 × 1.25/2.5 kW dual wattage
fresnel spots
4 × 2.5/5 kW softlights
10 × 1.25/2.5 kW softlights
6 × 1 kW profile spots
8 × floor stands

Cyc:
24 × 625 W single compartment top
units

or
30 × 625 W 4-compartment
groundrow units

400m²
Minimum power required: 340 kW
3 × 10 kW Fresnel spots
30 × 5 kW Fresnel spots
30 × 2 kW Fresnel spots
or
60 × 2.5/5 kW dual wattage
Fresnel spots
12 × 1 kW Fresnel spots
24 × 2.5/5 kW softlights
8 × 1 kW profile spots
12 floor stands

Cyc:
16 × 1.25 kW 4-compartment top
units
or
40 × 625 W 4-compartment
groundrow units

100m²
Minimum power required: 65 kW
16 × 2 kW Fresnel spots
10 × 1 kW Fresnel spots
6 × 1.25/5 kW softlights
4 × 1.25 kW softlights
4 × 1 kW profile spots
6 × floor stands
Cyc:
16 × 625 W single compartment top
units

250m²
Minimum power required: 210 kW
20 × 5 kW Fresnel spots
20 × 2 kW Fresnel spots

or
40 × 2.5/5 kW dual wattage fresnel
spots
10 × 1 kW Fresnel spots
6 × 2.5/5 kW softlight
6 × 1.25/2.5 kW softlights
6 × 1 kW profile spots
10 × floor stands
Cyc:
16 × 1.25 kW 2-compartment
top units

or
20 × 625 W 4-compartment
groundrow units

750m²
Minimum power required: 640 kW
6 × 10 kW Fresnel spots
70 × 5 kW Fresnel spots
35 × 2 kW Fresnel spots
or
105 × 2.5/5 kW dual wattage
Fresnel spots
20 × 1 kW Fresnel spots
40 × 2.5/5 kW softlights
12 × 1 kW profile spots
16 floor stands

Cyc:
32 × 1.25 4-compartment top
units
or
70 × 625 W 4-compartment
groundrow units

Basic lighting requirements for TV studios

anything up to three times. As an example of this, a BBC studio of 800m^2 will be supplied with approximately 450 kW of power and the 100 bars installed will each have two 5 kW luminaires rigged on them; thus the load presented by the luminaires to the system is 1 MW. In practice this is not a problem as only selected numbers of lights are used. The figures shown in the table on page 195 have been worked out from typical studio usage over many years and represent the reasonable requirements of any studio. It is obviously easy to start equipping a studio by covering the basic lighting requirements and in the fullness of time purchase more equipment to suit the installation. As an approximate guide, the 'luminaire power' required is divided into two-thirds hard sources and one-third soft sources.

10.7 Air conditioning requirements

If we install 100 kW of lighting in any area, we have to expect that, ultimately, all of this will appear as waste heat and most of it will rise vertically. From the point of view of air conditioning, two effects take place. The first is that the luminaires will radiate infra-red energy in the direction of the artistes. This radiation is in direct proportion to the efficiency of the luminaires themselves, and thus a luminaire with a claimed efficiency of 26% will have approximately 26% radiant energy in the light beam: the remainder will be contained within the luminaire and subsequently reradiated from the luminaire body or as exhaust from the ventilation system on the luminaire itself. Generally older premises are never provided with adequate air conditioning systems and in fact, in older theatres, it always seems 'that you have to sweat to earn your money'! However, in new premises or where premises are capable of being successfully converted, it is possible to have adequate air conditioning installed. There are thus two important areas from the point of view of the air conditioning man – first, the conditions that create a comfortable atmosphere at the acting level, and secondly, the conditions for people working either in the flies or at grid level itself – and it is at grid level where the maximum heat will eventually settle, assuming nothing is done to prevent it.

Heat loads are rather like the domestic electrical load and are subject, somewhat, to diversity of use. It is very seldom that *all* the installed lighting in any system will be used simultaneously, and over a period of some years it has been established, certainly in television and the theatre, that an average load of 66% of the maximum installed kilowatts will be used over a period of time. So, for a studio using 400 kW of power, we need to worry about 264 kW worth, thus easing the burden on the air conditioning man. Theatre practices have not changed very much over the years so the situation from the air conditioning point of view is fairly well established. In film studios, although large amounts of power are used on film sets, it is for reasonably short periods of time with breaks between, which allows the temperature, although perhaps having reached high levels, to be dissipated fairly quickly by the use of large fans in the roof or walls. Television has changed greatly in recent years and the technique of rehearse/shoot generally means that perhaps only one or two sets of the possible 13 sets in a large studio are in use at any one time; thus the load on the air conditioning system is considerably less and it may be in the future that the estimating figure of 66% has to be looked at once again and possibly reduced.

It is all very well having air conditioning that works effectively and keeps the ambient temperature to reasonable limits, to the relief of everybody concerned; however, air conditioning can only be achieved by moving a large volume of air down small ducting or an equal volume of air down a large ducting system. The latter will create, in general, much less noise, and in fact for television use, we have to be extremely careful with the generation of noise from the air conditioning system. An interesting coincidence occurs inasmuch that by moving large volumes of air we do not create some of the air movement that causes problems in practice, such as a cyc cloth being moved by the sheer volume of air flowing around a studio. Other than the needs of the studio, air conditioning will be required in the dimmer room, as there is a reasonable amount of waste heat generated. This is particularly important if the dimmer room doubles as a maintenance room for the electricians to use. In a large studio it may be that the air conditioning engineer concerned will be able to have a zonal control system so that when only one quarter of the studio is used only that quarter is conditioned to any reasonable degree. The requirement for a large volume of air to be moved down large ducting obviously implies a large space being occupied by the air conditioning at grid level. Thus, it is extremely important when planning a studio to integrate the air conditioning system and the lighting grid system together, so that a clash of interest does not occur and certainly access to the lighting equipment is not prevented. Others affected by the requirements of air conditioning are the sound and vision technicians, who also require the use of certain portions of the grid for some of their systems.

Some air conditioning systems, when moving the volumes of air suggested in this section, require large rooms in which to put the plant, and these rooms can almost approach the size of some of the studios they service. Further problems associated with air conditioning are that chilled water is required, and if compressor units are used, it is important they do not create any undue noise in the studio. It also happens that introduction of air conditioning breaches the walls around the area which consequently cause problems for the acoustic specialist. This latter problem will be discussed in Section 10.9.

10.8 Power requirements

Irrespective of whether we use 1 kW, 2 kW or 10 kW luminaires, or whatever type of dimmers drive them, power has to flow from one area to another in the theatre or the studio, and this involves large numbers of cables which have to be routed from one location to another with absolute safety. The system that supplies the power has to be carefully worked out, conditioned by whether or not it is a new installation or the refurbishment of an old installation. Various parameters concern us when we move power from one location to another and the most important of these is cable size.

What affects the cable size? All cables have a small resistance and the larger the cable the less they impede the flow of current. Therefore if we use cables which are high in resistance to the flow of current we will waste some power in the cables themselves and this can cause problems from two aspects; one of which is that the cables heat, which is dangerous, and secondly, we lose valuable power in the cables and do not deliver it to the lamps, and thus we get a volts drop and the lamps do not work at their maximum efficiency. How do we get around this problem?

The best method is to use generous sized cables and keep the distance from the dimmers to the luminaires as short as possible, bearing in mind possible acoustic noise problems. Unlike the film and TV industries, the theatre luminaires tend to be used with reasonably short flexible leads attached so that most of the volts drop is in the fixed wiring. The loss of volts in theatre installations is not a serious problem from the production's point of view, as the change of colour temperature of the lamps will generally not be noticeable. The heating of the cables by not being large enough in current carrying capacity is, however, very serious. With new installations the present legislation in the UK prevents cables being used which are quite simply not up to the job. However, in old installations, it is more than likely, if refurbished, they will have to have a completely new electrical system.

Most of the lighting circuits at 240 V in theatres are 2.5 kW (10 A), although sometimes 5 kWs are used and occasionally 10 kWs may be employed. It is preferable that all dimmers are grouped together in a purpose-built room where the noise can be contained and ventilation controlled fairly easily. Circuits should be run as phase/neutral pairs usually with a common earth provided either by large cables to groups of sockets or by the trunking used to distribute the power system. Unswitched sockets should be used and at the present time in the United Kingdom theatre industry, 15 A plugs and sockets are common. It is much better that modern plugs and sockets to BS 4343 are used in 16 A, 32 A and 63 A ratings, and these should be installed as a matter of course in a new installation and wherever possible as replacements in existing installations. Parallel sockets are provided for convenience on the radial circuits used with the responsibility for the electrical loading of the system being placed on the operators.

Most dimmers in use today are of the thyristor type, and we have already discussed the interference that these units can generate. Because there is usually good separation between the power wiring and the microphone cables, particularly with the use of radio microphones, high specification dimmers with low interference, such as used in TV, are not usually required in stage installations. In addition to the thyristor dimming circuits, independent or 'non-dimmable' circuits are also required. These are used for electrical loads such as the motors on effects lighting units, fan units and discharge lights, including follow spots. It is relatively easy to provide such circuits from contactor switched power, although most dimmer manufacturers offer 'non-dim' circuits through their dimmer racks, either by bypassing the action of the thyristors or having thyristor dimmers that, in full conduction, stay relatively stable when this type of load is applied. Other than the permanently supplied lighting power for the units contained within the premises, there is a need for additional power supplies when temporary lighting and sound equipment are provided by touring companies. From the point of view of cost, it is important that the dimmer room is as near as possible to the socket outlets used for the lighting system, thus cutting down the amount of cables required between the dimmers and the lights.

The requirements of the film studio for luminaires and dimmers are less demanding than those for a theatre installation and the majority of cables used will be flexible feeders and not part of the fixed installation. The biggest difference will be the provision of much larger power supplies. Whereas for years the film industry generated its own dc voltage, it now relies on the incoming ac mains supply.

The requirements of TV in most respects are very similar to those of the theatre with large numbers of dimmers used and a multiplicity of light sources. The type of luminaires employed will vary much more and thus their power needs will be different. The dimmers provided will be of the highest specification to prevent interference in practice. The majority of the wiring will be fixed although the length of cable runs will mean keeping a close eye on the voltage drop.

10.9 Acoustic requirements

The Greeks and the Romans together with the builders of cathedrals and concert halls of the past had little or no knowledge of the *decibel*. A mixture of luck and the fact that all buildings appear to be structurally designed for at least three times the strength needed, seems to play a part in the acoustics of old buildings. Apparently, with the high technology of today's construction methods, there is a greater need for acoustic architects than ever before. Just why is this so?

It is no good having a wonderful building where we are unable to hear the artistes perform – or for that matter resolve the sound spectrum fairly accurately within a broadcast studio. It is somewhat distracting when sitting in an auditorium to hear a jet aircraft overhead. This is one area where the architects of old had no problems; they weren't confronted with jet engined aircraft or the motor vehicle going by on the roads outside. The buildings of old did not seem to require much air conditioning as such as, due to their massive construction, they appear to be inherently cool in the hot weather and not too cold in the coldest of weather. They were constructed more like a storage heater rather than a slim line radiator. It is pretty obvious if we don't get the construction right and the building does not meet the requirements for good acoustics then all is lost.

What has lighting got that influences the acoustics to any degree? In the theatre, probably not a lot; the only problems arise usually with the noise generated by dimmer units which may be loud enough to take people's attention away from the performance; secondly the installation of lots of pieces of metal at high level over a stage area introduces many reflecting surfaces. The fly tower, if we are not careful, reacts just a little bit like a large organ pipe. The architect when designing theatres and similar premises still has to worry about the natural acoustics without much consideration to sound reinforcement or the use of radio microphones. Because we need walkways over the front of the theatre to position some of the front of house lighting, we breach the ceiling with slots which may give problems to the acoustic architect and be somewhat of a compromise between decor and the needs of audibility. The air conditioning in the theatre will not be of the levels required for the film and television studio and thus it may be relatively easy to keep the noise from the air movement to a low level. What would be important however is that the noise of the ventilation plant be kept separate from the structure so as to reduce noise through the building.

In the film and television studios, where large power feeders are used, there may be a requirement to ensure that noise does not come from any of the electrical plant into the studio area. In film studios, this should not cause too much of a problem as dimmers are not the norm in this situation. They will probably have more problems with the use of discharge light sources on the sets themselves and the ballast units used with them. In television, however, a problem with the use of many dimmers often positioned very close to the studio, is that we make holes in the walls by taking the trunking from one area through to the studio and hence allow a degree of vibration to go through the structures. Even if we inhibit vibration by using rubber mounts, or even discontinuous pieces of trunking, it may be that the noise comes from around the hole made in the wall, which can be a real problem in studios.

It is very convenient to have a door from the studio through to the dimmer room, but in most cases these have to be carefully selected acoustic doors, and usually double ones, to prevent noise coming from the dimmer room to the studio. Studios are usually formed as rather large box like structures with a metal grid, some 3m below the actual roof. TV studios are generally designed to have a fairly 'dead' sound and any reverberation required is added artificially; thus the acoustic specialist has to provide some form of acoustic boxes on the ceilings above the grid where space is at a premium. There is little or nothing he can do below the grid owing to the nature of productions and the usage of the system. The acoustic specialist will also want to cover the walls in acoustic cladding of some description, but unfortunately is bedeviled by lots of trunking and large control consoles at fairly regular intervals around the walls of the studios which cater for the lighting or the sound and vision system. However good the acoustic specialist is, matters are not always controlled by his skills. The biggest problem in studios can be the noise generated by the lights. If the choice of luminaires leads to creaking bodywork on heating up and cooling down of a luminaire, this is absolutely disastrous. *Lamp sing* can penetrate the quietest of conversations. One of the reasons that discharge lighting is not generally used for live performance is that the starting mechanism really is very, very noisy; thus whether we like it or not, the lighting industry does play a major part in the acoustics and sound quality of any building.

11   Automated lighting systems

Introduction

The dictionary defines automation as 'a high degree of mechanization in manufacture, the handling of material between processes being automatic, and the whole automatically controlled'. A technical dictionary defines automation as 'industrial closed loop control system in which manual operation of controls is replaced by servo operation'.

In the entertainment industry we have come to use the word 'automation' incorrectly, to describe several different types of system which are, in the main, generally motorized and responsive to some degree, with human intervention. The whole point about an automatic process is that it does occur without human intervention and with many robotic machines in use today a learning process takes place and after that process the machine works without a human operator. On car assembly lines, with this type of machine the operator goes through the motions of, say, a paint spraying process on a car body. The machine follows every movement of the human being and then replicates these when returned to the automatic mode. If we use the definition as laid down, the only automatic system we have in use today is the memory playback on lighting control consoles. In addition to this, we also have fairly basic motorized luminaire control systems that are memorized and then replayed. However, it is doubtful if we will ever get to the stage where the lighting system responds 'automatically' without human intervention. Although this section of the book discusses automated lighting systems, it really should be entitled: 'Mechanized systems with some form of memory control and its application to lighting'.

Before looking at modern systems, it is worthwhile going back to examine the events and reasons for the mechanization of the lighting system. At the turn of the century, film makers had studios that were able to rotate on trackways, so that they took advantage of the sun's direction, this being the main source of illumination. With some of the earlier studios, although labour was relatively cheap during this period, operational needs sometimes required some form of mechanization, the earliest example in film studios being that of long poles to adjust the lighting. Owing to the nature of luminaires being used it was more than likely to adjust the 'on/off' function. As the film industry developed electricians tended to rig luminaires from grid structures by means of block and tackle arrangements, either with single light sources or using 'boats'. In the theatre, quite complicated and involved hoist systems were being used. It was unfortunate, however, that the film industry did not take account of some of these earlier experiments with mechanized lifting and suspension systems and operated a very labour intensive lighting system which has remained unchanged – even today. The film industry's motto seems to be: 'Why use one person when two will suffice?'. Television, in its earlier days, adopted the techniques of the film studios and in the ensuing years rapidly learnt that productivity was extremely low when using this means of rigging. This either meant that the producers had to reduce the rehearsal time to meet programme deadlines, or it necessitated the building of many more studios to meet the needs of the programme makers. To make cost-effective television requires high utilization of studio premises with a rapid turnround of programmes. In the days of monochrome television, the first attempt to increase productivity was by the introduction of mechanized lifting systems, together with simple pole-operated luminaires. This was followed by experiments with dual purpose luminaires where soft and hard lights were combined in one unit. In the late 1960s, the introduction of colour to British television caused a dramatic rethink of many systems. The BBC, for example, commenced the use of dual source luminaires with pole operation, which enabled switching between the soft source and the hard source. The power output could be varied between 2.5 kW and 5 kW and it was easy to adjust the spot/flood mechanism together with the pan and tilt controls. The purpose of the introduction of this unit was to allow the same rigging time as previously used for black and white television. In other areas, the needs of the studio required that the control of intensity of lights was also improved, thus lessening the necessity for light reducing scrims to be placed in the older

Figure 11.1   Manual shift controlled dimmers

type of luminaires. Over a very short period of time, television moved away from the old resistance dimmer units, as used in film studios and theatres, to thyristor dimming units so that instantaneous control of all luminaires in the studio was achieved. The original control systems, inherited from the theatre industry, were replaced by systems using digital electronics, with relatively unlimited capability.

Earlier attempts in America with computerized lighting control were not brought into general service use there as rapidly as those introduced in Europe. Television required that the methods of rigging traditionally used by the film industry had to be mechanized. This was done mainly by two methods:

(i)   Using single point suspension units, such as the monopole or pantograph, to enable accurate rigging of light sources. Even from an early stage of development mechanical control, such as portable electrical or air driven tools, was used to reduce the amount of staff required to operate the monopole systems.
(ii) By using lighting winch units, which generally consisted of barrels approximately 2.5m long being raised by motors mounted at grid level.

Theatres also introduced motorized barrel units to ease rigging problems with lighting systems. It should be appreciated that it was very much easier to introduce up-to-date mechanized systems into new television studios than to convert old theatres to new systems. Generally, with old premises the mere weight of new equipment might impose loads on the structure that were unacceptable to the architects concerned.

In recent years, units such as self-climbing barrel winches have been introduced to enable fairly simple structures to be adapted to motorized units. Control of suspension systems was usually by switches controlling analogue circuits which often required several kilometres of multicore cable to be installed, whereas some systems being installed today use digital information to control the suspension system.

Applying controlled mechanization to the luminaires is not new and attempts were made in Europe during the 1970s to achieve some crude form of control. The units themselves were fairly cumbersome, utilizing standard drive systems, such as small ac or dc motors.

Remote controlled luminaires for entertainment were introduced on a large scale for the pop groups on tour doing roadshows and live concerts, and the idea of moving the luminaires was a progression from purely placing colour in them. The added dimension of controlling pan and tilt was soon discovered: with each luminaire's position controlled from a memory, scores of luminaires could be directed simultaneously from a multitude of different angles onto one single subject such as a lead guitar. This simple, controlled movement has an emotional effect on the audience, producing nervous reactions, such as tingling of the skin, or making the hair stand up on the back of the viewer's neck.

Eventually, television and film borrowed the techniques to create, in their own media, a simulation of a live pop show. Having experienced the joy of moving a luminaire with fingertip control, without getting anywhere near the luminaire itself, the television industry promoted the idea to manufacturers of developing all-singing, all-dancing studio luminaires. The theatre industry, whilst recognizing the desirability of such units, thought it would never have enough money so would watch the development in television and see what ideas and products could be picked up afterwards.

The technical designers soon discovered that the pop industry, theatre and television requirements were poles apart. The pop industry wanted extremely fast movement for effect, as many colour changes as one could imagine, sometimes as many as 100 using multilayer dichroic coatings inside the unit, all combined in an extremely lightweight portable unit that could be rigged on slender overhead trusses. The theatre and television systems, however, do not require the same degree of speed and number of colour changes, but do require very accurate positioning.

The most arduous requirement for a motorized luminaire is the profile spot with hard edged focus used in the theatre. With a projected distance of, say, 10 m the beam must stop within a repeatable accuracy of at least 10 cm; having achieved this degree of accuracy, all other movements are less demanding and can use the same technique. In the case of Fresnel or PC luminaires, focusing from flood to spot does not require a great accuracy of setting; similarly hard edge to soft edge focus on a profile spot. How many functions does the operator require for remote control of the luminaire? A Fresnel with a barndoor requires four movements of the barndoor flaps and a clockwise/anticlockwise rotation. A colour changing system is essential in the theatre, with a suggested requirement of 20 colours. With the theatre profile projector, two lenses have to be moved to change the spot size, four beam shaping shutters with some degree of rotation to shape the beam, and a flat peaky setting of the lamp to produce the beam distribution required. Ask any LD for a desirable list of requirements and he will cite all of the above, generally performed by him standing in the middle of the acting area, pointing a magic wand at the luminaire and creating any one of these changes. Added to these requirements is a memory system that would record every movement, the time of that movement and the position of the end result.

The acoustic noise associated with movement and accuracy of alignment can be overcome by either reducing the speed of movement or by using very high grade drive systems. The motorized luminaires in theatre and television are not intended to stimulate emotional effects; their aim is to produce fast turnround times in a television studio and in the theatre, with the demands of 'rep', to allow different luminaire settings without having to get to those difficult luminaires tucked away up in the 'gods'.

The major British broadcasting organizations have not progressed into full-scale automation whereas Radio Telefís Éireann in Dublin have started down that road. A system installed in one of the RTE studios consists of motorized monopoles with each monopole being equipped with a fully motorized multipurpose luminaire. The system gives control of monopole vertical movement, together with luminaire control of the following functions: pan, tilt, focus, all barndoor functions (which include rotation and control of each individual flap), the softlight/hardlight mode and the power output of the lamps. The present system does not have memory and feedback but a proposed Mk. II system does have these facilities.

One of the stated aims of the automation of lighting systems is that the LD would be able to sit at his desk, hopefully at home, and via his computer draw a lighting plot which will then be automatically rigged at the touch of a button. It would also be possible to memorize and replay lighting plots on a repertory basis so that set rigs could be rapidly brought into use.

A TV studio using something like 100 luminaires would have its cost raised, for the provision of those luminaires, from around £100,000 to something in the region of £400,000. The difference of £300,000 would have to be paid back over a reasonable period of time to keep the accountants happy. If we assume a four-year payback period, we require to save something like £75,000 per annum and this would be approximately three electricians, although we doubt if the figure includes their overtime.

Maintenance

It is therefore fairly obvious that savings can be made in the operation of the system but we may be confronted with a higher maintenance load. Based on the experience of lighting control systems, which these days are extremely robust, it is more than likely that the actual control system will give few problems over a 10 year period. The major problem would be with the electromechanical devices used when they are working in areas which are alien to them. Although dampness would certainly not be a problem in the majority of cases, heat and dust obviously will create problems. If the new luminaires are more complex than the luminaires they have replaced, they will have to be taken out for longer periods of time for maintenance. Most luminaires used in the TV and film industry give very little trouble if a small amount of relatively simple basic maintenance is performed every year. In the case of fully automated luminaires this maintenance will have to be much more stringent.

In discussing maintenance, we have to bear in mind that this is generally only required because of breakdowns. What actually does happen if a fully automated luminaire breaks down? If, as we have stated already, it was replacing three luminaires, the loss would be most noticeable in a theatre production. It might be that due to the nature of TV and film the breakdown might not be so severe providing access to the device that failed is reasonably easy; the main point being that we are not so concerned with the live performance any more in these industries.

Finally, and most important of all, what happens when the control systems malfunction and every cue is uncontrollable? Perhaps we are looking at two systems, one for rigging and one for performance.

Although this overview appears gloomy, there are some real benefits in mechanization when correctly applied, and hopefully this section will provoke ideas for the reader.

11.1 Grid system functions

Control of lighting breaks down into three distinct areas:

(a) Control of the intensity of luminaires and their on/off function in some combination.

    (b)   The elevation and positioning of the luminaires themselves by motorized lifting systems.

    (c)   Control of the directional properties of luminaires and further functions for effect such as iris, shutters and barndoors together with the control of the colour output.

First of all, what is the basic function we require if we apply mechanization to a grid system? It would be nice to be able to control the hanging of any luminaire in three planes, i.e. its attitude across and along the acting area, coupled with the height of the luminaire over the acting area. The control of height is very straightforward. When using motorized pantographs and motorized monopoles, control of direction in either the 'x' or 'y co-ordinates of the studio is easy as the unit will invariably only have to motor backwards and forwards along a fixed trackway consisting of either barrel or RSJ, or a 'C' section channel system. Movement in the other plane would be more difficult to accomplish although not impossible. When rigging a monopole and its associated luminaire, the only problem that exists for the operators is to have a nominated position for the luminaire to be hung in the studio and also sufficient space to hang it in the position required. Motorized barrel systems require a slightly differing technique inasmuch as there is no individual control of any single luminaire, except when using short barrels, other than by use of supplementary spring pantographs on the barrel unit itself.

The height of a motorized barrel unit is generally dictated by the LD's requirements. The luminaire on its associated trolley is then moved along the bar to a point as near as possible to the nominated position in the studio rig. As has already been stated, this is somewhat of a compromise in practice. Where a horizontal bar some 2.5 m long is raised and lowered in a studio, its position in relation to the scenery is extremely important and, in fact, it might be impossible to put the bar at the desired position due to the height of intervening scenery.

Motorized pantographs pose similar positioning problems to the motorized monopole – with one big distinction. Where necessary, monopoles can be removed from their associated trackways and either lifted out to another trackway or, by using crossover point systems between trackways, be diverted to adjacent trackways. The motorized pantograph system is generally permanently installed to the trackways and not normally rigged or de-rigged.

If we motorize the elevation of monopoles, barrel winches or pantographs, the safety cutout systems employed on them should guarantee not too many mishaps in operational use. The slack wire cutout operates very rapidly on these devices when meeting an obstruction on their downward travel: however, when individual units are not fully loaded the overload system may not trip even when starting to pick up inadvertently a relatively large piece of scenery. This highlights one of the major problems with total mechanization of winching systems in that dangers are always inherent with scenery flats and other obstructions in the acting area, which really do require human supervision to ensure no malfunction of the system.

It is relatively easy to add a motor to allow a unit to traverse along its trackway but what happens to the luminaire at the base of the lifting device? Does it know that a scenery flat is in the way or that a luminaire in the trackway is in the position which we have nominated for the new luminaire? At what speed will our nominated luminaire approach the fixed luminaires within the rig? If we are using barrel systems, it might be that only one motorized traversing unit has to be fitted to each barrel. However, to cover the studio area adequately, we would have to provide a large number of short barrels all over the studio. If we extend this principle of restricting the movement of the traversing system, would it not be sensible to restrict the movement of the monopoles in their trackways and the motorized pantographs in theirs, so that they are only allowed to travel in 'safe space'? It is strongly suspected that this would be operationally extremely undesirable!

Let us now look a little closer at the individual systems themselves and the problems they may pose.

Barrel systems

Barrels which may be 2.4 m long or a shorter one at 1.2 m long are installed to give as much coverage as possible within the studio. The length of the bars dictates the actual operational flexibility of the system. More short bars are obviously preferable to fewer long bars. The BBC, for instance, uses systems where two luminaires are permanently rigged to 2.4 m bars and one luminaire is permanently rigged to a 1.2 m bar, but there is always the provision to add extra lights to any of the bars in use for special requirements within a production. How would we get over the problem of the peak demand of studios where we do not necessarily always require the largest number of luminaires to be permanently rigged?

This brings us to the point as to how do we set about rigging a studio with motorized luminaires which are attached to barrel units? Although the barrel unit only has the problem of finding its nominated height as dictated by the LD, the luminaires, if motorized, would have to pan and tilt to meet the requirements of the LD. Two problems exist with motor driven pan and tilt with luminaires on barrel systems used in this way. One is to avoid a luminaire on panning around crashing into its neighbour; secondly, if the starting torque is high, it is more than likely this would impart motion to the barrel unit itself which would probably react by swinging like a pendulum for some time during the rigging period. The problem comes when adjustments are made to the lights in the rehearsal period, where motion is totally undesirable and would be extremely annoying from the point of view of the LD and even more so from that of the programme directors.

Barrel units always have a tendency for some motion generally caused by their position near the floor which involves relatively long wire rope drops from the grid level. This statement holds true for standard winches with motors at grid level or for self-climbing winches with integral motors. Other problems exist with installing mechanized luminaires on barrel rigs. Firstly, there is the cost of installing fully automated luminaires on the bars themselves; and secondly, what functions are required and how are these units actually controlled? The existing barrel systems usually have a reasonably generous SWL but it is marginal when additional temporary equipment is rigged. The additional loads presented by the motorized units may prohibit some types of temporary equipment being used.

Motorized pantograph systems

The BBC has installed three studios, varying from $140\,\mathrm{m}^2$ to $220\,\mathrm{m}^2$, with motorized pantograph systems. The reasons for their introduction are twofold: one is that they are much safer than the traditional spring pantographs used in small studios and secondly, if they are motorized for elevation and track position, they can be controlled from a remote point by one man relatively easily. The basic premise of the original system installed was that if each motorized pantograph unit was fitted with a multipurpose luminaire, a man with a pole in one hand and a remote control unit in the other could rig and adjust the lighting in the studio with consummate ease. This system, although mechanized, has no inherent positional memory provided and thus cannot be claimed to be an automated lighting system. Additionally, the luminaires chosen for use have no motorized functions and are standard multipurpose units.

The pantograph trackways are spaced at intervals so that the luminaires can pass each other when moving along their associated trackways, generally with the barndoors open. It is possible to obtain greater flexibility by having the trackways spaced at smaller intervals but the barndoors may have to be closed when units pass each other. It is also possible to lower the luminaire to the floor so that its supporting pantograph, which is smaller in cross section, can pass between adjacent luminaires. Grids in this type of studio are approximately 6m above floor level, and thus extra long pantograph units are not necessarily required. The pantograph only needs to reach one metre above floor level so that luminaires can be rigged and de-rigged with ease. The signals coming from the control system could be in many forms, but in the BBC they were chosen to be ac mains signals, so that the amount of control gear built within any pantograph unit was kept to a minimum, thus reducing the possibility of operational failure. The electrical signals required for any unit are the 'up/down' and the 'traverse' functions. In the event of control system failure, it was felt necessary to provide a pole operated control switch on the pantograph unit that could, by injecting mains signals, replace the incoming control signals and allow for local control of up/down and traverse motion. To avoid damage to adjacent units, buffers were fitted to the trolley units at the top of the pantograph rather in the style of an elongated version of buffers as fitted to railway locomotives. It is important that the traversing speed is not too high, so that the units themselves do not swing when in a lowered condition. To this end, all the pantographs have to be fitted with pivoting mechanisms at high level to avoid damage.

If either of the motor units fails, this is a severe operational problem in practice; therefore, the unit should be relatively easy to move off the trackway if the need arises. They would be rather unwieldy for the operational personnel to manhandle without safety problems being encountered, so this operation will probably require the use of a small local winch unit to raise and lower the old and new pantograph units into position, and in practice this type of unit has proved to be extremely reliable.

As the units are fitted with one luminaire, only one 5 kW supply cable and socket for lighting power is needed at the base of each pantograph unit. The controlling ac mains feeds, together with the lighting power, are fed to the motor unit at high level by a catenary cable system rather like those used with overhead electrical cranes.

At the moment it sounds as though we are discussing one unit in the track, which of course in practice is not the case, and more than likely six motorized pantograph units will be used in each trackway. If we assume three units would be fed by catenary cables from each side of the studio, then some degree of flexibility has to be inbuilt to the cabling system. It has to be noted that to reduce the amount of trackways for the cable systems, bunches of cable are suspended from either one or two trackways. These trackways are adjacent to their respective pantographs and carry one set of triple cables from one side of the studio and another triple set from the other. The flexibility requires that all the units can be positioned anywhere along the trackway, the only limitation being the space taken up by adjacent units. To achieve this means that the cables themselves must be sufficiently long to permit any unit to reach its maximum towards the other side of the studio, allowing for parked luminaires, and that the cable between each unit also has to be long enough (say 8 m) to offer precise positioning of the luminaire.

The operator in charge of the rigging is provided with a small hand-held controller. This controller, although it could be connected by flexible cable back to a wall termination point, is much better for use if it is not constrained by a length of cable. The hand-held unit could be infra-red, rather like the controller for TV/video systems, but generally is radio controlled, the reason for this being that some problems have occurred in practice when using infra-red systems and their reception, usually occasioned by flats and cloths and other devices being in the way in the studio area. The intensity of lighting itself, however, has proved little or no problem for IR systems in the studios and experiments did take place where receptor units were exposed to the light of a fully spotted 5 kW luminaire and still were able to distinguish the infra-red signals being received.

The small hand-held controller is used to select the luminaire required in the studio and its associated pantograph and controls the luminaire's 'on/off' function. It also enables the control of the 'up/down' and 'traversing' motion of the pantograph unit while the channel is selected. It is possible, having selected the channel to be 'on' or 'off', to leave it in either state so that all the lights on any one area can be controlled easily. Initially, it was felt desirable to control the mechanical functions of only one unit at a time, thus avoiding any dangerous situations, such as a unit being moved inadvertently out of the operator's eyeline. It would be possible, however, to control more units if it is assumed that the operator has a clear view of all units selected.

If radio control is used in an area, it is essential that the control unit is not operated outside of that area as the signals will be received by the base station and this would mean that the units in the studio would be controlled by somebody having no idea of what was happening. In practice this is overcome by making sure that only trained operators use the system with strict instructions that *under no circumstances is the controller unit to be used outside the studio*. To prevent malpractice, the operators have to input an access code to the system.

Upon completion of the rigging period, the studio control system is switched off and the normal lighting control console takes over control of the luminaires themselves. The actual rig is now in position and unless small adjustments are required is left unattended.

The biggest advantage of the motorized pantograph unit is the fact that springs are not required, and thus the unit itself is not load dependent. Any luminaire – from the smallest to the largest – allowed on the unit may be rigged and de-rigged in absolute safety.

Motorized monopole systems

We now come to studios which are utilizing motorized monopole units for mechanization. One of the problems with monopoles, as has been noted elsewhere in this book, is that to move them around requires personnel working at grid level, possibly above artistes and other people during rehearsals. In recent times, with the advent of stricter safety legislation, this practice has had to be tightened up considerably and for safety reasons people are sometimes moved away from the area in which monopoles are being rigged and de-rigged. It would be difficult to move the monopoles in their 'x' and 'y' axes without very complicated mechanical arrangements being made and it is preferable that they only traverse along sections of trackway. It would be desirable to limit that movement to certain sections of trackway, due to the need to avoid one unit hitting another or the possibility of fouling other pieces of studio equipment.

If we limit the traversing of units to a specific distance, what distance should be involved? Probably, as a guide, it could be similar to that of the barrels on barrel winches – approximately 1.5 m. Monopole studios are usually constructed with trackways that are very close to each other to enable luminaires to be positioned almost anywhere. If we have a system where traversing is allowed even over short distances, we have to make allowances for luminaires to pass each other for overlap purposes and this would dictate the spacing of the trackways and invariably make them wider spaced. By doing this, we have negated one of the great advantages of monopole rigs, which is that luminaires can be positioned anywhere. If we follow this argument to its logical conclusion, it would seem more acceptable to rig monopoles incapable of traverse in a standard monopole grid and only use 'up and down' motors on the units themselves. Having done this, we have taken away another advantage of monopole systems, as rigging still has to take place to a considerable degree, requiring a reasonable number of electrical staff.

If we make the systems more efficient, it is the reduction of staff that is important from the point of view of cost saving. Rigging is the situation where the most staff are required, but any studio, once rigged, requires very few electricians to do the fine 'trim' desired by the LDs. If we automate a monopole situation, what type of luminaires should be used on the monopoles themselves? RTE in Dublin have opted for a motorized version of a multipurpose luminaire as this seems to be the most logical choice to accomplish any degree of automation.

11.2 Automated luminaires

What functions need to be automated on any luminaire? First of all we will examine what types of luminaire should be automated for their particular application and the functions used for that application.

A high proportion of lighting used in discotheques is a motorized form of illumination. Due to the need to create mood and atmosphere in fairly dark conditions, the intensity of source illumination is not too high. There is also a need to shape the light beam in many ways and to introduce a multiplicity of colour effects. In the luminaires provided by manufacturers for the discotheque and leisure industry, much of the movement is created by the use of mirrors moving at high velocity to divert the light beam in various directions. Mirrors are used because they are extremely lightweight devices in comparison to the luminaire itself, and to move luminaires at high velocity to achieve the rapidly moving effects desired by the pop industry would require quite sophisticated drive systems. For the television, film and theatre industries, the movements we often require from our automated luminaires are slower. We also want to move higher intensity sources and many of our luminaires are larger in size. Let us therefore examine the basic functions required for any type of automated luminaire.

Pan and tilt

With motorized 'pan and tilt' mechanisms, we can remotely direct the luminaire to the position required in the studio or on the stage. On the surface this seems relatively straightforward to achieve but there are several snags that have to be watched for and these are:

(a) What is the speed of motion required?
(b) How is the speed controlled?
(c) Is it variable and does it have a finite maximum to avoid any structural damage to any component parts of the luminaire?
(d) What happens if the unit meets an obstruction?

If the speed is too low it will be annoying to the operator viewing the result, and if too fast probably not very well controlled. How far do we take the directional movement? It would obviously be quite ludicrous to have a device that allowed the 'tilt' mode to keep travelling in the same direction and thus rotate within its yoke. This would cause rather a lot of damage to any power feeding cables or control cables used, either internally or externally. By the same token the 'pan' has to be restricted in some way with a feedback system that tells the control that it has reached a finite distance of travel. It is suggested that for 'pan' the motion must be restricted to just over 360° to cover for all situations. Is the device equipped with a system that allows control of 'pan and tilt' simultaneously and does the device have sufficient intelligence to work out its final destination from two co-ordinates being provided? Perhaps most important of all is how accurately does the device position itself and how noisy is it in operation? As an example, let us take the case of an effects luminaire with a beam width of 30° and a throw of 10 m: the beam diameter would be 5.36 m. On the assumption that an error of 50 mm at the edge of the beam would not produce too disturbing a result, we discover that this is caused by the beam being misaligned by 0.29°. In the world of digital electronics where the binary system is used, we find that 2 raised to the power of 10 gives 1024. As this would be a convenient number to use within our digital electronic control system, if we divide 360° (the maximum rotation within one full circle) by 1024 we discover it produces 0.35° and in fact most of the systems in use today work to an accuracy of roughly this amount: in most manufacturers' literature, called 'one third of a degree'. This error, applied to our original beam at 10 m throw, produces an error of 61 mm, which is just over 1% of the width of the beam. Obviously as the beam width becomes narrower, the proportion of error in relation to the projected beam is greater. With wide beam luminaires, the result would not be so noticeable. The accuracy of the electronics involved is still, however, greatly influenced by the mechanical coupling of the systems themselves and if much slack exists in either the 'pan' or 'tilt' mechanism accuracies such as those discussed will not be attained. The practical limitations of 'pan and tilt' would appear to be a fraction over 360° in 'pan' and 270° for the 'tilt' operation. One point to be observed when going through the 'tilt' angles is that it would be quite possible to exceed the lamp manufacturer's stated operating angles when using tungsten halogen lamps, although possibly quite satisfactory for discharge sources. Because a fixed speed of movement would be a disadvantage it is preferable that it is a smoothly controlled variable, governed by the control electronics. One manufacturer publishes figures of a minimum velocity of 0.5° per second, and a maximum velocity of 120° per second, which, translated into more meaningful terms, means rotations varying from three seconds in duration to 12 minutes. The 'pan and tilt' drive motors and decoding mechanisms are generally contained within the yoke fitted to the luminaire.

Mechanical slipping clutches should be fitted to the 'pan and tilt' system so that in the event of hitting an obstruction the unit will not drive against a motor. This avoids the possibility of either damaging scenery or the luminaire body or burning out the motors.

Focus of luminaire

Having adjusted the 'pan and tilt' so that the luminaire is pointing in the right direction, what type of beam do we require? There are two ways of varying the beam angle of a luminaire, one of which is to adjust the lamp in relation to the optics to give varying outputs. This would be the case with

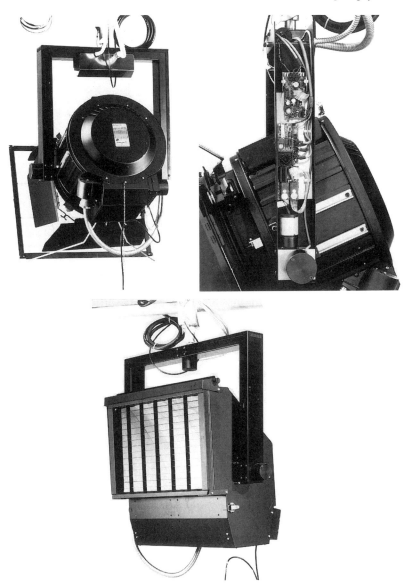

Figure 11.2 Motorized luminaires

Fresnel lens type luminaires. If we were focusing projector type luminaires, such as the profile spot, it would be desirable to have adjustment of the optics or, if fitted, zoom optics, thereby being able to give a continuously variable beam angle over the operating range of the optics. Another desirable feature on a luminaire and also with profile projectors used in the theatre is to have a soft or hard edge to the light beam. Obviously it is difficult to put a time or speed to the adjustment of the focus or any of the optics as this would probably be observed and adjusted accordingly by the operators concerned but the main criterion is that the movement must not be too fast, so making it easier to stop at the correct point. With all types of luminaire in use, patterns or 'gobos' will be desired and these should obviously be inbuilt to the device so that a small number are instantly available upon selection.

Colour

Many of today's effects luminaires are fitted with discharge lamps, and when integrated with other units, it must be remembered that their colour output will probably be around 5600K, so that to match with other sources within sets or on the stage, they may have to be colour corrected to 3200K. Even allowing for the colour of the source, we may wish to change the basic colour of the light output for effects purposes in any of the venues where these devices may be used. There are two ways by which this can be accomplished, one of which is to put electromechanically driven colour changing units on the front of the luminaires or have integral colour changing usually accomplished by a 'dichroic' system. Electromechanical colour changers are invariably noisy whereas the use of integral dichroics may be less obtrusive from the point of view of acoustics. A dichroic colour changer has to be able to feature a wide range of colours; one manufacturer gives a range of 120 different colours. Colour changes should occur fairly rapidly so that it would appear to the viewer that a snap change between two independent light sources had occurred, not a slow mix of colour on one source which would probably not give the effects desired by the operators. It may be, of course, that slow changes are required and that the system should allow for colour mixing within its programme (Figure 11.3(a), (b)).

Light output

If we are using tungsten luminaires obviously these can be dimmed by electronic dimmers in the normal way. However, if we are using discharge

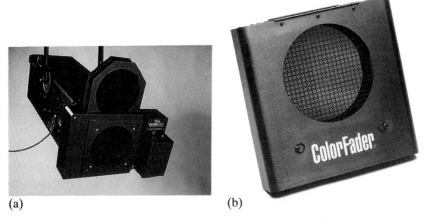

(a)   (b)

Figure 11.3   (a) Semaphore colour changer. (b) Scroll colour changer

sources, even if they are of the 'instant restrike' type, they always have to go through a period of colour and intensity change upon any degree of warming up after being activated. Generally discharge sources require separate mains supply and do not work well from dimming circuits, and therefore the most satisfactory method is to use a mechanical dimming shutter to control the light output. This possibly would take the form of an iris which works in a similar manner to that of a still camera. Although the iris would give good control of the light beam, we would have to allow for complete blackout for effect and the time from maximum 'open' to maximum 'close' has to be carefully controlled. Two variations of operation occur, one of which is the appearance of the luminaire having been switched off, which implies a very rapid shutdown of the iris, or it might be programmable over a long period of time to give the effect of a very slow fade, as used in the theatre world. Being a mechanical device, it once again is a source of acoustic noise.

Barndoor systems

If we are using automated lighting for television or film, the larger luminaires used will always have barndoor systems fitted. Some barndoors come with four flaps, each with adjustable width of flap, and some with eight independent flaps. However, we will examine the effect of mechanization on a four door system. Because barndoors are made with two small and two large flaps, the orientation of the doors allows oblong shapes at various rotational angles to be projected onto the sets. We must be able to regulate this rotation and it can be seen immediately that we also require some method by which the rotation is carefully governed so as not to exceed a reasonable operating range and run into problems with control cable feeds, etc. Thus the rotation of the barndoor flaps is similar to that of the 'pan' system which allows for just over 360° of rotation. Each of the individual barndoor flaps must be adjustable from fully open to fully closed, and one of the problems with this is that if two flaps are allowed to operate simultaneously and intermesh there must be some safeguard so

Figure 11.4   Motorized barndoors

that they intermesh safely and do not cause mechanical jamming. This obviously requires a great deal of feedback from the angle of flap movement to the control system to compare the angle of each flap to ensure correct intermeshing. How far do we take the control of the barndoor system? Should we be able to rotate and adjust all four flaps at the same time? If so, this probably poses more problems for the control system.

One of the biggest problems with having small motors attached to the flaps of barndoors is that the barndoor system regulates the light beam, which unfortunately is one of the hottest parts of the luminaire; thus all the devices used on the doors have to be either carefully insulated or be in such a position that they are not affected too much by the heat of the light beam. Having said that, the same would be true of any motors that are close to the body of a high powered light source in use, due to the radiant heat from the luminaire body.

In a manner similar to that of the 'pan and tilt' the repeatability of barndoor positioning must obviously be high. If, for instance, a set of barndoors is used to project an oblong shape on a doorway within a film or TV set, such positioning needs to be extremely accurate.

Having established some of the basic functions required, with what type of luminaires are we concerned? The requirements would seem to break down into two distinct areas: those of the theatre and pop world against those of the TV and film industry.

In the pop world, the greatest need would seem to be for moving beams of light to heighten the effect of the performers on stage; thus the luminaires concerned could be from a Parcan through to the high intensity movable Xenon sources used rather like searchlights. All of these, of course, have to be controlled in some way and the degree of accuracy of their requirements depends upon the effects desired. The world of the theatre, however, will probably use motorized luminaires with remote control systems, quite often tied into the lighting control system of the theatre concerned, to achieve a lower rate of luminaire usage. In other words, where before two or three lights were used to create an effect, mainly on the grounds that colours had to be changed, one luminaire with its integral control of beam and colour may replace three luminaires. All these changes have to meet two criteria:

1. They have to be extremely quiet to avoid being a nuisance to the audience enjoying the theatre show.
2. They must provide rapid response to their positional or colour changes so that the effect is virtually instantaneous from the audience viewpoint.

The trouble is, speed and quietness are not easy bedfellows. We come to the requirements of the TV and film industries. Any luminaires used in these industries would invariably have to be supplied to go with rigging systems and the whole integrated very carefully. In TV one luminaire without lateral movement will not be able to take the place of three other luminaires. One of the problems in TV and film is that we have always got an obtrusive object called a boom microphone that hovers around creating rather nasty shadows if the lighting is not correctly positioned; therefore the position of the luminaire is extremely critical.

There would appear to be two forms of control desirable when using automated lighting for the film and TV industries, one of which is the ability of an LD to implement his intended plot from his home computer to the studio. The second form of control would be that when the rehearsals and takes or transmissions are involved, he has full control of the luminaires from a control room adjacent to the studio. In television the control of the lights is relatively easy because the LD will have camera preview monitors to see the effect of any adjustments made; in the film industry, however, this might not be the case although some systems do use combined video/film techniques. The biggest snag in the TV and film industries is the fact that the units would probably be too noisy for the quiet conditions demanded by the realization team in any studio.

11.3 System control

We have talked at great length about the actual system applied to the luminaires themselves but somehow all the functions have to be controlled from a console of some description. It is more than likely that the console we have will bear a great similarity to a lighting control system and in many cases the two are integrated as one unit. With more functions requiring control, the system has to be more complex, which brings us to the point of how do the control signals go from the console to the functional parts on the luminaires? Well, we turn to our friend the 'digit' which rapidly goes down pieces of wire from the control area to the luminaires themselves. If the control system used means that a luminaire has to wait until another luminaire has finished all its functional movements, then this is much slower than a system which allows two or more luminaires to be adjusted simultaneously. The limiting point in the speed of operation is that, as more functions are required, each luminaire needs more control signals. These take a finite time to be accepted and made operable. If a large number of adjustments are having to be made at the same time, the system itself may become slow and cumbersome. Thus, the effects are observable and not acceptable as far as the LD is concerned.

Having decided that we require to get signals from point A to point B to control the luminaires, how are these signals distributed in the premises? It is impractical to take a set of control wires for each function to each luminaire, and therefore a superior way is to provide a digital control 'bus' with provision made for take-off points for the luminaires involved. This then means that each luminaire plugged into the 'bus' must have a code number recognized by the control system itself. The fact that the luminaire must be capable of communicating to the master control system means that a 'bi-directional' control system has to be provided. If any luminaire is changed within the lighting rig due to possible failure or a requirement change, a definite code must be sent, on substitution, so that the system recognizes the type of luminaire in use and its position in the system.

One of the reasons for using motorized systems is the requirement to reduce operating costs and, as can be imagined, the cost of automated lighting systems is fairly high. The cost of any system will be dictated by the complexity of the luminaires concerned: if simple functions such as 'pan and tilt' only are desired to be automated then this is obviously much cheaper than a TV studio full of multipurpose luminaires where many functions would have to be controlled. It may be that our need for using motorized luminaires is that it makes life so much easier when the number of luminaires in a lighting rig is reduced; this would be particularly so on large-scale musicals mounted on the West End stage.

11.4 Studio installations

What type of studio is suitable for an automated lighting system? If we start at the lower end of the scale with small interview situations, there is probably no need to automate any small studio that has only two or three-handed interview situations as the lighting could be left for the majority of the time and even when changes were desired, these would be small and relatively insignificant. Studios of this type often run with little or no electrical staff and in fact the lighting may be adjusted by any of the vision operators concerned. Moving up a notch, we get to a small studio of approximately $150\,m^2$ which would be the kind used for small regional programmes and local news input. In this type of studio the programmes are usually based around an anchor man/woman sitting at one position with two or three set-ups to cover for much of the news intake of the day and local current affairs programmes. They have, on past occasions, been used for small dramas and for small audience participation shows – all of which lead to variations in the lighting rig itself. Owing to the repertory nature and repeatability of the lighting over quite long periods, possibly over a programme period of 13/26/52 weeks, there is a definite need for a repeatable rigging system, and an automated lighting control system in a studio such as this is highly desirable. The idea is that the LD could have the studio rigged with about eight basic but different set-ups to cover most of the situations he is likely to encounter on a day-to-day basis. Having received the information as to the programme content, it would then be very easy for the LD to dial up 'Set 1', 'Set 2', and so on, until he has the combination of sets so desired for the programme content of the day. If the luminaires are fixed in their application, such as a 'key' light, these will invariably be Fresnel spotlights, together with a requirement for softlights as fillers. However, to allow the LD a greater degree of flexibility, the use of multipurposes is to be encouraged so that any luminaire can perform any function – within reason. Subsequently, there will probably be a reduction in the overall size of the rig. This type of installation lends itself to the use of the motorized pantograph working within a reasonable range of lateral flexibility and height, together with a multipurpose luminaire. This system, as already noted, allows space for luminaires to move alongside each other, so accuracy of rigging is reasonable. It might be that the control system is clever enough to know that if one luminaire is not within striking distance of another luminaire it can move to a new position, thus allowing accurate rigging. It may be an operational requirement that all luminaires are parked at one end of any trackway and the system should be intelligent enough to allow this operation to take place without any problems.

What happens when we go to a main line studio, say of about $500\,\text{m}^2$, where we would expect to cover any production such as drama, dance, music, light entertainment, audience participation, comedy shows, etc.? If we take drama, it is quite possible that we will not necessarily be confined to single storey sets, but we may have multiple storey sets which cause problems because of their height. There could be scaffold arrangements built in studios of this type, which might be for high cameras, for example. It might be that we need special follow spot positions rigged, which again involve scaffolding towers and special positions within the studio. There will be a need to light the cyc cloths to a higher degree of evenness than would be required in a smaller studio and this would therefore require special cyc lights to be rigged at high level. There will also be a need in the largest studio for scenery to be suspended from the grid itself, necessitating the use of spot winching systems, lines and supplementary barrels or drapes to be positioned, all of which conspire against the movement of luminaires along the grid system: thus traversing becomes extremely difficult. The problem can be eased in a monopole studio by restricting the lateral movement of the units themselves. If we are considering a barrel rigged studio, such as the BBC uses, then the problem is not so acute because the basic barrel system allows spaces for the scenery suspension system. It is only where supplementary barrels have to be placed, possibly at right angles to normal, that there could be problems.

The major drawback to automation in studios of this size is that the programmes are not repertory by nature and are usually 'one offs'. A series of six situation comedy programmes will be different in their content on a weekly basis. It is no good pretending that although we have a 'stock set' every week, such as a police station in a series of programmes, lighting within that set will stay the same, because it will vary according to the action within that area. Therefore 'normal' lighting does not exist. This highlights the main problem when trying to apply automated systems to large studios. The lighting is extremely varied, there are difficulties in moving the lights themselves and this also requires that on every individual programme the LD would have to reprogramme most of the lights in the studio on that production, even on the repetitive week-to-week series that may be shot. If the system could be made as sophisticated as possible then, as stated previously, the LD would have the pleasure of sitting at home with his computer, working out the lighting plot and then sending it down the modem to the studio centre to have it rigged automatically. The problem comes – when does it get rigged? We are certain that the scenery department will be most indignant while they are rigging to find that lights keep moving around. Do the scenery department have to say to the lighting man's computer: 'We've finished, you can carry on now'?

Large studio productions rely for speed and efficiency upon scene crews and electrical crews largely integrating their work output so that time is reduced in the rig and pre-light session. If we have to have a situation where the lighting has to be allowed to reset itself, and rejig itself to new positions, is this done before the sets are placed in position? Because this is not the normal way of doing things. At the present time, sets are rigged and the lights are dropped in to suit the action on the sets. What happens if the scenic designer has made a change, or for that matter the sets have been placed off their marks in the studio? This actually happened to one of the authors, working on a very famous police programme in the 1960s, where the whole studio had to be relit from scratch, due to a design mix-up prior to the first day of rehearsals. Would the lighting man's computer know this? And when his luminaires position themselves, would they be able to ascertain this? Not without extremely good intelligence which would require enormous computer capacity with a very sophisticated feedback system from the luminaires.

It would seem therefore that there is a case for automation in the smaller to medium sized studio but its application to large production studios is probably a remote dream and most likely will never be realized. Even if we could have equipment of the intelligence required to solve many of the problems, could we actually afford it all? Would our capital costs be recovered by the savings on the operating costs? Possibly with some of the clever young accountants of today this might be the case; but we believe in actual practice this is unlikely. With regard to the larger studio, what is desired is a better degree of control of the luminaires to help the LD. Remote control of the functions on a key light would allow the LD to adjust the effect while sitting in the correct viewing position. This applies equally to all forms of entertainment lighting.

In conclusion, it must be realized that there is no magic solution for productivity in television or film studios. Each studio has unique problems of its own and thus must be designed for the purpose to which its major functions are best met. It is, however, an inescapable fact that unless television studios throughout the world reduce costs, by whatever means are necessary, we will for evermore be looking at the same jaded mixture of programmes every night on every channel.

12 Electrical distribution

Introduction

In the past, and indeed up to recently, film studios often generated their own power. This was in the form of a dc voltage, usually at 120 V and mainly used because of the need to supply carbon arc sources used in the film industry. The basis of the 120 V was the importation from America of the lighting technology used in film studios. As the public supply authorities did not in general supply dc voltage, it was necessary for the film studio to install large diesel driven generators. Associated with the 120 V systems used was the need to have much larger copper feeder cables than would be normal in the United Kingdom, due to the current being used. With the advent of much more sophisticated dc power supplies, particularly of a size such as the film industry would demand, it was easier to supply systems with ac voltage and transform and rectify it to the 120 V needed.

Nearly all entertainment premises these days use ac power supplies provided by the local electricity authority. In the smaller installation one three-phase transformer will usually be fed from an 11 kV high voltage main. In the larger installations, it is quite possible that a high voltage ring main will be used with several substations to transform from 11 kV to 415 V within the building and positioned adjacent to the areas of maximum demand. A big problem for supply authorities these days is that the supply system itself contains a high proportion of harmonics created by the use of discharge lighting systems such as fluorescent and in many cases the use of solid state semi-conductor equipment such as computer power supplies. Unfortunately in large entertainment premises using lighting systems we do have a high proportion of fluorescent lighting in the offices, we may have a high proportion of discharge lighting on the sets, and we certainly have many dimmer racks full of solid state equipment generating harmonics. In theory, in a balanced three-phase system all the current will flow in the phase conductors and not in the neutral. Unfortunately in the situations quoted, it is possible to have as much current in the neutral as contained in the phases themselves.

So far we have discussed the supply of power for use in an entertainment situation from the public supply system but of course it is possible to have a back-up generator used within the premises to prevent any problems if the public power supply fails. If back-up power systems are used only for technical equipment then the loads may not be too great and small diesel generators are a good proposition. When applied to the lighting systems where considerable amounts of power are required, it is not always economically viable to install standby power equipment. Most television companies install a small generator, sufficiently large to keep a small amount of crucial equipment operating and capable of being used for transmission, with sufficient power spare to enable, say, captions and one announcer to be lit.

In very large installations, it is probable that two incoming supplies from the local 11 kV distribution system are provided to the premises with an arrangement made for changeover facilities in the event of failure. It is extremely advantageous in a large building to use a ring main for the high voltage supplies so that in the event of damage or faults to equipment, an alternative supply route can be utilized. In premises such as a large television studio complex there is a need to keep the studios working as much as possible, and therefore when maintenance is required, it is important that the local transformer can be bypassed and the area supplied from another source to enable essential maintenance to be carried out. Routine maintenance on all the switchgear will obviously have to be done on a regular basis.

Within any installation, the siting of the main transformers and switchgear connected with either high voltage or low voltage systems has to be carefully considered and the installation well planned. In the smaller installation, only one low voltage substation will probably be provided; additionally one switch room will be installed close to the incoming supply and within this room will be a factory-built assembly from specialist manufacturers which will incorporate the circuit breakers, fuses, mcbs and metering systems. A very important point in the selection of the electrical power systems is that the electrical designer concerned should ensure that most equipment is fairly standard, so that any problems can be quickly overcome and the spares holding is reasonable in size. Usually the lighting power is controlled by a special switch on the lighting console, probably remotely engaging a large contactor in the switch room. Although it would be nice to think that this contactor would be operated as a 'no load' device, thus ensuring that the contacts within the switchgear are not burnt by opening under large electrical loads and thus causing arcing, there is no guarantee that this will not happen. In practice therefore the switchgear has to interrupt large currents.

In general in the entertainment industry, it is not a good idea to install systems that would automatically shut off the supply in the event of an overload. In the theatre, this would spoil the audience's enjoyment of the production and in television, where large audiences may be watching a live programme, an auto switchdown of the system would be annoying in the extreme. Systems are therefore generally designed to have warnings displayed for overloads so that the operating staff can take avoiding action. As already pointed out in Chapter 10 the installed capacity of luminaires can quite often exceed that of the power allowed for any installation, and therefore good discipline of the operators is required to prevent an overload of the system.

For ease of operation and to minimize disruption in the event of faults, generally with lighting installations, it is wise to have several small pieces of switchgear feeding dimmer racks, thus ensuring no one item of equipment on failing would take the whole system out of action. One good thing about most modern dimming equipment is that it is generally well protected by fuses or mcbs and therefore faults are contained within individual parts of the system and not reflected back into the main system.

In the theatre and generally in film studios and television studios, lighting creates the greatest demand for electricity. With demands ranging from hundreds of kilowatts to possibly even thousands of kilowatts, lighting has to be considered almost separately from the rest of the installation. The loads it can impose on a three-phase system can have quite severe effects on the rest of that system.

Theatres have always traditionally used 15 A plugs but today the situation has changed somewhat and most installations in the UK will use BS 4343 plugs and sockets in either 16 A, 32 A or 63 A rating. This also holds true for most TV installations. One great advantage of using this range for plugs and sockets is that they are very readily available from many sources and are relatively cheap. In practice, they have proved to be extremely rugged and very adaptable.

There are no hard and fast rules with regard to the provision of lighting power outlets in any installation. The numbers involved will require liaison for the individual installation between the lighting consultant and the user of the premises. The factors, however, to be taken into account include maximum usage of any premises so that on installation all needs are catered for because it is so much easier and cheaper to do it in the first place than modify systems at a later date.

Film studios are a slightly different case when compared with TV and theatre, because their power intakes do not generally feed dimming systems. So the main requirement is to have banks of switchgear with individual contactors or isolators supplying large distribution frames somewhere within the studio. These are usually at floor level although there could be some power distribution at high level if a grid is installed or a gallery provided around the studio itself. Film power distribution tends to be rather flexible in nature, using long leads to distribute power to various parts of the sets involved. These days the requirements of British Standards for power distribution, be it on outside broadcasts or filming, involve the use of specified distribution units so that an installation is somewhat safer than the old style of production. These distribution units contain circuit breakers, fuses, and at times RCDs, to prevent any harmful electric shock. Other types of power connectors are also allowed for under British Standards for the distribution of power on film and TV, but generally it is preferable to use the BS 4343 range because of ease of replacement.

12.1 Substation and switchgear

When using power of hundreds of kilowatts, it makes sense to have large transformers very close to the areas concerned. This enables high voltage feeds, say 11 kV, to be fed to local substations and then be transformed down to a 415 V three-phase system. One snag with having the transformer very close to the dimmer room is that the impedance of the cables between the dimmer cabinets and the transformer is extremely low, allowing very high fault currents to occur. This means that the dimming equipment supplied will have to meet exacting tests.

In the smaller installation, it will not be practical to allow the lighting system to be fed from its own transformer and it will have to share power requirements with the remainder of the building. In larger installations, however, it is preferable that the lighting system has its own transformer and when systems are of the order of 500 kW this makes life so much easier. It may also be possible in the very large installation that two studios can share a transformer and even bigger transformers can be installed. It can be advantageous to have a dimmer room with two sets of switchgear, fed by a common transformer, covering two studios.

Lighting loads in a studio, when the console is being used in anger, on some types of shows, might vary from the solo spotlight on a performer, perhaps at 2 kW, to a complete lighting change of 300–400 kW of power, and this imposes enormous surges on the power system. Thus, the inherent stability of the lighting power system has to be good and the requirement met by high quality transformers as well as modern self-stabilizing dimming systems.

If we take the distribution in a large dimmer room the main incoming power from the adjacent transformer will be fed through armoured cables to the switchgear and then via a busbar system through the switchgear. The switchgear provides for an isolator per dimmer rack. This is for (a) safe

Figure 12.1   Main switchgear/dimmer room

isolation for maintenance; and (b) to isolate parts of the equipment in the event of a major fault. It is important to have individual isolators for the equipment and not a common isolator to more than one piece of equipment which could cause a problem during the normal operation of the premises; and of course it is not very useful when you have to shut down the entire system just to maintain one dimmer. All the lighting power will usually be under the control of a contactor on the input to the switchboard, so that lighting power can be remotely switched from the lighting control room. This contactor will have to be quite large: it will also need to be rated for live working conditions. There is no guarantee that 'no load' conditions will exist at the time the contactor operates.

It is usual to feed from the isolators on the switchgear to the dimmer racks with armoured multicore cable and, as this has a definite bending radius, it is often advantageous to use parallel multicore cables of a slightly smaller physical size so that they may be manipulated easily within the dimmer room. Generally dimmer racks are fed via the top of the units which makes access fairly easy, although on some occasions we are likely to find the air conditioning installation technicians trying to impose their trunking in the most awkward places. Other than armoured cables, the use of trunking to enclose PVC power feeder cables can be advantageous, because PVC cables are much easier to manipulate than their armoured counterparts. We have already noted in Chapter 8 that it is extremely important to provide sufficient space for the termination of the mains input cables. The racks' incoming cables may range from $16\,mm^2$ cables on smaller installations up to $400\,mm^2$ cables or the equivalent on very large dimmer racks.

12.2 Power and balance for three phases

In the past, due to the British regulations pertaining at the time which treated single and three-phase working voltages differently, it was very difficult to feed the lighting system effectively from three-phase supplies, owing to the need for defined limits of separation between socket outlets on different phases. In practice, this often meant that all floor sockets were often on the same phase as the technical equipment. In trunking arrangements with socket outlets fitted, and especially on barrels, it was difficult to prevent clusters of equipment appearing on the same phase causing large imbalances over the three phases. The main reason was that studios had to have the individual barrel outlets on the same phase; thus one-third of the barrels would be connected to the 'red' phase, one-third to 'yellow' and the remainder 'blue'. Generally, the barrels were interspersed as sets of three for phase distribution. Thus barrel 1 would be red, barrel 2 blue, barrel 3 yellow and so on. Sometimes to get around loading problems in an installation, yellow and red phases would be used for lighting and blue for the remainder of the installation. Due to a change of IEE specification, which defines *any voltage up to that of 1000 V ac between conductors, or 600 V ac between conductors and earth, as low voltage*, we are now covered for both 240 V and 415 V in one voltage range and the requirement for separation has lapsed. We can now quite happily design the lighting distribution to be spread over three phases for the ease of balancing the power system. Although it is possible to design the studio to work on three phases, and also to arrange some form of uniform distribution throughout the grid system and lighting sockets generally, we have no guarantee that the luminaires will be plugged in a balanced way or that the use of the lights controlled by the lighting console will not, by coincidence, use only one phase.

When the lighting director is producing his lighting plot for the electricians to use in the studio to plug the luminaires into the electrical supply system, he will have to bear in mind the phase of the various lighting power socket outlets in the area concerned so that he can ensure a reasonable balance over three phases. If systems are using any form of 'patch' it may be that the LD indicates the lighting positions that he requires and allows the electricians to plug these into appropriate sockets. With a soft patch system in use it may be that the LD upon being given the dimmer numbers, can programme his console to suit the channel numbers in use. The main point that the LD will have to watch is the maximum capacity of each phase.

How is the lighting apportioned over the three phases so that one phase is not highly loaded in comparison to the others? It may be that the maximum current allowed on a phase dictates the amount of luminaires that the LD can use at any one time. Thus it is not always a simple matter for the lighting director to ask for various combinations of lighting equipment without having some regard for the supply concerned. For example, if the maximum current allowed is 200 A per phase, it will not be possible to allocate more than ten 5 kW luminaires to that phase. If there were some guarantee that diversity was applied, i.e. all the dimmers were never to be higher than, say '8', then more luminaires could be allocated per phase due to the lower individual current consumption.

These days, where many installations do not have permanent lighting directors but most are brought in on contract, it is more than likely that any LD does not have an intimate knowledge of the premises concerned. It is extremely important, therefore, that any technical literature that may be given to a guest lighting director in any premises is extremely accurate and reflects faithfully the lighting electrical system together with details of the lighting console installation and any quirks within the installation with regard to the general power supplies. In practice, it is no good calling for six 10 kW luminaires to be used when the system does not even have any 10 kW dimmers, or even sockets, supplied.

12.3 Distribution systems

Probably the best place to start in our distribution system is to look at an individual circuit and see the initial effects of lighting power in a practical way and then how it affects the rest of the system. The current carrying capacity of a 4 mm² PVC cable is 30 A and a 240 V 5 kW circuit will draw 20.83 A, and therefore superficially it would appear that this cable would be sufficient for our purposes; but unfortunately that is not the end of the story. It is important in any installation that the volts dropped by the currents flowing down the cables do not exceed certain limits. The concern with voltage drop is that items of equipment might cease to operate correctly and therefore constitute some form of danger. In the British IEE wiring regulations, the maximum volt drop stipulated until recently was 2.5% which on a 240 V system represents a maximum drop of 6 V. In the light of experience, the latest edition (16th of the IEE wiring regulations) proposes that the volt drop limit can be extended to a 4% band, thus allowing a maximum drop of 9.6 V. Although this proposal widens the tolerance, it still expects equipment to work correctly. Obviously with the majority of lighting equipment, we are not so much concerned with the volt drop to the luminaire as the tungsten lamps will operate on any voltage from zero to their maximum. Our problem, in practice, if we lose too many volts down the cable, is that the lamps will commence to burn at a lower colour temperature than that desired even at maximum applied volts, and although not critical in a theatre, this might prove to be a problem with aligning cameras. Voltage drop on a domestic installation will not be very high as the lengths of cables involved are relatively short. However, let us take a practical example in an installation using a 240 V 5 kW dimmer, feeding a socket in the acting area and where the cable from the dimmer to the socket is 80 metres long.

PVC single core cable (in trunking)	V drop for 80 m
4 mm^2 11 mV per amp per metre of run	= 18.3 V
6 mm^2 7.3 mV per amp per metre of run	= 12.2 V
10 mm^2 4.4 mV per amp per metre of run	= 7.3V

It will be readily appreciated that all of these voltage drops exceed the 2.5% limits as laid down by the present 15th Edition IEE regulations, and only the 10 mm^2 cable would be acceptable under the revised 16th Edition of the regulations. It is therefore possible that the 10 mm^2 cable figures of 7.3 V at the present time would be acceptable.

A further problem now arises. Most luminaires are fed via flexible cables and if we assume this to be a 4 mm^2 3-cored flexible cable, then even a short lead, 5 m long, will give us 1.3 V of voltage drop on a 5 kW luminaire. This has to be added to the 10 mm^2 figure.

Yet an even bigger problem occurs, when the 80 metres of 10 mm^2 cable is terminated at grid level, instead of going directly to a socket in the acting area. This is usually to allow the inter-connection of a 4 mm^2 flexible cable from the termination point, via a flip flop cable system, down to a socket on a suspension bar. If this cable was 15 m long, we would get a further voltage drop of 4 V. If we run all the figures together, which might be possible in a TV studio installation, we therefore have, using 10 mm^2 cable, a loss of 7.3 V. We have a further loss of 4 V on the feeder from the grid system to the bar outlet socket and the luminaire lead will also have a loss amounting to 1.3 V, so our total loss is 12.6 V, which is above the desired IEE technical parameters.

However, in the studio, this might not give a problem with the intensity of light, but we do have to bear in mind that if this were a 240 V system, we would have a colour temperature change of 5 K per volt. When calculated this gives $12.6 \times 5\,K = 63\,K$. It is not unknown in practice, unfortunately, that lamps are delivered from manufacturers with low operating colour temperatures and these may be around 3100 K for a nominal 3200 K lamp. So instead of our system now producing a start point of 3200 K, it may be we are closer to 3000 K, and of course we intended lining the TV cameras up around this point. If we reduce the dimmer to '7' which would be our normal starting point for technical line up, we would have a colour temperature output from the lamp of about 2850 K, which is really at the lower acceptable limit of the video camera and so does not allow for any further dimming of the light sources if we are to maintain the cameras' colour integrity.

Thus it is extremely important that cables between the areas and on the equipment themselves are as generous as possible to avoid voltage drop. It is, of course, possible to have the input transformers feeding the switchgear and dimmer racks adjusted so that they deliver high volts on input, say 250 V, to offset some of the voltage drop in a system, but this is a practice which should not be encouraged. By starting with high volts at the input to the dimming system, and then getting a voltage surge, it might be that the safe voltage limits on the dimmer control circuits are exceeded and this would be quite disastrous.

In most installations in the entertainment industry these days, electrical services will be conveyed by trunking or cable trays. Due to the amount of cables used in installations, which may be pairs of single conductors or multicore cables, it requires that the trunking and tray systems installed will have to be prefabricated from steel, due to its strength and rigidity. Cables fed by either system at high level in the premises will, unfortunately, be in the area of the highest temperatures. It may be that the use of cable trays is more advantageous with the cables being exposed to the air, particularly if not bunched, and probably not having the same electrical requirements of those that are totally enclosed. However, due to the need to keep the EM interference as low as possible, it is preferable to keep all cables from dimming systems in trunking rather than on trays and this is particularly important when the dimmers are feeding low level sockets within the premises where they may be in close proximity to sound circuits. As a guide, if separations of approximately 300 mm or greater are used between the lighting power cables, and any other installed cables, there will not be a problem.

Another major advantage of metal trunking systems is that they can provide an extremely good earth continuity throughout the installation and in addition afford a high degree of mechanical protection to the cables. In the theatre, the trunking systems will be provided generally to the periphery of the stage area so that power feeds can be taken across to the lighting bars on flexible cables. In film studios, as already noted, most of the distribution will be at floor level. In television studios, however, nearly all the distribution is at high level and this means that the system has to be carefully integrated with the layout of any monopole system, bar system, motorized pantograph system or even a fairly simple lighting system such as fixed barrels. If we require clearance above a grid for access, it is important that trunking is not put in the most awkward places, thus creating possible hazards to the operational staff working in the area. As can be seen from Figure 12.2, most systems will use trunking at high level, dropping it down to outlet points on a fairly regular basis and usually this will be a central box feeding four winch units at the same time. In the case of monopoles, quite complex socket arrangements are provided.

Figure 12.2 Typical BBC grid showing power distribution trunking

One problem with using dimmer systems is that the harmonic content of the waveforms is extremely high when they are in 90° conduction, and if we are not careful we will have high circulating currents in the neutral and earth conductors.

There are two basic rules which are extremely important: *all circuits wired from the dimmer room to the acting area should be wired as live/neutral pairs of conductors in the same conductor size.* The use of several small independent phase conductors with a large common neutral is to be deprecated, because this in itself can cause a problem. For example, in one large broadcasting studio that was converted from saturable reactors to thyristor dimmers using common neutral systems, the circulating harmonics caused severe eddy currents in the trunking in the studio and created conditions where it was extremely difficult to hold a conversation against the noise, and also the trunking was getting rather hot. It is worth noting that it cost quite a lot of money to correct this design error.

Equally important and at times capable of causing more problems, is the correct earthing of the system. It is essential that the earthing system does not form a ring conductor within the system but all earths should be radial conductors and, if possible, taken to a nominated star point. To avoid problems on most installations these days, it is usual practice to adopt a 'clean earth' policy where the technical equipment is on a separate earth system to the dimming system – if this is at all possible. Any circulating earth currents can cause a greater problem with the sound and vision equipment than the electromagnetic interference radiated by the cables from the dimmers.

In addition to the power cables for the individual circuits from dimmer racks, there are control system inputs from the control room to all dimmer racks and these will be conveyed in either separate trunking or by small flexible cables fed within the racks themselves. On the whole, the control cable is relatively immune from interference problems. The main precaution to take with analogue signal cables is to ensure that the cables are well screened internally. With digital inputs now becoming more normal, control system interference is virtually non-existent, as any random signals can be prevented from causing problems by checking all the data for error signals.

Other than the power wiring in the studio, there will be a need for additional trunking which provides for the control cables to and from the various control consoles within the studio and these would be as follows:

1. Local electricians' panel.
2. Lighting hoist control panel.
3. Scenery winch control panel.

These may be placed anywhere at studio floor level for the ease of the local operators, but they tend to be grouped, particularly those for the electricians' panel and the lighting hoist panel.

12.4 Plugs, sockets and distribution

Most of the sockets used in the theatre are supplied by 2.5 kW dimmers although there are requirements for some 5 kW circuits and on occasions 10 kW circuits are used. In the theatre, parallel sockets can be advantageous on the dimmer outputs to enable pairs of light sources to be coupled together. This is obviously very convenient for two cross lights on the artistes. Many theatres, even today, still use the traditional 15 A plugs and sockets. There is, however, a slow change taking place over to BS 4343 (CEE 17), 16 A, 32 A and 63 A plugs and sockets.

With a limited number of dimmers, it is possible to have a power patch system so that the sockets to be powered in the 'active lit' area can be connected to dimmers as appropriate to the area concerned. This is often done in smaller installations where perhaps 24 dimmers are provided feeding 48 sockets. A good thing about patch systems is that, usually, the power from the dimmer to the socket is on a 'one to one' basis with very little chance of circuit overloads occurring. If, however, the dimmer units are provided with parallel sockets on the front panels for convenience, there is the danger of overloads when the operators are not careful.

Due to the flexible nature of monopole grids, it is necessary to provide a reasonable number of dimmers which cater for the maximum size of production in the studio but because of the need to keep continually repositioning monopoles and to prevent long flexible leads, several parallel sockets at high level are required. Either we have a very clever switching system to prevent any of the individual circuits being overloaded or we rely upon the operators making the right decision when plugging up the various luminaire feeder cables.

In pantograph systems, when permanent catenary systems are employed feeding the individual luminaires on the base of the pantographs one seldom finds circuit overloads. This is because the system is strictly 'one to one'.

Motorized barrel systems will employ a variety of sockets mounted adjacent to the suspension barrel for the luminaires. In general, the circuits will be 5 kW and the minimum number usually supplied per 2.5 metre bar, for example, will be three circuits. It is possible that one or more of these circuits may be installed with parallel sockets across the dimmer circuit so that two small luminaires can be patched to one dimmer from the bar itself. In addition to the normal outlets for the Fresnels and softlights used, there will be a requirement for either additional standard sockets or for special sockets for cyclorama lighting units.

The distribution system will also feed floor outlets but the circuits are usually connected directly to the dimmer units. On occasions, it may be advantageous to switch between floor lighting power sockets and high level lighting power sockets, but if this is switched in the correct manner the power can only be in one place at any one time, and therefore a circuit overload is avoided.

In a television studio, other than the need for the power sockets for the normal lighting on any of the types of suspension used, there is a need for additional sockets to be used for effects lighting, cyc lighting and discharge lighting which may require connection to a three-phase system, and this is usually provided by special sockets in selected locations to suit the installation.

One area where special sockets are required is for the lighting of cyclorama cloths. Groundrow cyclorama units invariably are supplied with 625 W lamps per compartment. If we use four-compartment groundrow units for four-colour mixing, we can feed a string of eight of the same colour compartments from one dimmer, i.e. $8 \times 625\,W = 5\,kW$. Special cables are supplied by manufacturers to allow the linking of several units. These may be integral to the unit itself or supplied as preformed cables in eight, four and single way configurations.

Cyclorama lighting units when employed at the top of cycs invariably use 1250 W lamps and we could therefore light four of the same compartments from one dimmer, i.e. $4 \times 1250\,W = 5\,kW$. Top cyc units can be supplied by manufacturers with input cables to suit the installation power sockets. They can vary from a single cable and plug attached to each compartment to a nine-pin male connector, used for the four circuits, going to special sockets provided in the grid system.

Figure 12.3   Electrical distribution box

As an example, let us take the case of overhead cyc lighting with four units used, each with four compartments fed from four 5 kW dimmers, Dimmer A feeding the first colour, Dimmer B the second colour, Dimmer C the third colour and finally Dimmer D the fourth colour. In the case of groundrow units, obviously the four dimmers are still required but we now can feed eight sets of four compartment units rather than the four used at high level. For convenience, we can install sockets in groups of four

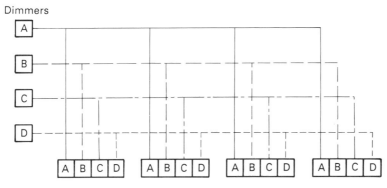

Dimmers

Four-compartment CYC lighting units

Figure 12.4   Cyclorama lighting distribution

representing A,B,C,D, for use by either cyclorama system. It may be that the barrel system at high level also has a permanent cyclorama lighting installation which would utilize groups of A,B,C,D, sockets where the sockets would be paralleled in groups of four, i.e. $4 \times$ A, $4 \times$ B, $4 \times$ C, $4 \times$ D, across one dimmer output.

In addition to this type of socket used in the studio, there will be a need for a distribution, in some studios, of 10 kW sockets when higher powered luminaires may be required. When the 10 kW socket is not being used, it is preferable to supply two 5 kW sockets in parallel, switched from and

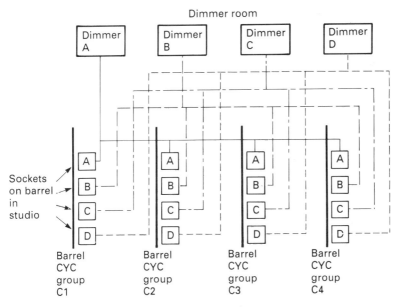

Dimmer room

Studio barrels

Figure 12.5   Permanently installed cyclorama distribution

adjoining the 10 kW socket and all fed from the same 10 kW dimmer; thus upon selection, one 10 kW socket could be used or two parallel 5 kW sockets. These 5 kW sockets would have to be sub-fused on the adjacent panel next to the selection switch.

12.5 Fuses and circuit breakers

There are two functions required from the protective devices we use, one of which is to protect for normal overload conditions, such as lamps failing or incorrectly plugged luminaires creating too much current on a circuit. In addition, the devices have to be adequately rated so that they safely stand fault currents caused by short circuits.

The wiring going from the switchgear to the dimmer racks has to be protected either by fuses or some form of circuit breaker. Before we go any further it would perhaps be wise to look at the magnitude of currents that flow from the main switchgear to the dimmer racks. In a fairly straightforward simple installation using packs of 6 × 2.5 kW dimmers each pack, which would probably be connected to 240 V single phase, would consume 62.5 A on full load. At the other end of the scale, using a high density dimmer rack containing 192 5 kW dimmers, spread over three phases, we would have 1333 A per phase on full load. With smaller systems it is probably just as easy to protect the input to the dimmer racks by fuses. However, with higher current systems, it is more than likely that the electrical installation engineer will install circuit breakers of sufficient rating to meet the demands of the dimmer racks. As far as the output of the individual dimmers themselves goes these can be protected either by mcbs or fuses.

At this point it would be worthwhile looking at fault currents. What do we mean by fault current? If we are stupid enough to place a piece of wire across a 240 V supply and switch on, the wire disappears rather quickly. By using a simple bit of Ohm's law it will soon be realized that the current is governed by the resistance of the piece of wire and if the piece of wire does not have much resistance the current can become quite large. For example, if a piece of wire with a resistance of 1/100 Ω is placed across a 240 V supply, the current flowing through the piece of wire would be 24,000 A. It is reasonably obvious that with a current flow of this magnitude, unless we are using an enormously thick piece of wire, the wire would actually vaporize and thus fuse. In practice we would not just be concerned with a piece of wire across the 240 V supply, because in addition to the resistance of the wire will be the resistance of all the cables feeding to the initial point where the wire is inserted in the circuit. Thus, the nearer we are to the point of supply the greater will be the fault current. On the input to the main switchgear from the substation and its transformer we can get very high fault currents indeed. If, however, the fault occurs at the end of a 100 metres of cable run the fault current will be relatively low. Although in practice it would be rare to have a short circuit at the output of a dimmer, for example, the rules and regulations regarding protection state that we have to protect for a short circuit at this point. Thus the prospective fault current has to be verified for this point. Why should we be worried about a short circuit in the wiring system? We are concerned with avoiding short circuits in our lighting feeders because of the danger due to the magnetic and thermal effects they can produce in the conductors and on busbar systems. We must therefore place protective devices in the conductors which must operate sufficiently quickly and in absolute safety to prevent this kind of danger. If we are going to use a fuse, we can meet the fault current requirement by selecting fuses with a high rupturing capacity; for example BS 88 in the United Kingdom allows for a rupturing capacity of 80 kA. Another method of protecting circuits is by using an air circuit breaker (acb) or a moulded case circuit breaker (mccb). These will also have to be rated to meet the prospective fault current.

Thus the switchgear feeding the dimmer racks will be provided with, say, fuses to handle 400 A running current and if a normal overload occurs will rupture relatively quickly. In addition, they will have to fuse immediately with a fault current of around 20,000 A. Acbs and mccbs are often specified for high current applications of about 400 A and greater on switchgear. Fuses are generally used below this point.

Many mcbs that are used for circuits with much lower current capacity have fault current ratings of somewhere between 6000 A and 9000 A, particularly in the type that we would select for dimmers. It is more than likely that the potential fault current of the circuits involved will exceed these values. It would seem at this point that an mcb could not be used to protect our outgoing circuits; however, in practice this is not the case, because we are allowed to use a device which is not quite adequate if we back it up with a fuse which adequately protects the complete circuit. Thus, if the prospective fault current was 8000 A and the breaking capacity of the mcb we had selected was 6000 A, we would have to back up the mcb with a fuse with a breaking capacity in excess of 8000 A so that the circuit was fully protected.

Most of the devices to protect the installation will have to be carefully selected. We have to bear in mind that there will be more than one device protecting the circuits so the protection devices have to be carefully integrated with each other so that discrimination is achieved. For example, it is no good having the mccb feeding the dimmer rack failing when only one outgoing dimmer circuit has a fault.

12.6 Meters

It is fairly obvious that the fault conditions can be calculated and appropriate measures incorporated in the switchgear, dimmer racks and any ancillary equipment feeding a stage or studio area. Overload conditions are catered for by the selection of devices that disconnect the supply when a certain current level is reached.

From an operational point of view it is important that we monitor the parameters of the supply so that we do not create overloads on the main power intake. It may be that if you are on a special tariff, going 'over the top' costs real money. By putting voltmeters across the phases it will be possible to see the state of the voltage within the premises, although in general these are somewhat of a luxury because even if the volts are wrong you can do little or nothing about it. One of the problems with supplying voltmeters is: 'Where do you actually take the reading? If it is taken at the switchgear, it is quite possible that the voltage will be reasonable; if we take it at a studio socket it is more than likely it will be several volts lower and, due to the varying lengths of run in a studio, it would be highly impractical to adopt a policy of looking at socket voltage outputs. Therefore the master voltage of the studio is the only one, but unfortunately this is rather misleading in practice.

What can be done, however, is to ensure that the capacity of the system is not exceeded by trying to draw too much current. If ammeters are

Figure 12.6   Power meters

supplied which monitor the current of the total system, and individually monitor supply to various parts of the system, then we can ensure an overload does not take place. On any lighting system it is preferable that an ammeter is placed in the incoming supply to the dimmer rack installation so that the total current can be monitored. This can then be displayed on remote metering systems in control rooms and in the dimmer room and at stage or studio floor level. Modern metering systems use low volt signals to convey the information from special transducers built into the equipment. The metering systems should be placed for the operators' benefit and it is essential that the operators can read clearly what is indicated. It is very frustrating to have a meter with a red segment indicating the overload area, when you actually cannot see the needle and where it is pointing. Thus, generally, if meters are supplied they will require little lights to illuminate the panels. Of course, self-illuminating meters could be used and in recent years some use of gas discharge bar graphs have been used where rising columns of bars indicate the voltage and current levels reached. On the whole, analogue meters are preferable, although there's much to be said for a digital display where the current level is clearly displayed in figures and not open to the operator's interpretation.

It is not a good idea to have a trip system which on sensing an overload would shut down that phase to avoid any further problems because from an operational point of view this would be highly undesirable. Warning systems have been incorporated into metering systems in the past which, for instance, give some indication of either approaching the danger point or the actual overload condition per phase, but unfortunately the buzzers themselves can become a nuisance in practice and they have never been brought into general use.

It is essential that there is no leakage of any currents down to earth; they should always come back up the correct paths. To ensure this, it is preferable that the earth leakage currents are monitored at the input to each dimmer rack, and this can be achieved by having a current transformer mounted at the input of any rack where the input cables are taken through and then terminated. This will make certain that the current flowing into the rack equals the current flowing back up the return conductors and thus cancels out. Any imbalance would indicate a current flowing elsewhere and hence a fault condition. Earth leakage can be monitored in each rack and then, if a fault occurs, a local indicator is activated. All the individual rack EL warning systems can be fed to a central unit which in turn sends a master warning signal to all interested parties. Isolating the problem is simply achieved by going to the dimmer room and seeing which individual rack has the fault.

13 Working lights and emergency systems

Introduction

In any area used for entertainment, there will be a requirement for four types of lighting:

1. Lighting for performance.
2. Lighting for working practices when the performance lights are not in use.
3. Houselights; provided for the benefit of audiences.
4. In the event of failure of the performance lighting, the working lights or the house lighting, an emergency lighting system has to be provided.

Houselights and working lights tend to describe lighting systems that may be achieving a somewhat similar result. In theatres, we would describe houselights as those used to illuminate the auditorium for the benefit of the audience. Working lights are used in the more technically orientated areas of the installation. In television and film studios, houselights describe the fittings provided in a studio for general illumination and they are also the working lights.

When not using the performance lighting, we need to be able to see to work on rigging sets and to make changes to the production lighting within a building. In the so called 'good old days' this seemed to be answered, if one views any Hollywood movie, with a 60 W lamp stuck in a stand in the centre of a stage. Unfortunately, that is not now good enough, because with the new measures to increase safety within working premises used for entertainment, light levels have to be sufficiently high so that hazards to staff and artistes are avoided. There are no hard and fast rules for light levels for working lights and it is generally left for the users to decide what is best for their installation. Guidance for light levels in various areas is given by the IES Code For Interior Lighting in the UK.

13.1 Types of sources

Before we discuss where to put working lights in any premises let us review the light sources available, their advantages and disadvantages.

For many years, tungsten lamps have been used for house lighting and working lights and there really is not much of a problem when using this type of source. By choosing the correct lamp it is possible to get a reasonable light level commensurate with a reasonably long life. It is helpful if lamps do not have to be changed too frequently, because they are invariably in slightly inaccessible positions. The main snag with tungsten lamps is that their efficiency is low and they produce quite large amounts of waste heat. In big theatres, film and TV studio installations a considerable amount of power can be used for the house and working lights and which, in some studios, might be as high as 30 or 40 kilowatts.

It would seem advantageous, therefore, to go to other sources of light, the first of which would be the fluorescent lamp. Fluorescent lamps, which are more efficient, generate much less waste heat, and this is advantageous from both electrical and air conditioning viewpoints. One of the problems, however, of fluorescent lamps, is that unless used close to the working area they provide broad sources of illumination and are not as convenient as focused downlights which may be required when the working area has a high grid. It would seem fairly obvious that we might be able to employ high bay lighting, such as in factories, using mercury discharge lights. The advantage of this type of lighting is that it is more efficient with much less wastage of power. But mercury discharge lights have one major drawback – they take time to reach full light output; and if they fail whilst they are burning – and thus are hot – they take a long time to cool down. This means a long wait before the lamps can be restruck.

During the 1970s, the BBC experimented with the use of discharge lighting in a studio at Television Centre in London. The installation made use of reasonable quality mercury discharge lamps in parabolic reflectors aimed down to the studio floor area. To get around the problem of the warm-up time of a discharge lamp, a tungsten lamp was positioned adjacent to each of the discharge sources. Upon initial 'switch-on' the tungsten light was activated as well as the discharge lamp; after about 10 minutes, the tungsten lamp was extinguished because by this time the discharge lamps had reached their stable working condition. In normal use, if the supply to the discharge sources was interrupted, either by the operators switching 'off' the working lights, or by failure of the incoming mains, the tungsten lamps were reactivated and the control circuits waited for the discharge lights to cool down before reapplying their ignition pulses. This required a reasonable amount of intelligence to be built into the control system for the studio, particularly as the working lights were split into four quadrants and each was treated independently.

Several facts emerged from this experimental installation, one of which was that the lamps used did not maintain a good colour over their operational life and therefore some distortion was caused in the colour rendering of materials and drawings in use, being particularly troublesome to the lighting and scene crews involved. There was also a reasonably high degree of flicker present from the discharge sources. The periods of changeover from tungsten to discharge were annoying in practice and the operators much preferred the tungsten light, although it had a slightly lower light intensity. Finally, but not least, the installation of the system incurred high capital costs and although it was felt that these costs would be recovered in a reasonable period of time, this was not the case in practice.

A major problem that has emerged in recent times in the application of discharge lamps for working lights is the need to have an emergency switch to turn off the production lighting in the event of any electrical hazard occurring in the working area. When the main production lighting is removed, the working lights need to be activated immediately, and discharge sources take too long to come up to full light output. Having looked at the light output of sources used for working lights, what about the colour? We find tungsten lights will invariably give good colour rendition and cause very few problems in practice. If we choose to use fluorescent tubes for lighting the working area we have to be careful in the choice of tube so that the colour rendition is of a high order. Modern discharge sources can now be obtained with very good colour rendition and greater stability throughout their working life but for the reasons stated are not being adopted for general use in entertainment working lights.

The following light levels are given as guidance for installations: theatre auditorium (houselights) 100 lux; theatre stage area (working lights) 100–300 lux; film studios (working/houselights) 200–400 lux; TV studios (working/houselights) 300–400 lux.

13.2 Integration of working lights into the general system

Having decided upon the type of light source that we will use for a working light, where will we provide it? In the theatre, the main areas will be in the wings, above the grid, on the fly galleries and a general illumination on the stage itself. In all these areas a reasonably high illumination is required so that the operators can see clearly what they are doing, thus avoiding any accidents when handling scenery, luminaires and counterweight sets. Other than the working lights in any area, there is also a need to have some level of lighting backstage during the performance. This is to enable the stage operatives to react to cues and thus perform lighting and scene changes. It is fairly obvious that this should not disrupt the performance lighting on the stage itself and thus interfere with the effect intended by the LD. This background lighting must be of a sufficiently high level so that it too avoids any safety problems.

All of this activity is occasioned by the 'live' performance. In television and film this is not the case! Having set up the scene, movement is then restricted to keeping background noise to a minimum whilst the scene is recorded on either film or via television cameras. Thus, the need in television and film studios is for working lights over the whole area to enable sets to be erected, dressed and lit and then ultimately used for production shooting when the working lights will be switched off. In film and television, if there is a need for some special working lights within a production area, due, for example, to quick-change dressing room facilities being required, localized lighting is usually provided.

In the larger television and film studios fluorescent lights are rarely used, tungsten sources being preferred and these are usually in the form of long life 1000 W linear lamps mounted in floodlight fittings pointing downwards or in the general direction of the acting area. This enables a reasonably high illumination level in the main area. In smaller studios, it is quite possible to use fluorescent fittings to provide an adequate light level on the studio floor. However, it may require several twin units to produce the light level required as it is more difficult to provide focused beams with fluorescent lamps as a source. One of the problems of mounting any form of working light in a grid system is that there are so many objects hanging from the grid, obscuring the working light. In a large studio, we get the crazy situation that when all the winches are raised towards the grid level, we have unobstructed lighting of the studio floor, but when we lower the winches to their operational height, which would be the main requirement when rigging and setting, the working lights are obscured.

When illuminating the acting area it is bad enough trying to position a small floodlight fitting about 300 mm square within a grid system, but when attempting to install fluorescent fittings up to two metres in length, it is almost impossible. Small lighting units can be installed between the ends of barrel winch units and not interfere with the main production lighting layout. Fluorescent fittings, however, can only be positioned between rows of production lighting units and this in practice means valuable space is occupied.

Other than the fittings below the grid level which illuminate the main area, there is also a requirement to illuminate above the grid for operators working at that level, although these lights will only be used occasionally and not permanently switched on.

In large studios there is usually a provision for some emergency lighting that is left on permanently, and fed from a central battery power supply. This has to be carefully integrated with the rest of the system, although the light level provided is low in comparison to the main house lighting and therefore generally does not affect the production lighting.

We've now got lights all over the place! How do we switch them on and off? It's pretty obvious that switching them all off at the same time may be inconvenient and possibly dangerous. Most studios have the lights switched in four quadrants; thus it is possible to have a quarter of the working lights on, with three-quarters off and this switching arrangement can be in any combination for convenience. One big problem with high level working lights in a studio is that they are also a major source of illumination and can project quite obtrusive, unwanted shadows. So although the lighting can be removed in certain segments, it is usually necessary to switch off most of the working lights during a production to avoid any undesired effects.

It is necessary to have an emergency 'off' button which operates the main lighting power. This is provided to remove the power from the active area in the event of fire or any electrical hazard. The application of this switch, which removes the main lighting, could plunge the area into darkness; so to prevent this, an interlock system has to be provided so that when the production lighting is switched 'off', the working lights are immediately switched 'on', thus avoiding any danger. The emergency 'off' buttons operate on a latching system and are not allowed to be reset until an authorized person investigates the problem and clears the situation for normal operation again.

Whatever type of lights we choose for our working lights, there will be a need to maintain them. This might be simply changing a lamp when it fails or cleaning the fittings on a regular basis to ensure maximum light output.

Figure 13.1   Houselights – unwanted shadows

This requirement means we have to consider carefully where we put the fittings and how they are accessed in normal use. In a small studio, using tungsten or fluorescent fittings, or, for that matter, a theatre using fluorescent lighting for some of its peripheral illumination around fly galleries, a pair of steps or a reasonably short ladder may be used by operators to gain access. In premises where high grids are installed, there will be a need to provide access to the working lights, generally from the grid system itself to avoid the use of high portable towers. On occasions there will also be a need to lower the fittings to the floor and this requires lifting devices to be installed for every lighting unit.

Tungsten working lights and houselight systems usually have thyristor dimmers to control them. Some modern studio installations have sophisticated control systems in an attempt to save power. The method of control is generally to have a period when the lights are fully on, which is usually worked out from normal rigging practices and amounting, say, to four hours. At this point the lights will slowly fade down to half brightness, thus saving some energy. If the operators are still working and require the higher light level, the action of touching the 'on' button of the system reactivates the circuits to maximum and a further four hour cycle commences.

On all types of working lights where there is a lamp involved we obviously have to take safety precautions. It is rather unnerving to have a lamp explode above members of staff or the public. Having only a mesh in front of any of these working luminaires is insufficient, and it is essential that no material escapes from one of these fittings when it is above people. In the case of tungsten or discharge fittings, it is possible to have toughened safety glasses fitted and also have a mesh to prevent pieces of the safety glass falling to the floor level. With fluorescent fittings, specially designed units can be obtained that are generally safe in most aspects. All these fittings must of course be fireproof!!

We have already mentioned that around the edge of a stage area there will have to be working lights left on to enable staff to perform some of the functions during a live performance. In television, particularly, there is a need for items of equipment to be illuminated around the edge of the studio for normal use, but which must not be too obtrusive when using the studio for recordings or transmissions.

Many television studios are fitted with cyclorama cloths that at times can encompass two thirds of the periphery of a studio and this can pose a problem inasmuch that direct access towards an exit doorway is not possible, and an alternative route has to be available. There are strict rules concerning how much of a studio can be encompassed by pieces of cloth or sets and there must be definite access ways provided for safety. A problem that often occurs in television studios is that the exit lights have to be left on and if a cyclorama cloth is hung across the face of the exit light the camera will see the outline of the 'exit' sign through the cloth; thus the exit sign has to be obscured in some way. The safest method, by far, in these circumstances is to hang some kind of material in front of the sign but this must be hung as near to the cyc cloth as possible so that the normal sight line to the 'exit' from the fire lane at the rear of the cyc is maintained.

Additionally, around the edge of the studio there will be consoles for local control of the winches, pantographs, monopoles, together with controls for switching lights on and off. All of these need illumination for the operators to see what they are doing, and this is generally accomplished by having fluorescent downlighters mounted above the panels which can be obscured from the view of the camera. Unfortunately at times the outline of the panels can be seen through cloths, and therefore local switching arrangements have to be provided so that the fluorescent units can be switched off if the camera is looking in that direction.

A fire lane will invariably be provided all the way round the edge of the studio and to ensure that illumination is sufficient for rapid access in the case of an emergency, fluorescent lights attached to the studio walls are provided at frequent intervals. These also require baffles so that the cameras cannot see this illumination.

In a theatre, there will be permanent arrangements for an audience, this being part of the normal operation. However, in film and television studios, audiences are not the 'norm'. When they are there, it is essential that the safety arrangements made are as good as those in theatres. Special arrangements have to be made to indicate clearly the exit routes, although in most modern studios the audience seating is generally integrated into the building, so there are definite access routes. If, however, the audience seating is placed in the area on an 'ad hoc' basis, then this must be taken into account, particularly with regard to the lighting. In the event of an emergency it is essential that the audience is safely conveyed away from the technical area being used for the production, which is the high risk area.

Thus special temporary lighting arrangements have to be made to light the exit routes, particularly around the audience rostra.

13.3 Lighting in control areas and dressing rooms

Although not usually of direct concern to a technical consultant planning lighting systems, he should be aware of the requirements for control rooms and dressing rooms. In the control room used by the LD, there will be a need for downlighters onto the desk adjacent to the lighting console so that the LD can interpret the prepared lighting plot for the production in question. It may be that he has used colour coded symbols to indicate cyc lighting colours, for instance, so that, in addition to a reasonable light level, there is also a requirement to have faithful colour rendition. In television, the lighting director is intimately involved with the technical picture quality from the cameras and therefore has to use high grade monitors in good viewing conditions, which implies almost dark surroundings and where the only areas of light will be those on the control desk. Desk lighting these days is usually achieved by having fluorescent fittings to give a general background illumination along the working edge of the desk, with small tungsten spotlights to pick out areas of special interest. Both the fluorescent and tungsten lighting have to be provided with dimmers so that a balanced working light level is achieved.

Traditionally, dressing rooms are lit by banks of tungsten lamps around a make up mirror. Recently, however, fluorescent lighting has been used in an attempt to give a more even illumination, which is both kinder on the performers' eyes and also helps to save electrical energy. To achieve good colour reduction, it is important that *all* fluorescent tables, including those over the control desks, are of very good quality.

13.4 Emergency systems

Emergency lighting can take two forms:

1. **Standby lighting**
   Used where essential work is allowed to continue (this would obviously be more applicable to a hospital operating theatre). Normally in the entertainment industry, standby lighting is not installed but it may be provided on occasions in those areas concerned with television master transmission suites which have generators backing the public electrical supply systems, and feeding the technical plant, so that a minimum 'on air' presence is maintained.
2. **Escape lighting**
   This is required in areas occupied by staff, artistes and audiences so that in the event of fire a rapid, but controlled, exit can be made from an entertainment area. It is the most important form of emergency lighting as its main purpose is to save life.

The essential requirement for emergency lighting is that it will operate reliably from an independent source other than the mains supply. The light level for safety lighting is often remarkably low and in fact for most areas a level of one lux is considered sufficient. However, the light level is really up to the installers and operators of the premises to review and, if necessary, increase upon this base level. Other important purposes of emergency lighting are:

1. It must clearly define the exits and all the emergency exits.
2. All escape routes must be clearly indicated and adequately lit so that people can see their way to exits.
3. It is essential that the lighting along escape routes is relatively even and without wide variations in light level.
4. It is absolutely essential that, having got out of the building, all the people evacuated do not blunder into pitch blackness, and therefore outside illumination must be provided.

One of the most onerous requirements of emergency lighting is that it has to reach the desired light level within five seconds of failure of the main lighting system. It is possible that the response time of the emergency system can be increased up to 15 seconds with the permission of the local authority, provided that people in the building concerned are very familiar with their surroundings. However, in most cases it is preferable if the five seconds is maintained. Due to the five second limitation, it would obviously be impossible to use discharge sources for emergency lighting, and in fact the only types of lamps preferred for emergency lighting are from the tungsten and fluorescent families.

It is also extremely difficult to use a generator for the emergency lighting system because a generator also needs a finite time to run up and in most cases will probably exceed the five second limit. The main source of supply for emergency lighting is a battery system. This can be either a central system where the emergency power is distributed to the areas concerned, or a self-contained system where each individual luminaire used comes complete with its own battery. In the past, some installations used large banks of batteries contained within a battery room in the premises to provide dc voltage to the emergency lighting system. In essence, the battery system works rather like the battery on a car: in normal use, any drain on the battery systems by maintained exit signs or house lights would be catered for by a charging plant in the same manner that the alternator on a car keeps a battery topped up. With failure of the mains, the batteries are always in a state to provide an emergency power source for a reasonable period of time. Battery powered emergency lighting is usually designed to be activated for a period of up to three hours, according to the size of the premises and with due regard to all the problems of escape from the building.

Battery backed luminaires used for emergency systems are usually reliant upon the normal mains input to provide a trickle charge so that the batteries are maintained in a working condition at all times. Luminaires for emergency systems come in three types:

(a)   Where a lamp is 'off' until any emergency arises, in which case the lamp will be powered from the internal battery pack. Normally the mains feeding the unit will trickle charge the battery pack.
(b)   Where the lamp is always in use and under normal circumstances powered from the mains, but in an emergency situation will use the internal battery supply. Once again, the incoming mains trickle charges the battery.
(c)   It is possible to combine the two types of operation in a third sort of luminaire for emergency systems. This luminaire contains two lamps, one which is used normally powered from the mains, and a second lamp for use only in emergency conditions, powered from the internal battery pack. In the event of mains failure the second lamp will switch on. As before, the unit relies upon a trickle charge from the normal mains to keep the batteries in good condition.

A problem that arises with emergency lighting luminaires is that if the lamp in the fitting is used all the time it is in a constant process of ageing; hence some notice must be taken of its life cycle so that lamps are changed to avoid failure in emergency conditions. Units that employ lamps which are only switched on in emergency conditions need to have these lamps checked at fairly frequent intervals to ensure no possible malfunction when used. It is also extremely important that all units installed in the premises are switched onto the emergency state at fairly frequent intervals to check that the batteries are working correctly.

In the entertainment industry members of staff working in the premises will be aware of the escape routes, and emergency exits. Unfortunately, many members of the public may come into these premises and be totally unfamiliar with the layout of the building. This requires that the operators of the premises must ensure that all exits, permanent or temporary, be clearly marked. As well as the need to have clear exit signs and lighting for the emergency routes, there is a requirement for additional lighting where hazards may exist along a route, such as stairways and any other type of obstruction. Obviously these must be clearly lit so that no additional problems are caused by people tripping over obstacles. It goes without saying that, if in doubt, put more emergency lighting in.

It is extremely foolish to short change on people's lives!

14 Tendering, contracts and purchasing

14.1 Writing a specification

The average person when buying a car goes to endless lengths to ascertain all the bells and whistles they will get when they complete the purchase, such as the colour, engine size, service cycle, type of engine, type of seats, how big is the boot, has it got a sunroof, how good is the radio, has it got a CD player and . . . . the list is endless. The same person going into a shop to buy a fridge usually accepts that it looks reasonable on the surface and appears the right size and as an aside perhaps asks if it has a plug fitted when it is delivered. These two situations highlight the process of looking at a specification and being aware of what is being purchased. Although the person buying the car will not necessarily write down a specification, he will detail at great length to the salesman what he wants, and in fact, this is tantamount to a specification, usually called by most people 'a requirement'.

Specifications can range from a fairly basic written list of requirements to the very elongated variety issued by government departments and particularly by large broadcasting organizations. The simple one may not cover all the points sufficiently but the other specification is so long that it bores the pants off the person reading it because it goes into such great detail and leaves no room for manoeuvre whatsoever. Does the specification 'refer to existing equipment and materials', or is it requesting the development of certain items? If it is for the use of engineers to develop some apparatus then the specification needs to be highly detailed and has to relate to all the parameters to be observed by the operatives. If, however, it is a specification so that the supplier of some equipment knows exactly what the purchaser desires, then this is relatively straightforward. Perhaps if we start at the top and work our way through the basic outline of a specification, we can then appreciate some of the points that have to be included.

Let us begin with the front cover. This needs to tell the person looking at the specification what its general contents are and where the work will take place and have some form of reference number. A reference number is very important on a specification and so is the date of issue, because it might be that we have amended an original specification for some reason, and hopefully any reissue ensures that the original copy is destroyed. From personal experience, we are not entirely happy with a system that suggests odd pages are removed and new ones substituted, because this does not always work well in practice. The reader should be told on the first one or two pages by whom the specification has been written and how to contact the author(s) so that any problems can be ironed out. Having covered the main description of the premises and work required, there should be a contents page listing all the items to be considered and where to find them in the specification document. With the specification, there will probably be drawings of the buildings or plant concerned and these need to be described with their drawing numbers so that there is no doubt as to the purpose of the drawing. In addition to this main specification there could be subsidiary specifications for standard items of equipment to be used by the purchaser, such as special requirements for any solid state equipment used within his premises for example. Obviously this could apply to many items of equipment being used, particularly in a television studio where it may cover the power unit of a video camera down to a ballast system for a discharge source.

A brief introduction should be provided which describes the work to take place and any related work to be done by other contractors. It should also set out the timetable for the delivery, installation and commissioning of all the equipment. The company receiving the specification will need to know how to tender for the work and, when tendering, what conditions will be laid down by the customer for the contract.

In the entertainment industry, the type of work that will normally take place will be either building new premises or refurbishing old ones and would encompass mechanical work, electrical work, purchasing luminaires, lighting control systems, dimmers and scenery equipment.

Let us look at a brief outline of the main requirements in, say, a small television installation. First of all, it is useful to give the dimensions of the studio because this has an implication on the equipment to be used. Let us assume that the studio has been in use and this is a refurbishment.

Item 1: Remove all existing lighting suspension equipment, luminaires, dimmers and lighting control console.
(At this point it should be decided whether the company concerned or contractor will dispose of the equipment.)
Item 2: Design, manufacture and supply 16 self-climbing winches.
Item 3: Design, manufacture and supply a winch control console for the self-climbing winches.
Item 4: Manufacture and supply 16 2 kW Fresnel luminaires; eight 1 kW Fresnel luminaires; eight 2.5 kW softlights.
Item 5: Manufacture and supply 40 5 kW dimmers together with a 40-way two preset control console.
Item 6: Deliver to site, install, test and commission.

Having outlined the main requirements for the specification, we now need to detail the individual parts so that the supplier is in no doubt as to what is expected from the specification.

Self-climbing barrel units

The self-climbing units should weigh no more than 160 kg excluding the load on the bar. Each unit should be equipped with a barrel 2.5 m long capable of a safe working load of 150 kg. The units are required to work over an operating range of 6.25 m. It is preferable that the unit is as small as possible so as not to restrict the studio headroom. The unit must be provided with top and bottom limits; overload and slack wire system. It is preferred that a simple flip flop cable tray system is integrated with the main unit. The lighting power outlets mounted adjacent to the suspension barrel should be capable of 5 kW each and comprise four individual circuits provided with BS 4343 240 V 32 A socket outlets. The unit must be provided with all electrical terminations in a box that can be installed at grid level. Wiring to and from the box at grid level will be the responsibility of other contractors. The unit must be as quiet as possible in operation and conform to the necessary safety regulations with regard to this item of equipment. (Obviously the safety regulations could be quoted but are dependent upon where the unit is being used and the country of use.)

We could extend the details of the specification for these winch units but the ones listed highlight some of the main areas of concern for a potential customer. It should be borne in mind that the details form part of the contract.

A further section discusses the luminaires to be provided and in general these are standard items from manufacturers' lists, although it may be possible that some small modifications are required by the purchaser. The equipment list is as follows:

Sixteen 240 V 2 kW studio Fresnels, pole operated, complete with four-leaf barndoor, wire guard, colour frame, CP41/73 240 V 2 kW lamp, safety bond and 4.5 m of mains cable fitted with a 240 V 32 A BS 4343 plug.

Eight 240 V 1 kW studio Fresnels, pole operated, complete with four-leaf barndoor, wire guard, colour frame, CP40 240 V 1 kW lamp, safety bond and 3 m of mains cable fitted with a 240 V 16 A BS 4343 plug.

Eight 240 V 2.5 kW softlights, pole operated, complete with eggcrate, colour frame, two P2/12 240 V 1.25 kW lamps, safety bond and 2 m of mains cable fitted with 240 V 32 A BS 4343 plug.

Dimmer rack and lighting console requirements

Note: The dimmer room is rather small in the premises to be re-equipped; therefore the dimmer rack must be physically small in size and as the unit is to be positioned very close to a wall *front access only* is to be provided.

The unit must be capable of three-phase working and contain all the dimmers. The power input wiring to the rack and the wiring from the rack to the studio will be carried out by other contractors. As the supplier of the rack, however, you will be expected to terminate the connections from the studio to the individual dimmers. Obviously the specification will go into more detail with regard to the requirements of the dimmers, such as do they need to meet high interference specifications, etc.

Finally we need to specify a lighting control console to drive the 40 dimmers. The lighting console must be as small in size as possible and lightweight as it is required to use it from two different positions in the building. Position one will be when it is mounted on a desk adjacent to the vision control position in the main control room; the second position is to be used as a lighting director's control from the studio floor where it will be plugged into a convenient socket mounted adjacent to the sound and vision panel in the studio. The console must come equipped with 10m of flexible lead so that it can be plugged into these socket outlets. The form of control can either be analogue or digital, the main criterion being cost effectiveness.

The lighting console is required to be a two-preset with master control. It must be equipped with a dipless cross-fade system and it is essential that each of the channel faders is provided with a 'cut' button. The preferred colours for the faders are white and green for the presets and red and blue for the master faders. Indicators should be provided adjacent to the individual master faders to ascertain the state of fade. It should be possible to memorize the various fader settings and record them into a memory system. The memory system should provide at least 20 memories. Simple playback via the red master fader only is required.

This is obviously a rather odd console that has been specified but we hope the reader gets the general idea that it covers for many of the items and gives the supplier a pretty good idea of what the customer requires.

One of the points about writing specifications is to be aware of standard items of equipment available from the various manufacturers concerned with the industry, so that rather than writing nebulous specifications which would require special modifications to be carried out, it is preferable to buy standard items. One of the problems with specifications is that your particular requirements may very quickly preclude several sources of supply.

Although writing a specification seems a chore, most people when equipping the area in which they work have a pretty good idea of their requirements and in general are quite willing to talk about them but very reluctant to put them down on paper. It really does not take many minutes to do this, however, and it makes the life of the supplier and the user so much easier to discuss detailed items over the phone when they have been carefully catalogued.

14.2 Tendering – who to invite

Having written the specification, who do you send it to? We all have our favourite suppliers because they are the ones who often give us good service, possibly a reasonable price and, most important of all, they are rather nice people to deal with. Unfortunately that doesn't help when trying to negotiate good prices all the time; it's no good going back to the same old supplier because eventually you end up in their pockets. It is also essential to widen the net to see what is becoming available throughout the industry. To that end, therefore, it is important to tender to as many companies within reason – as possible – and as a good guide at least six would be a base figure. The choice of the companies to be invited to tender for the work is governed by their past track record, or it may be that you have to invite a new company to tender when you have no knowledge of its capabilities. In this case, it is essential to get an up-to-date résumé of its activities and recent installations; then you are able to check with people who have had work done whether or not the work was satisfactorily completed.

In many fields of engineering, it is possible to have companies on tender lists who have years of experience in the field, are well established and have a firm financial base. In the entertainment industry, however, a firm financial base is a very doubtful thing and many companies make a precarious living out of the entertainment industry. Thus, there is an element of risk involved and one of the great problems with tendering is how to minimize the risks. Having established that the company being invited to tender will not go into liquidation, the prime consideration generally, assuming prices throughout are reasonably even with not too many extremes, is the quality of the people you will deal with. Your specification will be looked at by an engineer and it is essential that this engineer is conversant with your needs, thus enabling a very easy discussion to take place with regard to your requirements. In our experience, no specification covers all the points that may arise; therefore detailed discussions have to take place, invariably at the factory concerned, where any equipment relative to the specification can be inspected and points of detail resolved.

It may be that at the time of tendering, you have said in your covering letter with the specification that you will not necessarily award a contract for all the equipment to one individual company, and it is possible that items are individually purchased from various companies, such as the self-climbing winches from one company and the dimmers and control system from another. By splitting the contract, it may be necessary to have meetings with two or more of the tenderers at the same time to resolve points of detail where interface difficulties may arise. Other than the well-established companies in the industry, perhaps a new company has risen rather rapidly through the ranks with some new idea, and the application of this idea may be ideal for your situation in the premises concerned. However, you have to be very careful that you are assured that they can produce the equipment and meet delivery deadlines. As a rule, it is best to invite all of the people who are capable of doing the work, irrespective of the age of the company and the possible present situation, and then assess the tenders when they come in. Although not necessarily an ethical practice, it is not unknown for specifications to be written in terms which will almost guarantee that one specific tenderer will succeed in getting the work. This can and has been done to circumvent red tape in large organizations.

In addition to the senior engineers who are concerned with the design, you are also much concerned with the equipment installers. The reason for mentioning the installation team is that not all companies employ their own staff to perform this function, and therefore it is extremely important to know with whom they are associated and the capabilities of the sub-contractors. It is no good having very good quality equipment if it's botched when being installed. Unfortunately, other than looking superficially at the performance of companies and of the staff themselves, at the end of the day, when having to make a decision about who to invite to tender, it probably comes down to that good old 'gut feeling'.

14.3 Negotiation

It would be lovely to write the specification, send it out to four or five companies, get answers back and say: 'Yes, we'll have that one, it's the cheapest, they look pretty good, let's go for it!'. In practice, it is not as simple as that. It may be that the most desirable equipment, on receipt of the tenders, is the most expensive. The lower priced ones may not be desirable at all, but the rules say that the cheapest tender has to be used. The only thing to do is go back to the company concerned to see if some reduction in price can be negotiated. On the other hand, it may be that there is a limited budget for the work and with which to purchase the equipment. This then is also subject to negotiation to contain expenditure within the budget limits. There are two methods by which a price can be reduced. First, the equipment essentially stays the same but the company concerned reduces its profit margin. A second alternative is to cheapen parts of the equipment or remove certain items so that it comes within the stated financial limits. But having said that the equipment preferred is probably the best for the job, it is very difficult to take parts away and maintain the desired standard.

It might be that the company tendering has a slightly cheaper version of a similar type of equipment. Once again, it is a very hard thing for the customer to lower his sight lines from the point of view of equipment quality. Even if it were possible to accept the slightly cheaper item, it might be that this would conflict with the tenders from other suppliers, who also could be in a position to lower their prices in relation to the quality of equipment; thus it is very difficult not to get into a path of an ever downward spiral where companies are battling against each other.

Another aspect of negotiation is to confirm when the equipment will be ready for delivery. It may be that the preferred company is extremely busy and therefore unable to meet the dates set when responding to the tenders. At this stage, it could be said that the company tendering should know whether or not they have equipment available to meet the dates as set out, but unfortunately they may have work from other sources and the integration of this work in the factory may be sometimes difficult to control. Therefore the element of negotiation at this point is whether the customer can move the installation date, but bearing in mind that if more than one company is involved, several moves may have to be made by other sub-contractors and this can be quite difficult to achieve with success. Hopefully, at the end of the day, you have talked with all the companies concerned, have ironed out all the manufacturing problems and points of detail with the equipment involved, and ascertained that the companies will be able to deliver on time and that they are capable of installing the equipment satisfactorily and can also work with other sub-contractors without any problems.

Just a little point of detail with regard to using several sub-contractors: it is essential when writing the specifications for the various parts of the work that the divisions between each section should be very clear, in black and white. Grey areas are to be avoided at all costs, because you invariably end up with contractor 'A' saying: It's is not my responsibility, it was contractor 'B'! and vice versa, and you are the unfortunate person in the middle trying to resolve the conflict. This may cost money and time and delay the whole installation.

14.4 Awarding contracts

Having established that company 'A' are the 'bees knees' as far as your work goes, you would then write a letter formally awarding them the contract based on their tender and any subsequent negotiations, which will all have been carefully documented. The contract will mention the original specification, and any document subsequent to that specification and any other correspondence. Thus in law, there is no doubt as to what you expect to get and from the point of view of the contractor, he knows what you are expecting.

Part of the contract process is how will you pay for the work. With most manufacturing processes the company concerned will have to purchase raw materials and possibly buy in manufactured items from other companies to make the product that you are installing. It is therefore not unreasonable that the company concerned would expect some money fairly early in the contract period to cover some of the costs of raw materials. It is suggested that this is best carried out by a percentage payment against goods received. Sometimes it may be a gesture of goodwill to pay a small amount of money with the initial contract. A further stage of payment may be when the equipment is complete at the manufacturers' works, and upon satisfactory inspection by the customer, money is released to the percentage of work completed. When the equipment has been delivered and installed satisfactorily, a payment will be made which might be for the remainder of the contract sum of money, or a small amount of money is retained by the customer as a guarantee in the first year following completion of contract.

There will be certain conditions attached to the contract itself and in the UK these may be the contract conditions as prepared by the Institution of Electrical Engineers and Institution of Mechanical Engineers. In large organizations, it is possible that they will have their own interpretation of conditions of tender and contract and these will be applied. Additionally, there could be special conditions laid down with regard to safety procedures when working in the premises of the purchaser.

Subject to the contract being awarded, it might be that the purchaser has to carry out tests at the manufacturers' premises to ascertain the suitability of the equipment being offered for his purposes. Additionally it might be that an engineering prototype has been requested to see that it meets the requirements of the specification prior to general manufacture being carried out. Or it may be an inspection of a standard item to ensure that it meets all known parameters. It goes without saying that the 'hands on' approach to any equipment being purchased far outweighs what may be written in the specification.

14.5 Deliveries, timetables and penalties

With a reasonably simple installation of new equipment, the main requirement will be to deliver the equipment on time, and install it fairly quickly so that the premises concerned can resume normal operation. However, in larger installations, there can be problems with deliveries and timetables. A good example of this would be a busy television studio where many activities are taking place at the same time with the danger of conflicting work patterns. If there is a large delivery of equipment, will it be put into use immediately or just lie around in temporary storage? Problems with 'out of service' periods occur quite often when the air conditioning and subsequently the heating is switched off; thus part of the building concerned may be subject to condensation problems. It is not helpful having 200 luminaires in boxes delivered to site and cluttering up the place so that other people cannot get on with their work. Most premises do not have facilities to store huge quantities of equipment. This is certainly true of television studios and in the theatre it is intolerable! Thus the time of delivery has to be carefully worked out, and a timetable for all the events taking place with an installation is essential.

Some companies employ 'critical path programmes' to ensure no hold ups with installations. At the planning stage these can be invaluable in working out the delivery and installation programme so that the work progresses smoothly. However, these are generally only as good as the last piece of information input to the programme. They may give the desired programme of work and installation, but unfortunately, never allow for firms having manufacturing problems or, say, the sub-contractor who suddenly goes out of business!

If timetables are not met for any reason, arguments invariably ensue as to whose fault it was. In large companies, it is sometimes par for the course to blame other sections of the organization for any delays within the installation programme. This also goes for the contractors who will blame each other for any snags arising. The solution to all these problems is to have very strict project control: this will be performed by the project manager concerned together with senior staff from all the contractors and sub-contractors. Lateness in installation or delivery of any equipment may be quite costly to the customer. For instance, in the theatre, the loss of revenue from the paying audience is somewhat embarrassing. In television, the loss of every day of shooting might be reckoned to be about £100,000. It could be that the delay occasions a postponement of programmes to a later date owing to the unavailability of the actors and actresses concerned. Thus it would not be unreasonable to have a penalty clause written into the contract for late delivery or installation. However, as already mentioned, where more than one company is involved, there usually ensues an argument at this stage as to whose fault it was and, in our experience, penalty payments are very difficult to apply in practice. If only one company or contractor is involved, it is obviously somewhat easier to apply a penalty clause, because if that company had any problems they could eventually pass the penalties on to their sub-contractors, but the customer has been saved the headache of argument.

14.6 Standardization for maintenance and spares

One of the problems with a variety of equipment used is that its maintenance requires different procedures for each type of equipment. This generally poses a problem for the maintenance engineer and also it can lead to items being overlooked because the staff are unfamiliar with all the equipment. When assessing tenders it is therefore essential in any installation to try to reach a standardization of the equipment and of parts used.

Although a 1 kW profile spot luminaire may appear to be very similar between two manufacturers, there are many points of detail that will vary in its construction: it is quite possible, for example, that parts used are sourced from different manufacturers. It might be that different lampbases are used on very similar pieces of equipment and this will cause a problem when trying to repair them. This leads us on to spares holding.

It is very well worth repeating at this point that it is essential to keep the amount of spares held on premises as low as possible, because it is plant that just gathers dust and usually accomplishes no useful purpose, other than tying up sums of money that could be well spent elsewhere. If we are lucky, it may be that the solid state devices used by three or four dimmer manufacturers are common to other pieces of equipment. For example, it may be that the output thyristors on a 5 kW dimmer need to be 40 A devices, say, and these could be sourced, provided they meet the technical specification, from several manufacturers. This enables prices to be kept low. A good example of standardization is with motorized winches. In an installation containing, say, 100 units, it would be nice to think that only one motor unit had to be kept in stores in case of failure. It would also be preferable that any limit switches in use on the units were the same type of microswitch. Although sometimes necessary, it is not desirable to have several types of switch on any unit because it only puts up the spares holding within the premises. In the negotiation process with a company when tendering for work, a point that has to be discussed is how many items need to be kept as spares for the particular pieces of equipment. Items of equipment such as monopoles, winch systems and mechanical items require very few spares to be held as most components will be relatively lightly used. Similarly, lighting consoles and dimmers have very low failure rates. It would also be nice if the same could be said of the luminaires, but unfortunately they are subject to heat, to mechanical movement, to being rigged and de-rigged and thus suffer more damage in use.

One of the problems with standardization of products is that a company may hesitate before going in another direction for the supply of equipment. Hopefully, in practice, this is not usual because it would inhibit any development work by the various manufacturers servicing the entertainment industry. However, the point remains that some standardization is beneficial to the customer and can also be beneficial to the manufacturer. One of the best examples of standardization is where luminaires for discharge and tungsten lighting can use the same luminaire body, yoke and pole operation controls, the only items varying being the reflector, lens combination and the lampholders.

15 Servicing, maintenance and hired equipment

15.1 Maintenance rooms and test equipment

In Europe we have a wonderful legacy of splendid theatres handed down to us over the ages; some have beautiful architecture, some have splendid auditoria but they all have one thing in common – a dividing line drawn at the proscenium arch separating the paying audience from the theatre's working area. The average theatregoer would not believe the cramped conditions and in some cases the squalor that exists in the world beyond the proscenium arch. To find any space for a maintenance area is difficult and the electrician often resorts to a bench in a dark corner somewhere. The luxury of a purpose-designed maintenance room in a modern theatre can only be upstaged by the maintenance areas provided in the modern television studios. So if we are given an opportunity to plan our own maintenance area in film, television or theatre, what should we look for?

The first requirement is an area large enough to store the spare lights and equipment plus enough room to stack the equipment requiring repair, leaving room to light and test luminaires and have enough racking for spares and consumables such as lamps and filters. Obviously we would require a good electrical supply terminated into a purpose-built distribution board which will provide all the types of socket outlets required and three phase; a large bench, with an equally large vice, covered in a thick linoleum that is also a good insulator; a large lock-up cupboard stocked with taps and dyes and nuts and bolts of all sizes, complete with all of the normal tools, including an electric drill, large and small soldering irons and an adequate supply of various plugs, sockets and cables. Test equipment should include a good quality multimeter, a lux meter and a tri-stimulus colour meter to perform light tests. To comply with the Electricity at Work Regulations 1989, each piece of electrical equipment must be entered into a register and periodically tested (see Chapter 16). Facilities are available to perform all the electrical test requirements in one instrument, a good investment both for everyday use and for the periodic tests. To be given these conditions and a good lock on the door is no more than the electrical staff deserve to enable them to keep a well ordered house in good working condition.

15.2 Luminaire maintenance

A common misunderstanding of maintenance is that the electrician walks round with a duster, flicking dust from lights and repairing the ones that do not work. Nothing could be further from the truth. Electrical maintenance is a legal requirement, laid down in the Electricity at Work Regulations 1989 (see Chapter 16, section 16.3).

Over and above the electrical safety tests, there are three main problem areas to be considered when carrying out luminaire maintenance: (a) heat; (b) mechanical damage; and (c) the ingress of dirt. It is inevitable that a luminaire will attract the dust and dirt in the air by virtue of the fact that the instrument is designed to have a cold air intake to cool the lamp and electrical equipment which also sucks in the associated grime. As it does so, it deposits the dirt on the lens, the reflector and any other surface subject to change of temperature. Therefore, periodic cleaning is required to maintain the efficiency of the luminaire. Most reflectors are made from brightly polished anodized aluminium. These are surface reflectors and should only be cleaned by wiping them with a damp cloth and liquid soap; a conventional wipe down with a wet rag afterwards to remove the soap will suffice and they can be dried with a lint-free rag. The same method can be used to clean the lenses; however, in the case of the tungsten halogen lamps which do have a large deposit of grime on them, these should be wiped clean with alcohol and then polished with a clean lint-free rag. Fingermarks must be avoided on tungsten halogen lamps to prevent the fingerprints becoming etched into the envelope when they are hot, causing hot spots which can collect extra heat and form a blister on the envelope.

In addition to the electrical test required in the Electricity at Work Regulations, examination should take place in the luminaire of the cables which are flexed when the unit is focused to determine if the insulation has been damaged. The switch is also a target for excessive heat and the lampholders. One indication of a lampholder overheating is to remove the lamp and inspect the pins. If they show signs of 'arcing' then the lampholder must be replaced, because if a new lamp is inserted into a lampholder that already has arcing on the contacts, it will transmit the same problem to the new lamp. The safety bond must be visually inspected for damaged or frayed strands. Any bond or chain must be replaced if it has arrested one fall of the luminaire so any distortion in its shape should alert you to this problem. Barndoors and colour frames are retained by safety catches which must be in good working order. If cables are to be replaced they must be of the recommended temperature range: do not be tempted to use just any old cable. Lenses must be examined for chips or cracks; the most obvious place is around the edge of the lens which when continuously heated and cooled expands the chip into a crack, causing the lens to ultimately fracture. Change any damaged lenses. Look for dents in the housing that could cause problems to the electrical internal switches and wiring. The yoke must be examined to determine that it is mechanically sound. And the last plea is to management – *please take maintenance seriously.*

Suspension system maintenance

Motorized bars, barrels, telescopes and pantographs are basically the same device, a means of supporting luminaires from above with variable height. They employ electrical drives, with limit switches and support cables or springs. We can therefore generalize about support systems and state that a secondary means of support should be provided. This takes the form of a secondary cable or a safety bond, in short a means of arresting the device if the primary means of support is broken. Therefore the first step in mechanical maintenance must be to inspect these areas which provide the ultimate safety.

Well designed winches allow inspection of the cable termination on the winding drum and at the bottom end of the cables. Look for loose or frayed ends; examine the whole length of the cable as it is wound in and out for any loose threads. If any such signs are seen, the cables must be changed. Each lifting apparatus has a safe working load (SWL) stated on it, and a periodic inspection must include the application of a test load to determine that the unit is safe. Many insurance companies require such tests annually. Most designs employ a top and bottom limit; the unit should be run through the whole range to determine that both limits are working and also the overload and underload limits. These are normally provided to switch the device off in the event of its picking up an additional load such as piece of scenery or as a safeguard against the operator placing too many luminaires on the barrel. The underload switch is required in the event of the luminaire being lowered onto the top of a set where cable would be spewed out until the luminaire toppled off the set and presented a real hazard. This test can easily be simulated by lowering the luminaire onto a rostrum where it should cut out immediately it touches the floor. Traversing monopoles and pantographs are normally fitted with end stop switches for traverse, which must be tested, and the electrical cables should be examined for damage, particularly in the case of pantographs where cable is laced up the side of the links and can easily be caught between them.

In general, gearboxes should not require maintenance, unless they have been stripped down for repair. Care should be taken with the type of grease or oil used; some types of gearbox rely on a heavy lubricant to help them to become self-sustaining to avoid the luminaire running away under a no volt condition. Any lubricants used must be at the recommendation of the manufacturer. A good guide to all lifting devices is that two turns should be left on the hoisting drum when the device is at the bottom limit. This will determine that the cables retain the load and not the end fixing. The cables used in lifting devices are special and normally of a flexible nature. Use only the manufacturer's replacements. Pantographs should be inspected for mechanical damage of the links and the hinge pin retaining clips; these have been known to pop off and not affect the operation until the pin slides out. The springs used on pantographs normally have a 10,000 cycle working life: this does not mean that they will fall to pieces in 10,000 cycles but an early warning of fatigue can be found by inspecting the edge of the springs, which show small cracks developing along the edges towards the end of life. At any sign of fractures, the springs should be replaced.

Extreme care must be taken in removing the springs from pantographs: with a pantograph on a bench, the spring should be pulled down by the ring provided and allowed up slowly until it touches its winding drum. In this state, the spring will be stationary and can be released. The assembly can be removed from the pantograph. Under no circumstances attempt to remove the spring from the drum; it is under considerable tension and can only be removed from the drum by the manufacturer. Barrel roller trolleys have stops screwed to them which engage under the barrel to prevent the trolley jumping off. Inspect these for inclusion and damage. Where monopoles are concerned, sticking tubes are often caused by external damage. If this is the case, it is recommended that a complete set of tubes is replaced, because these are mated during manufacture for not only size tolerance but also the bow that occurs in their length. Any attempt to replace one particular tube could result in many hours of work and problems of fit and alignment that you had not envisaged.

15.3 Holding spares and expendables

The seemingly simple task of holding spare parts and replacement items is anything but simple. The problems are mainly trying to identify the parts required and the quantities to hold in stock and monitoring the usage of expendable items.

Major items of equipment, such as winch systems, dimmers and luminaires will be changed with replacement of worn out plant programmes and these may vary in length of time from a seven to 20-year cycle. However, on a day-to-day basis, we have operating costs that are concerned with the maintenance of plant and the use of lamps, filters and certain types of accessories.

With a new installation it is a good policy to ask the manufacturer for a 'spares list' identifying all the likely parts that will be required to keep the product in good repair. This request in itself causes some manufacturers to research their own products to determine the likely spares requirement for the future; whereas other manufacturers produce pictorial spares sheets, with photographs of the parts for easy identification. This practice also helps the user to determine his particular model in the years to come after the product has undergone several modifications and upgrades, and also overcomes the language problem when trying to describe the parts that are required. If your make of equipment does not provide this luxury it is expedient to ask for a written parts list which will identify your model and the parts required at that point in time.

If you are fortunate enough to be at the planning meeting when the products that are to be ordered are chosen, then it will be advisable to include the spares at the same time and as a condition of the original purchase. That part is easy. The question is: how many spares should be held?

Manufacturers have often taken part in discussions with the user to determine a sensible spares holding. In the first place this can only be an educated estimate from past experience and a percentage applied to the purchase order. A typical spares list for a luminaire could be as follows, with a percentage applied for orders from 100 to 300 units.

Lenses	5%
Lampholders	6%
Switches	5%
Internal electrical harnesses	3%
Yokes	2%
Reflector	6%
Wire guard	2%
Barndoors	4%
Colour frames	10%
Housing	1%
Mains cable assembly	5%

This could be a good starting point but do not forget that paradoxically the older the equipment gets, and therefore the more likely to require spares, the less likely they are to be available; because the manufacturer has moved on to other designs. However, most reputable manufacturers keep spares for seven years from the first model – so beware if you have purchased in the last year of manufacture.

Holding spares in an existing installation reduces the problem of how many to stock, because a good record of purchases over the years will give a good guide to the likely requirement. The main problem is availability, because many luminaires are kept working long after their useful life. If this is the case and the original equipment manufacturer cannot supply the spare parts, there are specialist companies that carry out repairs and make special parts for old products.

Expendable items are much easier to predict. With a good record of purchases a working quantity can be arrived at. Some of the most expensive items are the lamps. Fortunately, there are several main stockists that hold the large range of lamps used in TV, film and theatre, so the spares holding can be reduced to a nominal amount to cover day-to-day needs and the stock of the main stockists can be called on for unscheduled requirements. From records, a guide of lamp usage in theatre and TV studios is approximately 1.3 lamps per year per luminaire. This is assuming that the lamps are supplied from dimmers. In the theatre the lamps will be providing different light levels, but the average dimmer output level could be similar to that adopted in television, where it is common practice to line up the cameras with the dimmers set to level '7'. In both cases this has the effect of greatly extending the life of the lamp. However, in film lighting the lamps are normally run at full voltage, resulting in a much shorter life. Typically for a tungsten halogen lamp, rated at 3200K, this is likely to be from 200 to 400 hours. One way of easing the pain of the lamp costs in the first two years of a new installation is to order two lamps for each luminaire at the same time that the equipment is purchased. In this way it is paid for out of the capital investment and does not come out of the expendable budget. By the second year, sufficient experience will be gained to determine a fairly accurate expendable requirement.

Whereas lamp manufacturers supply figures of typical life in use, filter manufacturers do not. This is obviously extremely difficult to do, because the life of filters is dependent upon the light source being used. However, from the customer's point of view, it is very useful to do some tests to ascertain which filter material has a good life. This can be done very simply by putting up similar colours on the same light source and seeing which one deteriorates the most.

Stocking colour filters can be a big problem; the variables being 100 different colours sold in sheets and rolls. Although there are several good stockists who can normally respond quickly to your needs, it is expedient to keep a working stock of filter to call on. To remove one of the variables, it is normally a good practice to stock colour filters in rolls; this makes racking simple, with a colour swatch and number attached to the end of the roll. Rolls are also more economical because different sizes can be cut with the minimum of waste. However, the second variable of 100 colours needs a lot more thought. If one applies the 20/80 principle, which seems to work in most cases, then 80% of the filters used will be in 20% of the colours offered. This would appear to be a simple solution; just stock the 20 most popular colours. After much discussion and heated exchanges with the LDs, you might arrive at a compromise short list – but be prepared for a long and arduous debate.

Filters used for colour correction are, of course, out of this category and are stocked separately as the need dictates.

Some accessories disappear as if they were expendable items and require special attention, otherwise a constant state of annoyance will persist. Barndoors usually suffer from damage preventing them from rotating and the flaps suffer from that infuriating malady known in the trade as 'a droopy flap'. This is when the hinges have become so weak that they cannot support the weight of the flap. Replacements will save a lot of aggravation between the LDs and the electrical staff. Safety bonds have a habit of disappearing; whether an alternative use has been found for them that we have not yet discovered or a private hoard is hidden somewhere in the building, we will most likely never find out; but one thing that is certain is that every luminaire must have one to meet the safety requirements, so good replacement stocks must be maintained. Colour frames suffer from the same problems but have the additional requirement in theatre to be 'gelled up' between shows, so a complete set of spares is required as well as replacements.

Control and dimming should not require a large spares stock; the modern systems are very reliable and offer electronic card replacements and dimmer modules which should suffice. However, do not forget that when a tungsten halogen lamp ends its life with an arc-over across the filament, it draws a large current and normally blows the fuse, so it is necessary to keep a good stock of spare fuses. Finally be sure that you have made your case for expendable items by submitting your budget for next year in plenty of time. No one else in management is going to remind you to spend their money.

15.4 Monitoring equipment usage for replacement programmes

It is quite common for a lighting manufacturer to be asked for spares to repair a luminaire that is 30 years old, not for a sentimental enthusiast to restore the instrument as an antique, but by necessity to keep the luminaire working long past its useful life. It is normally not too difficult to get management to replace a control system after some years of service, because there is always a good case for having the latest development in 'thingummy bobs and wotsits' that the designers of lighting control systems are constantly adding to their products. The simple luminaire or lifting device stands very little chance of becoming more desirable just because it is a new model, so the attitude of some managements is: 'Light still comes out of it' or 'It still lifts up and down, doesn't it?', mainly brought on by the sudden realization of a big capital investment.

Whilst we can blame the management for not wanting to invest more money, what have we done over the preceding years to develop a replacement programme? In most establishments, the accountant will depreciate the capital equipment by 25% per year; in this way the book value will reduce to 23.72% of the original value in five years. This method of amortization will never remove the item from the books, but will show the management that the equipment that will be scrapped when it is replaced has very little capital value so that it can be written off. It is therefore a good practice to keep records of your own in the maintenance department of purchases and the date and cost, and make this information part of your inventory. To support your argument for replacements, you should keep a record of breakdowns, cause and effect and so build up a case for replacements because of the nuisance to the production. Other factors are size, weight and performance compared with a modern equivalent. In this way additional items can be introduced into your capital replacement budget each year in the hope that some money will be made available. If this is not forthcoming, keep the running total and add to it each year; then if you eventually get a percentage of your requested capital investment allowance, it will at least be a percentage of a much higher figure. The last question that management cannot ignore is: 'Does it conform to *current* safety standards?'

15.5 Hired equipment

At some time or other most lighting men will require the services of a lighting rental company to supply the extra equipment for a particular occasion or to provide a total installation on a temporary basis. There are many good rental companies available, providing an excellent service to the industry. Rental companies tend to specialize in film, television or theatre; normally dictated by the specialized equipment required in each of the lighting disciplines.

A film company usually registers a film as a business name and trades as a limited company for the duration of the film. This sometimes makes it advantageous for equipment and cameras to be hired from a rental company and they are therefore costed directly to that film. If the equipment had been purchased, it could present a problem at the end of the film of what to do with it.

In theatre, most professional houses have a small complement of lighting and control but do not provide the quantity or choice of equipment for a large production. This dictates that the production company rents the additional lighting control and dimming required. The advantages are that the desired type and make of equipment can be chosen with the cost paid weekly from the takings or in the event of a disaster the equipment can be returned.

In television the main requirement is for outside broadcast lighting and, on occasion, to supplement the normal studio lighting with special units used for effects lighting.

While the rental system is most helpful and seems to fill a very real need it should not be entered into lightly, without reading the small print, usually found on the back of acceptance delivery notes and contracts issued at the time of ordering. Each rental company has its own conditions. The following are some of the more important ones found by the authors.

> The customer hiring the equipment must check and test it before it is used and satisfy himself as to its fitness for the purpose. Further the customer must have adequate insurance cover to protect the rental company from claims against it for its products or personnel employed by the rental company for legal actions, proceedings, costs, charges, expenses and indemnity of third parties.
>
> The equipment must only be operated by people with the appropriate qualifications.
>
> If the customer uses labour provided by the rental company, the customer is responsible for them whilst on site, including any damages done, expenses or consequential indirect loss.

Finally, many an expensive argument can be avoided by determining if the cost of the lighting equipment includes the lamps.

16 Safety

16.1 EN 60598 and its implications

After the 1939–45 war, the European countries continued to follow their own electrical and mechanical standards without regard to their neighbours or the adverse effect that this created on their export trade. Germany and Britain were the dominant standard makers and adopted the attitude that the other countries should fall in line with one of them. The thought of getting together and thrashing out a common set of safety standards was not only unheard of, but would have been tantamount to heresy. However, in 1979, commonsense prevailed and the International Electrotechnical Commission (IEC) published the first edition of a safety standard for luminaires that had been agreed by 23 participating countries. This standard was called *Luminaires: General Requirements and Tests Publication 598/1.*

In 1984 a proposed standard for luminaires used in the entertainment business was circulated to all participating countries to try to reach a common agreement in the industry. After six years of debate by all 23 countries, the proposed standard was at last adopted.

One of the authors of this book (modesty prevents us saying which one) sat on the United Kingdom Committee and cogitated with the rest of the team. Suffice it to say that our proud committee member sallied forth full of hope and encouragement to introduce a luminaire design to the whole of Europe with one set of European safety standards incorporated into it. The journey took our intrepid designer to many of the participating countries, and just to check on acceptance by the various national authorities he stopped by at the appropriate safety standards office in each country to say 'hello' and to gloat over our new-found commonality and to get agreement that we were working to the same set of rules. The results of his labours were best demonstrated in Norway, by the inspector of NEMKO.

Question: Do you accept IEC/598/2/17 in Norway?

Answer: Yes, of course; we are one of the participating countries.

The inspector then picked up a huge mound of books from his desk, placed them on top of IEC/598/2/17 and said: 'However, we still require you to conform to the NEMKO standards as well'. And so it was in each country visited.

Back in the UK a colleague put this into perspective by saying: 'You wouldn't expect British Standards or the Institute of Electrical Engineers to give up their regulations, would you?'

So there we were with all the different standards that we had before and a brand new one in addition.

Fortunately the situation was resolved several years later when the European Norms (ENs) modified and accepted the IEC 598/2/17 and issued them as EN 60598 in 1989, when it became a legal requirement to conform to them and British Standards issued EN 60598 as BS 4533 in 1990.

Luminaire design: consideration for safety

The following suggestions and remarks regarding safety considerations in the design and operation of luminaires should be taken as a guide to help you through most of the European standards but unfortunately you will still unearth local requirements that can only be solved at source.

The main basis of the following is the EN 60598 with an overlay of other standards that have been encountered. However, it is up to the individual to determine his own interpretation of the standards because the authors cannot accept responsibility for their accuracy. It is also assumed that the reader already has a sound knowledge of good electrical practice.

Glass fragments from luminaires

The luminaire should be designed in such a way that in the event of a lamp exploding, fragments of glass or quartz 3 mm in size do not escape directly in line, from a lamp, through a ventilator or other aperture. If the ventilation system is designed with a labyrinth or fitted with a mesh to prevent pieces of glass or quartz 3 mm in size coming out from a directly exploding lamp in such a way that the glass is caught within the labyrinth or by the mesh, this is accepted within the standard.

Safety glass/mesh

Open-faced luminaires require either a safety glass with a minimum thickness of 3 mm or a safety mesh that will not permit pieces of glass or quartz 3 mm in size to pass through it. Luminaires that have a lens require a safety mesh in front of the lens of such a size as to prevent 25 mm pieces of glass passing through it. Luminaires that have a safety glass require a safety mesh in front of it, of such a size as to prevent 12 mm pieces of glass passing through it. The glass and mesh must be captive in the luminaire. In the event of a safety glass or lens cracking, its mounting must retain the broken pieces in position. The mechanical heat test for the safety glass is carried out by placing the luminaire in the horizontal position and burning it until it reaches a stable temperature, then water at a temperature of 15°C is sprinkled onto it by hand. The unit is allowed to cool and reheated and the test is repeated three times; the glass can crack, but it must be retained in its position in the housing.

The yoke

The mechanical connection between the yoke and the luminaire must be locked against loosening. This is to prevent the pivots working loose, during operational use, by tilting the housing. Forms of locking consist of either fitting a locknut or drilling and pinning the pivot shaft. The yoke must have earth continuity to the housing. The mechanical safety of the yoke requires a 10:1 safety factor on each leg of the yoke so that if one side of the yoke is disconnected from the housing the remaining leg provides a 10:1 safety factor.

The test procedure is to hang the luminaire from its spigot and to disconnect the pivot on one side of the yoke so that all the weight is taken on the other pivot point. Since the safety factor is 10:1, a weight of *nine times* the total weight of the luminaire (including all accessories) is added to the housing, making a total of *ten times* the original weight. The yoke may deform under test, but it must not break. At the time of going to press, discussions are taking place to determine if the safety factor could be reduced to 6:1; but this is a matter for the future.

The male spigot (Coll: 'Spud')

The size and type of spigot to be used can be determined from the following: Luminaires weighing up to 7.5 kg may use a 16 mm diameter spigot made of either steel or aluminium. Over 7.5 kg a 28.6 mm spigot is required, which must be manufactured from steel (aluminium is not permitted). A hybrid spigot has been developed which dimensionally suits the German DIN specification together with the British and USA standards. This has not been accepted by the Standards committee but is suggested here as the only reasonable solution to a universal spigot (see Figure 16.1).

Safety anchor point and bond

A dedicated anchor point must be provided on the housing whereby the safety bond can be passed over the primary means of suspension and through the yoke and terminated at the anchor point. In this way the housing will be arrested even if the yoke breaks. The test procedure is as follows: the unit will have all its accessories attached and lifted 300 mm and allowed to free fall until it is arrested by the safety bond. This procedure is repeated 30 times. During the test it is not permitted for any part of the luminaire or its accessories to become detached although they may become deformed.

Barndoors and colour frames

A German DIN specification exists for the size of receptacles for colour frames and barndoors. This is to ensure a good mechanical fit of component parts together with ease of interchangeability with other manufacturers' items of equipment. Although this is not a formal requirement it represents a very desirable feature.

If possible, luminaires should be designed to cater for the sizes quoted in these standards. The major manufacturers in Europe have already adopted these sizes. Nominal size of colour frames – German DIN standard No. 15–560 part 38. The following dimensions (in millimetres) can be the diameter of a round colour frame or the size of a square frame: 120; 150; 160; 180; 210; 240; 270; 360; 390; 450; 480; 540.

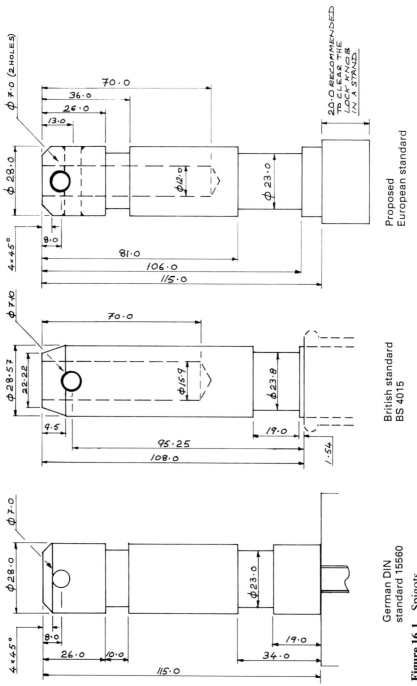

Proposed
European standard

British standard
BS 4015

German DIN
standard 15560

Figure 16.1   Spigots

The top latch, which is normally provided for retaining the colour frame and barndoors, must be self-applying so that it does not rely on the operator to close it. In this way, the operator is obliged to hold the retaining clip out of the way whilst he withdraws the barndoor or colour frame. On letting go of the catch, it returns to its locked position.

Cables

PVC or other plastic cables must not be used on luminaires. This is because the cable will deform with the heat if it touches the side of the housing. The mains input cable must have a sleeve of insulation where it is clamped at the cable entry. Any cable passing through a hole in sheet metal must be protected by a secondary sleeving to avoid mechanical damage to its insulation.

Electrical components and cables

All electrical components such as switches, cables, terminal blocks, lampholders, etc. must be manufactured to the appropriate standards for the individual items concerned, otherwise the luminaires could fail acceptance tests due to the use of non-standard component parts.

Earthing

The termination point of the incoming earth should be in view when the mains input terminals are exposed to enable an inspector to see that the earth is connected. The international earth symbol must be used adjacent to the incoming earth terminal. This must be punched into the metal or stuck onto it, so that it cannot be removed. The earth symbol must be a minimum of 5 mm high. Earthing washers are to be used to cut through the paint and ensure a good earth. The earthing screw is to be a minimum of 4 mm diameter with a machine cut thread; self-tapping screws are *not* acceptable. The screw size will increase with electrical current requirements but cannot be reduced for mechanical strength reasons. The screw must be plated steel or manufactured from brass or copper.

All metal parts that can be touched on the outside of the luminaire and that could come into contact with a live part under fault conditions, must be earthed. The lamp carriage must have a direct earth continuity wire; a scraping earth conducted along tracks is insufficient. Under no circumstances can push-on terminals be used for earth connections.

Terminal blocks

The terminal block should be designed so that it would allow one strand of wire to turn back from its connection by 8 mm and *not touch* adjacent terminals or metalwork in the luminaire. If the terminal block employed does not automatically perform this function, an insulating material must be placed under the block or used as a barrier between terminals so that isolation is achieved.

Warning labels required on the housing

The following recommended warnings are so numerous that it would require a larger housing just to display them on small luminaires. However, they are being quoted verbatim from the standards.

Before using the luminaire read the operating instructions
Before opening disconnect all poles from the electrical supply
(The minimum height for the lettering is to be not less than 2 mm)
The top of the unit must be indicated to prevent it being mounted upside down
(A broad arrow symbol may be used with the addition of the word 'TOP' or 'OBEN' in German. The minimum height of the arrow symbol is 5 mm).
Do not use without a lens and wire guard
To be serviced by qualified personnel
State the distance from the lens to a flammable surface
(When the temperature in the centre of the beam is 80°C with an ambient temperature of 25°C, the minimum recommended distance is 1 m. Use the international symbol)
The burning angle must be stated x° above horizontal, y° below horizontal
Observe the lamp manufacturers recommendations
Maximum voltage with an ac or dc symbol
The maximum current
The maximum wattage
(State if there is more than one lamp used, i.e. 4 × 1250 W)
The frequency of the supply
The maximum case temperature in degrees Celsius
(This is defined as the hottest part of the housing that could be touched from the outside)
The weight, complete with lamp and all accessories
The manufacturers name and type number
(The label must have permanent print and must be attached to the luminaire with rivets or stuck so that it cannot be removed)

Safety instruction sheet

This must be provided with every luminaire when it is sold.
The sheet must describe all the hazards involved with lamps and luminaires. (See 'Operating and safety instructions' below.)
   The following should also be noted:
Ambient temperature
All luminaires should be designed to work in a maximum ambient temperature of 45°C.
Fuses
The value of an integral fuse must be stated adjacent to the fuseholder, so that it is apparent to the operator when changing a fuse what value it should be.
Luminaire data sheet
This must be enclosed with each luminaire and include the following:
The same information that appears on the warning labels.
The fixing instructions of how the unit should be mounted or suspended.

A description and location of the safety bond anchor point and how to correctly attach the safety bond.

In addition, a description and reference numbers for the following items:
Safety glass
Wire guard
Lens
Safety bond
A list of all lamps that can be used in the luminaire with details of their voltage, wattage, life, colour temperature and any other parameters that are relevant.
A list of all accessories
Recommended stands
Spares
(*Note:* It is not a standard requirement to provide spares information, because the sheet will be particular to each unit. It is, however, a good opportunity for the manufacturer to identify the spares at this time.)

Additional requirements for discharge sources

Luminaires
These require the same standards as the tungsten halogen units, plus the following:
Safety glass
It is recommended that a glass of minimum thickness of 3 mm is provided to absorb UV radiation and provide adequate strength. However, with higher wattage luminaires, an increased thickness of glass will be required. In all other respects the same standards apply for safety glasses as described for tungsten halogen lamps.
UV radiation
It is prudent for a manufacturer to have an independent Test Certificate from a test house such as the National Physical Laboratory to determine that luminaires do not exceed any dangerous UV radiation levels.
Warning on housing
For UV protection, the safety glass must remain in position and be replaced if it is cracked, broken or has deep scratches.
Door opening
The lens door may be screwed closed, in which case it would not require a safety switch. In the event that the door can be opened without a tool, then a double pole mains isolation switch is required which must be activated by the glass of the lens so that the unit will not work if the lens is removed or the door is open. The activator must be designed so that it cannot be operated by hand, i.e. enclosed in a tube with a push rod to prevent the operator holding the switch closed and operating the unit. The same safety requirements apply to open fronted discharge luminaires that are fitted with a safety glass.
The following warning is required:
Do not open for 'x' seconds after switching off.
(*Note*: This is due to the hot lamps having high internal pressures and seeks to avoid explosions caused by cold air blowing on the lamp.)

Operating and safety instructions: lamps and luminaires

Manufacturers are required to provide the following information for the safe operation of luminaires and their associated lamps in the entertainment industry.

It is in the interests of every person purchasing or operating luminaires to read the following *typical* instructions, because the manufacturer is making you aware of the possible safety problems. This will prevent you being in the unenviable position, after an accident, of the manufacturer saying: 'I told you so!'

1. The equipment must be fitted with a suitable connector (the luminaire should be marked with the maximum operating current). Observe the following colour code (Europe)
    Brown wire   – live
    Blue wire   – neutral
    Green/yellow wire – earth
2. When connecting the luminaire to the mains supply, ensure that it is effectively earthed, that the mains supply is at the rated voltage and that the correct polarity is observed.
3. Each circuit must be protected by rapid acting, high rupturing capacity fuse or miniature circuit breaker of suitable voltage and current rating.
4. Lamp replacement must only be carried out after the luminaire has been disconnected from the electricity supply. Allow sufficient time for the lamp to cool before removing it from the equipment. (Cooling could take as long as five minutes.)
5. Only use lamps of the recommended type and observe the maximum wattage limitation marked on the luminaire. Observe the lamp manufacturer's recommendations relating to lamp type.
6. Insertion of the lamp into the lampholder by holding the envelope may cause mechanical breakage of the lamp and/or seal. For safety, install by holding the lamp cap or protective sleeve and use eye protection where appropriate.
7. Do not handle the quartz envelope with bare hands. Oil or grease from the skin may contaminate the surface of the envelope and in operation reduce performance and cause premature failure. If the quartz is accidentally handled, clean it before operation with a cloth moistened with alcohol or methylated spirit.
8. In certain circumstances, items made from quartz or glass may shatter. Prevent water droplets splashing onto a hot lamp as they may cause the envelope to break.
9. A suitable safety mesh or glass must be fitted to protect persons and property in the event of a lamp shattering – this is most important when lamps are used in open-fronted luminaires. If the safety glass or lens should become damaged with deep scratches or chipped edges, they must be replaced.
10. The lamp shall be changed if it has become damaged or thermally deformed.

11. At the end of life, lamps should be broken in a suitable robust container or wrapped to retain quartz fragments. The gas filling has a slight toxic content and large quantities of lamps should only be broken in a well ventilated area.

12. Direct exposure to discharge and tungsten halogen lamps can cause ultraviolet irritation to the skin and eyes. The use of glass or other UV filters is advised if the lamp is used in close proximity or for a prolonged period. When reflector fittings are used to concentrate the light in open-fronted luminaires, the safe exposure period will be reduced. Appropriate screening of people and surroundings must be provided.

13. The luminaire must be mounted on a firm support or stand and positioned at a safe distance from any flammable material, e.g. curtaining, background paper or scenery.

14. A high amount of radiant heat is produced and high surface temperatures are developed. Avoid operation in close proximity to human skin, as burns could result.

15. Avoid improper operation of the lamp, e.g. over voltage, or at burning angles not designed for the lamp type.

16. Luminaires must not be operated in explosive or flammable atmospheres or other hazardous areas.

17. All luminaires that are suspended must be fitted with a secondary independent means of support, i.e. a chain or bond. Removable accessories must be retained to prevent them falling if they become dislodged.

18. A dedicated anchor point should be provided on the housing so that the safety bond can be passed around a firm support through the yoke and terminated at the anchor point on the housing.

19. The top of the unit has been indicated to prevent its being mounted upside down.

20. Special care must be taken with portable luminaires and hand-held lamps. When demounting the luminaires, allow them to completely cool before standing them on a flammable surface or placing them in a carrying case.

21. For replacement parts, refer to the manufacturers' parts list for the recommended type of safety glass, wire guard, safety suspension bond and any relevant accessories.

22. Service and repairs must only be carried out by a qualified person.

16.2 The IEE Regulations in practice

In any installation that a lighting consultant is concerned with, the electrical engineer appointed will in the main make certain that the current regulations are adopted and enforced to ensure that the system is built to any required standards. There are, however, some aspects of the regulations which are of particular concern to the lighting consultant as well. The first of these is the selection of the equipment that meets the requirements of the permanently installed lighting system such as the dimmer racks. It is obviously no good having a piece of equipment that has a reasonable metal shell around it but leaves it possible to poke a finger through a ventilation louvre and touch a live terminal or a busbar.

There are several aspects to the safety of equipment such as this. Some of these items may seem very obvious but it is very useful to ensure that equipment meets some of the basic parameters. Any item of equipment selected must meet the requirements of the voltages present in the installation, together with the normal current consumption; additionally it has to perform satisfactorily and not create any danger by the abnormal current flow during fault conditions.

In the case of dimmer systems, we have to be aware of the voltage and frequency of the mains used. Dimmer racks are defined as 'factory built assemblies' and the rules for these must be complied with. There are various levels of protection required in a dimmer rack and without going into all the details, the first of these that we are concerned with is a degree of protection to IP2X. This means that the rack is protected against the entry of solid objects greater than **12 mm** across and is defined as a 'finger' or a similar object not exceeding 80 mm in length. This can be checked by using a 'Standard Test finger'. This degree of protection is required on all vertical surfaces of a dimmer rack. On the horizontal top surface, however, an even greater protection is needed, which is IP4X, where the top surface must be protected against the entry of solid objects greater than **1 mm**. The definition refers to wire or strips of metal in thickness greater than 1 mm and solid objects exceeding 1 mm in diameter. This requirement is to protect against the dropping of small screwdrivers through slots on the top of a rack or strands of copper wire being used for the installation penetrating the slots, thus 'shorting out' equipment within the rack, and possibly causing an electrical explosion.

The IEE regulations state that: 'Where an opening larger than that permitted for IP2X is necessary to allow the replacement of parts' two requirements will apply:

suitable precautions shall be taken to prevent persons from unintentionally touching live parts;

it shall be established as far as practicable that persons will be aware that live parts can be touched through the opening and should not be touched.

It is this particular requirement that makes the use of 'plug-in' dimmers particularly onerous. When a plug-in dimmer is removed from a rack, quite a large space is left and terminals at the rear of the dimmer are exposed. Most dimmer racks these days have dimmers that are totally enclosed with terminals that are either very difficult to reach from the front surface of a dimmer rack or meet an IP2X requirement.

One of the most important regulations that concerns us with dimmer racks, is the one that states:

Where it is necessary to remove a barrier or open an enclosure, or to remove a part of an enclosure, one or more of the following requirements shall be satisfied:

I   The removal or opening shall be possible only by use of a key or tool.

II   The removal or opening shall be possible only after disconnection of the supply to the live part against which the barrier or enclosure affords protection, restoration of the supply being possible only after replacement or reclosure of the barrier or enclosure.

III   An intermediate barrier shall be provided to prevent contact with a live part, such a barrier affording a degree of protection of at least IP2X and removable only by the use of a tool.

Item I is generally met on dimmer racks by a front door being fitted which is usually locked with a key, and by the fact that any rear access requires screwdrivers or special tools to remove screws or nuts. Item II is met by an automatic disconnection of a supply, probably realized by having a microswitch operating a contactor, for example, but this is not usually used in our installation systems although a micro switch on the lens door of a discharge luminaire is somewhat similar in operation.

An example of an intermediate barrier, such as quoted in III, would be a perspex cover such as that provided to enclose the terminals on a transformer or across terminals at the input of the rack.

Each of the pieces of equipment that we wish to install will require a label or other suitable means of identification to indicate its purpose. There will be wiring going to and from any apparatus installed and this must ensure that colour codes for identification of cables meet the requirements of the country where the system is to be used. It is essential that correct colour codes are maintained so there are no misunderstandings as to their purpose.

When using armoured cables for the input circuits to dimmer racks, there are strict rules regarding the type of cable used. One of the most important is that single core cables armoured with steel wire or tape should not be used, thus preventing any eddy currents being induced in the armour system. At the input to the dimmer rack, which is usually constructed from steel, an arrangement has to be made so that the individual conductors are not surrounded by a ferrous material thus preventing eddy (induced) currents. It is fairly obvious that any system using electrical conductors should provide a method of self-cancellation to prevent harmful electromagnetic fields.

Conductors of a.c. circuits installed in ferromagnetic enclosures shall be arranged so that the conductors of all phases and the neutral conductor (if any) and the appropriate protective conductor of each circuit are contained in the same enclosure.'

Every cable has to have adequate strength and be installed so that it can withstand any electromechanical forces caused by high fault currents or any other current that may occur in service. The same principle is applied to any busbar systems within dimmer racks.

As well as having regard for the regulations when we take the cables from the dimmer room to the production area, as has already been discussed, we must remember that any outlets either at the bottom of bars, along bars, attached to monopoles or pantographs, are all governed by regulations to ensure electrical safety is maintained.

An important element of the installation is the ambient temperatures that the racks and wiring can be subjected to: and there are rules regarding the limits and these have to be kept. The type of fusing, or protection afforded by mcbs, has to be carefully integrated with the size of cables and the loads that they are handling, although in practice the use of, say, a 20 A fuse on a 240 V 5 kW dimmer circuit will more than adequately protect the wiring installed which will invariably be generous in size to prevent voltage drop.

Another important element covered by regulations is concerned with the mechanical strength of the equipment. We have to be aware of areas of high humidity which, although not usually a cause for concern in the UK, can be a problem with equipment in other countries. Much of the equipment used for entertainment will be subject to vibration, and this is another area governed by modern regulations.

If we could ensure a balanced distribution through our three-phase network, we would not have to worry too much about the neutral conductor and it could be of a reasonable size in relation to the phase conductors. However, in many of our installations we will have out of balance three-phase systems, and therefore the neutral conductor must always have a cross-sectional area appropriate to the expected value of the neutral current. In general this means that the neutral conductor and the three-phase conductors are of similar size.

In a lighting system we have to make many electrical connections and there are strict rules with regard to these. The most obvious one is that the terminals should be large enough to make a good connection with the type of cable in use. Thus the means of connection have to take into account the following.

1. The material of the conductor and its insulation.
2. The number and shape of the wires forming the conductor.
3. The cross-sectional area of the conductor.
4. The number of conductors to be connected together.
5. The temperature attained by the terminals in normal service such that the effectiveness of the insulation of the conductors connected to them is not impaired.
6. Where a soldered connection is used the design shall take account of creep, mechanical stress and temperature rise under fault current conditions.
7. The provision of adequate locking arrangements in situations subject to vibration or thermal cycling.

Items 1, 2, 3 and 4 cover the size of terminals including the provision of two or more parallel connections; item 5 covers for high temperature switches where deterioration of the insulation will cause problems in practice; item 6 prevents the melting and breaking of soldered connections which could lead to wires floating about in cabinets; item 7 seeks to prevent terminals coming loose either by the extremes of cold and heat or by vibration which again could lead to wires floating about.

We are obviously concerned with the spread of fire within the systems we install, and another IEE regulation states:

Where a wiring system passes through elements of building construction, such as floors, walls, roofs, ceilings, partitions or cavity barriers, the openings remaining after passage of the wiring system shall be sealed according to the degree of fire resistance required of the element concerned (if any).

In addition

Where a wiring system such as conduit, cable ducting, cable trunking, busbar or busbar trunking penetrates elements of building construction having specified fire resistance it shall be internally sealed so as to maintain the degree of fire resistance of the respective element as well as being externally sealed to maintain the required fire resistance.

The two regulations quoted cover for the instances when we go from one area to another and thus create holes in the structure. The first covers for unenclosed wiring systems where it may be just cables going from one area to another. The second regulation quoted covers where we might have trunking going through a wall and the trunking itself is sealed to the wall surround but unfortunately the internal part of the trunking allows fire to move from one area to another and this, of course, would be just as dangerous.

The regulation that covers all of the above states:

Each sealing arrangement used in accordance with the regulations shall comply with the following requirements:
1. It should be compatible with the material of the wiring system with which it is in contact.
2. It shall permit thermal movement of the wiring system without reduction of the sealing quality.
3. It shall be removable without damage to existing cable where space permits future extension to be made.
4. It shall resist relevant external influences to the same degree as the wiring system with which it is used.
5. Each sealing arrangement shall be visually inspected at an appropriate time during erection to verify that it conforms to the manufacturers' erection instructions and the details shall be recorded.

Regulation 1 above seeks to prevent harmful chemical reactions between the wiring system itself and any materials used for fireproofing; 2 is fairly obvious, in that it would be no good having fireproofing that with gradual movement allowed gaps to appear. Unfortunately fire doesn't need too much of a gap to go from one area to another; 3 covers for the situation where it would be quite easy to spray, for instance, around cables with some foam which would be fire retardant but unfortunately, if you then needed to do anything with the cables, it would be physically impossible because they'd all be glued together.

Thus we have to be careful with the methods used for fire prevention because by covering for this eventuality it may make life difficult when expansion of a system is required.

During an installation temporary sealing arrangements have to be provided as appropriate, and when any work is done any sealing that has been disturbed has to be reinstated as soon as possible.

In lighting systems we have the normal mains supply cable going to the luminaires; in addition we will have low voltage multicore cables or smaller digital signal cables provided for the control systems. This type of situation is covered by the regulations which state that we are not allowed to mix cables with various voltages present unless all the cables are insulated for the highest voltage present in any of the cables, or alternative methods are adopted.

1.   Each conductor in a multicore cable is insulated for the highest voltage present in the cable, or is enclosed within an earthed metallic screen of a current carrying capacity equivalent to that of the largest conductor enclosed within the screen.
2.   The cables are insulated for their respective system voltage and installed in a separate compartment of a cable ducting or cable trunking system, or have an earthed metallic covering.

It is obviously extremely dangerous to pick up a conductor where we expect to find safe low voltage and instead find mains, and the above regulations seek to prevent this happening. The two methods are either to have good insulation of the systems so voltages cannot travel from one cable to another, or conductors that are surrounded by an earthed shield where any harmful voltage will be conveyed safely away.

In practice, we generally run the mains feeds around the building separately from the control feeds, and the only time where they may come into close proximity is perhaps on monopoles, pantographs or motorized barrel units where technical cables for the sound and vision system are installed in addition to the lighting circuits.

In places of entertainment and for those concerned with the production of entertainment we use a multiplicity of plugs and sockets. These may be the normal 13 A supplies for domestic use, or special sockets for lighting outlets and there will invariably be provision for three-phase supplies for portable machinery. We have to be extremely careful that we do not intermix any of these socket outlets or plugs so that people are not placed in danger or machines receive voltages for which they are not designed. The main requirements for plugs and socket outlets are as follows:

1.   It shall not be possible for any pin of a plug to make contact with any live contact of its associated socket outlet while any other pin of the plug is completely exposed.
2.   It shall not be possible for any pin of a plug to make contact with any live contact of any socket outlet within the same installation other than the type of socket outlet for which the plug is designed.
3.   Every plug and socket outlet shall be of the non reversible type with provision for the connection of a protective conductor.

Finally, but certainly not least, is the provision of devices for emergency switching. The regulations require that a means of interrupting the supply for the purpose of emergency switching shall be capable of cutting off the full load current of the relevant part of the installation.

Means for emergency switching shall consist of:
1. A single switching device directly cutting off the incoming supply, or
2. A combination of several items of equipment operated by a single action and resulting in the removal of the hazard by cutting off the appropriate supply; emergency stopping may include the retention of supply electric braking facilities.

The regulations go on to state:

> Where practical a device for emergency switching shall be manually operated directly interrupting the main circuit. A device such as a circuit breaker or a contactor operated by remote control shall open on de-energisation of the coil, or another technique of suitable reliability shall be employed.

> The operating means (such as handle or push button) for a device for emergency switching shall be clearly identifiable and preferably coloured 'red'. It shall be installed in a readily accessible position where the hazard might occur and where appropriate, further devices shall be provided where additional emergency switching may be needed.

> The operating means of a device for emergency switching shall be of the latching type or capable of being restrained in the 'OFF' or 'STOP' position. The release of the emergency switching device shall not re-energize the equipment concerned.

Although it is possible, in a further qualified part of the regulations, to allow an automatic reset under specified conditions, we in the entertainment industry are mainly concerned with the fact that nearly all the operatives involved with a production could de-energize the system by operating the emergency switching. The re-energizing of the equipment has to be carried out by approved personnel, such as the engineers or electricians concerned, to ensure that the hazard that caused the 'emergency' has been dealt with correctly.

16.3 The Electricity at Work Regulations in practice

The Health and Safety Executive issued the Electricity at Work Regulations 1989 and they came into force on 1 April 1990. The Regulations are mandatory, so they are enforceable by law. The intention of the Regulations is to require precautions to be taken against the risk of death or personal injury from electricity in the place of work. Whilst the Regulations cover all electrical supplies and equipment, we will restrict our coverage to portable items that can be plugged into the mains via a plug and socket. These are obviously the most vulnerable to damage and are by definition the most likely to be handled.

The Regulations cover every portable item to be found on the premises, from luminaires to kettles, from typewriters to electric drills; in fact every item with a plug fitted must be included. The house wiring and permanently connected machinery and apparatus are also included, but are not being considered by us at this time. The question is how to comply with the Regulations. The first step is to obtain a copy of 'Electricity at Work Regulations 1989' and 'Statutory Instrument No. 635'. There are also two very useful Guidance Notes PM 32 'The Safe Use of Portable Electrical Apparatus' and GS 37 'Flexible Leads, Plugs and Sockets'. All are issued by the Health & Safety Executive, Her Majesty's Stationery Office, or just ask the Safety Officer for your area. The following notes are our interpretation of some of the requirements and should not be taken as a statement of the Regulations.

The statement that all portable electrical equipment must be as far as possible electrically safe is the starting point and it really means *all and every item* found on the premises and does not take into account who owns it. It can be a personal radio or a rented item, it still comes under the umbrella of the Regulations. When the Area Safety Officer calls to inspect your premises, he will ask to see the Duty Holder. This is any responsible person who has been nominated to keep a register of every item of electrical equipment; he will ask the Duty Holder for the register and expect to find certain information in it. Identify the item, the date that it was tested, the result of the test, which can only be pass or fail, action taken and the date of the next test. The period between tests can only be established by the Duty Holder and the operator and will depend on how often the appliance is used and the history of damage that can be sustained by the environment in which it is used. Examples could be: an electric drill being used every day, all day on a production line, in which case three-monthly tests could be deemed appropriate; equipment in frequent use and subject to transit damage could be tested every six months, and so on. Until a history is built up in the register no definite period can be established.

Most portable items in entertainment that are not out on rental or travelling shows, and are normally used in the same premises, could be considered to have light duty and an annual test might be appropriate. Portable electrical equipment can be divided into three classes:

Class I   Requiring an earth connection to any metal part that could become live in a fault condition.
Class II   A totally insulated electrical device where no part can become live in the event of a fault condition. This type of equipment does not require an earth wire.
Class III   Low voltage equipment that has its own regulations.

A typical test for Class I equipment could be as follows: A visual inspection of the cable, the plug, the cord grip at the plug and the cord grip at the appliance. Any damage to these items would fail the test and the equipment would not be allowed to continue to the electrical test. The reported accidents show that 80% of electrical accidents could have been avoided by a visual inspection. If the equipment passes the visual test it will be tested electrically for earth continuity from the plug to the frame of the appliance and the earth resistance will be recorded and must be within the Regulations' requirements. The insulation is tested from the plug through the earth and live conductors and must have the required resistance.

Finally, a run test is conducted to determine that the equipment conforms to the Regulations in its working state. Other tests are available on some products; a high voltage test might be carried out, normally 1500 V for Class I equipment and 3000 V for Class II, but these are made at the discretion of the electrical engineer conducting the tests.

16.4 Safety checklists and inspections

It is quite amazing that the majority of people who drive around in their cars, except for having a routine service done (which generally means the oil is replaced and the spark plugs are still there), very seldom inspect to see if the car is safe or otherwise. It is generally assumed that this is the case.

Much of the equipment used in the entertainment industry is well built and a superficial examination usually would lead one to expect the equipment would work safely for long periods of time with little or nothing going wrong. However, life is not as easy as that, and modern legislation requires that moving equipment such as monopoles, winches, pantographs and devices used to suspend equipment over stage areas, studio areas and particularly above audiences, is regularly inspected to see that no danger is present. Many items concerned with mechanical safety can be verified by visual inspection, but this is not necessarily the case with electrical equipment when the fault may lie in a piece of copper somewhere.

Mechanical equipment is required to be inspected at regular intervals these days and, to ensure that this is done correctly, all items of equipment must be properly coded and numbered and a register of equipment and tests kept on the premises. When items of lifting and suspension equipment are purchased, they must be marked with an identification number, the safe working load (SWL) of the particular piece of equipment. The manufacturer must ensure that each item or a batch test of a particular piece of equipment is carried out so that test certificates can be issued.

Routine testing of lifting equipment has to provide checks against the following items:

1. Undue wear of any part.
2. The wire ropes used for lifting must be inspected to ensure they have not been damaged and that no strands are broken.
3. The points where wire ropes are made off to provide permanent anchor points to other parts of the structure are to be inspected to ensure they are not loose or damaged.
4. All parts of the motor assembly are firmly in place and not loose in any way.
5. All pulleys or scroll drums to be examined for undue signs of wear which would indicate possible problems with the winding of the wire ropes.
6. All diverter pulleys to be examined for signs of wear and the fact that they are free to rotate.
7. A visual inspection of the top and bottom limit system in addition to visual inspection of overload and slack wire system.

8.   To apply load tests to ensure that the slack wire and overload system works correctly. In addition, to traverse the unit from top to bottom to see that limit switches are operating correctly.
9.   Ensure that all warning labels are present and all indicators are fully functional.
10. Ensure that the equipment is capable of being controlled from all nominated control positions, e.g. studio floor level or on the local controls at grid level.
11. All covers and guards are correctly positioned and fastened securely.

All of the above tests are to be carried out by approved test houses, usually employed by the insurance companies covering the premises concerned.

Electrical safety is covered, in the main, in the UK, by the Electricity at Work Regulations 1989, which covers for items of equipment that are portable, and in addition the latest edition of the IEE regulations pertaining to the installation of the electrical system in the building. As well as the regular checks for electrical safety under the Electricity at Work Regulations 1989, it is also wise to check for the mechanical safety of any luminaire or other type of light source used in the entertainment industry. Most premises will, on a fairly regular basis, do some maintenance to ensure the equipment works correctly, and this obviously makes life much easier from the point of view of the electricians concerned with lighting equipment. At the time these checks for maintenance are made, it is very easy to go over some of the mechanical items to ensure that they are not damaged in any way. Testing the pan and tilt mechanism for movement and slackness might reveal problems, but a visual examination of a yoke, for instance, would not necessarily indicate something wrong with the devices used to lock the yoke to the body of the luminaire. A fairly careful examination of the bodywork of any luminaire would reveal any loose parts that may be suspect and therefore in danger of falling off.

To give an example of a problem that can occur, and in fact did, many years ago and also had tremendous implications for safety in the studio, a luminaire mounted above two actors suddenly discharged molten aluminium down to the studio floor. The amount was quite considerable and would have caused a severe burn had it hit one of the actors. An investigation was carried out and revealed that a small internal aluminium cover in the luminaire had come loose, possibly through vibration by being raised and lowered in the studio on a bar unit. This small aluminium cover had fallen across the primary reflector of a 1250 W linear lamp. Instead of melting the offending piece of aluminium that had become dislodged, the lamp chose to melt the reflector around it. The amount of molten aluminium fell through the bottom louvres used for air flow in the unit concerned and dropped to the studio floor. One horrifying aspect of this case was that during the tests to reproduce the fault, it was found that with the dimmer held at about '7' and thus applying about 200 V to a 240 V 1250 W linear lamp, no problem occurred and, in fact, this might have been the case for a long period of time. However, as soon as the lamp was raised to full output the fault was reproduced. Thus, it was rather like playing Russian roulette with molten aluminium.

Therefore a suggested checklist for luminaires is as follows:

1. Is the yoke functioning correctly and are the pan and tilt controls, if fitted, working satisfactorily?
2. Do all locking knobs fitted correctly tighten the moving part so it can be held in the position as set?
3. Examine the spud fitted to see that it has not become loose from the yoke assembly.
4. Check internally for any loose parts, particularly with regard to reflectors and lampholder assemblies.
5. Check internal wiring for any signs of wear.
6. Check all switches fitted to see that mechanically they function correctly. Although they may appear to be satisfactory from an electrical standpoint, it might be that they are not mechanically perfect. This generally avoids any arcing problems within switches, caused by springs or levers being slack.
7. Check to see that all accessories attached to the luminaire are not loose, i.e. barndoors, colour frames, etc.
8. Check all louvres which allow air flow through the luminaire for signs of damage and ensure they are working correctly to make certain that the luminaire does not get over hot. This can usually be ascertained by signs of burning on the bodywork.
9. Check to see that barndoors function correctly and are sufficiently tight to do the job.
10. If a base or feet are provided to stand a luminaire on, ensure they have not become damaged in any way. Luminaire leads and plugs should be inspected once a year but it is useful to inspect them on a more frequent basis to see that no arcing is occurring on any of the pins, which would also indicate deterioration in any of the permanent sockets fitted in the system.
11. A useful point is to listen out whilst in operation for any nasty frying noises, which would indicate lamp contacts arcing and thus a lampholder would need replacing.

Although all the foregoing seems a bit of a chore and probably many people would say, 'It's not my responsibility', if the tests listed above are carried out, it will ensure a safe working environment and one which is easier to work in because all the equipment is functioning correctly.

Appendix 1 Glossary of terms

Absorption filter A filter which transmits selected wavelengths. The absorbed energy is converted to heat which raises the temperature of the filter.

Acb Air circuit breaker.

Acting area That portion of a stage used by the actors during a performance.

Additive colour mixing The superimposition of light beams, usually consisting of the primary colours, whereby the resultant light is the *addition* of the various wavelengths concerned. (See **Subtractive colour mixing**.)

Ambient light General background light.

American National Standards Institute (ANSI) An independent association that establishes standards to promote consistency and interchangeability among manufacturers. This organization was formerly known as the United States of America Standards Institute (USASI or ASI) and previously as the American Standards Association (ASA).

Arc light A luminaire using a carbon arc discharge as the source of illumination.

Aspect ratio The ratio of the width to the height of any imaging system. Generally refers to the final picture on the television or film screen. Nearly always expressed with the height as 'unity'.

Automation The ability of a piece of equipment to go to predetermined operational points by means of a closed loop servo system without the need for human intervention. Often confused with 'power assisted systems'.

Backing Scenery used behind sets to limit the view of the audience or a camera through openings such as doorways or windows.

Backing lighting The illumination provided for scenery and backcloths.

Back light A luminaire used to light the subject from the rear to help separation from backings and to increase the three-dimensional effect.

Ballast The electrical device, required for all discharge lamps, that limits current through the lamp. Additional functions may be incorporated in the basic unit such as starting circuits and dimming control.

Barndoor Movable flaps attached to a Fresnel or PC luminaire to shape the light beam.

Barrel (Colloq. Bar) A metal tube, generally 48 mm diameter, for suspending luminaires or scenery. Usually manufactured from steel or aluminium.

Base light   The basic intensity of 'soft' lighting required to satisfy the minimum viewing or technical requirements.

Batten   (a) Horizontal pipe on which luminaires or scenery can be hung; (b) Compartmented multicolour floodlight unit for theatrical lighting.

Beam   The unidirectional flow of total light output from a source, usually a luminaire.

Beam angle   Those points on the light output curve which are 50% of maximum output. The included angle between these two points is the beam angle. Sometimes referred to as the 'half peak angle'.

Beam light   Lensless luminaire with a parabolic reflector to give a parallel light beam.

Blackbody   A body which completely absorbs any heat or light radiation falling upon it.

Blackbody radiation   Radiation that comes from an ideal blackbody. The distribution of energy is dependent only on the temperature of the blackbody and is governed by Planck's radiation law.

Blackout   To switch off all illumination (except exit lights).

Blackout switch   A master on/off switch used for controlling the overall production lighting for either stage or studios.

Bounce lighting   Directing light onto a large diffuse surface to produce a soft reflected light.

Brail   To pull a lighting suspension or piece of scenery out of its normal hanging position by means of attached rope lines.

Bridge   A narrow platform suspended over the acting area. Luminaires and projection devices mounted on the bridge are accessible during performance.

Brightness   (See **Luminance**.)

Brightness ratio   Ratio of maximum-to-minimum luminances occurring within a scene.

British Standards Institute (BSI)   Produces technical specifications and other documents which are made generally available. The main aim of the Institute is to maintain standards, quality and safety in goods and products.

Broad   A wide-angle floodlight.

Brute   A 225 ampere dc high intensity carbon spotlight with a 24 inch diameter Fresnel lens.

Bubble   Slang term used in the television and film industries to describe lamps of any type.

Bulb   An old term describing the bulbous glass envelope of an electric lamp.

'C' Clamp   (See **Hook clamp**.)

Camera light   A luminaire mounted on a camera for lighting along or near the optical axis, usually to provide catch lights for the subject's eyes.

Candela   Unit of luminous intensity.

Candlepower   A term that was used for intensity but has been replaced by the candela.

Carbon arc   A dc arc source in which the arc is produced in air between a pair of carbon electrodes. These electrodes burn away and must be advanced during operation.

Channel   The circuit from the fader on the lighting control console to its associated dimmer.

Chaser lights   A linear string of lamps wired and controlled so that the lights appear to be following in sequence.

Chroma   In television, the information which gives the colour of the image as distinct from its luminance (brightness).

Chroma key   A television special effect which uses a monochromatic coloured background to allow electronic switching to another picture. Deep blue is commonly used for the background when the foreground involves people.

Chromaticity   The colour of light, as defined by its chromaticity co-ordinates, generally using the CIE diagram.

Circuit breaker   An electrical switch positioned in the circuit that will automatically operate to break the flow of current under abnormal conditions.

Cold mirror   A dichroic coated glass surface which reflects visible light but allows infra-red energy to pass through the reflector so that the reflected light contains less heat.

Colour   A sensation of light induced in the eye by electromagnetic waves of a certain frequency – the colour being determined by that frequency.

Colour frame   A frame used to support colour media at the front of the luminaire.

Colour media   Any coloured transparent material that can be placed in front of a luminaire, often referred to as 'gels' (for gelatin). Glass and other plastic materials are also used.

Colour rendering index (Ra)   The evaluation of the effect of a light source on a set of coloured test pieces representing portions of the visible spectrum. The higher the index towards its maximum of '100' the better the colour reproduction. Sources in general require an index greater than 90 to prevent noticeable colour distortion.

Colour temperature   A method of specifying the colour of a source which emits light in a continuous spectrum. Expressed in Kelvin units, the range used in media lighting is from 2600 K (white lights with a high red content) to 6000 K (white light with a high blue content). *Note*: Cannot be used with discharge sources, although sometimes used as a guide to approximation of colour. (See **Correlated colour temperature**.)

Colour wheel   A circular mechanism holding several different colours mounted in front of a luminaire which can be rotated by hand or by a motor drive.

Complementary colours   A pair of colours in the additive colour mixing system which combine to make white light.

Condenser   A lens or mirror used in an optical system to collect the light being radiated from a source, which is then directed onto the gate of the projection system.

Contactor   Large electrical switch used within the input electrical system to control the on/off state of the supply. Usually operated by an electromagnetic coil.

Contrast range   This is the ratio of the brightness between the lightest and darkest areas in a subject. In a video system, it is the range between the maximum signal which can be satisfactorily handled without distortion and the acceptable electronic noise level of the system.

Correlated colour temperature (CCT) Many sources of light energy do not have the same characteristics as blackbody radiators, but sources which have a mainly white light output can be given a correlated colour temperature. This is defined as that temperature of the blackbody radiator which *most closely* matches that of the light source in question. It therefore gives a rough guide to the blueness or redness of the source.

Cosine law The equation which allows the calculation of illumination on a surface which is at an angle to the incident light.

Counterweight system Mechanical system for flying scenery in which the weight of the pieces of scenery is balanced by adjustable weights in a cradle running up and down in guides in a frame normally at the side of the stage. The system is also used for lighting bars.

Cross barrel Used between barrels to allow accurate positioning of luminaires.

Cross fade A lighting change where one set of channels reduces in light intensity and another set increases in light intensity.

Crosslighting Illumination from two luminaires at approximately 180° to each other on opposite sides of the subject. They are generally hard sources.

CSI A discharge lamp which approximates to sunlight for colour balance (CCT 4000 K).

Cue A signal, which may be written, verbal or by action, that causes motivation of artistes or technical staff.

Cyclorama A backing, mounted in the studio, to provide a continuous surface and an illusion of infinity.

Cyclorama (cyc) lights Luminaires with specially designed reflectors used either at the base or at the top of cycloramas to light in a smooth manner.

Daylight filter (a) A blue filter used to change the colour of a light source from tungsten at 3200 K to approximately 5600 K; (b) A blue filter used on a camera to allow daylight balanced film stock to be used with tungsten lighting.

Devitrification The process which causes a change from a 'glassy' state to a crystalline state.

Dichroic filter A filter which reflects chosen wavelengths and transmits the remainder.

Diffuser Sheets of frosted plastic or spun glass fibre used to soften the shadows produced by the light beam.

Dimmer An electronic device used to reduce current flow to a lamp and therefore allow its light intensity to be adjusted.

Dimmer curve A graph which shows the light output or voltage output of a dimmer against the channel control setting.

Dimmer room The area allocated for the equipment racks which contain the dimmers and associated equipment.

Discharge sources Light produced by the passage of electricity, through a gas, across two electrodes enclosed in a quartz envelope, e.g. Xenon, CSI, HMI, MSR lamps.

Double broad   This is a twin lamp floodlight generally used on studio floors as a local filler.

Double purchase   A suspension system used on counterweight bars which gears the movement of the counterweight bucket to half that of the bar itself. (See **Single purchase**.)

Douser   A small metal flag used in follow spots to cut off the light beam without having to switch off the electrical supply to the source.

Downlighter   Usually refers to small ceiling mounted luminaires in control areas.

Downstage   The stage or studio area which is nearest the audience.

Drop arm   A device used to hang a luminaire lower than the normal suspension system permits.

Effects projector   A focusing luminaire used to project slides or shapes. The effects can also be motor driven.

Efficacy   This is the efficiency of a light source in converting the electrical input power to light and is expressed in 'lumens per watt'.

Efficiency   This is a measure of the *useful* light output in lumens against the total lumens generated by the light source.

Eggcrate   A device consisting of small cross baffle plates to restrict the spread of the light beam on a softlight.

Ellipsoidal spotlight (profile projector)   A luminaire which uses an ellipsoidal reflector and a reasonable quality optical system to project shapes and patterns with a hard edge.

Extension bar   This is used to extend lighting barrels for accurate positioning of luminaires.

Fader   A control device for indirectly setting the current output of a dimmer and thus varying the light intensity. Originally were levers, but are often 'wheels' in modern lighting control systems.

Field angle   Those points on the light output curve which are 10% of maximum output. The included angle between these two points is the field angle.

Filler   Light used to control shade areas. Usually a softlight but can be controlled hard light.

Film speed   (a) A measure of the film's sensitivity to light expressed in numerical terms to given an 'exposure index' which is used in the ISO and ASA system on light meters; (b) The velocity of film passing through movie cameras or projectors is measured in frames per second or in metres per minute.

Five K   A colloquial term for a five kilowatt spotlight.

Flag   A sheet of metal or card mounted a short distance in front of the luminaire to give a sharp cut off to the light beam.

Flood   By focusing a lamp close to a lens, the diameter of the light beam is enlarged and thus gives the widest field of illumination.

Floodlight   A luminaire which has only a reflector to control the beam and has wide angle distribution. (See **Softlight** and **Cyclorama light**.)

Fluorescence   The ability of some materials to convert ultraviolet energy into visible light.

Fly   To suspend scenery or equipment above a stage or studio floor by means of a suspension system which can be manually operated or driven by motorized units.

Fly gallery   The gallery which extends around the side walls of the stage area approximately 10m above the stage floor. It is used for operating the ropes which adjust the counterweight system and hence the height of the bars above the stage.

Fly tower   The upper part of the stage area which is formed as a tower, usually with galleries, to suspend scenery out of sight of the audience.

F-number   A set of numbers used to express the aperture of a lens which represents its light transmission. It is worked out by dividing the focal length of the lens by the diameter of the opening in the lens diaphragm. It is also colloquially known as the 'stop'.

Focal length   The distance of the focal point from the lens is called the focal length of the lens.

Focal point   The point where the incident parallel rays, which are bent by a lens, meet in focus.

Focus   In optics, the adjustment to give a clearly defined image. Used in the lighting industry to indicate the process of 'spotting' or 'flooding' the light beam of a luminaire.

Follow spot   A narrow angle, focusing hard edged spotlight used to follow moving artistes.

Footcandle   An old unit, now superseded by 'lux', used to describe illumination which was measured in 'lumens per square foot'.

Footlambert   The old unit for luminance (brightness) which has been replaced by the 'nit'.

Footlights   Lights mounted along the edge of a stage to provide uplighting.

Fresnel lens   A convex lens built with concentric steps to enable its thickness to be reduced.

Fresnel spotlight (colloq. Fresnel)   Luminaires fitted with Fresnel lenses of varying sizes; the width of the beam can be changed by varying the spacing between the lens and the lamp/reflector assembly.

Front of house lights (FOH)   Luminaires usually mounted on barrels, and generally concealed, above the audience seats.

Frost   Translucent gel or plastic used to diffuse light sources.

Fuse   A protective device for electrical circuits; originally a piece of special wire but nowadays nearly always a metal link contained in a ceramic cartridge.

Gaffer   Term used in the film industry to describe the chief technician.

Gate   The optical centre of a profile projector where the shutters are positioned and an iris or 'gobo' can be inserted.

Gel   (See **Colour media**.)

Gobo   A mask placed in the gate of a profile spot to shape the beam. It is a simple form of outline projection.

Grid   (See **Lighting grid**.)

Groundrow   Compartmented lighting units usually arranged in linear fashion for lighting from the base of cyclorama.

Half scrim   A semicircular scrim used to attenuate part of the light beam. (See **Scrim**.)

Hard glass halogen lamp   A tungsten halogen lamp with an envelope of borosilicate glass.

Hardlight   A luminaire that produces well-defined shadows, normally a spotlight.

Heat filter   A light filter which removes infra-red from the beam to reduce heat from the source of illumination.

Hertz (Hz)   The unit of frequency which is measured in cycles per second. Other units are kilohertz (kHz) and megahertz (MHz).

High key   Describes a scene containing mainly light tones well illuminated without large areas of strong shadow.

HMI (also CID and MSR)   Discharge lamps which have a daylight colour balance (5600 K).

Hoist (See **Winch**)   Old term used to describe either manual or motorized lifting equipment.

Hook clamp   A clamp used for suspending luminaires from lighting bars.

House electrician   An electrician permanently employed by a theatre or concert hall to maintain and operate the electrical equipment in the premises.

House lights   A lighting system permanently installed to either illuminate an audience area or provide worklights in studios.

Hue   The quality by which one colour is distinguished from another as a result of their wavelengths. It does not take into account the brightness or intensity of the colour.

Illumination   The luminous flux falling on unit area of a surface. The unit of illumination is the lux (1 lumen per square metre) and it is the measure of the quantity of *incident light*.

Incandescence   The emission of light by raising a material to a high temperature.

Internal reflector   An integral reflector formed on the inner rear surface of the envelope of a lamp and is usually parabolic or elliptic in shape.

Inverse square law   The equation which is used to calculate the illumination at a given distance from a source of light.

Iris   A series of adjustable metal plates arranged to give a variable circular aperture. Used in lighting projectors to alter the size of the light beam.

Kelvin   The SI unit of thermodynamic temperature. It uses the same size of degree as the Celsius scale. (Zero K = −273°C.)

Key light   The principal modelling light, usually a spotlight.

Kicker   Generally a hard light source used to provide obvious highlights.

Kilowatt   Electrical power term for 1000 watts.

Lamp   A glass or quartz envelope which contains filaments or electrodes. The term lamp is often used to describe a luminaire, which is to be avoided as it can cause confusion. (Colloquial terms include globe, bubble, source.)

Lantern   (See **Luminaire**.)

LD   Abbreviation for lighting designer or lighting director.

Leko   A slang term used in America to describe ellipsoidal spotlights.

Life   Usually refers to the manufacturer's rates life in hours of a lamp at its normal voltage and is based on the average life of a number of lamps which have been tested.

Light centre length (LCL)   The distance from the centre of the filament to a standard point at the base of the lamp.

Lighting batten A barrel assembly with integral power feeders for luminaires.

Lighting control console A unit which contains the controls for adjusting the channel levels and thus the dimmer outputs, 'group channel' control, memory control, playback system and special effects.

Lighting designer (director) The person who creates and implements the lighting design for a production.

Lighting grid In *television* a structure mounted at high level above the operational area, usually made from steel or aluminium or a combination of the two, for the purposes of suspending luminaires and ancillary lighting equipment. In *theatre*, it is the framework above the stage in a close gridiron formation to allow operators access for positioning lights and scenery.

Lighting plot A scale drawing which shows the disposition of the lighting equipment in relation to the production concerned. Used by the LD and electricians.

Limbo Describes a state of lighting where the background details are suppressed. In television this is usually created by 'blackness' whereas the film industry tends to use a white background.

Linnebach projector A lighting unit, basically a box without a lens, which contains a small point source of illumination to project soft diffused images of cutouts or glass slides.

Louvres Thin black metallic strips located on a luminaire to reduce spill light. (See **Eggcrate**.) When fitted in front of a luminaire may also be adjustable at various angles to provide dimming without colour change.

Low key Describes a scene containing mostly dark tones with large areas of shadow and is often used to create a dramatic mood.

Lumen The lumen is the unit of 'luminous flux' and is defined as the amount of light which falls on one square metre of a surface at a *constant* distance of one metre from a source of one candela.

Lumens per watt The light output in lumens produced by a source for each watt of electrical power supplied to the source.

Luminaire A general term for a complete lighting unit. It includes the housing, the reflector, lens and lamps. (Colloquial terms include light, lantern, fixture, unit, instrument, fitting.)

Luminance The measure of brightness of a surface. It is measured in 'nits'. The old unit was the 'foot lambert'.

Luminous intensity A measure of the energy from a light source emitted in a particular direction. It is measured in candelas.

Lux The unit of illuminance (illumination). It is the unit of measurement for the incident light arriving at a surface. The old measuring system used footcandles. (One footcandle equals 10.76 lux.)

Mcb Miniature circuit breaker.

Mccb Moulded case circuit breaker.

Master/group master Usually refers to a lighting control system fader which over-rides by electrical means a group of individual faders.

Maximum overall length (MOL) The overall physical length of a lamp including all electrical contacts.

Memory The term used to denote 'filed' information which controls the lighting channels.

Microphony   The interference caused by the mechanical vibration of any electrode system. Particularly troublesome on the older type of camera pickup tube, such as the Image Orthicon and the Plumbicon tubes used in colour cameras.

Mirror ball   A motor driven ball with its surface covered in small mirrors. When rotated, with spotlights shining to it, it produces moving points of light.

Modelling light   The term is used to describe any luminaire, generally a hard source, that reveals the depth, shade and texture of subjects.

Nanometre (nm)   A unit of metric measurement equal to one billionth of a metre, which is used to measure light wavelengths.

Neutral density filter   A filter which attenuates the light passing through it without affecting the colour of that light.

Nit   The unit of luminance, which is one candela per square metre of surface radiation. It is therefore the measure of the *brightness* of a surface.

Non-dim   Describes the circuit which replaces the normal dimmer function, where the circuit is switched 'on' or 'off' *only*, either by a switch or relay system.

Objective lens   (See **Projection lens**.)

Offstage   Areas that are out of the eyeline of an audience.

Onstage   In view of the audience.

Opaque   Absorbance of electromagnetic radiation at specific wavelengths, generally refers to the fact that light is not transmitted.

Open-faced luminaire   Describes luminaires with no lens system, such as the 'Redhead'.

Pcb   Printed circuit board.

Pan   Term describing the horizontal movement, about a point, of luminaires or equipment.

Pantograph   A mechanical cross-armed device for varying the height of luminaires or other fittings. It is generally spring balanced but can be operated by a motor or manually driven gear system.

Par-can   A simple luminaire, basically a metal tube, with a Par lamp mounted in it. The type of lamp determines the beam spread.

Patch   A term describing the connections made on low voltage control or power systems.

Patch panel   A system rather like an old telephone operator's interconnection system (switchboard) to connect low voltage circuits or high voltage circuits.

Pin matrix   A method of coupling control channels into groups by the insertion of special pins into a 'x' and 'y' matrix, where the 'x' axis may represent channels and the 'y' represent groups.

Pixel   A picture element. The smallest element of a CCD array. The definition is governed by the number of 'pixels per area', the higher the amount the better the definition.

Plano-convex lens   A lens which has one flat side and one convex side.

Plano-convex spotlight (PC spot)   A luminaire that gives a reasonably even beam with a very sharp edge.

Playback   That part of a lighting control system where the lighting memories and/or other lighting states are combined and controlled by output master faders or switches.

Pole operation (Colloq. pole op)   The control of electrical and mechanical functions on luminaires and suspension equipment by means of a long metal pole.

Power assisted systems   Luminaires and suspension equipment under the direct control of an operator, e.g. winch control motor systems.

Practical   Describes a light, e.g. table lamp, that can be effectively switched on and off by an actor within a scene. In television, the light will usually be remotely switched from the lighting control console.

Prefocus   Denotes special lamp caps so that the filament lines up precisely to the optics of a luminaire.

Preset (blind mode)   A facility on lighting control systems that enables a lighting plot to be set up without affecting the lights already operative.

Primary colours   The primary *additive* colours are red, green and blue. The primary *subtractive* colours are cyan, magenta and yellow.

Profile spot   A luminaire used to project shapes or patterns.

Projection lens   A lens specially designed to project slides or shapes onto a surface with considerable enlargement of the slide or original material.

Proscenium arch (opening)   The surround to the stage area and through which the audience views the performance.

Pup   A colloquial term for a one kilowatt spotlight.

Quartz   Crystalline silica which is glass like and used to make envelopes for lamps. It is generally transparent to ultraviolet radiation.

Record (or file)   The action of memorizing a lighting state on a lighting control system.

Reflectance (reflection factor)   The ratio of the reflected light to the incident light falling on a surface, measured in lumens.

Rig   To set up scenery equipment and lighting.

Rigging   Collective term for suspension equipment.

Rigger's control   A remote portable hand-held control unit for controlling either luminaires or winch systems.

Risers   The flat surfaces on the Fresnel lens rings that form the division between segments.

rms   Abbreviation of root-mean-square. The rms value of the current is a measure of its effectiveness in producing the same heating effect in a resistance as a direct current. It therefore allows for various wave shapes and directly relates to the power in watts.

Safety bond (also safety chain)   A short length of wire rope or chain formed into a loop around a suspension point to act as a secondary means of suspension in the event of failure of the primary system.

Saturated rig   A lighting installation where luminaires are installed in sufficient numbers to cover the total acting area without rigging and de-rigging.

Saturation   A term used to describe the density of a colour between the pure colour concerned and white, i.e. a deep red or pink.

Scoop   A simple elliptical shaped floodlight usually fitted with a large GLS lamp giving a soft light output.

Secondary colours   Those colours produced by mixing either additive primary colours or subtractive primary colours.

SCR (silicon controlled rectifier).   A solid state current switching device, used in dimmers for lighting systems. It comes from the *thyristor* family.

Scrim   A fine mesh used in front of a luminaire to attenuate the light beam. They are made with various meshes to give different attenuation characteristics. (See **Half scrim**.)

Shutter   Metal flags of various shapes used within a luminaire to block light. They are used to shape the light beam from effects spotlights and follow spots.

Single purchase   A suspension system for counterweight bars where no gearing is used. The distance of travel of the counterweight bucket will be the same as the barrel. (See **Double purchase**.)

Skycloth   A scenery unit used to convey the impression of a open sky. (See **Cyclorama**.)

Skypan   A very shallow scoop used in the film industry, rather like a metal dustbin lid with a bare lamp in the middle.

Snoot   A conical metal tube fitted to the front of the luminaire to enable a reduction in beam size.

Softlight   A luminaire designed to produce virtually shadowless light; generally used to control contrast.

Specular   Describes a mirror-like surface.

Spigot   The male member attached to a yoke used for the suspension of the luminaire and also for insertion into a floor stand. (Colloq. 'spud'.)

Spill light   Extraneous uncontrolled light from a luminaire.

Spot   To focus a luminaire by moving the lamp/reflector away from the lens, giving a narrow beam.

Spotlight   A luminaire with a focusing system to concentrate the light beam and thus give greater operational control.

Stage left/right   The performers' left and right as they face the audience.

Stand   A telescopic floor-mounted tripod device which provides a means of adjusting the height of luminaires above floor level. Can be manual lift, or by a geared wind-up system.

Studio area   The total floor area contained within the walls of a studio which may not always be used as the acting area, due to fire lanes, etc.

Subtractive colour mixing   The removal of light of various wavelengths, by filtering or reflection, e.g. a magenta filter *subtracts* the green from the light path, whereas the pigment of yellow paint reflects the red and green components of the incident light but absorbs (*subtracts*) the blue. (See **Additive Colour Mixing**.)

Telescope   A grid-mounted device made from retractable sets of tubes used to suspend luminaires at varying heights in the studio. Older types of telescopes were driven by portable power tools; modern systems are generally equipped with integral electric motors.

Throw   Generally describes the direction of light from a luminaire and also the effective distance between the luminaire and the area being lit.

Tilt   Term describing the vertical movement, about a point, of luminaires or equipment.

Tower   A temporary platform, usually made from scaffolding, on which to mount luminaires.

Truss   A framework, generally made from alloy bars together with cross-bracing, to provide lightweight rigging structures.

Tungsten halogen   Describes a family of lamps with either hard glass or quartz envelopes, tungsten filaments and halogen (usually iodine or bromine) fillings.

Two K   A colloquial term for a two kilowatt spotlight.

Ultraviolet (UV)   The band of short-wave radiation from 400 nm to 10 nm; although invisible to the eye the energy is extremely powerful and produces reddening of the skin (sunburn); it can also cause damage to the eye.

Underwriters laboratory (UL)   An American independent test laboratory that ensures minimum safety standards of equipment.

Voltage drop   That loss of volts that occurs through energy wastage when a current passes through a cable or electronic device.

Wash   General ambient light on the acting area.

Winch   Term used to describe either manual or motorized lifting equipment.

Wire rope   Ropes formed from fine wires woven in complex patterns to give great strength.

Working lights   (See **House lights**.)

Yoke   The suspension frame of a luminaire; possibly containing the drive mechanism for pan and tilt. (Colloq. fork, stirrup, trunnion.)

Zoom   Used in profile spots and scenic projectors, consisting of the relative movement of two lenses in an optical system to change beam width and focus.

Appendix II   World television systems and mains voltages

Country	Population (millions)	Language	Television standard	Supply voltage	Supply frequency
Afghanistan	17.5	Pashtu/Persian	PAL	220	50
Algeria	20.6	Arabic/French	PAL	127/220	50
Angola	8.5	French/Portuguese	PAL	220	50
Antigua & Barbuda	0.077	English	NTSC	230	60
Argentina	28.9	Spanish/Castellano	PAL	220/225	50
Australia	16.25	English	PAL	240	50
Austria	7.6	German	PAL	220	50
Bahamas	0.22	English	NTSC	120/240	60
Bahrain	0.4	Arabic/English	PAL	230/110	50/60
Bangladesh	100.0	Bengali	PAL	230	50
Barbados	0.252	English	NTSC	115/200/230	50
Belgium	9.9	Dutch/French	PAL	127/220	50
Benin	3.93	French	PAL	220	50
Bermuda	0.055	English	NTSC	120/240	60
Bolivia	6.4	Spanish	NTSC	115/230	50
Bophutatswana	1.7	English/Sitswana	PAL	220	50
Brazil	138.6	Portuguese	PAL	127/220	60
Brunei	0.3	Malay/English	PAL	230	50
Bulgaria	8.9	Bulgarian	SECAM	220	50
Burma	38.0	Burmese	NTSC	230	50
Burundi	4.46	French	Mono	220	50
Cameroon	9.564	English/French	PAL	220	50
Canada	25.6	English/French	NTSC	120/240	60
Canary Islands	0.14	Spanish	PAL	127/220	50
Central African Rep.	2.465	French/Sango	Mono	220	50
Chile	12.17	Spanish Castellano	NTSC	220	50
China	1000.0+	Chinese – regional	PAL	220	50
Colombia	27.5	Spanish	NTSC	120/240	60
Congo	1.77	French	SECAM	220	50
Costa Rica	2.9	Spanish	NTSC	120	60
Cuba	9.9	Spanish	NTSC	115/120	60
Curacao & Aruba	0.231	Dutch	NTSC	127/220	50
Cyprus	0.7	Greek/Turkish/English	PAL	240	50
Czechoslovakia	15.5	English/Czechoslovak	SECAM	220	50
Denmark	5.1	Danish	PAL	220	50
Djibouti	0.34	French/Arabic	SECAM	220	50
Dominican Rep.	5.8	Spanish	NTSC	110	60
Ecuador	9.25	Spanish	NTSC	110/120/127	60
Egypt	42.2	Arabic/English	SECAM	220	50
El Salvador	6.0	Spanish/English	NTSC	120/240	60
Ethiopia	33.9	Amharic/English	Mono	220	50
Finland	4.9	Finnish	PAL	220	50

Country	Population (millions)	Language	Television standard	Supply voltage	Supply frequency
France	55.4	French	SECAM	127/220	50
Gabon	0.7	French/Fang	SECAM	230	50
Gambia	0.7	English	Mono	230	50
Germany	77.4	German	PAL/ SECAM	127/220	50
Ghana	12.68	English/Acan	PAL	250	50
Gibraltar	0.06	English	PAL	240	50
Greece	10.0	Greek	SECAM	220	50
Grenada	0.115	English	NTSC	230	50
Guadeloupe	0.328	French	SECAM	220	50/60
Guatemala	8.0	Spanish	NTSC	120/240	60
Guinea Rep.	6.0	French	SECAM	220	50
Haiti	5.2	French/Creole	SECAM	115/220/230	60
Honduras	4.1	Spanish	NTSC	110	60
Hong Kong	5.5	Cantonese/English	PAL	200	50
Hungary	10.6	Hungarian	SECAM	220	50
Iceland	0.245	Icelandic	PAL	220	50
India	750.0	Hindi/Urdu	PAL	230/250	50
Indonesia	160.0	Indonesian	PAL	127/220	50
Iran	43.0	Farsi/Kurdish/Arabic	PAL/ SECAM	220	50
Iraq	15.0	Arabic/Kurdish	SECAM	220	50
Ireland	3.6	English	PAL	220	50
Israel	4.33	Hebrew/Yiddish/Arabic	PAL	230	50
Italy	57.2	Italian	PAL	127/220	50
Ivory Coast	9.3	French	SECAM	220	50
Jamaica	2.27	English/Spanish	NTSC	110/220	50
Japan	121.0	Japanese	NTSC	100/200/210	50/60
Jordan	3.5	Arabic/English	PAL	220	50
Kenya	19.0	English/Swahili	PAL	240	50
Korea (N)	19.63	Korean	SECAM/ NTSC	220	60
Korea (S)	40.0	Korean	NTSC	100	60
Kuwait	1.7	Arabic/English	PAL	240	50
Laos	4.0	Lao	PAL	220	50
Lebanon	2.7	Arabic/French	SECAM	110/220	50
Lesotho	1.5	English	Mono	220	50
Liberia	2.1	English	PAL	120/240	60
Libya	3.5	Arabic/Italian/English	PAL	17/230	50
Luxembourg	0.366	French	PAL/ SECAM	120/127/220	50
Macau	0.35	Portuguese/Cantonese/ English	PAL	110/220	50
Madagascar	9.5	Malagsy/French	PAL	127/220	50
Madeira	0.36	Portuguese	PAL	220	50
Malaysia	5.0	Malay	PAL	240	50
Mali	7.3	French	Mono	127/220	50
Malta	0.327	English	PAL	240	50
Mauretania	1.63	Hassaniya Arabic/ French	SECAM	230	50
Mauritius	1.1	English/Creole	SECAM	230	50
Mexico	74.9	Spanish	NTSC	120/127/220	60
Mongolia	18.5	Mongol	SECAM	127/220	50
Morocco	21.0	Arabic/French	SECAM	115/127/220	50
Mozambique	13.5	Portuguese	PAL	220	50
Nepal	16.0	Nepali	PAL	220	50
Netherlands	14.5	Dutch	PAL	220	50

Country	Population (millions)	Language	Television standard	Supply voltage	Supply frequency
New Zealand	3.1	English	PAL	230/240	50
Nicaragua	2.8	Spanish	NTSC	120/240	60
Niger	2.8	French	Mono	220	50
Nigeria	9.4	English	PAL	220/230	50
Norway	4.2	Norwegian	PAL	230	50
Oman	1.5	Arabic/English	PAL	240	50
Pakistan	90.0	Urdu/English/Punjabi	PAL	230	50
Panama	1.9	Spanish/English	NTSC	120/240	60
Papua New Guinea	3.5	English	PAL	240	50
Paraguay	3.6	Spanish	PAL	220	50
Peru	19.69	Spanish	NTSC	225	60
Philippines	56.0	Filipino	NTSC	120/220/240	60
Poland	37.0	Polish	SECAM	220	50
Portugal	10.1	Portuguese	PAL	220	50
Puerto Rico	3.5	Spanish	NTSC	120/240	60
Qatar	0.29	Arabic/Farsi	PAL	240	50
Reunion	0.516	French	SECAM	220	50
Romania	22.6	Romanian	SECAM	220	50
Saudi Arabia	10.5	Arabic	SECAM	127/220	50
Senegal	6.3	French	SECAM	127	50
Seychelles	0.065	English/French	Mono	230	50
Sierra Leone	3.3	English	PAL	230	50
Singapore	1.5	Mandarin/English	PAL	230	50
Somalia	4.6	Arabic/Italian/English	Mono	110/220/230	50
South Africa	23.4	English/Afrikaans	PAL	220/230/250	50
Spain	38.8	Spanish	PAL	127/220	50
Sri Lanka	16.0	English/Sinhala/Tamil	PAL	230	50
St Vincent	0.138	English	NTSC	230	50
Sudan	20.66	Arabic	PAL	240	50
Suriname	0.372	Dutch/English	NTSC	115/127	50/60
Swaziland	0.7	English	PAL	230	50
Sweden	8.4	Swedish	PAL	220	50
Switzerland	6.5	French/German/Italian	PAL	220	50
Syria	10.0	Arabic/Kurdish	SECAM	115/220	50
Taiwan	20.0	Mandarin	NTSC	110/220	60
Tanzania	20.4	Swahili/English	PAL	230	50
Thailand	53.0	English/Thai	PAL	220	50
Togo	3.0	French	SECAM	220	50
Trinidad & Tobago	1.13	English	NTSC	115/230	60
Tunisia	6.84	Arabic/French	SECAM	220	50
Turkey	52.3	Turkish	PAL	220	50
Uganda	14.0	English	PAL	240	50
United Arab Emirates	1.2	Arabic/Farsi	PAL	220/240	50
United Kingdom	56.6	English	PAL	220/230/240	50
Uruguay	3.0	Spanish	PAL	220	50
USA	241.0	English	NTSC	120/208/240	60
USSR	280.0	Russian	SECAM	127/220	50
Venezuela	17.79	Spanish	NTSC	120/208/240	60
Vietnam	62.0	Vietnamese	SECAM	120/220	60
Virgin Islands	0.11	English	NTSC	110/220	60
Yemen Arab Rep.	7.7	Arabic	PAL	220	50
Yemen Dem. Rep.	2.1	Arabic	NTSC	250	50
Yugoslavia	22.6	Croatian	PAL	220	50
Zaire	31.6	French/English	SECAM	220	50
Zambia	6.26	English	PAL	230	50
Zimbabwe	7.8	English	PAL	225	50

Appendix III   Lamp tables and cross-references

In general, lamps for film, TV and theatre in Europe can be divided into three groups, having the codes of CP, P and T. The designations are given by the Lighting Industries Federation (LIF) and are broadly described as follows:

CP Originally stood for Colour Photography, because the first lamps were imported from the USA by the film industry. All CP lamps are 3200 K and are single-ended, ranging in size from 300–10,000 W.

P Class lamps are also 3200 K but they are linear, double-ended types, ranging in size from 250–2,000 W.

T Indicates lamps designed for theatre, because they are of the order 2900–3000 K with an appropriately longer life, ranging in size from 500–2,000 W.

The American National Standards Institute (ANSI) has a different coding system, being three letters arranged in alphabetical order. The cross-reference table gives the equivalent types in both systems and can be used not only as a substitute guide, but also to help the user to find alternative lamps of different wattage and voltage for his luminaire. To do this, identify the lamp base and the Light Centre Length (LCL) and look for alternative lamps that have the same. The only caution is not to exceed the maximum rated wattage of the luminaire as this will cause the lamp to overheat and shorten its life; it can also damage the housing and present a safety hazard. The tables have been collated from many different manufacturers' catalogues so it is not an easy task to select one catalogue and expect to find that it provides information on all types of lamps, but a good wholesaler should have the required information, if you supply him with the code and the voltage required. When ordering lamps for Europe, be careful to specify 220 V or 240 V because if 220 V lamps LCLs are used at 240 V, the life will be reduced to only 30% of the manufacturer's stated life. In the tables that follow the lamps LCLs are given in millimetres, Life is given in hours and the colour temperature (CT) is in Kelvins.

Film, theatre, television single-ended tungsten halogen incandescent lamps. European/USA cross-reference

	European code (LIF)	USA code (ANSI)	Volts	Colour temp.	LIFE	LCL	Base
250 W	–	DYG	30	3400	15	36.0	GY 9.5
300 W	CP-81	FKW	120	3200	150	46.5	GY 9.5
	CP-81	FSL	220	3200	150	46.5	GY 9.5
	CP-81	FSK	240	3200	150	46.5	GY 9.5
	M-38	–	220/240	2900	2000	46.5	GY 9.5
500 W	T-18	FRF	120	3050	400	46.5	GY 9.5
	T-18	GCV	220	3050	400	46.5	GY 9.5
	T-18	GCW	240	3050	400	46.5	GY 9.5
	CP-82	FRG	120	3200	150	46.5	GY 9.5
	CP-82	FRH	220	3200	150	46.5	GY 9.5
	CP-82	FRJ	240	3200	150	46.5	GY 9.5
	M-40	–	220/240	2900	2000	46.5	GY 9.5
	T-1	DNW	240	2900	200	55.5	P28s
	T-17	FKF	220/240	2950	750	55.5	P28s
	T-28	–	220/240	3000	300	55.5	P28s
	–	BTL	120	2950	750	55.5	P28s
	–	BTM	120	3200	150	55.5	P28s
	–	EHC	120	3200	300	60.5	G 9.5
	–	EHD	120	2900	2000	60.5	G 9.5
	–	EGN	120	3200	150	63.5	G 22
	–	EGE	120	2900	2000	88.9	P28s
650 W	–	DYR	220/240	3200	50	36.0	GY 9.5
	–	DYS	120	3200	75	36.0	GY 9.5
	–	EKD	120	3400	25	36.0	GY 9.5
	T-26	FRE	120	3050	400	46.5	GY 9.5
	T-26	GCT	220	3050	400	46.5	GY 9.5
	T-26	GCS	240	3050	400	46.5	GY 9.5
	CP-89	FRK	120	3200	200	46.5	GY 9.5
	CP-89	FRL	220	3200	150	46.5	GY 9.5
	CP-89	FRM	240	3200	150	46.5	GY 9.5
	T-12	–	220/240	3000	750	55.0	GX 9.5
	CP-23	–	120	3200	100	55.0	GX 9.5
	CP-23	–	220/240	3200	100	55.0	GX 9.5
	T-13	FKA	120	3000	750	55.5	P28s
	T-13	FKB	220/240	3000	750	55.5	P28s
	CP-51	FKL	120	3200	100	55.5	P28s
	CP-51	FKM	220/240	3200	100	55.5	P28s
	–	FKR	220/240	3100	300	60.5	G 9.5
	–	FKV	120	3150	300	60.5	G 9.5
	CP-39	FKG	120	3200	100	63.5	G22
	CP-39	FKH	220/240	3200	100	63.5	G22
	–	DTA	120	3200	300	87.0	P40s
750 W	–	BTN	120	3000	750	55.5	P28s
	–	BTP	120	3200	200	55.5	P28s
	–	EHF	120	3200	300	60.5	G 9.5
	–	EHG	120	3000	2000	60.5	G 9.5
	–	EGR	120	3200	200	63.5	G22
	–	EGG	120	2900	2000	88.9	P28s

	European code (LIF)	USA code (ANSI)	Volts	Colour temp.	LIFE	LCL	Base
1000 W	T-11	–	120	3050	750	55.0	GX 9.5
	T-11	–	220/240	3050	750	55.0	GX 9.5
	T-19	FWP	220	3050	750	55.0	GX 9.5
	T-19	FWR	240	3050	750	55.0	GX 9.5
	CP-24	–	120	3200	200	55.0	GX 9.5
	CP-24	–	220/240	3200	200	55.0	GX 9.5
	CP-70	FVA	220	3200	200	55.0	GX 9.5
	CP-70	FVB	240	3200	200	55.0	GX 9.5
	T-14	–	120	3050	750	55.5	P28s
	T-14	FKD	220/240	3050	750	55.5	P28s
	CP-52	FKN	220/240	3200	200	55.5	P28s
	–	BTR	120	3200	250	55.5	P28s
	CP-77	FEL	120	3200	300	60.5	G 9.5
	CP-77	FEP	220/240	3200	300	60.5	G 9.5
	T-30	–	220/240	3000	750	63.5	G22
	CP-40	FKJ	220/240	3200	200	63.5	G22
	–	EGT	120	3200	250	63.5	G22
	T-16	–	220/240	3050	750	87.0	P40s
	T-15	FKE	220/240	3050	750	88.9	P28s
	–	EGJ	120	3200	500	88.9	P28s
	–	EWE	220/240	3200	250	88.9	P28s
	–	BVT	120	3050	500	100.0	P40s
	–	BVV	120	3200	250	100.0	P40s
	–	CYV	120	3200	250	127.0	G 38
	–	DSE	120	3200	500	N/A	E40s
1200 W	T-31	–	220/240	3050	400	63.5	G22
	CP-93	–	120	3200	200	63.5	G22
	CP-93	–	220/240	3200	200	63.5	G22
	T-29	–	120	3050	400	67.0	GX 9.5
	T-29	FWS	220	3050	400	67.0	GX 9.5
	T-29	FWT	240	3050	400	67.0	GX 9.5
	CP-90	–	120	3200	200	67.0	GX 9.5
	CP-90	–	220/240	3200	200	67.0	GX 9.5
1500 W	–	DTA	120	3200	300	87.0	P40s
	–	CWZ	120	3200	300	100.0	P40s
	–	CXZ	120	3200	300	127.0	G 38
	–	DSF	120	3200	750	241.0	E40s
2000 W	CP-43	–	120	3200	400	70.0	GY 16
	CP-43	FTM	220	3200	400	70.0	GY 16
	CP-43	FTL	240	3200	400	70.0	GY 16
	CP-79	–	220/240	3200	350	70.0	GY 16
	CP-53	–	120	3200	400	87.0	P40s
	CP-53	–	220/240	3200	400	87.0	P40s
	CP-92	–	220/240	3200	400	90.0	G22
	–	BVW	120	3200	400	100.0	P40s
	CP-41	FKK	220/240	3200	400	127.0	G 38
	–	CYX	120	3200	400	127.0	G 38
	–	FWG	120	3200	500	128.0	E40s
	CP-59	–	220/240	3200	300	133.0	E40s
	–	BWF	120	3200	400	133.0	E40s
	–	FWH	120	3200	500	171.0	E40s

	European code (LIF)	USA code (ANSI)	Volts	Colour temp.	LIFE	LCL	Base
2500 W	CP-91	–	220/240	3200	400	90.0	G22
	CP-94	–	220/240	3200	400	127.0	G 38
2500 W (2 filaments, each 1250 W)							
	CP-22	–	220/240	3200	100	143.0	GX 38q
	CP-30	–	220/240	·3200	300	143.0	GX 38q
3750 W (2 filaments: 2500 W + 1250 W)							
	CP-57	–	220/240	3200	100	143.0	GX 38q
	CP-58	–	220/240	3200	300	143.0	GX 38q
5000 W (2 filaments, each 2500 W)							
	CP-20	–	220/240	3200	100	143.0	GX 38q
	CP-32	–	220/240	3200	300	143.0	GX 38q
5000 W	CP-29	–	220/240	3200	500	165.0	G 38
	CP-29	DPY	120	3200	500	165.0	G 38
	CP-46	–	220/240	3200	400	165.0	G 38
	CP-46	ECN	120	3200	400	165.0	G 38
10000 W	CP-80	–	220/240	3200	400	254.0	G 38
	CP-80	EBA	120	3200	400	254.0	G 38
	CP-83	–	220/240	3200	500	254.0	G 38
	CP-83	DTY	120	3200	500	254.0	G 38

Film, theatre, television double-ended tungsten halogen incandescent linear lamps: European/USA cross-reference

	European code (LIF)	USA code (ANSI)	Volts	Colour temp.	LIFE	Length	Cap
250 W	P1/8	–	30	3400	12	78.0	R7s
400 W	–	EHR	120	2900	2000	78.0	R7s
500 W	P2/30	FDF	120	3200	400	118.0	R7s
	K1	–	220/240	2900	2000	118.0	R7s
625 W	P2/10	–	220/240	3200	200	189.0	R7s
	P2/10	–	120	3200	200	189.0	R7s
650 W	P2/6	FAD	120	3200	100	78.0	R7s
800 W	P2/13	DXX	220/240	3200	75	78.0	R7s
	P2/11	EME	220/240	3200	150	118.0	R7s
1000 W	–	DXW	120	3200	150	93.0	R7s
	P2/35	–	220/240	3200	150	93.0	R7s
	P2/28	FCM	120	3200	300	118.0	R7s
	P2/28	–	220/240	3200	300	118.0	R7s
	P2/29	FHM	120	3200	300	118.0	R7s
	P2/20	–	220/240	3200	300	118.0	R7s
	K4	–	220/240	3000	2000	118.0	R7s
	–	FFT	120	3200	500	167.0	R7s
	P2/7	EKM	220/240	3200	200	189.0	R7s
1250 W	P2/12	–	220/240	3200	200	189.0	R7s
1500 W	–	FDB	120	3200	400	167.0	R7s
2000 W	P2/27	FEX	220/240	3200	300	143.0	RX7s
	–	FEY	120	3200	300	143.0	RX7s

Appendix IV Comparison of luminaire performance

All measurements are at 240 V

	Spot		Flood	
Distance (m)	*Output (lux)*	*Size (m)*	*Output (lux)*	*Size (m)*
575 W HMI				
4	12500	0.70	1250	4.00
6	5555	1.05	556	6.00
8	3125	1.40	313	8.00
10	2000	1.75	200	10.00
1.2 kW HMI				
6	10278	1.16	1944	6.11
8	5781	1.54	1094	8.15
10	3700	1.93	700	10.20
12	2570	2.31	486	12.23
14	1888	2.70	357	14.27
16	1445	3.08	273	16.30
2.5 kW HMI				
8	17187	1.19	1562	10.00
10	11000	1.49	1000	12.50
12	7638	1.78	694	15.00
14	5612	2.08	510	17.50
16	4297	2.38	390	20.00
18	3395	2.68	309	22.50
20	2750	2.97	250	25.00
4 kW HMI				
10	30000	1.57	2000	9.97
14	15306	2.20	1020	14.00
18	9260	2.83	617	18.00
22	6198	3.46	413	21.94
26	4438	4.09	296	25.93
30	3333	4.72	222	29.91
6 kW HMI				
14	24439	1.84	1531	12.47
18	14784	2.36	926	16.03
22	9897	2.88	620	19.60
26	7086	3.41	444	23.15
30	5322	3.93	333	26.71
34	4144	4.46	260	30.28
8 kW HMI				
14	32653	1.47	2041	14.27
18	19753	1.89	1235	18.34
22	13223	2.31	826	22.42
26	9467	2.73	592	26.50

Distance (m)	Spot		Flood	
	Output (lux)	Size (m)	Output (lux)	Size (m)
30	7111	3.14	444	30.57
34	5536	3.56	346	34.65
38	4432	3.98	277	38.72
12 kW HMI				
18	30864	1.82	1543	18.74
22	20661	2.23	1033	22.90
26	14793	2.63	740	27.07
30	11111	3.04	556	31.23
34	8650	3.44	433	35.40
38	6925	3.85	346	39.56
42	5669	4.26	283	43.73
Redhead				
4	2539	3.07	429	7.46
6	1128	4.60	191	11.19
8	634	6.15	107	14.90
Blonde				
4	13593	1.63	1719	5.60
6	6042	2.44	764	8.40
8	3398	3.26	430	11.20
10	2175	4.07	275	14.00
12	1510	4.88	191	16.80
1 kW Fresnel				
4	4609	0.77	675	4.8
6	2048	1.16	300	7.2
8	1152	1.54	169	9.61
2 kW Fresnel				
4	11562	0.70	1563	4.53
6	5139	1.05	694	6.79
8	2891	1.40	391	9.05
10	1850	1.75	250	11.32
12	1284	2.10	174	13.58
5 kW Fresnel				
6	13889	1.31	2083	6.79
8	7812	1.75	1172	9.05
10	5000	2.20	750	11.32
12	3472	2.63	521	13.58
14	2551	3.07	383	15.80
10 kW Fresnel				
8	19531	1.40	2656	7.30
10	12500	1.75	1700	9.10
12	8680	2.10	1181	10.90
14	6378	2.45	867	12.80
16	4883	2.80	664	14.60
18	3858	3.15	524	16.40
20	3125	3.50	425	18.20

2.5 kW Softlite: 120° horizontal, 90° vertical

Distance (m)	Output (lux)
4	781
6	347
8	195

5 kW Softlite: 120° horizontal, 90° vertical

Distance (m)	Output (lux)
4	1563
6	694
8	390
10	250

650 W Profile projector: 25° fixed

Distance (m)	Output (lux)	Size (m)
6	972	2.66
8	547	3.55
10	350	4.43
12	243	5.32

1200 W Profile projector: 11°/26°

Distance (m)	Narrow		Wide	
	Output (lux)	Size (m)	Output (lux)	Size (m)
6	7083	1.15	3611	2.77
8	3984	1.54	2031	3.70
10	2550	1.92	1300	4.62
12	1771	2.31	903	5.54
14	1301	2.70	663	6.46

2 kW Profile projector: 12°/22°

10	4288	2.10	1856	3.90
12	2978	2.52	1289	4.66
14	2188	2.94	947	5.44
16	1675	3.36	725	6.22
18	1323	3.78	573	7.00
20	1072	4.20	464	7.78

2 kW Tungsten follow spot: 9°/15°

12	3955	1.89	1733	3.16
14	2906	2.20	1273	3.68
16	2225	2.52	975	4.21
18	1758	2.83	770	4.74
20	1424	3.15	624	5.27

1 kW CSI Discharge follow spot: 9°/15°

20	4284	3.00	2556	5.34
22	3540	3.31	2112	5.87
24	2975	3.61	1775	6.40
26	2535	3.91	1512	6.94
28	2186	4.21	1304	7.47
30	1904	4.51	1136	8.00

Appendix V Measurements, formulae and conversion factors

Measurements

Most scientific measurements are made using the International System of Units (Systéme International d'Units) or SI for short.

The three basic units are the **metre, kilogram** and the **second**. From these are derived the whole range of units which cover the world of physics. For the ease of our readers we have chosen only those units which are applicable to the subject matter in this book.

Measurement of length
Basic unit: **metre** (m)
Other units:
centimetre (cm) = one hundredth of a metre (10^{-2}m)
millimetre (mm) = one thousandth of a metre (10^{-3}m)
nanometre (nm) = one thousandth millionth of a metre (10^{-9}m)

Measurement of area
Basic unit: **square metre** (m^2)
Other units:
square centimetre = one ten thousandth of a square metre (10^{-4}m^2)

Measurement of mass
Basic unit: **kilogram** (kg)
Other units:
gram (g) = one thousandth of a kilogram (10^{-3}kg)
tonne (t) = one thousand kilograms (10^{3}kg)

Measurement of electric current
Basic unit: **ampere** (A)
Other units:
milliampere = one thousandth of an ampere (10^{-3}A)

Measurement of thermodynamic temperature
Basic unit: **kelvin** (K)
Note: The kelvin scale used the same interval of degrees as the Celsius scale. 'Absolute zero' on the kelvin scale is *minus* 273 degrees Celsius. Thus: K = (°C) + 273.

Measurement of light
Basic unit: **candela** (cd)
The unit of luminous intensity (I) and the amount of luminous flux in a given direction.
Other units:
lumen
The unit of luminous flux and the measurement of luminous energy.
lux
The unit of illuminance (E) and the measurement of luminous flux falling on an area.

$$\text{Thus: lux} = \frac{\text{lumens}}{\text{area in sq. metres}}$$

Laws of illumination

Inverse square law $E = \dfrac{I}{d^2}$

where E = illuminance in lux
      I = luminous intensity in candelas
      d = distance of source to surface being illuminated

Cosine law $E = \dfrac{I}{d^2}\cos.A$

where A = the angle to the normal of the incident light.
Note: This is a modification to the inverse square law to take account of the angle of incidence.

Electrical formulae

Ohm's law states that the current (I) flowing in a circuit is directly proportional to the applied voltage (V) and inversely proportional to the resistance (R), thus:

$$I = \frac{V}{R} \qquad V = IR \qquad R = \frac{V}{I}$$

Power (P) in the circuit is given by the product of voltage (V) and current (I). The unit of power is the watt (W), thus:

$P = V \times I$ watts

alternatively   as $V = IR$ therefore $P = I^2R$ watts

as $I = \dfrac{V}{R}$ therefore $P = \dfrac{V^2}{R}$ watts

The above formulae are those used for direct current (dc) circuits.

For alternating current (ac) circuits, the formulae only hold true when the circuit is purely resistive. That is, the voltage and current are in phase with each other. If the circuit contains inductance or capacitance the voltage and current will be out of phase to some degree. To allow for this discrepancy we have to modify the formulae as follows:

In an ac circuit the ratio of applied voltage (V) divided by current (I) is called the impedance (Z):

$$Z = \frac{V}{I}$$

The power is given by: $P = VI \cos \phi$ watts where ϕ is the phase difference between the current and supply voltage.

Cos ϕ is called the power factor (PF)

The power factor is also given by: $\dfrac{\text{power in watts}}{\text{rms volts} \times \text{rms amperes}}$

For most practical measurements: $PF = \dfrac{\text{kilowatts}}{\text{kilovoltamperes}}$

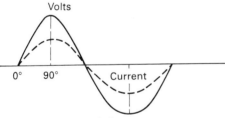

(a) Single phase resistive current

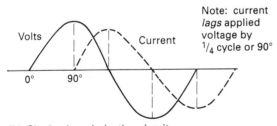

(b) Single phase inductive circuit

Note: current *lags* applied voltage by $^1/_4$ cycle or 90°

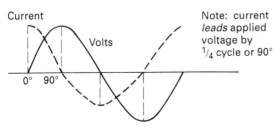

(c) Single phase capacitive circuit

Note: current *leads* applied voltage by $^1/_4$ cycle or 90°

Figure AV.1   Single-phase sine wave

Electrical energy

This is the measurement of power used over a period of time.
Thus: watts × seconds = watt-seconds or 'joules' (J)

$$1\,kWh = 1000 \times 3600 \text{ watt-seconds}$$
$$= 3{,}600{,}000\,J$$

For practical purposes the units most used are:
kilowatts × hours = kilowatt-hours (kW h)
Generally called a unit of electricity.

Three-phase systems

Star connection and neutral point.

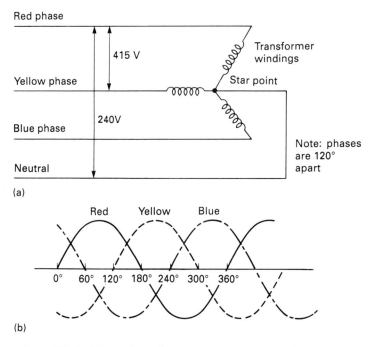

Figure AV.2   Three-phase sine wave

Conversion factors

Imperial to metric		**Metric to imperial**	

Length

Inches × 25.4	= millimetres	millimetres × 0.03937	= inches
Inches × 2.54	= centimetres	centimetres × 0.3937	= inches
Feet × 0.3048	= metres	metres × 3.281	= feet

Area

| Sq. inches × 6.452 | = sq. cms. | Sq. cms. × 0.155 | = Sq. ins. |
| Sq. feet × 0.0929 | = sq. metres | Sq. metres × 10.76 | = sq. feet |

Volume

| Cubic ft. × 0.02832 | = cubic metres |
| Cubic metres × 35.311 | = cubic ft. |

Mass

Pounds × 0.4536	= kilograms	kilograms × 2.205	= pounds
Tons × 1016	= kilograms	kilograms × 0.0009844	= tons
Tons × 0.9844	= tonnes	tonnes × 1.016	= tons

Appendix VI CIE luminare symbols

Floodlight
A luminaire with a beam angle of 100° or more

Special floodlight
A luminaire with a beam angle of less than 100°

Reflector spotlight
A luminaire with a variable beam produced by movement of the lamp in relation to its reflector, e.g. Beamlight

Sealed beam light
A unit where filament, reflector and lens are all fixed in relation to each other, e.g. Par 64, etc.

Lens spotlight
A luminaire with a variable beam using a lens with combined lamp and reflector movement, e.g. PC unit

Fresnel spotlight
The same principle as the 'lens spotlight' but uses a 'stepped' Fresnel lens to give a softer beam edge

Figure AVI.1 CIE symbols

Profile (ellipsoidal)

A luminaire which has a hard edged beam. The shape of the beam is variable by the use of diaphragms, shutters or sihouette cutouts

Effects spotlight

Projects stationary or moving effects, produces an even field by using an objective lens

Softlight

A luminaire with a large lit surface area to produce a diffused light with indefinite shadow boundaries

Further reading

The Technique of Lighting for Television and Film, Gerald Millerson, Focal Press, 1991.

The Stage Lighting Handbook, Francis Reid, A & C Black, 1992.

Light, Michael Freeman, Collins, 1990.

Thorn Technical Handbook (Various), Thorn Lighting.

The Reproduction of Colour in Photography, Printing and Television, R W G Hunt, Fountain Press, 1975.

Light and Vision (Various), Time Life, 1969.

Light and Colour, R Daniel Overheim, David L Wagner, John Wiley & Sons, 1982.

Light, Michael I Sobell, University of Chicago Press, 1987.

IEE Wiring Regulations, 15th and 16th Editions, IEE London, 1989–91.

Theatres, Roderick Ham, Butterworth Architecure, 1988.

Handbook of Electrical Installation and Practice Pts. 1 & 2 (Various), Granada, 1983.

Theatre Lighting in the Age of Gas, Terence Rees, The Society for Theatre Research, 1978.

Guide to Acoustic Practice, BBC Engineering, 1990.

Science & Technology Dictionary, Chambers, 1988.

Index

acoustic engineers 176, 180
acoustic noise *see* sound
additive colour mixing 26–7
air circuit breakers (acb) 235
air conditioning 140, 176, 180, 196–7
American National Standards Institute
    (ANSI) 299
analogue control of dimmers 152
angle of lighting 129
annular reflectors 66
apparent brightness 45
arc lights 55–61, 75–7
architects 176, 179
audience, sight lines of 182
auto transformer dimmers 144, 157–8
automated control systems 161–5
automated lighting systems 201–20

back lighting 91–3, 130, 131, 132, 136
back-up control systems 164
back-up power supplies 221–2, 245
ballast units 60–61
ballet lighting 130
barndoors 99, 215–17, 262, 267, 269
barrel winches 167–71
barrels 111, 117
    control of 207–8
    counterweight 111, 190–1
    motorized 103, 121–2, 168–9, 184, 206,
        207–8
    rigging of 167–71
    roller 106–10
    self-climbing 110
Basher 77, 78
battery emergency lighting 245–6
battery hand lamps 95–6
beam lights 67, 89–90
beam splitting 34
blackbody radiation 12, 19–21, 22, 45, 59
blacklight 12
Blonde performance 305
blue 15, 16–18, 20, 23, 25, 27, 128
boats 102, 137, 184
Bohr, N. 21
Boll, F. 6
borosilicate glass lamps 55, 60
breakdowns 205

brightness 13, 14, 45
British Standards
    BS88 154, 235
    BS4343 117, 223, 230
    BS4533 266
bromine lamps 54
Brute spotlight 56–7, 77, 78, 135
budgets 262–3
building construction 177, 180–8, 189–94
burning angle 100

cables:
    colour coding 275
    heating of 198, 228, 229
    of luminaires 110, 172–3, 258, 269
    mixing of voltages 278
    safety 197–8, 275
    size of 221, 225, 226–8
    travelling equipment 118, 119, 120, 123–4,
        170, 171, 199
cameras, light conversion in 30–35
candela 36–7
candles 36–7
carbon arc lights 56–7, 75–7
carbon dioxide lamps 57
carbon filament lamps 48
cellulose acetate filters 24
centre of gravity (C of G) of luminaires 73–4,
    97
charge coupled devices (CCDs) 35, 141
checklists, safety 281–3
chlorine lamps 54
chokes for dimmers 147
chopped waveform dimmers 51, 60–61,
    145–9
chroma 14
chromacity diagram 18
CIE:
    chromacity diagram 18
    colorimetric system 15–19
    colour rendering index 15
    luminaire symbols 312–13
    relative photopic luminosity curve 17, 43,
        44
circuit breakers and fuses 51, 140, 154–5,
    157, 172, 223, 234–5, 262, 275–6
circular true radius reflectors 64–5